The Concise Rāmāyaṇa of Vālmīki

The Concise Rāmāyaṇa of Vālmīki

Swami Venkatesananda

State University of New York Press

Published by
State University of New York Press, Albany

Printed in the United States of America

For information, address the State University of New York Press, 90 State Street, Suite 700, Albany, NY 12207

Library of Congress Cataloging in Publication Data

Vālmīki.
[Rāmāyaṇa. English]
The concise Ramayana of Valmiki / Swami Venkatesananda.
p. cm.
ISBN 0-88706-862-6. ISBN 0-88706-863-4 (pbk.)
I. Venkatesananda, Swami. II. Title.
BL1139.22.E54 1988
294.5'922—dc19 88-2057
CIP

10 9

The cover of this book differs from that of the original printing. In order for the State University of New York Press to maintain its extensive backlist, it has been necessary to use digital printing technology to minimize the cost to reprint small quantities. This has made it possible for our books to remain in print much longer and maintain reasonable pricing. We assure you that the content is identical to the previous printing with the possible exception of minor text corrections.

Contents

Preface

This is a condensed version of a long epic, written between 750 and 500 B.C., consisting of 50,000 lines of Sanskrit verse. Divided into seven Kāṇḍas, or books, it tells the story of Rāma from his birth to this death. At regular intervals throughout the text, the chapters being condensed are designated by Kāṇḍa title and numbers. Each interval is appropriate in length for a daily reading and there are 365 intervals.

The cast of characters is provided by a glossary of proper names. It is suggested that this be read first.

Cast of Characters

Agastya: a sage

Ahalyā: wife of a sage, seduced by Indra and redeemed by Rāma

Akṣa: Rāvana's son, killed by Hanumān

Aṅgada: Vāli's son

Añjanā: in previous life a celestial Puñjīkasthalā, daughter of Kuñjara, mother of Hanumān

Aśoka: the grove where Sītā had been interned

Ayodhyā: the capital city of the Kosala kingdom of Daśaratha

Bharadvāja: a sage and a great friend of Rāma and his brothers

Bharata: a brother of Rāma; born of Kaikeyī; he refuses to rule during Rāma's exile but lives an ascetic life in Nandigrāma with Rāma's sandals on the throne

Brahmā: the Creator of the universe (Brahma-loka is the region of Brahmā)

Brahmacarya: the vow of celibacy, the period of student-life

Brāhmaṇa: a person belonging to the priest-class

Citrakooṭa: a hill on which Rāma spent some time during his exile

Daṇḍakāraṇya: the great forest where Rāma spent his exile

Daśaratha: the king of Kosala, father of Rāma

Dūṣaṇa: The commander-in-chief of the forces of Khara

Gandharva: a celestial musician

Gaṅgā: the holy river, sometimes personified

Garuḍa: said to be a bird, demi-god and vehicle of Viṣṇu

Godāvarī: a river

Guha: a tribal chief greatly devoted to Rāma and his brothers whom he entertains on their way to the forest

Hanumān: a vānara-chief, son of Añjanā and Kesari (offspring of vāyu, the wind-god), of great strength, who discovered the whereabouts of Sītā, and in countless ways contributed to the success of Rāma's mission

Ikṣvāku: an ancestor of Rāma

Indra: the king of heaven

Indrajit: the son of Rāvana, who conquered even Indra; Indrajit was killed by Lakṣmaṇa

Jāmbavān: said to be a bear, a tribal chief and ally of Rāma

Jambumālī: the first demon killed by Hanumān in Laṅkā

Janaka: king of Mithilā, adopted father of Sīta

Janasthāna: part of the forest, where sages lived and where Khara and his forces harassed the sages

Jaṭāyu: said to be a vulture which fought with Rāvaṇa as he flew away with Sītā

Kabandha: a demon of unusual shape, whom Rāma encounters in the forest (also known as Danu)

Kaikeyī: wife of Daśaratha, mother of Bharata; she demanded that Rāma be exiled and Bharata crowned king

Kailāsa: the legendary abode of lord Śiva

Kausalyā: wife of Daśaratha, mother of Rāma

Kesari: father of Hanumān

Khara: the demon-chief who with thousands of demon-warriors was killed by Rāma in Janasthāna

Kiṣkindhā: the kingdom of Vāli and Sugrīva

Kosala: the kingdom of Daśaratha

Kṣatriya: a prince, a warrior

Kubera: the demi-god of wealth, said to be a brother of Rāvaṇa

Kumbhakarṇa: the demon-brother of Rāvaṇa; a warrior of terrible power, he slept for long and ate a lot

Kuśa: the son of Rāma; Sītā gave birth to twins Lava and Kuśa

Lakṣmaṇa: son of Daśaratha and Sumitrā; of the three brothers, Lakṣmaṇa was Rāma's constant companion

Lakṣmī: goddess of wealth; consort of lord Viṣṇu

Laṅkā: the kingdom over which Rāvaṇa ruled

Lava: son of Rāma and Sītā

Maināka: a hill that sprang from the ocean during Hanumān's historic flight to Laṅkā

Māṇḍavi: wife of Bharata

Maṇḍodarī: Rāvaṇa's wife

Mantharā: the servant-maid of Kaikeyī, who instigated the latter to have Rāma exiled

Mārīca: a demon and accomplice of Rāvaṇa; he was hit by Rāma but not killed; later he took the form of a golden deer, luring Rāma away; Rāma killed him

Māyāvī: son of Maya; Māyāvī fought with Vāli and was killed by the latter after a bitter fight in a cave

Mithilā: the capital of Janaka's kingdom

Nala: an ally of Sugrīva; Nala was the architect who had the bridge built for Rāma and the army to cross over to Laṅkā

Nandigrāma: the suburb of Ayodhayā where Bharata lived an ascetic life during Rāma's exile

Nārāyaṇa: one of the Trinity; the protector of the universe; also known as Viṣṇu

Nīla: the commander-in-chief of the vānaras

Pampā: a lake in the Daṇḍaka forest

Pañcavati: the spot where Rāma had a cottage built for his dwelling during the exile

Paraśurāma: said to be a previous incarnation of Viṣṇu; born in a brāhmaṇa family, Paraśurāma killed the wicked kings of the world

Pulastya: the father of Rāvaṇa who was also known as Paulastya (and the Rāmāyaṇa was also known as Paulastya-vadaṁ or the killing of the son of Pulastya)

Puṣpaka: an aircraft of extraordinary manoeuvrability. It originally belonged to Kubera; Rāvaṇa took it away from him; Rāma used it to return to Ayodhyā

Rāma: son of Daśaratha and Kausalyā; said to be an incarnation of Viṣṇu; the hero of the Rāmāyaṇa

Rāvaṇa: born of a sage, Rāvana got a boon of near-invincibility from the Creator; he oppressed the sages, abducted Sītā, fought with Rāma and was killed by him. He had other nicknames like Daś-agrīva

Ṛṣyamūka: the hill where the defeated Sugrīva lived before he met Rāma

Rudra: the third member of the Trinity; also known as Śiva, Try-aṁbaka etc

Śabarī: a female ascetic who was devoted to Rāma and who helped him in his search for Sītā

Sagara: a king

Sāgara: the ocean

Sampatī: said to be a vulture; son of Supārśva; brother of Jaṭāyu; helps Hanumān find Sītā

Śarabhaṅga: a sage who lived in the Daṇḍaka forest

Śaramā: though a demoness, she was Sītā's friend in the Aśoka-grove

Sarayū: a river, near Ayodhyā

Śatabalī: a tribal chief and leader of the vānara forces

Śatrughna: a brother of Rāma; son of Daśaratha and Sumitrā; he was devoted to Bharata

Siddha: a perfected sage (Siddhāśrama-hermitage of such sages)

Simhikā: a demoness who obstructed Hanumān's flight to Laṅkā

Simśapā: the tree under which Sītā was kept in the Aśoka-grove

Sītā: adopted daughter of king Janaka; she was the wife of Rāma

Śrutakīrti: the wife of Śatrughna

Subāhu: a demon who polluted the forest and the sacred rite of Viśvāmitra; he was killed by Rāma

Sugrīva: a vānara-chief; brother of Vāli whom he offends on account of a misunderstanding; driven away from the kingdom, Sugrīva lives on a nearby hill till Rāma kills Vāli and installs him on the throne; an ally of Rāma, he organised the invasion of Laṅkā. Rumā was his wife

Sumantrā: the charioteer of Rāma

Sumitrā: one of the wives of Daśaratha; mother of Lakṣmaṇa and Śatrughna

Surasā: mother of nāgās; she was an obstacle to Hanumān during his flight to Laṅkā

Śūrpaṇakhā: Rāvaṇa's sister who tried to seduce Rāma in the forest and had her face mutilated by Lakṣmaṇa

Suṣeṇa: a tribal chief, leader of Sugrīva's forces; also Sugrīva's father-in-law

Tārā: wife of Vāli

Tāṭakā: a demoness who obstructed Viśvāmitra's religious rite and was killed by Rāma (the first demon killed by him)

Trijaṭā: a demoness, but a friend of Sītā in the Aśoka-grove

Trikūṭa: the hill on which Rāvaṇa's capital stood

Ūrmilā: Lakṣmaṇa's wife

Vāli: a vānara-chief; brother of Sugrīva; after Rāma's alliance with Sugrīva, Rāma killed Vāli

Vālmīki: sage and the author of the Rāmāyaṇa; when Rāma banished Sītā, she lived in his hermitage, where the twins Lava and Kuśa were born, to whom the sage transmitted the Rāmāyaṇa

Vānara: said to be monkeys; they were probably 'dwellers in the forest'; tribesmen

Vasiṣṭha: a sage; the spiritual teacher of Janaka and Daśaratha

Veda: the basic scriptures; books of knowledge; four of them were known: Ṛg, Yajur, Sāma, and Atharva

Vibhīṣaṇa: the pious brother of Rāvaṇa who abandoned him and sought Rāma's asylum; he played a vital part in the defeat of Rāvaṇa; he was crowned king of Laṅkā, after the death of Rāvaṇa

Virādha: the first demon whom Rāma killed in the forest life; born of Java and Śatahradā; in former life he was the sage Tumburū

Viśvakarma: the architect of the gods

Viśvāmitra: a sage who taught the science of warfare to Rāma and also gave him many missiles; Viśvāmitra was a kṣatriya who became a brāhmaṇa sage by self-effort

Yamunā: a river

Yudhājit: brother of Kaikeyī

Yuga: a world-cycle; there are four of them—Kṛta, Tretā, Dvāpara, and Kali

Yuvarāja: crown prince

Narada tells story
to Valmiki
↓
Tell it to Rama's Sons
↓
Tell it to Rama

Bāla Kāṇḍa
Boyhood of Rāma

Everything has a frame
Every story
beginning

Vālmīki asked the foremost among sages, Nārada: "Who is there in this world who is of good nature, powerful, righteous, alert in action, truthful in speech, firm in resolve, exemplary in conduct, devoted to the welfare of all beings, learned, skilful, with a pleasant presence, self-controlled, with anger overcome, resplendent and free from jealousy, of whom even the gods are afraid when he is angered?"

Delighted, the sage Nārada narrated in brief the whole of the Rāmāyaṇa, after extolling the glories of lord Rāma who was the one person that matched the description implied in Vālmīki's question. "Rāma is the peer of lord Viṣṇu! And in his nature he is like the ocean, the Himālayas, mother earth, the god of wealth and dharma himself." Nārada recounted the story of Rāma.

Friend of Rama

After the narration, Nārada went his way. Vālmīki, accompanied by his disciple Bharadvāja, went towards the Tamasā River for his noon bath and ablutions. Just then he saw a hunter mercilessly kill a male crane while it was sporting with its female companion, and heard the female's heart-rending cry. Overcome by pity and angered by the hunter's heartless cruelty, Vālmīki uttered a curse; "For this sin, you will lose your peace of mind for countless years." Regaining his composure at once, Vālmīki regretted the curse (which had taken the form of a verse couched in delightful metre) and countermanded the curse saying: "It shall be a verse and not a curse." Yet, the mystery that even he could lose his temper and thus risk losing the merit of his asceticism intrigued him.

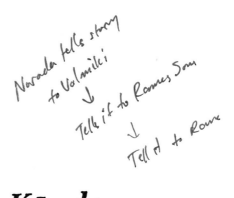

Thus musing, he returned to his hermitage. There he beheld the divine Brahmā, the creator. Vālmīki worhipped the creator. Divining the ascetic's mental state, Brahmā said: "The metre in which you uttered those words, O Vālmīki, will bring you great blessings. In the same metre sing the glory and the story of Śrī Rāma; elaborate on what Nārada has already told you. All the details concerning the story of Rāma will be revealed to your vision; nothing that is expressed by you will prove to be false. Your composition will be sung by people so long as the sun and the moon shine."

After thus blessing him, lord Brahmā departed for his own realm. Immediately thereupon, Vālmīki began the immortal epic, the Rāmāyaṇa, in the same style in which he had uttered his first verse which was directed to the hunter.

Bāla 3–4

Vālmīki entered into deep meditation and in his superconscious state he actually saw all that took place in the past, as clearly as he would see a fruit lying on his palm. The entire story unfolded itself in his consciousness, in all its details, even as to what the characters in the story said or thought, and how they laughed or behaved. And, the narration flowed from his lips in the form of an exquisite poem, and though its central theme is the detailed exposition of dharma and mokṣa (liberation), it also deals with prosperity (artha) and pleasure (kāma), and it delights the mind as much as it enlightens the soul. The story that thus unfolded covered from the birth of Rāma to his coronation and his later reign as the monarch. It consisted of twenty-four thousand verses.

Vālmīki wondered: "Who is that intelligent man endowed with almost superhuman memory who will commit the whole poem to his memory and pass it on to posterity?" At that instant, Kuśa and Lava entered his presence and bowed to him. They were the sons of Rāma and Sītā, born in Vālmīki's own hermitage, after Sītā had been banished from Rāma's court and had taken the asylum of Vālmīki's hermitage. Kuśa and Lava were his own pupils, and foremost among them. Unto them Vālmīki committed the epic poem, the entire Rāmāyaṇa which embodies the great story of Sītā, calling it Paulastya Vadhaṁ as it deals with the conquest of Rāvaṇa or Paulastya.

The two boys quickly memorised the entire epic. They were endowed with melodious voices; and they were masters of music. In appearance they naturally were the very images of Śrī Rāma. One day they recited the epic in an assembly of sages and saints, who were all enchanted by the music and transported by the sublimity of the epic itself. They exclaimed that Vālmīki's portraiture of the story of Rāma kept it alive for all time, and that it was so vivid that to listen to it was to see it all over again. They rewarded the two boys with suitable presents.

Thus encouraged, the two boys travelled, narrating the divine story wherever they went. They reached Ayodhyā, the capital of Kosala over which Śrī Rāma ruled. Here, too, they were warmly received by the people. Their fame reached Rāma's ears. He invited them to his palace, received them with due honour (the honour due to ascetics and sages) and seated them in his court. He then said to his brothers: "Listen carefully to the epic poem that these two young boys are going to sing."

Thereupon, the two boys began to sing the story, as commanded by Śrī Rāma, in a style befitting the dignity of the poem; Rāma himself was in the audience and soon his mind was absorbed in the narrative.

Bāla 5–6

His sons are reciting his poem to him?

Kuśa and Lava said:

The sublime story that we are about to narrate is of the descendants of the great king Ikṣvāku among whose ancestors was the famous Sagara. It is known as the Rāmāyaṇa. Listen without prejudice, as we relate the story from the very beginning.

King

There is a mighty kingdom known as the Kosala on the bank of the holy river Sarayū. Its capital is Ayodhyā, a city which was built by the Vaivasvata Manu himself, the first ruler of the earth during the present world-cycle. This vast city is twelve yojanas (over ninety-six miles) long and three yojanas (over twenty-four miles) wide. It is a powerful and prosperous city. The city is well planned and laid out, surrounded by an impassable moat. In it are embassies of kings who pay tribute to the emperor; and in it are traders from many countries of the world. Its roads are clean and wide; and its faultless water-supply system provides good and sweet water for all its inhabitants. It has seven-storeyed buildings decorated with precious stones and it is resplendent like a celestial body. It is protected on all sides by mighty and faithful warriors who make it utterly invulnerable.

In that foremost among cities, the citizens are happy, devoted to righteousness, learned and wise, truthful, contented with the wealth they have and therefore free from avarice. No one in that city is poor or destitute. No one is ignorant or cruel. Everyone leads a well-regulated life of piety and charity. Everyone has faith in God and the scriptures; and every member of the twice-born communities is well versed in the sacred lore. Narrow-mindedness and pettiness are unknown in that city. The brāhmaṇas are zealously devoted to the study of the sacred texts, to a self-controlled life free from desire and hate and to the promotion of righteousness in the world. And, the members of the other three communities (the rulers and warriors, the farmers and businessmen, and the servants of the people) follow the leadership of the brāhmaṇas.

It was over such a kingdom and in such a city that the famous king Daśaratha ruled. He was himself learned in the Vedas. He was as mighty as he was wise. He was in truth a royal sage, a sage who happened to occupy a throne. He led an austere life, his mind and senses fully controlled. From Ayodhyā the capital city (its name itself significant viz., invincible), made impregnable by its strong gates, made resplendent by its lovely houses and inhabited by thousands of people, the lord of the world, Daśaratha, governed the kingdom as Indra rules the heaven.

Bāla 7–8

The king Daśaratha had eight ministers. Vasiṣṭha and Vāmadeva were his preceptors. He also had other counsellors.

The ministers were endowed with noble qualities of statesmanship. They were affluent and modest, powerful and self-restrained, majestic and truthful. They were courteous in their manners and a smile always played upon their lips. They were strict but never lost their temper even when provoked. They were tactful, but they did not swerve from the path of truth. They were just: they did not hesitate to punish the guilty even if the latter were their own sons, and they did not persecute even an enemy who was not found guilty. They ensured that the state coffers were full, but did not resort to unrighteous means to achieve this end. While meting out punishment, they invariably took into consideration the weakness or the strength of the guilty. Their conduct earned the approval of the preceptors. They were famous and powerful, and their reputation for statesmanship and wisdom travelled even to foreign lands.

Though the king was so righteous and though he was eager to have a son and heir to the throne, he was not blessed with a son. One day the king said to himself: "Why should I not perform the horse-rite in order to earn the blessing of a son?" He had his preceptors and priests immediately invited to his court.

The king said: "Though I enjoy all the blessings in this world, yet I do not have the blessing of looking at the face of a son and this makes me sad. In order to earn that blessing, I consider that I should perform the horse-rite. May you be pleased to make this possible!" The preceptors applauded this idea. They advised that a good horse be released and its safety ensured. They asked for the ground on the northern bank of the river Sarayū to be got ready for the sacred ritual.

The king thereupon decreed that all this should be done forthwith. He entrusted the care of the horse to a noble prince. He ensured that the preliminary rites connected with the horse-rite be duly performed by the priests so that there might be no flaw in its conclusion, as otherwise, the performer of the rite would forfeit his prosperity. The ministers and the priests got busy immediately with their allotted tasks.

The king then announced his intention to his wives: "Undergo the necessary consecration along with me," said the king. And when they heard this, their faces blossomed like lotuses at the end of the winter season.

Bāla 9–10

Minister Sumantra said to the king:

The following story was originally attributed to Sanatkumāra, who prophesied the birth of four sons to you. He further prophesied as follows:

The sage Kaśyapa has a son known as Vibhāṇḍaka who will beget a son called Ṛṣyaśṛṅga. This latter will constantly dwell in the forest, devoted to the service and the holy and only company of his father. And therefore Ṛṣyaśṛṅga will observe brahmacarya in both its aspects: physical continence and also the spiritual transmutation of the whole being. Having never set his eyes on members of the opposite sex, he will possess the innocence of ignorance.

During the same period, a mighty king called Romapāda will be the ruler of Aṅga. And, the kingdom will suffer from a severe drought as the fruit of the karma of the king and his subjects. The king will seek the counsel of the learned brāhmaṇas who will proffer the only solution to the crisis: "If you will bring the young sage Ṛṣyaśṛṅga to your kingdom and give him Śāntā, your adopted daughter, in marriage, the gods will be pleased and send abundant rain."

But who could lure the mighty sage away from his father? The king will entrust the task to the brāhmaṇas. The family priest will suggest to the king: "Let the best among your courtesans be employed to achieve the royal purpose." The king will consent. A bevy of the most beautiful young women will go to the forest where the sage will live. By the will of benign providence, Ṛṣyaśṛṅga too, will happen to notice their presence outside the hermitage. He will invite them to the hermitage where he will duly worship them as guests should be worshipped. They, in their turn will give him some fruits and take leave of him, for fear of incurring the displeasure of his father.

Their touch, their fond embrace and their company will arouse in the young innocent a desire for their further company. Very soon he will leave the hermitage and trail after the courtesans. Lo and behold, as he enters the kingdom of Aṅga, there will be the most welcome shower of rain.

The king will receive the young ascetic with due honours and immediately beg of him to confer a boon: "May your father be not angry with us nor curse us!" And this will be granted. The king will lead the young sage into the inner apartments and there will give his adopted daughter Śāntā in marriage to the sage. The glorious sage Ṛṣyaśṛṅga will thus spend his time in the company of his wife Śāntā.

Bāla 11–12

Minister Sumantra continued:

The sage Sanatkumāra further prophesied as follows: "A descendant of Ikṣvāku, king Daśaratha by name, will cultivate the friendship of king Romapāda. The former will one day approach the latter with the request: 'I have no sons O king. Therefore, please let Ṛṣyaśṛṅga be asked to conduct a sacred rite so that I may be blessed with a son.' In response to this request, Romapāda will depute the sage to conduct the sacred rite through which Daśaratha will be blessed with sons." I pray that the needful may speedily be done to persuade the sage Ṛṣyaśṛṅga to come here and preside over the sacred rite you have undertaken.

Forthwith, the king Daśaratha, with the permission of his preceptors and priests, sought the presence of the holy sage Ṛṣyaśṛṅga. Having reached the forest hermitage, he met king Romapāda in the company of the sage. Romapāda received Daśaratha with great joy, delight and respect. After spending a few days in the hermitage, king Daśaratha prayed to Romapāda: "Let your daughter and her sage husband come to Ayodhyā, to bless the sacred rite I am about to commence." Romapāda conveyed this request to the blessed couple who immediately consented.

All of them left the hermitage. King Daśaratha despatched fast messengers to Ayodhyā to convey to the citizens the glad tidings of the sage's visit and to ask them to give him a royal welcome. The delighted citizens celebrated the sage's entry into the capital with a festival. The sage and his wife enjoyed the royal hospitality for some days.

On the advent of spring, king Daśaratha approached Ṛṣyaśṛṅga with the prayer that the sacred rite may be commenced. The sage issued the necessay instruction. The king summoned he preceptors and priests and said. "I wish to perform the horse-rite in order to obtain the blessing of a son. And, I am sure that by the spiritual power of Ṛṣyaśṛṅga, I shall have my wish fulfilled." The priests and the preceptors applauded the king's words.

Ṛṣyaśṛṅga thereupon instructed as to the proper manner in which the sacred horse should be released and the ritual ground should be prepared. The king, on his part, requested the priests to ensure that the rite be conducted without the least flaw: for the least flaw in its conduct would have contrary results. And the priests responded suitably and got busy with the preparation for the sacred horse-rite. Having thus personally ensured the proper performance of the rite, the king Daśaratha retired to his own apartment.

Bāla 13–14

A year had gone by: as enjoined by the scriptures, the king was ready to commence the horse-rite. Humbly he approached his preceptor Vasiṣṭha and said: "You are a dear friend to me, my supreme preceptor, too: you alone can bear the burden of the proper execution of this rite." The sage Vasiṣṭha immediately assumed charge.

At Vasiṣṭha's behest, a whole new township sprang up on the northern bank of the holy river Sarayū with ritual pits, palaces for royal guests, mansions for the officiating priests, stables for horses, elephants and so on, wells and markets, all of them properly equipped to supply the needs of the numerous guests expected to grace the occasion. Vasiṣṭha personally instructed: "Every house should be well provided with food and other necessities. Ensure that the people of all the communities are nicely fed and attended to, with respect—never without respect and reverence. No one shall show the least disrespect or displeasure, leave alone anger, towards the guests." All those in charge humbly accepted the charge. Vasiṣṭha asked Sumantra to invite the princely neighbours, the kings of neighbouring kingdoms as also those afar, to attend the sacred rite. Very soon they began to arrive with rich presents for king Daśaratha. Everyone concerned reported back to Vasiṣṭha that the duty allotted to them had been accomplished. Once again, Vasiṣṭha warned them: "Serve and give all that is necessary to our guests, but give with respect; do not serve with disrespect or playfully; disrespectful service destroys the giver."

At the conclusion of the year of consecration, the sacred horse had also returned. With Ṛṣyaśṛṅga at their head the priests now commenced the horse-rite, which proceeded in strict accordance with scriptural injunctions. In fact, the priests in their eagerness not to let a flaw creep in, exceeded even the scriptural demands in the performance of the rite. There was no flaw in the rite, the mantras were correctly recited and the ordained procedure was strictly adhered to. Vasiṣṭha had said: "Give, give food and clothes to all," and those in charge literally fulfilled this command. All the guests were thoroughly satisfied and blessed the king. The various beasts through whom the different deities were to be worshipped had been brought to the hall. The horse itself was richly decked and worshipped by the queens. Delighted that the horse-rite had concluded without an obstacle, the king gave away the land to the priests who, however, returned it to the king and accepted more useful monetary gifts from the king. They were all highly pleased.

The king fell at the feet of Ṛṣyaśṛṅga and the sage reassured the king that his wish would be fulfilled.

Bāla 15–16

The holy sage Ṛṣyaśṛṅga contemplated deeply for a few minutes and then said to king Daśaratha: "I shall perform a sacred rite prescribed in the Atharva Veda, adopting the method of the perfected heavenly beings, for the sake of securing the boon of progeny for you." As the sage commenced this sacred rite, the gods and the siddhas (demi-gods) descended upon the hall of worship in their ethereal forms. They worshipfully addressed Brahmā the creator as follows: "Lord, relying on a boon you had conferred upon him, the demon Rāvaṇa is oppressing all of us. According to that boon he cannot be killed by gods, demi-gods and demons: and so we are powerless against him. Even the natural elements function in obedience to him. Pray, find some means of putting an end to our tormentor."

The creator was sorely distressed to hear this and replied: "Rāvaṇa, proud and haughty that he was, only prayed that the gods, demi-gods and demons should not kill him: he held man in such utter contempt that he did not include man in the list! Hence, he can only be killed by a human being." As Brahmā said this, the lord Viṣṇu descended upon the scene. The gods now turned to him in heartfelt prayer: "Lord, we lay the burden of our misery upon your shoulders. Pray, incarnate yourself as a human being and destroy this Rāvaṇa who is an enemy of the world; who is invincible by gods. All of us—gods, demi-gods, demons, sages and hermits seek your refuge for protection: you are indeed the supreme refuge for us all." The lord Viṣṇu assured them that he would do the needful.

Lord Viṣṇu quickly decided that he would become the son of Daśaratha, at the same time fulfilling the wish of the gods. The lord at once became invisible to them all.

At the same time, a divine being emerged from the sacred fire, holding in his hands a golden bowl containing pāyasaṁ (a preparation of milk and rice). He said to king Daśaratha: "I am a messenger of Viṣṇu. With this sacred rite you have propitiated the lord. This pāyasaṁ which has been prepared by the gods is capable of conferring the boon of progeny upon you; take it and give it to your wives." Saying thus, that messenger disappeared into the sacred fire. King Daśaratha at once gave the pāyasaṁ to his wives. Half of it he gave to Kausalyā, half of what remained he gave to Sumitrā, half of the rest to Kaikeyī, and what remained he gave again to Sumitrā. Such indeed was the potency of this divine pāyasaṁ that all of them instantly shone with the radiance appropriate to the presence of a divine being in their wombs.

Bāla 17–18

Brahmā, the creator, commanded the gods: "Project part of your energies into the mortal world so that mighty beings may be born of you, in order to aid the Lord."

Thus commanded by the creator, the gods begot through vānara-women offspring mighty, powerful and strong and with the form and the external appearance of their celestial parent. Hanumān, the offspring of the wind-god, was the cleverest and the ablest of them all.

A year had rolled by. At the end of the twelfth month after quaffing the celestial pāyasaṁ, on the ninth day of the lunar (bright) fortnight in the month of Caitra (April-May), Kausalyā gave birth to the resplendent Rāma, the Lord of the universe, adored by all, who was indeed the manifestation of one half of lord Viṣṇu. After this, Kaikeyī gave birth to Bharata who was a quarter-manifestation of lord Viṣṇu. Sumitrā gave birth to twins Lakṣmaṇa and Śatrughna, who, together formed the other quarter of lord Viṣṇu.

This was an occasion for great rejoicing not only in Ayodhyā and in the kingdom of Kosala, but in the celestial realm, for the Lord incarnate as the son of man would put an end to the reign of terror of the demon Rāvana. The citizens gave the fullest reins to their eagerness to celebrate the event.

The preceptor of the king, Vasiṣṭha, christened the four sons Rāma, Lakṣmaṇa, Bharata and Śatrughna, and also lavished gifts upon all, on behalf of the king. Lakṣmaṇa became an inseparable companion to Rāma; they were one life in bodies, and without Lakṣmaṇa Rāma would not even ȶ sleep. Even so, Bharata and Śatrughna were dear to each other.

All of them grew up into intelligent and wise young men, learned in the scriptures, exemplary in their conduct and devoted to the welfare of all. The king was supremely happy to see them thus grow into young men.

At this time, the sage Viśvāmitra came to Ayodhyā. He sent word through the guards at the palace gate to the king Daśaratha of his desire to meet the king. Daśaratha ran forward to receive the holy sage who was a Rājarṣi (because he was of royal descent) and had later become, by dint of great austerity, a brahmarṣi (equal to a brāhmaṇa-sage). The king worshipped the sage who warmly embraced the holy men in the royal court. The king then offered to do whatever lay in his power to serve Viśvāmitra, and this offer greatly pleased Viśvāmitra.

Bāla 19–20

Viśvāmitra was thrilled to hear the king's noble words, and he further fortified the king's noble intentions by saying: "There is no one in the world who is your equal, O foremost among kings! You have a glorious ancestry and, in addition, you have the sage Vasiṣṭha himself as your preceptor and spiritual guide." The sage continued: "I have undertaken the vows connected with the performance of a sacred rite which is being interfered with by a couple of demons. I could easily deal with them myself, but the vows prevent me from giving vent to my anger. Hence, I pray, send with me your son Rāma for the protection of this sacred rite. In my care and with his own prowess he will be able to do the needful. I assure you that the two demons are as good as dead, for I know the matchless might of Rāma, as even Vasiṣṭha and the other sages do. I need him only for ten days and nights, and it is imperative that the sacred rite be completed within that time and not be prolonged by interruptions."

When king Daśaratha heard this he promptly fainted, and regaining consciousness after a few minutes, he spoke falteringly to Viśvāmitra: "Rāma is hardly sixteen years of age; I do not see that he is qualified to fight, especially with demons. Tell me what I should do. I shall send you my vast army. I

In 10 days Rama was married ?

shall myself come with you and fight the demons, but without Rāma I cannot live even a few minutes. He is but a child and is incapable of assessing the strength of the enemies. After a long, long time I have been given this precious son as the gift of the gods; how can I even think of parting from him. Nay, I shall come with my army to fight the demons."

Viśvāmitra reiterated his demand in the following words: "There is a mighty demon called Rāvaṇa, a descendant of Pulastya. He himself does not personally interfere with sacred rites, but he sends two other demons, Mārīca and Subāhu, to disturb them, and they throw filth, blood and flesh into the sacred fire. It is against such foes that I seek the help of Rāma, for only he can restrain these demons."

Greatly disturbed in mind to hear this, the king replied: "Oh, no, even I cannot face the mighty Rāvaṇa in battle. But if it is only to deal with Mārīca and Subāhu, I shall come with my army, but I can in no circumstances send my beloved son Rāma. You are indeed a renowned sage and you know dharma: therefore kindly show mercy upon us. Do not ask that I send Rāma with you. If you like, I shall come with you. If that is not acceptable to you, kindly forgive my inability to do anything in the matter."

Bāla 21–22

In great anger, the sage Viśvāmitra said to king Daśaratha: "How disgraceful and how unworthy of a king, that having promised you go back on your own word! This is unworthy of the glorious clan you belong to. However, if that is your decision, I will go; enjoy the ignominious life!"

Seeing this, the sage Vasiṣṭha intervened and said to the king Daśaratha: "O king, you are descended from an unbroken line of the most righteous monarchs. It does not behove you to swerve from the path of truth. If you should break your promise to the sage Viśvāmitra, you would lose all the merit that you earned by the performance of the great religious rites. The sage Viśvāmitra is a pastmaster of the marshal arts. He has at his command all the most deadly missiles (astras) which he has acquired directly from lord Śiva himself. Moreover, he can even invent new and more deadly missiles. It is not as if he is afraid of these demons. He can surely deal with them; but he is asking for Rāma for the good of Rāma himself!

Therefore, do not hesitate to accede to Viśvāmitra's request; thus would you be fulfilling your own promise."

These words reassured the king who immediately regained his composure and self-confidence and made up his mind to send Rāma with the sage to protect his rite. He sent for Rāma, embraced him fondly, kissed the crown of his head and blessed him. The family preceptor Vasiṣṭha blessed Rāma, too, with sacred Vedic texts. Even nature blessed Rāma. As Rāma and the inseparable Lakṣmaṇa set out to follow the sage, there was a gentle breeze and a shower of flowers from above.

It was a sight for the gods to see—Rāma and Lakṣmaṇa with warlike weapons slung on their shoulders walking with the stern ascetic Viśvāmitra. While they were still walking along the southern bank of the holy river Sarayū, the sage addressed them: "Rāma, without the least loss of time I shall initiate you into mysteries of Balā and Atibalā (strength and supreme strength); when you acquire these, you will not be subjected to fatigue, to fever, nor will your lovely form undergo adverse change. Nor will the demons be able to overpower you even in your sleep, if you have these mysteries."

After the necessary preliminary purification, Rāma received the divine mysteries from the sage; and immediately he shone with a new brilliance. The three spent that night on the bank of the holy river Sarayū, and Rāma and Lakṣmaṇa rendered the sage all the personal service that a disciple is expected to render the preceptor.

Bāla 23–24

At dawn the next day, the sage lovingly awakened the princes and all three of them offered their morning prayers. The two princes devoutly saluted the preceptor, ready to do his bidding. Led by him, they continued their journey and soon reached the confluence of Sarayū and the holy Gaṅgā, where they beheld several hermitages. The princes were curious and the sage said to them: "Cupid was endowed with physical form in days of yore. Lord Śiva was once engaged in breathtaking austerities on this very spot: and Cupid sought to distract the Lord. By a mere 'huṁ'-sound, and with the fire that emanated from his eye, the Lord destroyed the body of Cupid who thenceforward became bodiless. Where the limbs (aṅga) of his body were shed became known as Aṅga-territory.

These hermits who are devoted to their austerities here are the followers of lord Śiva."

While fording the holy river near the confluence, Rāma heard a roaring sound in the water. Viśvāmitra allayed his curiosity again with the following story: "Near Mount Kailāsa there is a lake known as Mānasa Sarovar, because it was born of the mind of Brahmā. This river Sarayū is so called because it flows from that Sarovar. The sound you heard is caused by the force with which that river rushes to meet the holy Gaṅgā. Offer your salutations to the holy rivers at the confluence, O Rāma."

Soon they reached a terrible forest which was frightful to enter. Once again, Viśvāmitra explained: "This area was once a prosperous country. In days of yore when Indra slew the demon Vṛtra who was a brāhmaṇa by birth, he had to expiate the sin of having killed a brāhmaṇa. The holy sages and brāhmaṇas performed the ritual of atonement with the waters of the holy rivers. When the impurities had thus been washed away, Indra shone with his native radiance. The impurities thus washed away from Indra were deposited here. Indra was happy to be rid of them and wanted to show his gratitude to the place where they fell away. He blessed this country with prosperity and named it Maladā and Karūṣa.

"The principalities of Maladā and Karūṣa were thenceforth prosperous and wealthy, till Tāṭakā appeared on the scene. This demoness was the wife of the demon Suṇḍa, and they have a terrible son known as Mārīca. Tāṭakā strikes terror in the hearts of the inhabitants of Maladā and Karūṣa and has turned the prosperous and fertile country into a waste and a forest. Rāma, now it is for you to get rid of this demoniacal family and to restore to this countryside the prosperity and the glory that it once had."

Bāla 25–26

Rāma was bewildered: "How could a frail woman possess such might and such strength?" And, the sage Viśvāmitra told him the whole story of Tāṭakā which is as follows:

"Once upon a time there lived a powerful demi-god named Suketu. He had no children. Desirous of having an offspring he engaged himself in austerities. Brahmā, the creator, was highly pleased with this and conferred the boon of a daughter upon him, at the same time blessing this daughter with the strength of a thousand elephants. It is just as well that the creator did not bless Suketu with a male child! The girl was as beautiful as she was strong. Suketu gave her in marriage to a demon, Suṇḍa. Of them the terrible Mārīca was born.

"Suṇḍa had been cursed to death by the sage Agastya. Tāṭakā wished to avenge her husband's death and rushed at the sage. Agastya pronounced a curse upon Tāṭakā also: 'From now you will lose the appearance of a demi-goddess and you will roam about as a terrible demoness.'"

"Do not let the thought that she is a woman deter you. For the welfare of society you have to destroy her. Praiseworthy and non-praiseworthy actions may have to be done by a ruler for the protection of his subjects—even what appear to be unrighteous and sinful actions. This is indeed the eternal duty of those entrusted with the onerous task of administering the state. Therefore, destroy this wicked woman: she does not know what dharma means!"

Rāma at once responded; "My father commanded me to obey you in all respects when he entrusted me to your care. By obeying you, therefore, I shall have fulfilled my duty towards you as well as my duty to my father!" Saying this, he readied his weapon; and the sound that it produced terrified the dwellers of the forest and aroused the suspicions of Tāṭakā. She rushed towards the source of that sound and when she came into view, Rāma jokingly pointed out that terrible form to Lakṣmaṇa. "Look at this demoness, O Lakṣmaṇa. We shall make her immobile by amputating her arms and legs: I do not feel inclined to kill this woman." Viśvāmitra roared "huṁ" and spurred the princes on. She showered huge rocks upon Rāma. Rāma replied with missiles from his weapons. She disappeared from view. Viśvāmitra now warned Rāma: "Do not dally with this demoness any more, Rāma. They grow more powerful at nightfall. Kill her quickly." Though she remained invisible Rāma hit her, guided by sound alone. She fell down dead.

At that very instant the forest shone with its old splendour.

Bāla 27–28

Early in the morning of the subsequent day, the sage Viśvāmitra lovingly spoke to Rāma: "I am delighted with you,

Rāma. I shall therefore give you an armamentarium of the most powerful missiles with the help of which you will be able to subdue all your enemies whether they are earthlings or celestials. Here, take charge of the following foremost among the missiles:

"Dharma cakraṁ (cakraṁ may mean a revolver!), Kāla cakraṁ, Viṣṇu cakraṁ as also the fierce cakraṁ of Indra. I give you the Daṇḍa cakraṁ, as also the missile that has the power of the thunderbolt (Vajra), the Śūlaṁ (of Śiva), the Brahmāśiras and another known as aisikam which is like a blade of grass. I give you the most powerful Brahmā astram, the all-destroyer, and also mace-like missiles. And, here is the missile of the gandharvas which confuses and stupifies the enemy. These other missiles are capable of putting the enemy to sleep and changing his mood from one of anger to one of peace. I also give you other missiles which can produce a shower of rain or dry up the earth, or generate unbearable heat and scorch the enemy. Also, another missile which produces in the enemy a sort of intoxication and another which will rouse his passion. This missile here has the lustre of a sun and will bedazzle the enemy. I give you all these and many more which are powerful and valuable in war with even celestials."

Rāma saw all these missiles in front of him. Pleased, he resolved that he would use them only when such use was called for. Saluting the sage Viśvāmitra, Rāma submitted: "Sir, please also instruct me in the art of countering the effect of these missiles". The sage then instructed Rāma and also Lakṣmaṇa in the anti-missile system. In this connection, again, the sage gave them many more missiles with names that signify the way in which they function—some which can be seen, others which cannot be seen, some with a forward motion and others with reverse motion, some with ten 'heads', others with a hundred 'bellies', some giving the appearance of burning coal, others appearing like dense smoke. All these missiles and anti-missile missiles were spread out in front of Rāma, awaiting his command; they lay at his feet, as it were, offering their services to him. And, he made a mental note of them and resolved to use them when their use became absolutely necessary.

They had by now reached the verge of the dense forest. Just outside this they saw a beautiful and holy hermitage.

Rāma queried about this and sage Viśvāmitra narrated the following story concerning the Siddhāśrama.

Bāla 29–30

The sage Viśvāmitra said: "In days of yore, Viṣṇu himself dwelt here for thousands of years, practising austerities. Lord Vāmana's hermitage, known as Siddhāśrama, is also here. The following happened during the period king Bali ruled the earth and the heaven. Indra and the gods appealed to lord Viṣṇu for help. The demon king Bali performed a mighty rite, at the conclusion of which he would become Indra. Also, at the same time, the sage Kaśyapa had successfully concluded a sacred observance over a period of a thousand years. When the Lord appeared before him and offered to grant him a boon, the sage prayed: 'If, pleased with me, you are willing to grant a boon, then I pray to thee, become my son!' The Lord gladly incarnated as the son of the sage and his wife Aditī. He was dwarfish in appearance. He immediately went over to Bali's house of worship and begged of the king to give him three paces of land. When this was granted, the Lord measured the heaven and the earth with two paces (and thus recovered them for Indra) and with the third he blessed the king by placing his foot on his head. This āśrama (hermitage) which is so called because it removes śrama (physical and mental fatigue) was indwelt by the Lord himself and I, being his devotee, dwell in it now. Come, let us enter the hermitage, for it is yours as well as mine. I shall now commence the sacred rite and I pray, guard it from the demons' interferences."

The princes, too, joyously replied: "Blessed sir, please commence the sacred rite, and we shall abide by thy command." The next morning the rite commenced. The sage Viśvāmitra himself had taken on a vow of silence. Hence, the others instructed Rāma and Lakṣmaṇa: "Guard the house of prayer for six days and nights." And so they did, without a wink of sleep, vigilant throughout the day and night.

It was the last night. The ritual fire blazed with unusual brilliance. There was a loud roar in the sky. Like monsoon clouds, dark and turbulent, the two demons appeared in the sky. There was a shower of blood and flesh and all sorts of terrible things. "Lakṣmaṇa, see how I scatter them in all directions," said Rāma and fired the missile known as Śīteṣu (the cold missile) which hurled the demon Mārīca into mid-ocean, a distance of eight hundred miles, as wind disperses clouds. Mārīca was not killed. Then with a fire-missile Rāma destroyed the other demon Subāhu. Lastly, with the wind-missile, Rāma dispersed the lesser demons. The rite proceeded to conclusion without any obstacles.

Bāla 31–32

Their mission accomplished, the princes slept in the hermitage and woke up betimes the next morning; and after concluding their morning prayers, they approached the sage Viśvāmitra with joined palms, and submitted: "We are your humble servants, O Sage; command us, what shall we do?" The sage Viśvāmitra blessed them and replied: "King Janaka of Mithilā is about to perform a sacred rite and I would like you to attend it along with me. In Mithilā you will also see an extraordinary weapon which has baffled mighty men, gods and demons. It was actually a gift of the gods a long time ago; and since no one has so far been able to handle it, it has been worshipfully put away."

The sage at once got ready to move on. He bowed to the forest and sought permission of the trees: "God bless you, and I am now going from here to the Himālayas." Many sages, beasts and birds also accompanied Viśvāmitra! After a while, however, the sage persuaded the sages and the birds and beasts to return to the forest. The hermits accompanying Viśvāmitra covered some distance before they retired for the night on the bank of the river Sone.

Viśvāmitra said: "Once upon a time there was a king known as Kuśa who was a son of Brahmā, the creator. He had four sons Kuśāṁba, Kuśanābha, Asūrtarajasa and Vasu. Unto them he entrusted the task of protecting the people of the kingdom. The four sons built four cities, Kauśāṁbi, Mahodaya (Kanauj), Dharmāraṇya and Girivraja (Rajgir) respectively. These cities were surrounded by hills. The river Sone weaving through those hills was also known as Māgadhi because it flows through Māgadha territory.

"Kuśanābha had a hundred daughters born through a celestial nymph Ghṛtāci. When they had grown up into beautiful young women, the wind-god approached all of them and said; 'I wish to marry all of you. Give up the idea that you are human beings and attain longevity. Youth is evanescent; especially among humans. Become forever young and immortal, by accepting my proposal.' The girls were distressed to hear this. 'How can we accept you as our husband—you, who enter into all beings? Morever, our father is our lord and master, nay our god; he alone shall be our husband unto whom our father gives us away.' Offended by this rebuttal the wind-god entered into them all and caused deformity of their limbs (like arthritis).

"Thus they approached their father Kuśanābha with tearful eyes. The distressed king and father questioned them, 'Tell me, pray, who is the cause of this dreadful deformity of your lovely forms?'"

Bāla 33–34

"The girls narrated all that happened, to their father. The king Kuśanābha greatly applauded the conduct of his daughters and said: 'Forbearance is indeed the greatest ornament of women as also of men—the kind of forbearance that you have shown in your conduct towards the wind-god. Forbearance is the greatest gift, the truth, the best form of worship, glory, piety and the support of the world.'

"Soon, the king began to think of giving them away in marriage to a suitable man.

"It was about the same time that there lived a great ascetic by name Chūlī, who had undertaken unprecedented austerities. During this period, he was waited upon and served by a girl named Somadā. The ascetic, highly pleased with her devoted service, said to her: 'I am highly pleased with your service; name a boon.' At once she replied: 'I am unmarried, and I will not marry. Grant me, therefore, the boon of a son through the power of your asceticism.' Highly pleased with this prayer, the ascetic willed that she should conceive and give birth to a son: and the cosmic (Brāhmic) energy brought this about. The son thus conceived and delivered came to be known as Brahmadatta (gift of Brahmā), who became the king of Kāmpilyā. It was to this Brahmadatta that the king Kuśanābha gave away all his hundred daughters in marriage. During the ceremony, when Brahmadatta touched the hand of each girl, her deformity left her and she regained her beauty and charm.

"The king Kuśanābha now prayed for the birth of a son to him. His father Kuśa blessed him saying: 'A pious son will surely be born to you,' and immediately ascended to heaven. Soon Kuśanābha was blessed with a son whom he christened Gādhi, in accordance with the wishes of his noble father. That Gādhi is my father, O Rāma; and I am also called Kauśika because I am a descendant of Kuśa.

"I also had an elder sister known as Satyavatī who had been given in marriage to the sage Ṛcika. She was highly devoted to her husband. As a result, when the sage departed from this world, she ascended bodily to heaven, and later descended on earth as a river, the Kauśikī (Kosi), out of the largeness of her heart. As such she continues to be to this day, O Rāma. I was very fond of my sister and so spent some time on the bank of Kosi. After that, I left that spot and came to Siddhāśrama where, thanks to you, I have now successfully completed the most sacred rite.

"Thus have I told you, Rāma, the history of this place. The night is well advanced. It is time all of you retired to bed."

Bāla 35–36

Early in the morning, the sage again heralded the dawn and urged the princes to get up and get ready to move on. Crossing the river Sone, the party marched onwards. They saw the holy river Gaṅgā.

As usual, Rāma posed a question, for the benefit of the whole assembly: this time he wanted to know the story of the Gaṅgā. The sage Viśvāmitra said:

"Himavān (Himālayas) married the daughter of Meru (the polar ice-cap) who was known as Mena. They had two daughters: the elder is Gaṅgā and the younger is Umā. For the welfare of all the beings of the three worlds (heaven, earth and the intervening space) the gods begged Himavān to give Gaṅgā to them. The magnanimous Himavān, too, acceded to their request. Thus, the holy Gaṅgā ascended to heaven and became a celestial river; later she descended on earth in the form of a purifying stream. The other daughter Umā was given by Himavān in marriage to lord Śiva himself."

With his curiosity whetted by this brief narration of the sublime story, Rāma requested the sage to expand the narrative and give the account in greater detail. The sage, too, consented, and gave the following detailed account of the story of Umā, the consort of lord Śiva, and also the story of the descent of the Gaṅgā on earth:

"The lord Śiva had married Umā, the daughter of Himavān. And, they were engaged in enjoying conjugal pleasures for a long period of time. The Lord's creative energy grew more and more intense; and even the gods were afraid that the earth would not be able to support his progeny. They therefore made bold to interrupt the union of the divine couple, to offer a prayer: 'Lord, pray restrain your creative energy by your own self-control; the worlds will not be able to bear the full impact of your creative energy. By such self-restraint practised by you and your consort, alone, will the worlds survive.'

"The Lord at once agreed to the proposal. 'What shall we do with the energy already released?' he asked. This energy had covered the earth already. The gods sought the help of fire and wind. Fire concentrated the energy which now assumed the form of a mountain, and being blown around by the wind, it spread to a thicket of reeds—and eventually assumed the shape of Kārtikeya (lord Śiva's son).

"Umā, the Lord's consort, however, was annoyed by the gods' interference in her union with the Lord and cursed the gods that they would never have an offspring."

Bāla 37

"While lord Śiva and Umā returned to their austerities, the gods with Indra at their head approached Brahmā, the creator, and humbly submitted: 'Lord, the divine being Śiva had granted us our boon, which was to bless us with a commander: this commander can only be born of his energy. Having released this energy, lord Śiva has resumed his austerities, along with Umā, his consort. Pray, consider what should be done.'

"The creator Brahmā replied: 'Umā's words cannot be falsified. No god can receive lord Śiva's energy to give it a body. Here is the heavenly (celestial) Gaṅgā; let the god of fire convey the Lord's energy to Gaṅgā who will then deliver the son. Gaṅgā will doubtless regard the child to be hers; and Umā will also lavish her affections on him. Thus he will be the beloved of all.'

"The gods then approached the god of fire to accomplish the commands of the Creator. The god of fire in his turn approached the celestial Gaṅgā and prayed that she should carry the Lord's creative energy. Gaṅgā assumed a form of ethereal beauty. Seeing this the energy melted into her. The god of fire filled her with the divine energy.

"Unable to carry that divine energy for long, the holy Gaṅgā, on the advice of the god of fire, released it on the side of the Himālayas. Where the energy flowed, everything turned into gold. Whatever the energy touched turned into gold and silver of incomparable brilliance; the mere heat of the energy turned objects at a distance into copper and iron. Even its 'impurities' became tin and lead. Thus the minerals were created on earth.

"As I said before, the energy was spread among the reeds on the bank of the river Gaṅgā. The gods gathered that energy, which became a boy. The gods ordained the deities presiding over the constellation Kṛttikā to nurse the boy with their milk; hence he came to be known as Kārtikeya. He is known as Skanda because he 'flowed' with the river Gaṅgā.

"In a matter of days this divine boy grew mighty in strength and destroyed the host of demons who were harassing the gods. He became the commander of the divine hosts.

"This is the story of the birth of lord Śiva's son who is also known as Kumāra. He who is devoted to Kārtikeya will enjoy a long life, will be blessed with children and grandchildren and will eventually become one with lord Skanda."

Bāla 38–39

Rāma, I shall now tell you the story of the descent of Gaṅgā on earth.

One of your own ancestors was the mighty king Sagara. He was without an heir to the throne, though he had two wives—Keśinī, daughter of the king Vidarbha, and Sumati, daughter of the sage Ariṣṭanemi and sister of the divine bird Garuḍa. The king undertook austerities. Pleased with him, the sage Bhṛgu bestowed upon the king a strange boon: "One of your wives will give birth to one son for the perpetuation of your clan; and the other will give birth to sixty thousand sons."

In course of time, Keśinī gave birth to a son christened Asamanja; and Sumati delivered an egg (of the shape of a gourd) from which sixty thousand sons emerged. Sumati preserved them in pots of ghee; they soon grew to be youthful boys. Asamanja true to his name proved to be a wicked boy who had dangerously sadistic tendencies and who revelled in torturing and drowning even young children. Yet, again, his own son Aṁśumān was pious and noble and was greatly loved by the people.

King Sagara resolved to perform the sacred horse-rite. He chose the most holy piece of ground between the Himālayas and the Vindhyas, which is regarded by sages as specially suited for the performance of holy rites, and commenced the rite. The sacred horse was entrusted to the care of the valiant Aṁśumān, the king's grandson.

Indra the chief of the gods, disguised as a ghost, however, stole the horse away at a critical point in the rite. The priests exclaimed: "O king, catch hold of the thief and kill him; let the rite proceed to a successful conclusion; otherwise great misfortune will result." The king sent for the sixty thousand sons and commanded them to comb the earth and find the horse; they had his permission even to dig the earth.

The sixty thousand fell to their task. Not finding the horse on earth, they began to dig the earth. Seeing this wanton and ruthless destruction of the subterranean and other life, the gods and demons prayed to Brahmā, the creator: "Lord, life on earth is being destroyed by these sons of Sagara. Aquatic creatures and subterranean creatures are tormented, too. Suspecting that this or that may be the enemy of the horse-rite, and here or there the horse may be hidden, they are doing great harm to living beings."

Bāla 40–41

The creator, Brahmā, replied: "Earth is, as it were, the consort of lord Viṣṇu the protector of the universe. The sons of Sagara who thus ravage her and her creatures will surely meet their end at the hands of the Lord who himself dwells on earth at this time in the person of Kapila, the divine sage. The breaking up of the earth, too, does take place in every age: this is nothing unusual. And they who are endowed with vision see that those thoughtless people who are guilty of crimes against the good earth are justly punished." The thirty-three gods who preside over the natural elements returned to their abodes satisfied.

Sagara's sons could not find the horse, though they had searched everywhere and even dug up the earth. But the king urged them on: "Dig deep down, splitting the very earth into pieces." And so they did. As they went right through the earth, they encountered four elephants that looked like mountains (perhaps the other way round?)—Virūpākṣa in the east, Mahāpadma in the south, Saumanasa in the west, and Bhadra in the north. They paid their homage to each one of these and continued their search. Finally they proceeded in the north-easterly direction. They were frustrated and angry. At the end of the tunnel through the earth, when they emerged into the open, they saw Kapila seated in meditation. They mistook the sage for the horse-thief: for they saw the sacred horse too, peacefully grazing near the hermitage. They shouted in great anger and rushed at the sage. By mere utterance of 'huṁ' on the part of the sage Kapila of incomparable glory, all of them were reduced to ashes.

In the hall of worship, the king was impatiently waiting for the sons and the horse to return. When neither returned, he despatched his grandson Aṁśumān to find out what had happened. Aṁśumān took the same routes and met the same 'elephants' (and bowed to them) which reassured him that he would find the horse. Eventually reaching Kapila's hermitage, he saw the horse and the ashes of his uncles. While he was thinking of a suitable way in which to perform the obsequies to the departed, he saw the divine bird Garuḍa who advised him: "Grieve not, O brave one, the destruction of these your uncles by lord Kapila is just and as it should be. It is not right to use earthly water to propitiate their souls. When the divine Gaṅgā is brought down on this earth, and when their ashes are touched by the waters of the Gaṅgā, they will also ascend to heaven."

Aṁśumān returned to the house of worship and with the return of the horse the king brought the rite to a conclusion. However, he could not devise a method by which the celestial river Gaṅgā could be brought down to the earth. Sagara ruled for a long time and passed away, without accomplishing his cherished ambition of having the ashes of his sons purified by the holy Gaṅgā.

Bāla 42–43

On king Sagara's demise, the people lovingly elected Aṁśumān to occupy the throne. He for his part, engaged himself in protracted austerities over a number of years, in order to bring the Gaṅgā down: but he passed away before the austerities bore fruit. He had a son, Dilīpa by name. After the death of Aṁśumān, Dilīpa became king. But, he was so stricken with sorrow at the death of his granduncles, that he could not do anything about it. On his death, his son Bhagīratha ascended the throne.

Bhagīratha repaired to Mount Gokarṇa (perhaps Gomukh) in the Himālayas to perform intense austerities with view to bringing Gaṅgā down and also to gaining an offspring. He performed breath-taking austerities. Brahmā, pleased with his devotion, appeared before him and granted him the boon of his choice. And, Bhagīratha chose the two boons he had in mind. "Here is the Gaṅgā," said lord Brahmā, "but only lord Śiva can withstand the impact of her descent upon earth."

Bhagīratha now turned his devotion to lord Śiva. Standing on the tip of his toe for a full year, Bhagīratha invoked the grace of lord Śiva. The Lord, pleased with his devotion, appeared before him and said: "I shall satisfy your noble wish and bear the Gaṅgā on my head."

Soon, the celestial river Gaṅgā descended in all her power and majesty on the head of lord Śiva. The matted-locks of the Lord resembled the Himālayas themselves (perhaps the other way round?). Caught in the coils of the Lord's matted locks, the river tumbled down on her earthly course. The Lord let the river fall into the celestial lake Bindusāra: Gaṅgā emerged from here in three different directions, as seven streams. Bhagīratha rode in his chariot ahead of one of the streams or the main stream. The course of the river, like the course of our lives, was smooth in some places, tortuous in other places, quiet here, tumultuous there; twisting and turning, running straight and even turning back. The waters of the Gaṅgā, touched by the head of lord Śiva himself, are extremely pure. Even they who, on account of a curse, have fallen from heaven are purified by bathing in the Gaṅgā.

Bhagīratha thus led the Gaṅgā on the earth. They passed near the house of worship of the sage Jahnu who was engaged in a sacred rite. The waters of the Gaṅgā inundated the house of worship. Annoyed at this, the sage drank the entire river which thus disappeared within him. On the intercession of the gods and celestials, the sage allowed Gaṅgā to emerge from his ear! Once again Gaṅgā followed Bhagīratha's chariot. They eventually reached the tunnel made by the sons of Sagara. Bhagīratha reached the culmination of his superhuman efforts: the holy Gaṅgā actually flowed over the ashes of Sagara's sons who were instantly purified and liberated.

Bāla 44–45

The creator Brahmā congratulated Bhagīratha on achieving the end of his quest, after overcoming all obstacles by superhuman effort. He decreed that the holy river that Bhagīratha had thus brought on to the earth would henceforth be known as Bhāgīrathī (the daughter of Bhagīratha.) He also decreed that whoever listens to this glorious account of Bhagīratha's unprecedented, superhuman, determined and successful attempt to achieve the task set for himself (viz., bringing the Gaṅgā down to earth) will have all his desires fulfilled, all his sins wiped out, and will enjoy fame and longevity.

Thus the sage Viśvāmitra concluded the story of Gaṅgā. Early the next morning they crossed the Gaṅgā and reached the city of Viśāla. Once again Rāma asked Viśvāmitra to narrate the legends connected with Viśāla. The sage replied:

"During the epoch known as the Satya Yuga, there were two sisters, Diti and Aditi, who gave birth to many powerful children and many pious children respectively. They grew up. And the desire grew in them to be free from old age and illness, to become immortal. Looking at the ocean of milk (the Milky way) in the outer space, they felt that if they could find a suitable churning rod and rope, they could churn that ocean which would surely yield nectar that would confer immortality on them. They then used the Mount Mandara as the churning rod, the serpent Vāsukī as the rope, and began to churn the ocean.

"But the first gift of the ocean was disappointing and distressing: a terrible poison Hālāhala emerged. The frightened gods sought the refuge of lord Śiva. In order to save the gods and the whole of creation, lord Śiva at once drank this terrible poison, as if it were nectar.

"The churning continued. The churning rod, Mount Mandara began to sink. The gods prayed to the lord Viṣṇu who, assuming the form of a tortoise, supported the mountain on his back. After a long time there appeared the divine physician, Dhanvantari. Then came a bevy of celestial nymphs: as they were the very cream (rasa) of the ocean (ap), they were known as apsaras. Then there arose an intoxicating liquor known as Vāruṇī. The demons refused to take it; but the gods took it. Therefore, the demons are known as asuras (they who did not take liquor or sura) and the gods are known as suras (they who drank the liquor sura). Then followed a divine horse, a divine gem, and lastly the nectar which all the gods and the demons sought and began to fight over. Lord Viṣṇu, assuming the disguise of a beautiful woman, carried the nectar away. The demons who opposed the Lord were defeated and the gods, with Indra as the leader, attained sovereignty!"

Bāla 46–47

"Stricken with grief at the death of her sons (the demons) at the hands of her step-sons (the gods), Diti resolved to avenge their destruction. With tearful eyes she pleaded with her husband, the sage Kaśyapa: 'Bless me, pray, that I may give birth to a son who will kill Indra, the chief among your sons, through Aditi.' Caught on the horns of a dilemma, the sage cleverly worded his blessing: 'So be it: if you perform intense austerities for a thousand years, and if you are able to complete them without the least negligence, you will give birth to a son capable of killing Indra.'

"Diti immediately embarked upon intense austerities. And, Indra (her step-son) himself served her, fetching firewood and water, fruits and other articles needed by her, and devoutly shampooing her feet while she slept. A thousand years passed. Highly pleased with Indra, Diti said: 'I. am performing these austerities for the sake of a son to kill you! Yet, you have been devoutly serving me all these years. I am pleased with you. I shall, therefore, ensure that your new brother will be friendly with you, and that both of you will together conquer the world.'

"Soon after this, at midday, she fell asleep. Unfortunately on that particular day, her sleeping posture was unethical and impure. She had her head between her feet. Indra was quick to take advantage of this impurity. He entered her body through his own magic power, and, with his powerful weapon (thunderbolt) began to butcher the foetus, his unborn enemy. He had cut it into seven pieces, and they began to cry. He continued to cut them, telling them: 'Don't cry, don't cry.' He had cut them again, each into seven pieces (forty-nine pieces in all). Diti woke up and wailed: 'Don't kill them, don't kill them.' When Indra heard her wailing, he emerged from her body and prayed for forgiveness: 'You had committed an act of negligence and therefore forfeited the boon father gave you; hence I tried to destroy my unborn enemy. Kindly forgive me.'

"Though she was stricken with grief again at the loss, Diti realised that it was due to her own fault, and so forgave Indra. She said: 'These forty-nine pieces will be born as the windgods, in groups of seven. You yourself had christened them Marut (since you called out to them mā-ruda, don't cry). The seven groups of wind-gods will fill the heaven and earth and the intervening space, and move about under your direction.' Thus Indra and his step-mother reached an understanding. This is that sacred place, O Rāma, where Diti performed her austerities and Indra himself served her."

Bāla 48–49

Viśvāmitra and the princes, accompanied by the other sages, spent the night at Viśāla; the next morning they left for Mithilā.

On the outskirts of Mithilā, Rāma saw an abandoned hermitage and asked Viśvāmitra: "Pray, tell me whose hermitage was this—which is without a hermit and looks desolate?"

With a delighted heart, the sage Viśvāmitra narrated the following story in reply: "This wonderful hermitage, O Rāma, belonged to that foremost among sages Gautama in days of yore. He was living here with his faithful, devoted and most beautiful wife Ahalyā.

"One day, when the sage was absent from the hermitage, Indra, the chief of gods, in the disguise of Gautama himself, entered the hermitage and sought union with Ahalyā. The pious and devoted Ahalyā knew instantly that the man in disguise was Indra himself; yet, she yielded to his advances, as she was highly gratified that the chief of gods had thus approached her. As Indra was leaving the hermitage, she warned him of Gautama's wrath, and requested him to be careful;

however, Gautama entered the hermitage as Indra was leaving. In great anger, Gautama cursed Indra: 'Assuming my own form, you have committed a sinful act: you will, therefore, lose your virility'. Looking at his unfaithful wife, the sage cursed her, too: 'Living on air, lying on ashes, unseen by anyone, you will live here for a long, long time; when, however, Rāma will visit this hermitage, you will regain your purity.' Having thus cursed both of them, the sage went away to the Himālayas.

"Having lost his virility, Indra pleaded with the gods and other celestials: 'In what I did, I only sought to serve the gods: I angered the sage Gautama, who cursed me with the loss of virility and by doing so lost the energy he had gained by his austerities. Kindly do something by which my virility may be restored.' The gods then approached the chief of the manes and prayed: 'Transfer the genitals of this ram to the loins of Indra; the castrated ram will be a delight to you, too.' The chief of the manes acceded to the gods' request and restored Indra's virility by transplanting the ram's genitals.

"Now that you are here, O Rāma, the end of Ahalyā's curse is near, too. Step into the hermitage." As Rāma stepped into the hermitage, Ahalyā came forward to greet them all. With all her impurities removed by the very sight of Rāma, she shone with her ethereal beauty and splendour. She devoutly worshipped her divine guests. In the meantime, Gautama had also come there. Both of them offered their devotion and hospitality to Rāma; and then resumed their austerities. Rāma proceeded towards Mithilā.

Bāla 50–51

Soon the party reached Janaka's hall of worship where the sacred rite was in progress. A new township had come into being. Rāma admired the excellent arrangements made by Janaka. Thousands of brāhmaṇas well versed in the Vedas had come from different parts of the country, and they had been comfortably lodged.

When Janaka heard of the arrival of the sage Viśvāmitra, he rushed forward to greet him. The sage, for his part, enquired as to the king's welfare and the progress of the sacred rite. He also greeted suitably the other sages in the hall of worship. King Janaka said: "It is now that my devotion and the sacred rite I am engaged in have become fruitful: by your presence.

ɜed am I, most fortunate am I today." He also
sage that the sacred rite would last twelve days;
s would themselves appear on the last day, to
fferings personally.

Looking at the princes, the king humbly asked Viśvāmitra: "Who are these young boys? They look like gods. Their gait is like that of elephants. These heroic boys are like a tiger and a bull in strength. Their eyes resemble the petals of a lotus. They are handsome like the Aśvini Kumāras (celestial physicians)." He also enquired as to the object of their tour and their visit to Mithilā.

The sage Viśvāmitra explained to the king who Rāma and Lakṣmaṇa were and what they had accomplished thus far. Hearing of the account of their visit to Gautama's hermitage and the redemption of Ahalyā, Śatānanda who was the family priest of king Janaka, and who was the son of Gautama and Ahalyā, lovingly enquired as to the welfare of his parents. Viśvāmitra replied: "What needed to be done for both of them was done by us. Gautama and Ahalyā have been re-united."

Delighted with this, Śatānanda then turned to Rāma and said: "Welcome, O prince among men! It is indeed your great good fortune that you have come here, under the leadership of sage Viśvāmitra. This is a sage of incredible deeds, a brahmarṣi, full of the power of austerity and spiritual radiance. I know him to be the best refuge. Listen, I shall now tell you all that I know about him:"

This sage was a great and noble king, devoted to righteousness, who yet kept his enemies in check. He is the son of Gādhi, the grandson of Kuśa. On one occasion, the king Viśvāmitra went round the world with a huge army. During this expedition, he came to the hermitage of sage Vasiṣṭha. This extraordinary hermitage was the abode of gods, celestials, as also flowers and wild animals. It was equal in splendour to Brahmā's heaven!

Bāla 52–53

The sage Vasiṣṭha welcomed king Viśvāmitra and offered him the hospitality of the hermitage. The king, as was the custom, enquired if the religious activities of the hermitage were being carried out properly: in reply, the sage informed the king that all was well with the hermitage and the hermits dwelling in it. For his part, Vasiṣṭha enquired of the king: "Is all well with you, O king? Are you protecting your people, strictly adhering to dharma? Are your royal servants dutiful? Are your enemies well under your control? Is everything well with your army, your treasury, with your friends and family?" And, the king Viśvāmitra too, replied that even so all was well.

The sage Vasiṣṭha continued: "May I offer you and your vast army the hospitality of the hermitage? Please accept it and be my guests today." The king was bewildered: what had this ascetic and this hermitage to offer to the king and his vast army! Perhaps the offer was more of intention than deed: taking it to be so, the king politely turned down the offer. The sage obviously knew the mind of the king and repeated the offer again and again. Finally, intrigued by the proceedings, the king accepted the offer.

"Śabalā", called out Vasiṣṭha, and a cow appeared before him. "I wish to entertain this king and his vast army today; kindly do the needful. Whatever type of food that each one of our guests may desire, make that available." Even so the cow did! Food of every description, drinks of every description, as desired by each one of the members of the king's army, together with necessary plates and cutlery—in short, a royal banquet of unprecedented luxury and lavishness—was spread before the king Viśvāmitra and his vast army.

The king was wonderstruck at this unheard-of miracle. After the meal, he approached the sage Vasiṣṭha and said: "I have a request to make. This cow Śabalā is truly a gem among cows; and gems belong to the king. Therefore, give Śabalā to me, and I shall give you a hundred thousand cows in return." Politely but firmly Vasiṣṭha turned down the offer and refused to part with Śabalā. "All my religious activities, my sacred rites, depend upon her. I shall not part with her, even for a thousand million cows!" The king would not relent: he offered a lot more! Thousands of elephants, horses, millions of cows, any quantity of jewels and gems . . . limitless wealth the king was ready to give to Vasiṣṭha; but he wanted Śabalā. Equally adamant was the sage in turning down all the royal offers, again explaining that the cow was indispensable for his performance of the sacred rites and the daily charities, and finally clinching the issue, by declaring: "What is the use of too many words: I shall not give Śabalā."

Bāla 54–55

When Vasiṣṭha refused to part with the wish-yielding cow Śabalā, king Viśvāmitra took her away by force. But very soon the cow wrestled with her captors and returned to Vasiṣṭha and wailed: "O sage, why have you abandoned me?" The sage lovingly replied: "Śabalā, I have not abandoned you. But, the king has a vast army and therefore is more powerful than I am. What can I do now?" Quick was Śabalā's rejoinder: "But it is said that in this world truly the mighty rulers are not powerful; it is the wise ones who are powerful; the power of the mighty is limited to their arms, whereas the power of the wise ones is divine and infinitely superior. If it is your wish, I shall put an end to the king and his army." Vasiṣṭha, taking the hint, ordered Śabalā: "Produce a mighty army to destroy the king's army."

Śabalā at once created hundreds of warriors known as Pahlavas. When they were killed by the king's army, she produced hundreds of others who were of mixed Śāka-Yavana parentage, and of fair and light complexion. They fought furiously with the king's army. The king used whatever missiles he had: by these the Yavanas, Kāmbojas and Barvaras (all of them foreigners) were terribly harassed. Seeing this, Vasiṣṭha ordered Śabalā to produce more warriors. From her mouth emerged Kāmbojas, from her udder Barvaras, from her hind parts Yavanas and Śākas, from the very pores of her skin Haritas, Kirātas and other foreigners. In no time, all these together destroyed the entire army of Viśvāmitra and even his sons.

One son had survived the carnage. Entrusting the kingdom to him, Viśvāmitra went to the Himālayas to pray, worship and to meditate. Pleased by his austerities, lord Śiva appeared before him and granted a boon. Viśvāmitra prayed: "Whatever missiles are possessed by the gods, celestials and demons—I wish to know their secrets." Śiva granted this prayer and conveyed to him the vital secrets concerning the missiles. Armed with these, the king proudly assumed that the sage Vasiṣṭha could easily be defeated. Immediately he went to the hermitage of Vasiṣṭha and began sacking the holy abode with his missiles. A terrible fire raged in the hermitage; hermits began to run away out of fear, even though Vasiṣṭha tried to maintain their morale by asking them not to panic, and by promising to deal suitably with the king. Even birds and beasts fled the hermitage.

Greatly angered by this turn of events, the sage Vasiṣṭha said to king Viśvāmitra: "Cursed be thou: you have desecrated this holy hermitage, turning it into a desolate waste." The sage stood there with his staff uplifted—the mendicant's staff look like Yama's rod of chastisement, like the smokeless fire that portends cosmic dissolution.

Bāla 56–57

The king's confidence in military hardware and might was not shaken by the mendicant's staff which the sage Vasiṣṭha flourished: "Hold on a minute," said Viśvāmitra and hurled the deadly fire-missile at the sage. "Here I stand," said Vasiṣṭha. "Do your worst, O vile warrior! Can a foolish warrior's might face the spiritual power of a knower of Brahman the infinite?" To Viśvāmitra's astonishment, the fire-missile was neutralised by Vasiṣṭha's staff!

One after another, Viśvāmitra used all the missiles whose secrets had been revealed to him by lord Śiva—the soporific missile, the intoxicating missile, missiles that are unbearably hot, a missile that dries up everything, a missile that tears things apart, a missile which like the thunderbolt shatters everything, and yet another missile, as deadly as death itself. The energy released by all these missiles was effortlessly absorbed by the magic staff of the sage Vasiṣṭha!

Defeated in his purpose, Viśvāmitra now resolved to use the most powerful of all these missiles, the Brahmā-astra, which could destroy every created object. Even the gods and the celestials watched this with great anxiety and bated breath. But, the staff held in the hand of the sage rendered even the Brahmā-astra powerless. The impudence of the king, however, provoked the sage's ire: from every pore of the sage's skin, a supernormal energy emanated. Thereupon the gods and the celestials prayed to Vasiṣṭha: "Pray, arrest this flow of your divine energy." The sage calmed down. But, Viśvāmitra was utterly humiliated. "Shame on the might of a king; that is strength which a brāhmaṇa (knower of the absolute) possesses. With just his staff, this sage neutralised all my deadly missiles! I shall engage myself in austerities: for by austerities does one gain brāhmaṇa-hood." So saying he proceeded southward and began his austerities.

After years of intense austerities, the creator Brahmā himself appeared before Viśvāmitra and said: "I recognise you as a royal sage." But, the king was not satisfied. He wanted to be a brāhmaṇa! He continued his austerities.

At the same time, there was a king known as Triśaṅku. He had a desire to ascend to heaven with his body! He approached Vasiṣṭha with the request: "I wish to bodily ascend to heaven. I shall perform a hundred sacred rites with this end in view. Please conduct them." Vasiṣṭha, however, refused to do so. Triśaṅku was in no mood to give up his attempt. He, therefore, approached Vasiṣṭha's sons to do him the favour of conducting the hundred sacred rites so that he could bodily ascend to heaven.

Bāla 58–59

Greatly annoyed by Triśaṅku's request, sage Vasiṣṭha's sons replied: "The holy guru Vasiṣṭha is devoted to truth: and he has turned down your proposal—how then do you resort to others with the same proposal? If he has said it cannot be or should not be done, it should be abandoned! To do what has been forbidden by him would be insulting him." But, proud and greedy king Triśaṅku, though he was a pious and noble ruler, would not give up his pursuit! He said to the sons of Vasiṣṭha: "Well, then, I shall seek help elsewhere!" This was intolerable to them, and they therefore cursed him: "You have turned away from the light of truth (guru), and embraced the darkness of self-will. You will therefore become a dark being (caṇḍāla), your exterior as impure and filthy as your interior is."

The next morning king Triśaṅku woke up to find that even his appearance had changed and that everything he touched or that came into contact with him became polluted and filthy. Seeing him thus transformed, his ministers and followers abandoned him and returned to the city. The king who had become an untouchable sought refuge with Viśvāmitra.

With a heart full of compassion Viśvāmitra asked Triśaṅku the cause of the dreadful transformation; and the latter narrated all that had happened. He had gone to Vasiṣṭha and his sons with the best of intentions; but all that was of no avail. Far from bodily ascending to heaven, he had even lost his royal physical appearance, and had become a despicable being. "I have always been a truthful and righteous king. I wanted to perform a hundred religious rites which would enable me bodily to ascend to heaven. Look at my present state! The unseen will of the divine alone is supreme; self-effort is futile. The divine will overpowers everything; that divine will alone is our last resort. Today I take your refuge; I have no other refuge. Kindly find a way to overcome my fate through self-effort."

Greatly moved by the king's prayer, Viśvāmitra despatched his disciples in all directions to personally invite the holy men and priests to the sacred rite he had resolved to conduct on behalf of Triśaṅku, for the fulfilment of his wish. "Invite all, even the sons of Vasiṣṭha, on my behalf," said Viśvāmitra. All of them accepted the invitation and arrived at Viśvāmitra's hermitage forthwith—except the sons of Vasiṣṭha who contemptuously turned down the invitation. When he heard this, Viśvāmitra cursed them all in absentia: "Though they are supposed to be holy men engaged in austerities, they thus insult me! They will die and be born in seven hundred births to come as untouchables following despicable occupations."

Bāla 60

Viśvāmitra was about to commence the sacred rite so that Triśaṅku might bodily ascend to heaven. Viśvāmitra said to the great sages and priests, assembled with him: "Along with me, engage yourselves in such a sacred rite as will enable Triśaṅku to ascend to heaven with his physical body."

Viśvāmitra himself became the chief priest at the rite. All of them commenced the sacred rite in strict accordance with scriptural injunctions relating to such a rite. They invoked the presence of the gods so that they might receive the offerings: but the gods failed to arrive. Viśvāmitra's anger grew fierce. Pouring an oblation into the sacred fire, he declared: "As the sole reward for the austerities performed by me in the exercise of my own free will, I claim the bodily ascension of Triśaṅku to heaven. O king, behold the power of my will, my self-effort: by these I send you to heaven in your own physical form."

At once, to the astonishment of all, Triśaṅku began to rise towards heaven in his physical form. Indra, the chief of the gods and the king of heaven, turned Triśaṅku away from the gates of heaven, saying: "Triśaṅku, since you have earned the curse of your own guru, you have no place in heaven! Return to earth." With these words, Indra threw him out, and Triśaṅku began to fall down. As he was heading back to the earth, he cried out to Viśvāmitra: "Save me, protect me."

Viśvāmitra's anger knew no bounds. He cried out: "Stop!" And Triśaṅku's fall was arrested, and he stopped suspended in space. With the merit earned by his austerities, and with his own self-effort, defying the wills of the gods, as it were, Viśvāmitra began to create another heaven, another set of planets and stars, another set of 'seven constellations' (like the Great Bear) to go round Triśaṅku (as the others go round the pole star)—in short, a new galaxy in the southern quarter of the space. He was resolved even to create another Indra, or perhaps leave the new heaven without an Indra.

The outwitted gods and demons humbly approached Viśvāmitra and submitted: "Holy sir, this Triśaṅku had forfeited all his merits by provoking his guru to curse him, by defying his guru's counsel. Hence, he is incapable of ascending bodily to heaven." Viśvāmitra replied: "I have given my word that he will, and I cannot break my promise. Let him therefore enjoy heavenly bliss where he is. And let these heavenly bodies that I have created continue to exist during this world cycle." The gods agreed. They even granted that Triśaṅku would continue to remain suspended in space, but happy as a god.

Bāla 61–62

All this, however, was an obstacle to Viśvāmitra's penance: for this incident depleted the merits that he had earned by his previous austerities. He abandoned his abode in the south and moved to Pushkar in the west, and recommenced his penance.

At the time, king Aṁbarīṣa was king of Ayodhyā, and he was engaged in the performance of a horse rite. As usual, Indra stole the horse. The officiating priest was greatly distressed and said to the king: "By your neglect, the horse has been stolen; the sin of neglect destroys a monarch. If he cannot find the horse, the atonement prescribed is the offering of human sacrifice."

Shocked by this pronouncement, the king sought to find the horse. But he could not find it anywhere. In the course of his wanderings, he came to the hermitage of the sage Ṛcika and begged him to give him one of his sons for the purpose of the atonement. The sage refused to part with his first son; and similarly, his wife refused to part with the last son. The middle one, known as Sunaḥśepa, remarked: "The eldest son is indispensable to the father; the last one is indispensable to the mother; I guess I, the middle one, am the only dispensable one." Sunaḥśepa offered to go with the king who bestowed lavish presents on his parents, and left with the boy.

On the way, the boy Sunaḥśepa noticed Viśvāmitra engaged in austerities. The boy sought his refuge and prayed: "I have no one to look after me in this world, sir: so I seek your refuge. Kindly do something in such a way that the king's sacred rite might conclude successfully, and I might enjoy long life to practise austerities and go to heaven." Moved to compassion, the royal sage turned to his own sons and demanded who would take Sunaḥśepa's place and thus save him. One of his sons taunted the father: "How strange, father, that you wish to throw away your own sons, in order to save someone else's son!" Viśvāmitra was angered at the son's impudence. Such impudence had to be punished, whether it was others' children or his own who were involved. He pronounced a curse: "You will suffer the same fate as the sons of Vasiṣṭha."

Turning to Sunaḥśepa, Viśvāmitra said: "During the sacred rite, recite the two hymns I shall presently teach you. Your object will be achieved." Aṁbarīṣa resumed the interrupted rite and brought it to a conclusion. Sunaḥśepa recited the hymns and pleased with them Indra himself appeared on the spot, blessed Aṁbarīṣa and blessed Sunaḥśepa, with long life.

Viśvāmitra continued his austerities at Pushkar.

Bāla 63–64

After a thousand years of austerities, the gods headed by Brahmā the creator, went to the ascetic Viśvāmitra and announced: "You have now become a ṛṣi", not just a royal sage. But, Viśvāmitra continued his austerities with added zeal.

One day a celestial nymph Menaka came to the Pushkar lake to bathe. The ṛṣi saw her and lost his heart to her. She, too, responded to his invitation: and they began to live together in the ṛṣi's hermitage. For ten years they thus lived together, enjoying all the pleasures. One day he realised that this was again an obstacle to his penance! Sensing the change that had come over him, Menaka stood trembling with fear: but the ṛṣi took leave of her in affectionate words and went to the north.

Once again the austerities continued. Even the gods were astounded. They, and Brahmā the creator, came to Viśvāmitra again, and announced; "I am pleased with your austerities and you are now the foremost among the ṛṣis, and therefore a maharṣi." Viśvāmitra humbly submitted: "If you had called me a brahmarṣi, I would have thought that you considered me to have conquered my senses!" "Not yet," replied Brahmā, and said: "Carry on!" And, Viśvāmitra intensified his austerities. With uplifted arms, standing without support, eating nothing, surrounding himself with the five fires in summer, in the rainy season with nothing but the sky over-head, lying on bare ground in winter—he engaged himself in unprecedented austerities.

The gods were disturbed, for Viśvāmitra's austerities threatened their position and power. Indra said to another celestial nymph, Raṁbhā: "Go, and distract his mind." She was afraid that the sage might curse her! "Fear not, I am also with you," said Indra; "I shall be near you as a bird." And, so Raṁbhā went to the hermitage. Viśvāmitra saw her, and understood the trap! And, he cursed her: "You came to ruin my austerities; well, stay there petrified. After a long time, the sage Vasiṣṭha will enable you to regain your celestial form." Raṁbhā turned into a stone. Indra and Cupid quickly flew away!

But, Viśvāmitra did not rejoice. He had won a victory over lust; but he had succumbed to anger, and thereby lost the merit acquired by his austerities. "I shall conquer anger," said he to himself; "I shall not speak. I shall not even breathe. Till I attain the status of brāhmaṇa-hood I shall stand here, without food or drink, without even breath." Such a vow had not been taken by anyone before Viśvāmitra.

Bāla 65

For the last and final part of his penance, Viśvāmitra chose the east. This time it was more severe than ever. However greatly he was provoked, he did not get angry. After a thousand

years, when he had successfully completed the vow of
and silence, and he was about to break his fast and eat
himself appeared in the disguise of a mendicant and
for food. Quietly, without losing his patience, Viśvāmitra gave him the food he had prepared for himself, and, since nothing was left, continued his fasting and silence for another thousand years.

The 'fire' of his austerities, the psychic energy released by his penance, grew fierce. It appeared as if this energy would consume the whole world. The gods now approached Brahmā the creator and prayed: "The energy generated by Viśvāmitra's penance is scorching the whole world. We have all of us tried by several means to distract him; but undistracted his penance progresses. There is now no alternative but to grant him whatever he chooses, even if it be the rulership of the gods."

Brahmā and the gods went to where Viśvāmitra was engaged in penance, and the creator addressed Viśvāmitra: "I am highly pleased with your austerities, O Brahma-ṛṣi! You have truly attained to brāhmaṇa-hood by dint of your own austerities." Overjoyed to hear the blessings of the creator, Viśvāmitra submitted: "If such be thy will, Lord, let 'Om' and Vaṣaṭ, and let the Vedas come into my heart and become part of my being. Also I would like the recognition that I am now a brahmaṛṣi to come from the supreme sage Vasiṣṭha."

Brahmā and the gods then approached the sage Vasiṣṭha with the proposal. Vasiṣṭha immediately consented. He went over to Viśvāmitra, greeted him in a friendly way and said: "You are indeed a brahma-ṛṣi, and you are fully accomplished." Viśvāmitra's supreme austerities had borne fruit.

Such is the glorious life of this mighty sage Viśvāmitra, O Rāma: and you are indeed thrice blessed to enjoy his company and leadership, concluded Śatānanda.

Janaka who had also heard this most exalted story, now fell at the feet of the sage Viśvāmitra and exclaimed: "Truly blessed am I that, in the company of Rāma, you have blessed this sacred rite being conducted by me. I am highly inspired by this story of yours narrated by Śatānanda. I long to hear more. Yet, I must excuse myself now as the hour of evening worship draws near. Kindly bless me again with your presence tomorrow."

Bāla 66–67

Early next morning, king Janaka invited the sage Viśvāmitra and the princes Rāma and Lakṣmaṇa to the palace. On their arrival, he duly honoured them, and then addressed Viśvāmitra: "Holy sir, I await your commands: what can I do for you?" In reply, Viśvāmitra said: "These two sons of Daśaratha are eager to see the famous dhanuṣ you have."

The king sent for the dhanuṣ; and in the meantime, told the story of the weapon, which is as follows:

"You know how lord Rudra wrecked the sacred rite of Dakṣa in days of yore. He was annoyed that the gods had not reserved a portion of the ritual offering for him, and threatened to kill them all with this weapon. The gods fell on their knees and appeased the Lord. At once, the Lord became pleased and gave them the weapon as a memento. The gods in their turn gave it to an ancestor of mine known as king Devarāta.

"A few years ago a portion of my land was being ploughed, and I found a divine child in the furrow: I therefore called her Sītā, and adopted her as my own daughter. She grew up into a beautiful young woman, and many princes wooed her. I did not wish to give away Sītā, who was of immaculate birth, to an unworthy person. It was decided that only that hero who could fire this weapon would earn the hand of Sītā. All those princes and others tried their hand at it: but they did not even know what to do with it; they could not even touch it or hold it. If Rāma fires this weapon, then I shall give him in marriage Sītā of divine origin."

In the meantime, five thousand exceptionally strong men brought in the weapon with its strong casing, mounted on wheels. The sage Viśvāmitra said to Rāma: "Rāma, young man, please look at this weapon." Rāma opened the casing and remarked: "I see what it is: I think I shall be able to handle it and to fire it, too." And, as thousands of people were looking on, Rāma mounted it, and filled it, and then fired it: with a loud roar the weapon broke in the middle. King Janaka said: "Holy one, I have now seen the strength of Rāma, and I have seen with my own eyes, this supremely wonderful and incredible and indisputable feat. Sītā has found her spouse, and she will import to the family of Janakas great fame and glory."

The king Janaka and the sage thereupon sent swift messengers to Ayodhyā to inform king Daśaratha and to invite them all to Mithilā for the auspicious wedding of Rāma and Sītā.

Bāla 68–69

King Janaka's ambassadors soon reached Ayodhyā and sought an audience with the king Daśaratha. With folded palms and in a sweet voice, they submitted: "O king, the king Janaka conveys his greetings to you, through us his humble servants, and enquires after your welfare. He has sent through us, the following joyous message: 'You might already be aware that I had vowed that he who is able to put to use the mighty weapon of the gods which is in my possession will win the hand of Sītā, my daughter. That condition was duly fulfilled by your great and worthy son Rāma. I humbly pray that you will soon bless us with your presence so that I can fulfil my pledge and give Sītā in marriage to Rāma.' This message has the hearty approval of both Viśvāmitra and Śatānanda."

Daśaratha was overjoyed to hear this message. He forthwith summoned his counsellors and his preceptors, conveyed to them the happy tidings and begged for their advice: "If king Janaka's credentials are acceptable to you, then we shall proceed to his capital, without loss of time." The counsellors and others hailed the proposal, and the pleased king decided that they would leave the next day.

Under the king Daśaratha's instructions, he was preceded by his treasurers with vast wealth and precious gems, and by a mighty army, then by the sages and the preceptors, then by the household priests. King Janaka's ambassadors had in the meantime conveyed this news to him. He organised a suitable reception in Mithilā for the king Daśaratha. The meeting of these two monarchs was heart-warming and inspiring.

In his welcoming speech, king Janaka said: "I feel honoured and blessed by your visit to Mithilā, O best among men! You will soon behold your heroic sons. My house is exalted by this matrimonial alliance with the house of Raghu. Tomorrow morning after due ceremony, and with the blessings of the sages, you will witness the wedding."

In his reply, king Daśaratha said: "Thus have I heard: the recipient of a gift is in the hands of the giver! You are the giver, in as much as you wish to give your daughter in marriage to my son. And, I shall certainly do exactly as you say."

Such expression of goodwill and meekness on the part of the aged king Daśaratha moved the heart of king Janaka. Soon after this royal reception, Daśaratha saw and embraced Rāma and Lakṣmaṇa who humbly touched the father's feet. Then, all of them retired to their own apartments.

Bāla 70–71

The next morning, king Janaka sent for his brother Kuśadhvaja, the ruler of Sāṅkāśya, after informing him of the forthcoming event. Then he graciously invited king Daśaratha, with his preceptor and priests to the royal court. After taking his seat in the court, Daśaratha said: "The sage Vasiṣṭha is our spokesman, and I request him to acquaint you with my ancestry." Vasiṣṭha recounted the names of Daśaratha's ancestors, among whom were Marīci, Kaśyapa, the sun Vivasvān, Manu, Ikṣvāku, Māndhātā, and Asita. Asita died in the Himālayas, leaving two wives who were each expecting a child. One of them gave poison to the other, so that the foetus might be destroyed. Kālindī happened to meet the sage Chyavana, by whose grace the poisoned foetus was unharmed. This child who was poisoned before birth was known as Sagara as he was 'sa' (with) 'garena' (poison). After Sagara, Aṁśumān, Bhagīratha, Kākutstha, Raghu, and so on to Aja whose son is Daśaratha, whose sons are Rāma and Lakṣmaṇa. "Unsullied is the line of Daśaratha, from the very beginning, all the kings being pious and heroic and truthful. I seek the hands of your daughters for Rāma and Lakṣmaṇa. Worthy brides should be given to bridegrooms worthy of them," concluded Vasiṣṭha.

After this, king Janaka himself recounted his ancestry, as, he said: "On the occasion of the wedding of one's daughter to a worthy bridegroom, one belonging to a reputable dynasty should give an account of his ancestors." Among his ancestors were Nimi, Mithi, the first Janaka, Suketu, Devarāta, Mahāroma, Swarṇaroma, and Hṛasvaroma. "The last mentioned had two sons," Janaka continued; "myself and my brother Kuśadhvaja. After installing me on the throne, our father went away to the forest. Later, the powerful king of Sāṅkāśya, named Sudhanvā invaded Mithilā, but was defeated and killed by me. I then installed Kuśadhvaja on the throne of Sāṅkāśya. Such is my ancestry. I say, and I say it thrice beyond doubt, that I give you my two daughters, Sītā, who is of divine origin, and also my second daughter Ūrmilā to be your daughters-in-law, Sītā as the wife of Rāma and Ūrmilā as the wife of Lakṣmaṇa. Let therefore the auspicious ceremonies connected with the wedding be immediately commenced. And, on the third day from now, the wedding itself will be celebrated. May gifts be lavishly given for the welfare of Rāma and Lakṣmaṇa."

Bāla 72–73

The two mighty sages Vasiṣṭha and Viśvāmitra approached king Janaka and submitted as follows: "O king, the houses of king Daśaratha and your own are incredibly great and incomparable. It is therefore in the fitness of things that your daughters are to wed king Daśaratha's sons. But, there is more! We suggest that your brother Kuśadhvaja's two daughters may be given in marriage to the two other sons of king Daśaratha." The delighted king Janaka replied with great humility; "I consider it a matchless blessing that this proposal comes from you two sages. Let it be even so: may Kuśadhvaja's daughters become the wives of Bharata and Śatrughna."

Rising from his seat, the king Janaka pointed to two exalted seats in the wedding pavilion for the two sages and humbly begged of them: "You have conferred the greatest dharma (blessing or merit) upon me. I am your humble disciple, O best among sages! Kindly accept these exalted seats. Kindly conduct the auspicious ceremonies." King Daśaratha at the same time took leave of kings Janaka and Kuśadhvaja and retired to his camp for conducting the bridegrooms' part of the ceremonies. There he gave away in charity thousands of cows, adorned with gold, to the holy men, for the sake of his sons.

On the same day there arrived Yudhājit, the brother-in-law of king Daśaratha, and the brother of queen Kaikeyī, with the message that the queen's father was eager to behold his grandson Bharata and also Śatrughna.

The wedding ceremony proper commenced in the pavilion. Daśaratha approached it and sent word to Janaka who said: "This is the emperor Daśaratha's own house; need he seek anyone's permission to enter? Come, we are all eagerly awaiting your arrival." The worship of the sacred fire commenced, as a preliminary to the wedding. The holiest among sages themselves recited the mantras. At the climax to the ceremony, king Janaka led Sītā to Rāma and placing her hand in his, said to Rāma: "This is Sītā, my daughter, O Rāma, who is from today your partner in life. Accept her. Hold her hand in yours. She will always follow you as your shadow." The whole world and even the celestials rejoiced. Janaka then gave Ūrmilā to Lakṣmaṇa; and, on behalf of his brother, he gave Māṇḍavi to Bharata, and Śrutakīrti to Śatrughna.

All the four blessed couples then worshipped the sacred fire, and humbly bowed to and received the blessing of the sages and the parents. They then retired to their apartments; after following them up to those apartments, the kings and others retired to their lodgings.

Bāla 74–75

The next morning, all the kings and sages and guests were ready to depart. The sage Viśvāmitra took leave of the kings and immediately proceeded to the Himālayas. And, king Daśaratha, too, was getting ready to leave. At that time, king Janaka gave him a very large and rich dowry—thousands of cows, carpets, chariots, maid-servants, etc. King Janaka then returned to Mithilā.

As king Daśaratha was heading for Ayodhyā with his sons, daughters-in-law and others, there were mixed good and bad omens! Soon they saw at a distance a terrible dust-storm. And, then, there came into their view the powerful Paraśurāma with his axe and matted locks, the sworn enemy of kṣatriyas. The perplexed sages and priests in Daśaratha's entourage received Paraśurāma with great respect and devotion. Undeflected in his determination, however, Paraśurāma turned to Rāma and said:

"I heard of your marvellous exploit in firing the weapon which was in king Janaka's possession. I have brought another one with me! Fill it with ammunition and fire it, O Rāma, and show me your valour and your strength. If you succeed in doing so, I shall engage you in a duel."

Hearing this, king Daśaratha was shocked: "O brāhmaṇa," he said; "you had promised to desist from killing the rulers and kings (kṣatriyas), after having destroyed many of them. How is it that you are breaking your own word of honour? Surely, you have appeared here for my total annihilation; for without Rāma none of us here would continue to live." Paraśurāma ignored this and continued to address Rāma: "The weapon that you broke in Mithilā and the one with me were both fashioned by Viśvakarmā. Lord Śiva used the other one. This one was given to lord Viṣṇu. Once the gods wished to determine which of the two deities was the more powerful. At Brahmā's instigation they began to fight a duel. But, lord Viṣṇu silenced Śiva's weapon. They then made peace. Thus outwitted, lord Śiva then gave his weapon (which you broke recently) to Devarāta. This one was given by lord Viṣṇu to sage Ṛcika who in turn gave it to my father. He refused to use it: and taking advantage of this Sahasrabāhu killed him. To avenge his death, I have destroyed all the kṣatriyas, won the world and presented it to the sage Kaśyapa.

"Since then I have retired from active combat and am now living in the Mahendra Mountain. But, hearing of your feat in Mithilā I have come here, to challenge you. Fill this weapon, too, and fire it if you can; then I shall offer you a duel."

Bāla 76–77

After a respectful silence, in deference to the elders in the assembly, Rāma replied: "Holy one, I have heard of you and of the way in which you have avenged your father's murder: and I approve of it. Now, witness my prowess!" Rāma got hold of the weapon and loaded it and got it ready. In anger, Rāma then said to Paraśurāma: "I cannot kill you with this, O Paraśurāma, because you are a worshipful brāhmaṇa. But once readied it has to be fired. Tell me: at what shall I direct it? Either I shall make it impossible for you to move about; or, I can deprive you of the worlds you have earned (or, I can deprive you of your vision)."

Paraśurāma said: "I won the whole earth and gave it to the sage Kaśyapa as my offering. He then told me; 'You should not live in my kingdom.' Hence I retired to Mount Mahendra. But, please do not deprive me of locomotion. I shall go away to Mount Mahendra at once. You may deprive me of the worlds I have earned (or, my sight). I am not ashamed of having been defeated by you: for I know you are lord Viṣṇu himself, and that is why you knew this weapon so well! Fire the weapon, O Rāma, and I shall depart."

Rāma discharged the missile. And Paraśurāma went away to the Mount Mahendra, after humbly saluting Rāma.

Seeing that Daśaratha was still in a daze, Rāma respectfully informed him of Paraśurāma's departure. All of them continued their journey. Soon they reached Ayodhyā, the capital city. The citizens who had been informed of Rāma's achievements and of his wedding, gathered throughout the royal route to look at, to cheer and to bless Rāma. On arrival at the palace, the boys and their brides were lovingly received by the queens. Thenceforward, the four divine couples lived happily, fulfilling all their family, social and religious duties.

One day, king Daśaratha reminded Bharata and Śatrughna that Bharata's uncle was waiting to take them to meet his grandfather. Taking leave of his parents and also Rāma, Bharata, along with Śatrughna left for his grandfather's house.

Rāma and Lakṣmaṇa continued to serve their parents and preceptors. They did all the service which had to be done to their preceptors. They thus delighted the hearts of king Daśaratha, the holy ones and others. The people were highly pleased with the noble disposition of Rāma. Sītā and Rāma were exceedingly devoted to each other. Sītā knew even the unexpressed desires and intentions of Rāma, and lovingly fulfilled them.

→ Did Rama get married at 16 during his tenday travels with Visvamitra

Ayodhyā Kāṇḍa
Life in Ayodhyā

Queen Kausalyā was filled with supreme delight to behold beloved Rāma of unexcelled excellence grow into a young prince, even as Aditi rejoiced to see Indra. Rāma was a perfectly perfect young man. He had all the noble qualities. He was fully self-controlled. He was patient with others' wrongs, but would do no wrong himself. He sought the company of elders and wise men. He had a highly cultivated mind, and his behaviour was highly cultured, too. His actions were governed by the highest code of righteousness; and he was not interested in unworthy conduct. In the science of warfare he was a pastmaster. He knew when to use violence, and when to restrain himself. Even his body was perfect, healthy, strong and handsome. He was alert in mind and was able to read the mind and the intentions of everyone that came to him. He was highly learned in the scriptures, and was therefore well versed in the injunctions and prohibitions concerning the three pursuits of life (dharma, material wealth, and also pursuit of pleasure). He did not display his pleasure or displeasure in relation to others, and hence he earned the friendship of all. He was indeed the repository of all the good qualities, and he was, as it were, the very life of the people, moving outside their bodies.

King Daśaratha was delighted with all this: he was quite proud and fond of Rāma. At this time he noticed omens portending terrible evil. And he was growing old, too: naturally, therefore, he thought his own end was near. He mused: "How can I ensure that Rāma ascends the throne even while I am alive? Truly, he is more than worthy of being king. I am very old and have lived long enough. It would be the greatest blessing to see Rāma, the beloved of all, rule the earth before I go to heaven."

He did not lose much time before telling his ministers, preceptors and others about his wish. Since Rāma was extremely popular with all his subjects as well as with the ministers and preceptors there was really no problem, nor any impediment in the way of his ascending the throne. The king then invited to his court, the leaders of the community from all the towns and cities of his kingdom, to ascertain their view. He also invited the kings and rulers of all the neighbouring kingdoms and states, to ensure their approval, too, so that Rāma would be assured not only of the loyalty of his subjects but of the friendliness of all his neighbours. By an oversight, however, king Daśaratha had omitted to invite his own father-in-law the king of Kekayas and his son's father-in-law, king Janaka. All the invitees arrived, and assembled in the court.

Ayodhyā 2–3

King Daśaratha addressed the assembly in the following words: "I have lived long and shouldered the onerous duties of king for a very long time. This body is aged and fatigued. I wish to appoint my son to protect my people, and give this body its much-needed and well-earned rest in retirement. I am convinced that he will excel me and all my ancestors and that his rule will be a great good fortune to the earth. Is this acceptable to you all?" The assembly heartily applauded the king's proposal. Its spokesman said: "King, indeed you have ruled us well and for long. It is time that Rāma, the beloved of all of us, is enthroned."

The king addressed them, again: "I am pleased with your spontaneous response. But, tell me, pray, why is it that you wish to have Rāma enthroned even while I am alive?" The response was instantaneous and spontaneous again. The assembly assured the king that they were not displeased with him, but they adored Rāma. The spokesman spoke up again: "Rāma is a sat-puruṣa, the ideal man devoted to truth, the fountain of righteousness and welfare. He is richly endowed with knowledge, wisdom, valour, compassion, self-control, every good quality that the ideal man should possess, and he totally identifies himself with the joys and sorrows of the people and as such, is the ideal ruler. He is fit to rule the three worlds, not just this one: and neither his anger nor his pleasure is purposeless. We feel that the kingdom is eager to have Rāma installed on the throne. We know that all the people, especially the womenfolk daily pray that he should become their king." King Daśaratha was highly pleased and thanked them for their concurrence in his proposal.

After the assembly had dispersed, king Daśaratha humbly submitted to the sage Vasiṣṭha: "Holy sir, let everything needed by quickly done, to install Rāma on the throne." Vasiṣṭha in turn instructed the ministers. They reported back to the king that all had been arranged.

The king thereupon sent for Rāma who, on arrival, fell prostrate on the ground at the feet of his father. After embracing him, the king announced his intention: "You are my eldest and most beloved son; and you are the beloved of all our people. Hence ascend the throne as the yuvarājā (crown prince). You are excellent in every way: but on the eve of your enthronement I shall tender this friendly advice: 'Shun vices and adhere to righteousness. Do what is pleasing to your friends and the people, and they will be devoted to you.' " In the meantime, some of Rāma's friends went to his mother Kausalyā and conveyed the exceedingly glad tidings to her. She and all the citizens who heard it prayed to God for the success of the enthronement.

Ayodhyā 4–5

On second thoughts, king Daśaratha decided to send for Rāma once more! Seeing Sumantra again outside his apartments, Rāma wondered why he had come again, and encouraged him: "Tell me whatever you have in mind, unreservedly." Sumantra only said: "The king wants to see you again, immediately." Rāma went. The king spoke to Rāma again: "I have lived a very long life, and I have enjoyed all the royal pleasures, I have given away a lot in charity, and I have performed many religious rites. After much prayer, you were born to me. I have redeemed all the debts a man owes to the sages, gods and the manes. The only thing that remains for me to do is to see you on the throne of Ayodhyā. And, I see many ill omens, many terrible dreams, which portend calamity. Astrologers also say, that according to my stars a calamity is imminent. Hence, I wish to enthrone you immediately—tomorrow! I must do it before the fickle mind changes; for the mind of human beings is fickle. I called you again to tell you this; tomorrow is your enthronement. Therefore, you should fast tonight, along with Sītā, and observe strict discipline. I think it is better that you are enthroned when Bharata is away from Ayodhyā. He is indeed a noble boy; but no one can tell what the mind is capable of doing."

Rāma left the king's presence, went to his own apartment but instantly turned away and sought the presence of his mother. She, along with Sumitrā and her son Lakṣmaṇa, was at the temple, offering prayers to the Lord for the success of the enthronement. Rāma himself announced the king's intention to all of them and sought their blessings. Kausalyā was delighted and blessed Rāma: "Rāma, my son, may you live long, free from enemies. May you bring joy to my relations, and those of Sumitrā. I got you after years of unhappiness and austerities: but now they remain only like vague memories. My prayers have not gone in vain!" Rāma looked at Lakṣmaṇa and said: "I live for you, brother, and I accept even this crown for your sake. Rejoice and enjoy the sovereignty!" Then, Rāma retired for the night.

But the king did not rest yet! He sent for Vasiṣṭha and conveyed his decision. "Please go to Rāma and tell him all that he should do tonight." Vasiṣṭha went to Rāma's palace: but the going was not easy. Word of Rāma's enthronement had got round. There were crowds and crowds of people everywhere on the roads; and it was difficult to move—much less drive a vehicle! The roads of Ayodhyā got a thorough cleaning and sprinkling with scented water. There were flags and buntings everywhere. Somehow Vasiṣṭha reached Rāma's palace and instructed him to fast, etc. Then he returned to the king and informed him that the needful had been done. And, the king retired to his apartment.

Ayodhyā 6–7

When Vasiṣṭha had left his palace, Rāma bathed and went to the temple of lord Nārāyaṇa. After worshipping the Lord, he, along with Sītā, lay down on a grass mat, with his senses controlled, and mind offered at the feet of lord Nārāyaṇa. He awoke three hours before sunrise and busied himself with the worship of the Lord and the various religious rites to the enthronement ceremony.

Everywhere in the city, people were con discussing the glorious event of the day. Troup were performing, some of them enacting plays based on the lives of Rāma and his ancestors. Everywhere people had also erected 'dīpa-vṛkṣa' (trees with decorative lamps). Everybody was singing the glories of Rāma.

Somehow, Kaikeyī (the last wife of Daśaratha) had not been informed of all this. Her maid-servant Mantharā happened to see the festivities and the celebrations in the city, and also she noticed that Kausalyā's maid-servants were expensively dressed. On enquiry, she discovered the cause of all this. She rushed to Kaikeyī who had retired to bed and violently shook her saying in great agitation: "Get up! How can you rest? A great calamity awaits you. The person you love most, the person who pretends to love you dearly and whom you trust implicitly, is about to betray you and plunge you into misery." Calmly Kaikeyī asked her? "Are you sick? What are you saying?" Getting still more agitated Mantharā said: "Your ruin is at hand. King Daśaratha is going to crown Rāma tomorrow."

Mantharā went on: "You are the daughter of a king. You are the beloved consort of a great king. Yet, you do not realise the intricacies of palace intrigues. I am only your maid-servant who is devoted to your welfare. I can clearly see your downfall when Rāma and therefore his own mother Kausalyā, will become all-powerful, and your good fortune, and therefore mine, too, will come to an end. Oh, what a tragedy: you trusted and loved the king, not realising that you were holding a venomous reptile close to your bosom. You and your son Bharata have been deceived by the king. Awake, Kaikeyī, and act quickly to save yourself."

Pleased with the good news and not responding to Mantharā's panic, Kaikeyī gave rich and valuable presents to the maid-servant, saying: "I do not see any difference between Rāma and Bharata; therefore, I am delighted to hear that the king is going to crown Rāma."

Ayodhyā 8–9

Contemptuously throwing away the precious royal gifts, Mantharā continued: "How foolish of you to rejoice at the success of your enemy! Lucky Kausalyā! Very soon she will have you as her chief maid-servant. And, your beloved son Bharata who could be king, who has every right to be king, who is as much eligible to be king as Rāma is, might even be banished from the kingdom, if not from this earth!" Disgusted with the way Mantharā went on, Kaikeyī said firmly: "What has come over you, O Mantharā? Rāma is as dear to me as Bharata. Rāma, too, treats me with greater devotion and serves me more than he serves Kausalyā. If Rāma is crowned king, it is as good as if Bharata is crowned king, for Rāma treats Bharata as his own self." But Mantharā could not be silenced: she went on and on.

Mantharā's persistence paid off. Her evil counsel worked. Kaikeyī's anger was roused. She said: "Kindly devise a plan: what can I do?" Exulting over her victory, Mantharā quickly answered: "Of couse, I have the plan ready. You yourself told me that during a war between Indra and the demons, king Daśaratha lay wounded and unconscious on the field, and you saved his life, and that he then offered you two boons which, however, you did not choose at that time. Probably you have forgotten: because I love you, I remember that story. First make the king promise that he will now honour his offer and give the two boons of your choice. And these should be: first, Bharata should be installed on the throne, and second, Rāma should be banished from the kingdom for fourteen years. If Rāma goes away for fourteen years, Bharata who has all the qualities of a monarch, can win the confidence of the people and consolidate his position. The king loves you dearly and will not refuse the boons. He might, however, offer gold and jewels instead: refuse to accept them. Let nothing deflect you from this twofold purpose. Do not be content with Bharata's coronation: insist on Rāma's banishment."

Mantharā's persuasiveness made evil appear to be good! Kaikeyī fell for it. She even glorified Mantharā: "They say that deformed people are sinful and wicked, but in your case, the hunchback is packed with wonderful tricks. I should worship the hump which enhances your most charming form." Mantharā returned to her theme: "No one builds a dam after the water has flowed away! Do it now." Entering 'the chamber of displeasure' Kaikeyī threw around herself the jewelry that had adorned her and flung herself on the floor, and said to Mantharā: "Rāma shall go to the forest; Bharata shall be king or you will inform the king that I am dead." Finally, once more, Mantharā reminded Kaikeyī of the danger ahead and counselled her to stand fast on her decision.

Ayodhyā 10–11

When all the arrangements for the coronation had been made the king wanted to convey the happy news to his beloved wife Kaikeyī. He entered her palace which shone like a celestial mansion. He did not find her in the bed-chamber: overcome by an intense desire to be with her, he enquired about her whereabouts. Never before had she failed to lovingly greet him at that hour! A maid-servant informed the king: "In great anger, the queen is lying in the chamber of displeasure." Greatly distressed by this information, the king rushed to that chamber and saw his most beloved queen lying on the floor, with all her jewelry flung around her person. Sitting by her side, taking her hand into his, the king addressed her in the following consoling words: "My beloved, are you not well? Tell me: I shall have you served by the best and most able doctors. Has someone insulted you? Or, do you wish that someone should be killed who does not deserve to be killed, or do you wish a condemned person to be freed? Do you wish that I should enrich a pauper or deprive a wealthy man of his wealth? Myself and all that belongs to me are yours, and I cannot go against your wishes. Please get up and tell me what the matter is."

Thus comforted, Kaikeyī resolved to torment her husband still further. She said: "First, promise that you will do what I ask you to do; and then I shall let you know what I want." Delighted at the prospect of reconciliation, the king said: "In the name of Rāma whom I love most and without whom I cannot live even for a moment, I promise to do whatever you wish." And he thus promised thrice, and once again prayed to her to name her wish.

Taking the fullest and immediate advantage of this, Kaikeyī called the very gods to witness the proceedings, in the following words: "You are a righteous monarch: let the gods bear witness to your most solemn vow." Then, she proceeded: "Do you remember that on the battlefield when I saved your life, you offered me two boons? I said then that I would ask for them later. I want them now." The king patiently waited for her to name the boons. He was bound by his own vow. Kaikeyī continued: "You have made elaborate preparations to install Rāma on the throne. Using the same preparations, my son Bharata should be installed on the throne. This is my first boon. And the second boon is: let Rāma immediately proceed to Daṇḍaka forest and live there as a hermit for fourteen years. Wearing the bark of trees and deer skin, let Rāma become a hermit; and let Bharata enjoy the sovereignty of the kingdom. You are devoted to truth, and the wise say that truthfulness is the key to heaven. Therefore, adhere to your promise."

Ayodhyā 12

Hit by the cruel shafts of Kaikeyī's words, the king was stupefied for a few moments. He wondered: "Am I fancying all this, or is my mind deranged, or is my mind re-enacting a past event or am I sick?" But a look at Kaikeyī convinced him that it was none of these. It was real. He promptly fainted. When he came to, he spoke to Kaikeyī in great anger and anguish: "Wicked woman, what has Rāma done to you that you are so cruel to him? He is more devoted to you, than to his mother: and you yourself used to praise him to me. The whole world sings his glory; for what fault shall I exile him? Oh, no: I shall abandon Kausalyā, Sumitrā, all my wealth, and even my life: but I shall not abandon my beloved Rāma. If you wish, I shall crown Bharata."

But Kaikeyī was unyielding. She said: "Ah, well, if you wish to go back on your word, if you wish to disgrace the fame of your dynasty, if you wish to be the laughing stock of wise and noble men, do so! Forsaking righteousness would you like to enjoy life with Kausalyā and Rāma? Shame on you. If my boons are not granted, I shall take poison and die!" Daśaratha began to wail and rave: but Kaikeyī did not even seem to listen. Seeing her determination and the terrible promise made by him, Daśaratha thought of Rāma and fell down like a felled tree.

Daśaratha pleaded again: "If I agree to your demands, people will say of me: 'For the sake of a woman, the king banished the noble and righteous Rāma; how could such a fool rule Ayodhyā for so long?' For your sake I ignored all the loving service that Kausalyā rendered to me, though to me she was a servant, a friend, a wife, a sister and a mother all in

one, and she is the mother of my pet son. Ah, I did
that I was harbouring in you a venomous cobra in
of a wife! If I send Rāma away, Lakṣmaṇa also w
him. Unable to bear his separation I shall die. Yo
as a widow: and how cruelly you will govern my beloved
people! If I tell Rāma, 'Go to the forest', he will instantly obey me. He is incarnate dharma. How can you even conceive of this tender and glorious prince going to the forest, living on roots and fruits, wearing coarse apparel and roaming the forest on foot? If Bharata is pleased with this proposal to banish Rāma, he should not even perform my obsequies. Cruel woman, when you uttered those cruel words, your teeth should have broken into pieces and fallen from your mouth. I do not care if you faint, burn yourself, die, or enter the bowels of the earth: I will not do as you ask me to do. I bow down to you. I even touch your feet. Please bless me and save me." Daśaratha fell down, though his hands could not reach Kaikeyī's outstretched feet.

Ayodhyā 13–14

But, Kaikeyī was unmoved, and repeated: "I am only claiming the boons which I had already earned and which are due to me. You promise, you break your promise, and you also boast that you are righteous!" Once again, Daśaratha lost his consciousness. On regaining consciousness, he once again pleaded: "Surely I shall die when Rāma leaves Ayodhyā. If the gods question me in the other world, if I reply: 'On account of my love for Kaikeyī, Rāma went to the forest' even that would be untruth. How can I ask my beloved Rāma to go to Daṇḍaka forest? If I die before inflicting this undeserved pain on Rāma, that will indeed be better for me." Kaikeyī was unmoved; but time moved on.

It was getting close to dawn. The palace musicians began to play the music with which they usually awoke the king; but the king stopped them that day. He was awake, distressed and restless. Seeing this, Kaikeyī declared: "You have promised the boons; why are you lying down like this? You should get busy fulfilling your promise. The knowers of righteous conduct declare that truth alone is the highest dharma; standing firmly on truth I prompt you to do what is right. The king Sibi attained to the supreme state by adhering to truth and sacrificing his very body. By parting with his very eyes and giving them to a brāhmaṇa, the king Alārka attained fame. Adhering to truth and in fulfilment of its promise, the ocean does not transgress its bounds. Stick to truth. Send your son to the forest. If you do not, I shall die here in front of you."

Daśaratha clearly saw that he was bound by his own word. He cried: "I disown you and your son. When I die, let Rāma offer the libations. The libations should not be offered by you or your son. I have seen the joy on the faces of my people; how shall I see their grief-stricken faces on Rāma's departure to the forest?" But, Kaikeyī urged him: "Time is passing. Instead of wailing thus, call Rāma; when you send him away to the forest and install Bharata on the throne, you will have discharged your duty." Daśaratha agreed: "I am bound by the cords of dharma; I have lost my sense. I wish to see Rāma."

Eager to commence the auspicious ceremonies, Vasiṣṭha and his retinue arrived at the palace. He sent Sumantra to the king to announce his arrival and that everything was ready for the installation ceremony. Sumantra approached the room where the king was and in sublime words awakened him. They were hurtful to the agonised king who stopped him. The king could not speak: hence, Kaikeyī said on his behalf: "The king was awake the whole night and he is tired. He wishes to see Rāma." Puzzled, Sumantra looked at the king who confirmed: "Go and fetch Rāma." He left.

Ayodhyā 15-16

The brāhmaṇas had got everything ready for the coronation ceremonies. Gold pots of holy water from all the sacred rivers, most of them gathered at their very source, were ready. All the paraphernalia like the umbrella, the chowries, an elephant and a white horse, were ready, too.

But, the king did not emerge, though the sun had risen and the auspicious hour was fast approaching. The priests and the people wondered: "Who can awaken the king, and inform him that he had better hurry up!" At that moment, Sumantra emerged from the palace. Seeing them, he told them: "Under the king's orders I am going to fetch Rāma." But, on second thought, knowing that the preceptors and the priests commanded even the king's respect, he returned to the king's presence to announce that they were awaiting him. Standing near the king, Sumantra sang: "Arise, O king! Night has flown. Arise and do what should be done." The weary king asked: "I ordered you to fetch Rāma, and I am not asleep. Why do you not do as you are told to do?" This time, Sumantra hurried out of the palace and sped to Rāma's palace.

Entering the palace and proceeding unobstructed through the gates and entrances of the palace, Sumantra beheld the divine Rāma, and said to him: "Rāma, the king who is in the company of queen Kaikeyī desires to see you at once." Immediately, Rāma turned to Sītā and announced: "Surely, the king and mother Kaikeyī wish to discuss with me some important details in connection with the coronation ceremony. I shall go and return soon." Sītā, for her part, offered a heartfelt prayer to the gods: "May I have the blessing of humbly serving you during the auspicious coronation ceremony!"

As Rāma emerged from his palace there was great cheer among the people who hailed and applauded him. Ascending his swift chariot he proceeded to the king's palace, followed by the regalia. Women standing at the windows of their houses and richly adorned to express their joy, showered flowers on Rāma. They praised Kausalyā, the mother of Rāma; they praised Sītā, Rāma's consort: "Obviously she must have done great penance to get him as her husband." The people rejoiced as if they themselves were being installed on the throne. They said to one another: "Rāma's coronation is truly a blessing to all the people. While he rules, and he will rule for a long time, no one will even have an unpleasant experience, or ever suffer." Rāma too was happy to see the huge crowds of people, the elephants and the horses—indicating that people had come to Ayodhyā from afar to witness the coronation.

Ayodhyā 17–18

As Rāma proceeded in his radiant chariot towards his father's palace, the people were saying to one another: "We shall be supremely happy hereafter, now that Rāma will be king. But, who cares for all this happiness? When we behold Rāma on the throne, we shall attain eternal beatitude!" Rāma heard all this praise and the people's worshipful homage to him, with utter indifference as he drove along the royal road. The chariot entered the first gate to the palace. From there on Rāma went on foot and respectfully entered the king's apartments. The people who had accompanied him eagerly waited outside.

Rushing eagerly and respectfully to his father's presence, Rāma bowed to the feet of his father and then devoutly touched the feet of his mother Kaikeyī, too. "O Rāma!" said the king: he could not say anything more, because he was choked with tears and grief. He could neither see nor speak to Rāma. Rāma sensed great danger: as if he had trodden on a most poisonous serpent. Turning to Kaikeyī, Rāma asked her: "How is it that today the king does not speak kindly to me? Have I offended him in any way? Is he not well? Have I offended prince Bharata or any of my mothers? Oh, it is agonising: and incurring his displeasure I cannot live even for an hour. Kindly reveal the truth to me."

In a calm, measured and harsh tone, Kaikeyī now said to Rāma: "The king is neither sick nor angry with you. What he must tell you he does not wish to, for fear of displeasing you. He granted me two boons. When I named them, he recoiled. How can a truthful man, a righteous king, go back on his own word? Yet that is his predicament at the moment. I shall reveal the truth to you if you assure me that you will honour your father's promise." For the first time Rāma was distressed: "Ah, shame! Please do not say such things to me! For the sake of my father I can jump into fire. And, I assure you, Rāma does not indulge in double talk. Hence, tell me what the king wants to be done."

Kaikeyī lost no time. She said: "Long ago I rendered him a great service, and he granted me two boons. I claimed them now: and he promised. I asked for these boons: that Bharata should be crowned, and that you should go away to Daṇḍaka forest now. If you wish to establish that both you and your father are devoted to truth, let Bharata be crowned with the same paraphernalia that have been got ready for you, and go away to the forest for fourteen years. Do this, O best of men, for that is the word of your father; and thus would you redeem the king."

Ayodhyā 19–20

Promptly and without the least sign of the slightest displeasure, Rāma said: "So be it! I shall immediately proceed to the forest, to dwell there clad in bark and animal skin. But why does not the king speak to me, nor feel happy in my presence? Please do not misunderstand me; I shall go, and I myself will gladly give away to my brother Bharata the kingdom, wealth, Sītā and even my own life, and it is easier when all this is done in obedience to my father's command. Let Bharata be immediately requested to come. But it breaks my heart to see that father does not say a word to me directly."

Kaikeyī said sternly: "I shall attend to all that, and send for Bharata. I think, however, that you should not delay your departure from Ayodhyā even for a moment. Even the consideration that the father does not say so himself, should not stop you. Till you leave this city, he will neither bathe nor eat." Hearing this, the king groaned, and wailed aloud: "Alas, alas!" and became unconscious again. Rāma decided to leave at once and he said to Kaikeyī: "I am not fond of wealth and pleasure: but even as the sages are, I am devoted to truth. Even if father had not commanded me, and you had asked me to go the forest I would have done so! I shall presently let my mother and also Sītā know of the position and immediately leave for the forest."

Rāma was not affected at all by this sudden turn of events. As he emerged from the palace, with Lakṣmaṇa, the people tried to hold the royal umbrella over him: but he brushed them aside. Still talking pleasantly and sweetly with the people, he entered his mother's apartment. Delighted to see him, Kausalyā began to glorify and bless him and asked him to sit on a royal seat. Rāma did not, but calmly said to her: "Mother, the king has decided to crown Bharata as the yuvarājā and I am to go to the forest and live there as a hermit for fourteen years." When she heard this, the queen fell down unconscious and grief-stricken. In a voice choked with grief, she said: "If I had been barren, I would have been unhappy; but I would not have had to endure this terrible agony. I have not known a happy day throughout my life. I have had to endure the taunts and the insults of the other wives of the king. Nay, even he did not treat me with kindness or consideration: I have always been treated with less affection and respect than Kaikeyī's servants were treated. I thought that after your birth, and after your coronation my luck would change. My hopes have been shattered. Even death seems to spurn me. Surely, my heart is hard as it does not break into pieces at this moment of the greatest misfortune and sorrow. Life is not worth living so if you have to go to the forest, I shall follow

Lakṣmaṇa said: "I think Rāma should not go to the forest. The king has lost his mind, overpowered as he is by senility and lust. Rāma is innocent. And, no righteous man in his senses would forsake his innocent son. A prince with the least knowledge of statesmanship should ignore the childish command of a king who has lost his senses." Turning to Rāma, he said: "Rāma, here I stand, devoted to you, dedicated to your cause. I am ready to kill anyone who would interfere with your coronation—even if it is the king! Let the coronation proceed without delay."

Kausalyā said: "You have heard Lakṣmaṇa's view. You cannot go to the forest because Kaikeyī wants you to. If, as you say, you are devoted to dharma, then it is your duty to stay here and serve me, your mother. I, as your mother am as much worthy of your devotion and service as your father is: and I do not give you permission to go to the forest. If you disobey me in this, terrible will be your suffering in hell. I cannot live here without you. If you leave, I shall fast unto death."

Rāma, devoted as he was to dharma, spoke: "Among our ancestors were renowned kings who earned fame and heaven by doing their father's bidding. Mother, I am but following their noble example." To Lakṣmaṇa he said: "Lakṣmaṇa, I know your devotion to me, love for me, your prowess and your strength. The universe rests on truth: and I am devoted to truth. Mother has not understood my view of truth, and hence suffers. But I am unable to give up my resolve. Abandon your resolve based on the principle of might; resort to dharma; let not your intellect become aggressive. Dharma, prosperity and pleasure are the pursuit of mankind here; and prosperity and pleasure surely follow dharma: even as pleasure and the birth of a son follow a dutiful wife's service of her husband. One should turn away from that action or mode of life which does not ensure the attainment of all the three goals of life, particularly of dharma; for hate springs from wealth and the pursuit of pleasure is not praiseworthy. The commands of the guru, the king, and one's aged father, whether uttered in anger, cheerfully, or out of lust, should be obeyed by one who is not of despicable behaviour, with a view to the promotion of dharma. Hence, I cannot swerve from the path of dharma which demands that I should implicitly obey our father. It is not right for you, mother, to abandon father and follow me to the forest, as if you are a widow. Therefore, bless me, mother, so that I may have a pleasant and successful term in the forest."

Ayodhyā 22–23

Rāma addressed Lakṣmaṇa again: "Let there be no delay, Lakṣmaṇa. Get rid of these articles assembled for the coronation. And with equal expedition make preparations for my leaving the kingdom immediately. Only thus can we ensure that mother Kaikeyī attains peace of mind. Otherwise she might be worried that her wishes may not be fulfilled! Let father's promise be fulfilled. Yet, so long as the two objects of Kaikeyī's desire are not obtained, there is bound to be confusion in everyone's mind. I must immediately leave for the forest; then Kaikeyī will get Bharata here and have him installed on the throne. This is obviously the divine will and I must honour it without delay. My banishment from the kingdom as well as my return are all the fruits of my own doing (kṛtānta: end of action). Otherwise, how could such an unworthy thought enter the heart of noble Kaikeyī? I have never made any distinction between her and my mother; nor has she ever shown the least disaffection for me so far. The 'end' (reaction) of one's own action cannot be foreseen: and this which we call 'daiva' (providence or divine will) cannot be known and cannot be avoided by anyone. Pleasure, pain, fear, anger, gain, loss, life and death—all these are brought about by 'daiva'. Even sages and great ascetics are prompted by the divine will to give up their self-control and are subjected to lust and anger. It is unforeseen and inviolable. Hence, let there be no hostility towards Kaikeyī; she is not to blame. All this is not her doing, but the will of the divine."

Lakṣmaṇa listened to all this with mixed feelings: anger at the turn events had taken, and admiration for Rāma's attitude. Yet, he could not reconcile himself to the situation as Rāma had done. In great fury, he burst forth: "Your sense of duty is misdirected, O Rāma. Even so is your estimation of the divine will. How is it, Rāma, that being a shrewd statesman, you do not see that there are self-righteous people who merely pretend to be good for achieving their selfish and fraudulent ends? If all these boons and promises be true, they could have been asked for and given long ago! Why did they have to wait for the eve of coronation to enact this farce? You ignore this aspect and bring in your argument of the divine will! Only cowards and weak people believe in an unseen divine will: heroes and those who are endowed with a strong mind do not believe in the divine will. Ah, people will see today how my determination and strong action set aside any decrees of the divine will which may be involved in this unrighteous plot. Whoever planned your exile will go into exile! And you will be crowned today. These arms, Rāma, are not handsome limbs, nor are these weapons worn by me ornaments: they are for your service."

Ayodhyā 24–25

Kausalyā said again: "How can Rāma born of me and the mighty emperor Daśaratha live on food obtained by picking up grains and vegetables and fruits that have been discarded? He whose servants eat dainties and delicacies—how will he subsist on roots and fruits? Without you, Rāma, the fire of separation from you will soon burn me to death. Nay, take me with you, too, if you must go."

Rāma replied: "Mother, that would be extreme cruelty towards father. So long as father lives, please serve him: this is the eternal religion. To a woman her husband is verily god himself. I have no doubt that the noble Bharata will be very kind to you and serve you as I serve you. I am anxious that when I am gone, you should console the king so that he does not feel my separation at all. Even a pious woman who is otherwise righteous, if she does not serve her husband, is deemed to be sinner. On the other hand, she who serves her husband attains blessedness even if she does not worship the gods, perform the rituals or honour the holy men."

Seeing that Rāma was inflexible in his resolve, Kausalyā regained her composure and blessed him. "I shall eagerly await your return to Ayodhyā, after your fourteen years in the forest," said Kausalyā.

Quickly gathering the articles necessary, she performed a sacred rite to propitiate the deities and thus to ensure the health, safety, happy sojourn and quick return of Rāma. "May dharma which you have protected so zealously protect you always," said Kausalyā to Rāma. "May those to whom you bow along the roads and the shrines protect you! Even so, let the missiles which the sage Viśvāmitra gave you ensure your safety. May all the birds and beasts of the forest, celestial beings and gods, the mountains and the oceans, and the deities presiding over the lunar mansions, natural phenomena and the seasons be propitious to you. May the same blessedness be with you that Indra enjoyed on the destruction of his enemy Vṛtra, that Vinata bestowed upon her son Garuḍa, that Aditi pronounced upon her son Indra when he was fighting the demons, and that Viṣṇu enjoyed while he measured the heaven and earth. May the sages, the oceans, the continents, the Vedas and the heavens be propitious to you."

As Rāma bent low to touch her feet, Kausalyā fondly embraced him and kissed his forehead, and then respectfully went round him before giving him leave to go.

Ayodhyā 26–27

Taking leave of his mother, Rāma sought the presence of his beloved wife, Sītā. For her part, Sītā who had observed all the injunctions and prohibitions connected with the eve of the coronation and was getting ready to witness the auspicious event itself, perceived her divine spouse enter the palace and with a heart swelling with joy and pride, went forward to receive him. His demeanour, however, puzzled her: his countenance reflected sorrow and anxiety. Shrewd as she was she realised that something was amiss, and hence asked Rāma: "The auspicious hour is at hand; and yet what do I see! Lord, why are you not accompanied by the regalia, by men holding the ceremonial umbrella, by the royal elephant and the horses, by priests chanting the Vedas, by bards singing your glories? How is it that your countenance is shadowed by sorrow?"

Without losing time and without mincing words, Rāma announced: "Sītā, the king has decided to install Bharata on the throne and to send me to the forest for fourteen years. I am actually on my way to the forest and have come to say good-bye to you. Now that Bharata is the yuvarājā, nay king, please behave appropriately towards him. Remember: people who are in power do not put up with those who sing others' their presence: hence do not glorify me in the pres- arata. It is better not to sing my praises even in the f your companions. Be devoted to your religious ...vances and serve my father, my three mothers and my brothers. Bharata and Śatrughna should be treated as your own brothers or sons. Take great care to see that you do not give the least offence to Bharata, the king. Kings reject even their own sons if they are hostile, and are favourable to even strangers who may be friendly. This is my counsel."

Sītā feigned anger, though in fact she was amused. She replied to Rāma: "Your advice that I should stay here in the palace while you go to live in the forest is unworthy of a heroic prince like you, Lord. Whereas one's father, mother, brother, son and daughter-in-law enjoy their own good or misfortune, the wife alone shares the life of her husband. To a woman, neither father nor son nor mother nor friends but the husband alone is her sole refuge here in this world and in the other world, too. Hence I shall accompany you to the forest. I shall go ahead of you, clearing a path for you in the forest. Life with the husband is incomparably superior to life in a palace, or an aerial mansion, or a trip to heaven! I have had detailed instructions from my parents on how to conduct myself in Ayodhyā! But I shall not stay here. I assure you, I shall not be a burden, an impediment, to you in the forest. Nor will I regard life in the forest as exile or as suffering. With you it will be more than heaven to me. It will not be the least hardship to me; without you, even heaven is hell."

Ayodhyā 28–29

Thinking of the great hardships they would have to endure in the forest, however, Rāma tried to dissuade Sītā in the following words: "Sītā, you come of a very wealthy family dedicated to righteousness. It is therefore proper that you should stay behind and serve my people here. Thus, by avoiding the hardships of the forest and by lovingly serving my people here, would you gladden my heart. The forest is not a place for a princess like you. It is full of great dangers. Lions dwell in the caves; and it is frightening to hear their roar. These wild beasts are not used to seeing human beings; the way they attack human beings is horrifying even to think about. Even the paths are thorny and it is hard to walk on them. The food is a few fruits which might have fallen on their own accord from the trees: living on them, one has to be contented all day. Our garments will be bark and animal skins: and the hair will have to be matted and gathered on the top of the head. Anger and greed have to be given up, the mind must be directed towards austerity and one should overcome fear even where it is natural. Totally exposed to the inclemencies of nature, surrounded by wild animals, serpents and so on, the forest is full of untold hardships. It is not a place for you, my dear."

This reiteration on the part of Rāma moved Sītā to tears. "Your gracious solicitude for my happiness only makes my love for you more ardent, and my determination to follow you more firm. You mentioned animals: they will never come anywhere near me while you are there. You mentioned the righteousness of serving your people: but, your father's command that you should go to the forest demands I should go, too; I am your half: and because of this, again I cannot live without you. In fact you have often declared that a righteous wife will not be able to live separated from her husband. And listen! This is not new to me: for even when I was in my father's house, long before we were married, wise astrologers had rightly predicted that I would live in a forest for some time. If you remember, I have been longing to spend some time in the forest, for I have trained myself for that eventuality. Lord, I feel actually delighted at the very thought that I shall at last go to the forest, to serve you constantly. Serving you, I shall not incur the sin of leaving your parents: thus have I heard from those who are well-versed in the Vedas and other scriptures, that a devoted wife remains united with her husband even after they leave this earth-plane. There is therefore no valid reason why you should wish to leave me here and go. If you still refuse to take me with you, I have no alternative but to lay down my life."

Ayodhyā 30–31

To the further persuasive talk of Rāma, Sītā responded with a show of annoyance, courage and firmness. She even taunted Rāma in the following words: "While choosing you as his son-in-law, did my father Janaka realise that you were a woman at heart with a male body? Why, then are you, full of valour and courage, afraid even on my account? If you do not take me with you I shall surely die; but instead of waiting for such an event, I prefer to die in your presence. If you do not change your mind now, I shall take poison and die." In sheer anguish, the pitch of her voice rose higher and higher, and her eyes released a torrent of hot tears.

Rāma folded her in his arms and spoke to her lovingly, with great delight: "Sītā, I could not fathom your mind and therefore I tried to dissuade you from coming with me. Come, follow me. Of course I cannot drop the idea of going to the forest, even for your sake. I cannot live having disregarded the command of my parents. Indeed, I wonder how one could adore the unmanifest god, if one were unwilling to obey the commands of his parents and his guru whom he can see here. No religious activity nor even moral excellence can equal service of one's parents in bestowing supreme felicity on one. Whatever one desires, and whatever region one desires to ascend to after leaving this earth-plane, all this is secured by the service of parents. Hence I shall do as commanded by father; and this is the eternal dharma. And you have rightly resolved, to follow me to the forest. Come, and get ready soon. Give away generous gifts to the brāhmaṇas and distribute the rest of your possessions to the servants and others."

Lakṣmaṇa now spoke to Rāma: "If you are determined to go, then I shall go ahead of you." Rāma, however, tried to dissuade him: "Indeed, I know that you are my precious and best companion. Yet, I am anxious that you should stay behind and look after our mothers. Kaikeyī may not treat them well. By thus serving our mothers, you will prove your devotion to me." But Lakṣmaṇa replied quickly: "I am confident, Rāma, that Bharata will look after all the mothers, inspired by your spirit of renunciation and your adherence to dharma. If this does not prove to be the case, I can exterminate all of them in no time. Indeed, Kausalyā is great and powerful enough to look after herself: she gave birth to you! My place is near you; my duty to serve you."

Delighted to hear this, Rāma said: "Then let us all go. Before leaving I wish to give away in charity all that I possess to the holy brāhmaṇas. Please get them all together. Take leave of your friends and get our weapons ready, too."

Ayodhyā 32–33

First, on Rāma's list of worshipful beneficiaries of his gifts was Suyajña, a son of Vasiṣṭha, the family priest. Then came a son of the sage Agastya and a son of Viśvāmitra. Then the brāhmaṇa who attended to the religious rites that Kausalyā performed daily: to him was given a vehicle, servants, silken robes and much wealth. To Citraratha, the charioteer-minister, they gave jewels, garments and cattle. They now turned to the celibate students who were wholly devoted to the study of scriptures and who, therefore were non-earning young men: to them they gave camels loaded with jewels and bullocks loaded with foodstuff. Rāma distributed his own wealth to the brāhmaṇas, young people, aged ones, and the poor. Rāma requested them to take care of his as well as Lakṣmaṇa's palaces during the period of their absence in the forest.

There was a lighter side to this grand ceremony. In a suburb of Ayodhyā lived a brāhmaṇa named Trijaṭa who was poor but had many children. This day his wife happened to tell him: "Though as your wife, I should not instruct you, but serve you as my god, I suggest that you throw away the axe and the hatchet that you always carry and with which you dig up roots, etc., for our food, and go to Rāma. He will certainly give you some money with which to relieve our poverty." He arrived at the palace just as Rāma was distributing his wealth and prayed for help. Pointing to the cows standing on the farther bank of the river Sarayū, Rāma said to the brāhmaṇa: "Throw the staff you have with you, with all your strength. The number of cows that fall within the span of the staff will be yours." The emaciated and weak brāhmaṇa threw the staff with such force that it reached the farther bank of the river and fell near a bull. Rāma said to him smilingly: "I was joking with you to see your strength. These thousands of cows are yours. If you desire more ask! I have earned all my wealth only for the protection of the holy ones. By giving them to you I shall be blessed." The delighted brāhmaṇa went away with the cows. There was not a single brāhmaṇa, relation, servant or poor person in Ayodhyā who did not receive a share of Rāma's wealth.

Rāma then proceeded to Kaikeyī's palace to take leave of the king. People who had heard about the turn events had taken thronged to see Rāma, Lakṣmaṇa and even Sītā (who could not till then be seen walking along the roads) and they said to one another: "The king is surely possessed by an evil spirit to send Rāma to the forest. Like Lakṣmaṇa, we, too, shall go away to the forest. Then, the forest will become a city and this city will be turned into a forest. Let Kaikeyī rule over a ruined city inhabited only by rats and snakes."

Ayodhyā 34

Seeing the grief-stricken Sumantra outside the palace, Rāma requested him to inform the king of his arrival. The king said to Sumantra: "First bring all my wives here quickly. I wish to see Rāma only in the presence of all of them." Sumantra ran to the other apartments and urged the king's wives to rush to where the king was. Three hundred and fifty of them surrounded Kausalyā the principle queen, and hurried with her to Kaikeyī's palace. When they had arrived, the king said to Sumantra: "Bring in Rāma."

As Rāma entered the royal presence, followed by Lakṣmaṇa and Sītā, the king got up and rushed forward with outstretched arms, but fell down unconscious. Moved by this heart-rending scene, all those present there wailed aloud. When the king regained consciousness, Rāma said to him: "Father, I am ready to take leave of you and go to the forest: be pleased to bless me. Lakṣmaṇa and Sītā, too, insist on accompanying me, though I have tried my very best to dissuade them. Grant us leave to go." The king cried aloud: "Alas, I was not in my senses when I gave that boon to Kaikeyī. It is therefore proper for you to set aside my order, take me prisoner and enthrone yourself."

But Rāma humbly submitted: "I have no ambition for the throne, father; may you reign over the kingdom for a long, long time, so that on my return from the forest after fourteen years I may be able to bow down to your feet." At the same time, Kaikeyī also warned the king not to compromise on his pledge. The king said to Rāma: "My beloved son, go to the forest; and may your journey be happy and pleasant. You are wedded to truth and your resolve cannot be reversed. But, please stay today and go tomorrow. Rāma, I assure you that what has happened is not pleasing to me. It is the work of this woman who behaved like scorching fire hidden by cool

ashes. Yet, truth incarnate that you are, you have up
promise and the prestige of our dynasty."

Rāma politely replied: "The good things that I ca
today—who will give me tomorrow? I choose to go aw
itself. Father, one half of your promise to Kaikeyī has thus been fulfilled; fulfil the other half also. Let the crown pass on to Bharata. I do not desire for kingdom, nor for happiness, nor for this earth; neither for pleasures, nor even heaven, nor life: I wish to honour your word. Knowing this, pray grieve not, father. Mother Kaikeyī said: 'Go away to the forest at once,' and so shall it be. This is no hardship to us. I am certain that we shall be happy in the forest among the peaceful deer, beasts and birds. You ought to console others and wipe their tears: you ought not to grieve. May steps be taken immediately to install Bharata on the throne."

The king embraced Rāma: and immediately lost all consciousness.

Ayodhyā 35–36

The noble charioteer-minister Sumantra who was observing all this with a deeply agitated mind, now burst forth: he thought that by insulting Kaikeyī he might make her change her mind. He said: "I consider you the murderess of your husband and of your whole family; you do not seem to have a limit to your wickedness. You have cunningly set aside the time-honoured procedure of this dynasty; and that is, when the king dies his eldest son inherits the throne. Do you want your Bharata to rule Ayodhyā? Then, we shall all of us leave the country, along with Rāma. Abandoned by the brāhmaṇas, relations and the holy men, what will you gain by installing your son on the throne? Alas, why does not the earth open up under your feet and swallow you? It is a wonder, too, that the distress that the sages like Vasiṣṭha feel is not transformed into a flaming rod to consume you.

"Truly you have taken after your mother. Your father had earned from a sage the faculty of understanding bird-language. One night he heard two birds talk to each other: and he laughed. Your mother demanded the cause of his laughter. She would not yield even when your father told her that revealing the cause would mean his death! Upon the sage's advice, however, the king banished your mother and was at peace. Truly you have taken after your mother and do not value your husband's life. If you do not immediately give up this wicked course, you will earn eternal ignominy." Kaikeyī paid no attention to these words!

Daśaratha then commanded Sumantra: "Let it be so. Commanded by me, let a vast army, a host of maid-servants, bodyguards and also my entire treasury accompany Rāma to the forest, so that he might suffer no hardship during his long sojourn there." At this, Kaikeyī sprang up in great anger and displeasure: "Oh, no! this cannot be done. Bharata will not rule over an empty kingdom with an empty treasury!" Daśaratha was enraged and cried: "You did not stipulate this as a condition beforehand! Why are you countermanding my orders now?" But the inflexible Kaikeyī continued: "You own ancestor Sagara exiled his son Asamañja, and he did not provide the son with an army, servants and wealth. Rāma will go with nothing." The prime minister Siddhārtha said: "But Asamañja was of a sadistic and wicked disposition; he killed even babies. Hence, Sagara banished him. Rāma is not only faultless but is endowed with all the divine qualities. Banishing such a faultless person will deprive even Indra of his merits. Enough, queen, of all this. Let Rāma rule the kingdom." The king joined his plea with the prime minister's and said: "If your heart is not changed, I shall also go away to the forest with Rāma; rule the kingdom along with Bharata."

Ayodhyā 37–38

Rāma said: "Father, I have renounced the kingdom and all the pleasures incidental to it; what shall I do with the army and the treasury? Who but a fool will, after giving up an elephant hold on to the tether? The army and the treasury will all be of use to Bharata. I shall be content if Mother Kaikeyī's servants give me the gift of coarse robes worn by ascetics who dwell in the forest." Hearing this and without the least delay, Kaikeyī herself brought coarse dresses made of the bark of trees, for Rāma, Lakṣmaṇa and Sītā to wear. Rāma humbly received his share: and then and there dressed himself in the bark-dress, discarding the princely robe. Lakṣmaṇa immediately followed suit. But, Sītā was both puzzled and amused with the coarse fibre dress which Kaikeyī handed her: she tried it on in different ways, but did not know how to wear it. She turned to Rāma for help: and immediately Rāma himself wrapped it around her body. At the same time, the women present there lamented in irrepressible sorrow: Rāma took no notice of this.

Moved to tears by the spectacle before him, the sage Vasiṣṭha said: "Wicked Kaikeyī, the cup of your sin runneth over. Is it not enough that you deceived the king, extracted the two most unrighteous boons from him and earned disgrace for the whole dynasty? Princess Sītā need not and should not go to the forest. She is the very self of Rāma; for the wife is the very alter ego of the husband. If both of them go away, we shall all follow them. I am sure that even Bharata and Śatrughna will go. You will be the sole ruler of this deserted kingdom. You do not know Bharata; he will not consent to rule the kingdom abandoned by Rāma. You have therefore acted against your own son's interest. You only asked that Rāma should be exiled. Let then Sītā go adorned with princely garments and jewelry." Kaikeyī ignored all this. Sītā completed putting on her ascetic garments.

The people present shouted: "Shame, shame". Daśaratha, in the greatest anguish, begged of Kaikeyī: "Let at least Sītā be spared this cruelty, O Kaikeyī. What has she done to you? You tricked me into granting you the two terrible boons, for which surely I deserve to perish. But even those boons do not demand this cruel treatment of Sītā. You have indeed transcended all bounds of decency and righteousness; you have determined to go to hell." There was no response to this plea!

Rāma stepped up now and said to Daśaratha: "Father, give us leave to go. Before going I have one prayer: and that is, kindly treat my mother with greater consideration, for she is aged and stricken with grief; let not separation from me cause her greater suffering. Heart-broken, let her not depart from this world."

Ayodhyā 39–40

Daśaratha again wailed in agony: "I must have separated many calves from cows: hence I am suffering this way now. Seeing my beloved son clad in the robes of an ascetic, why does not life leave me?" He cried: "Rāma", lost consciousness, and regaining consciousness, he said to Sumantra: "Bring the best of chariots with the best of horses." The chariot arrived

. The king commanded the treasurer; "Remember Sītā will spend fourteen years in the forest. Bring enough robes and jewelry to last that long." This was immediately done. Sītā honoured her father-in-law's wishes and donned princely robes and jewelry.

Fondly embracing her, Kausalyā said: "Wicked women in the world desert even their beloved husband when he is overtaken by adversity. Their heart is inconstant; and neither their family status, nor what was done, nor learning, nor the gifts received nor even the marital vows hold them back. Pray, be like the good women, and ever treat Rāma as your god." Sītā immediately replied: "Surely, I shall abide by your advice, mother. A vīṇā without string is no vīṇā, a cart without wheel is no cart, and a woman without husband even if she has a hundred children has no happiness here. For, her father, brother and son, give only a little happiness to a woman; but the husband gives her illimitable happiness. How then will she not worship him?"

Rāma then prayed to his mother, in the same manner to continue to worship his father. Then he bowed to Kaikeyī and said: "Kindly forgive me if I have during the years that we have lived together offended you in any manner whatsoever." Hearing this, the ladies wailed aloud once again. Rāma, Lakṣmaṇa and Sītā then went round the king and took leave of him. Then they took leave of Kausalyā. They then went to Sumitrā (mother of Lakṣmaṇa) who was delighted that her son was accompanying Rāma. She blessed him and then instructed him: "Regard Rāma as Daśaratha (your father) himself; treat Sītā as your mother; consider the forest as Ayodhyā: and go forth happily, my beloved son."

The chariot was ready. When Rāma mounted the chariot Sumantra said: "The period of exile, which is fourteen years, commences this moment." The chariot moved. It moved the hearts of the people of Ayodhyā who ran behind the chariot shouting "Go slow". Daśaratha and Kausalyā also ran after the chariot shouting "Go slow". But Rāma urged Sumantra: "Go fast. Even if you are asked later, you can say: 'I did not hear'. The pain of separation should not be prolonged." The chariot picked up speed. The ministers advised the king to return to the palace: "You should not go too far to see off one you wish to return."

Ayodhyā 41–42

The people who had a last glimpse of Rāma, seated on the chariot, silently taking leave of all the citizens of Ayodhyā with folded palms, cried out in anguish: "Where goes our Lord who is the sole refuge and protector of the destitute, the weak and the men of austerity; and who did not lose his temper even when slighted, who tried to please even those who were angry with him, and to whom pleasure and pain were non-different? Rāma who treated us, his people with the same love, devotion and reverence with which he treated his own mother—where is he going? The king has surely lost all sense, to have banished such a prince." The king, too, heard what the people said, and it made him even more sad.

Stricken with grief, the people were in no mood to perform their daily tasks, mundane or religious. Even the animals were reluctant to graze or to eat. Nay, even the celestial bodies were thrown into utter confusion. Rāma's departure from the city to enter the forest was marked by menacing dark clouds and dust-storms and an earthquake in Ayodhyā. Dejected at the very thought that such unrighteousness could prevail in Ayodhyā, people seemed to have lost all interest in life itself and in one another. Their minds and their hearts were completely absorbed in the one thought of Rāma.

Daśaratha stood on the road watching the chariot disappear into the cloud of dust raised by itself. He craned his neck and strained his eyes in an effort to catch one more glimpse of his beloved son. When he could see no more, he fell down in a faint. Kausalyā and Kaikeyī at once knelt beside him to lift him up; but the king warned Kaikeyī: "Do not touch my body, sinful woman! I do not regard you as my wife any more. I cannot even bear to look at you." Walking with the help of Kausalyā, the king turned back. He looked at the ground and saw the marks left by the wheels of the chariot and the hoofs of the horses: "I see these," moaned the king, "but I do not see Rāma." He continued: "Soon he will lie down to rest, on hard and bare ground, and his body will be covered with dust. Even so, Sītā who is not used to forest-life will undergo untold hardship. Surely, the dwellers in the forest will behold Rāma, as the helpless perceive the lord of the world." Turning to Kaikeyī he said: "I am unable to live without Rāma, O Kaikeyī! I will pass away soon, and you will rule as a widow!"

Getting more and more restless, the king commanded his attendants: "I find no peace here. Take me to the palace of queen Kausalyā." They conveyed him to Kausalyā's palace. Lying on a couch there, he turned to Kausalyā and said: "Please touch me with your hand Kausalyā; I do not see you—my sight which followed Rāma has not returned to me."

Ayodhyā 43–44

Kausalyā now said to the king: "I would have preferred Rāma to be in Ayodhyā, even as a domestic servant of Kaikeyī if she had wished that. For, now that Rāma has gone to the forest, out of sight of all of us, I do not even know what is happening to him, and what she will do to him further. Kaikeyī's luck is in the ascendant; she is riding the waves: I wonder what she will do next. Will the time come when Rāma and Lakṣmaṇa return to Ayodhyā and thus bring joy and felicity to the people of Ayodhyā? How I long to behold the faces of the three children! Surely, in a past life I must have mutilated the udder of a cow and deprived the calves of their sustenance. Even as a lion overpowers a calf and thus deprives the cow of its calf, Kaikeyī has deprived me of my child."

The wise Sumitrā, mother of Lakṣmaṇa, who was very much more self-possessed, said to Kausalyā: "He whom you regard as your son is noble and strong: and you have no need to grieve over him. By his supreme renunciation of the kingdom he has earned great merit here and hereafter. Lakṣmaṇa too, has earned great merit by going away with Rāma to serve him. Look at the heroic princess Sītā who knowingly and bravely discarded the pleasures of the palace and has chosen to be with her husband, constantly serving him!

"I am certain that the entire nature will favourably respond to the spiritual glory and radiance of Rāma. Even the gentle breeze, and a pleasantly cool moon will render service to him. The missiles and the weapons which the sage Viśvāmitra has bestowed upon Rāma and which he has taken with him will surely provide him ample security. No enemy can face the splendour of Rāma's devotion to dharma. And, he will return soon, after completing the term of ascetic life.

"Devoted to dharma as he is, he is the light in the sun, the fieriness of fire; even so he is the prosperity of wealth, and he is the very essence of glory and patience. Not only this: I consider that he is the god of gods, the fore beings. Whether he lives in the forest or in the cit harm can fall to his lot? Sītā, who is goddess Lakṣmi accompanies him and he is constantly guarded by the powerful Lakṣmaṇa: how can any harm touch him! Fear not. Grieve not. Soon he will return to Ayodhyā. Soon your eyes will behold him. And, as you welcome him back to Ayodhyā, you will shed tears, not as now, but tears of love. Wipe these tears born of grief, blessed queen Kausalyā; very soon when Rāma will return and bow down to you and to all your friends—then it will be time to shed tears, tears of love."

These wise words of Sumitrā, mother of Lakṣmaṇa brought great solace to the queen Kausalyā.

Ayodhyā 45–46

The citizens of Ayodhyā who had followed Rāma's chariot would not return to the city. When he noticed that the sun was about to set, Rāma lovingly spoke to them once: "Blessed citizens of Ayodhyā! The love and adoration which you cherish for me, may the same love and devotion be shown to Bharata, for my sake. Bharata is of noble character and noble deeds and he will do all that is calculated to be pleasing and beneficial to you. Please behave in such a way as not to cause the least distress to the heart of the king, my father, for my sake."

Whatever he did to dissuade them seemed to persuade them that he alone was fit to rule them. The brāhmaṇas stepped forward as the spokesmen of the whole crowd: and they said, "Dear horses, do not take the chariot forward to the forest, but take your master, Rāma, back to Ayodhyā. This is the prayer of all beings." When Rāma saw the holy brāhmaṇas, he alighted from the chariot and walked humbly behind them, though he did not take any notice of their persuasion. The brāhmaṇas, seeing that Rāma was still proceeding towards the forest, prayed to him: "Rāma, our minds were so far devoted to the Vedas; now they are following you to the forest. Once our hearts have entered into your being, there is no going back; if you do not return to Ayodhyā how will dharma reign there? Don't you hear: trees which are unable to come with you, being held down by their roots pray, beg of you (by the creaking sound they produce) to return! Look at those birds: sitting motionless, they solicit you to return. Compassionate that you are, have mercy on all these created beings and return." While they were saying so, they came to the bank of the Tamasā river—even the river seemed to say: "Return", for it obstructed and lay across Rāma's path.

Sumantra unharnessed the horses and allowed them to graze. Rāma said to Lakṣmaṇa: "We shall spend the night here. We need not be anxious on account of our parents: Bharata who is incarnate dharma will look after them. I am glad you came, you will be of great help in looking after Sītā." After prayers, Sumantra prepared Rāma's bed. Upon the bed made of leaves of trees, Rāma and Sītā lay down to sleep; and were soon fast asleep. Lakṣmaṇa kept awake telling the glories of Rāma to Sumantra. When Rāma awoke, he found the citizens asleep still and said to Sumantra: "Bring the chariot quickly and we shall get away before the people awake. It is the duty of princes to save the people from unhappiness arising from the princes themselves." When the chariot was ready, Rāma asked Sumantra to take the northerly direction first and then quickly switch towards the forest, in order to confuse the mind of the people, so that they may give up their pursuit and return to the city.

Ayodhyā 47–48

The citizens of Ayodhyā who had accompanied Rāma had fallen asleep on the bank of the river Tamasā. When they woke up in the morning they found that Rāma had gone away. Sore distressed, they cursed sleep: "Fie on sleep by which we were deprived of our awareness, because of which we do not see Rāma now. Though he is most considerate of his devotees, how is it that Rāma has abandoned us and slipped away? He used to treat us, the people of Ayodhyā, as his very children; and yet he has gone away to the forest. We should all pursue him or meet with our end here itself. How can we ever face the people of Ayodhyā and announce: 'We went with Rāma, but we have returned without him.' "

They saw the tracks of the chariot-wheels in front of them. Rejoicing at the prospect of meeting Rāma, they followed them. But when they suddenly and abruptly ended without leaving any further trace, the people were broken-hearted and puzzled. Disappointed, they had to return to Ayodhyā, reconciled as they were that all this was the work of the gods. Yet, when they re-entered their houses, they found no joy in them; grief blinded their vision and they moved about as if deprived of their vision, deprived of their very life itself.

Thenceforward, nothing made the people of Ayodhyā happy. The womenfolk were literally possessed by grief and said to their husbands: "Of what use is wife, wealth, sons, pleasure and houses, to those who do not see Rāma? Lakṣmaṇa is indeed the only good man in the world, in as much as he has accompanied Rāma. The hills, the trees, the rivers of the forest are more fortunate than we are; all of them serve Rāma. Let us go to where he is: he is our only goal and refuge. Where Rāma is there is no fear and there is no defeat." They also resolved; "We shall never be subject to Kaikeyī's rule. Unable to bear the separation from Rāma, the king will perhaps soon die. Then perhaps Kaikeyī will rule the kingdom. In which case, we should either drink poison and die, or follow Rāma, or at least go far away. Oh, how cruel that Rāma, Lakṣmaṇa and Sītā have been banished to the forest. Surely Rāma illumines the forest now—Rāma whose face is like a full moon, with strong chest and long arms, who subdues his foes, with lotus-like eyes; who speaks first to everyone, and sweetly and truthfully, too; who is strong and good, who bestows joy on the whole world like the moon, the best among men who has the prowess of an elephant."

Thus, the people of Ayodhyā lamented and gave vent to their grief. Ayodhyā looked like a dead city.

Ayodhyā 49–50

Rāma continued his journey towards the forest. To Sumantra, Rāma said: "I look forward to the day when I shall return to Ayodhyā and roam in the forests of the neighbourhood on the pretext of hunting. I am not fond of hunting myself. Hunting wild animals was resorted to in days of yore for the sake of the royal sages or ascetics who lived in the forests. In course of time it became a sport for men who wielded weapons." As the Kosala territory receded into the background, Rāma turned towards it and with folded palms took leave of the city of Ayodhyā. Turning to the villagers who crowded around him, he bade them return with the words: "It is sinful to prolong sorrow; go and apply yourselves to your allotted tasks."

At a slower pace, because he was not pursued, he drove to the bank of the holy Gaṅgā. The holy river was flanked by many hermitages of sages. Gods (devotees of gods), demons and celestials ('gandharvas' = 'artists', too), nymphs and the wives of the gandharvas, all of them worshipped the Gaṅgā, and bathed in her waters. Turbulent and 'angry' at places, placid and pleasant at others; almost still and smooth at some places and swift and noisy at others, the river provided constant delight to all. With her origin in the lotus feet of lord Viṣṇu, the sinless river destroyed all sins.

Rāma reached the town known as Sṛṅgaverapura on the bank of the Gaṅgā. He decided to spend that night there. He saw at some distance a large ingudi tree and decided to camp under its shade. The chief of Sṛṅgaverapura was Guha who was a friend of Rāma. When he heard through his men that Rāma had arrived there, he rushed forward to greet him. On meeting, the two friends warmly embraced each other. Guha was mystified to see Rāma clad in ascetic's garb. He had food and other delicacies immediately brought and said to Rāma: "Welcome! Mighty one! The whole earth is yours. You are the Lord: we are all your humble servants. Kindly protect us and guide us. Here are four kinds of food: food that needs mastication, food that is soft, drink and delicacies that have been ground into paste. Here is food for the horses; and here again are excellent beds for your repose." Rāma embraced Guha again and said: "I am delighted to see you, Guha, and to see that you are well. Thank you for your hospitality, friend: but I do not need it now. I am under a vow to lead an ascetic life. However, I only ask for food for the horses which are the favourites of my father, king Daśaratha." Guha supplied food for the horses. Rāma took only the water of the river Gaṅgā. Rāma and Sītā slept under the tree; while Lakṣmaṇa and Guha kept awake under another tree.

Ayodhyā 51–52

Guha said to Lakṣmaṇa: "We are used to life in the forest, O brother; you are not. Here is a bed for you. Lie down and sleep. I shall keep awake and guard all of you." But Lakṣmaṇa declined, saying: "It is even as you say. Yet, I shall not lie down in the presence of my brother." As they both sat there vigilantly guarding Rāma and Sītā, Lakṣmaṇa expressed his anguish to Guha: "This night is perhaps the doom of Ayodhyā. Possibly our father has passed away. Possibly our mothers, too. And, the people are sunk in grief. Our only prayer is that the fourteen years may pass by soon, and Rāma may return to Ayodhyā."

At dawn, Rāma woke up and offered his prayers. To Guha he said: "Please arrange to have us ferried across the river Gaṅgā." When the boat was ready, he said to Sumantra: "I think you have come far enough, Sumantra: now you should return with the chariot to Ayodhyā." Sumantra could not even endure the thought for a moment. He cried bitterly: "How can I go back without you, Rāma? The life of brahmacarya and the study of the Vedas, the cultivation of virtues like kindness and truthfulness—all these appear to me fruitless, when I think that you can suffer this exile. Nay, permit me to be with you. If you refuse to let me come with you, I shall burn myself, chariot and everything."

Rāma, however, spoke gently to the grieving Sumantra: "Sumantra, you are the only true well-wisher of our family. You are our wise counsellor. Hence you should return to Ayodhyā and console the king with this message from me—'Neither myself nor Lakṣmaṇa are sorry that we have left Ayodhyā and are to live in the forest'. Please behave towards the king in such a manner as not to cause the least displeasure. Kindly convey a message to Bharata: 'Treat all our mothers with equal love and reverence'. It is important that you should return to Ayodhyā, Sumantra. Only when mother Kaikeyī sees that you have returned to the city without me will she be convinced that I have gone to the forest. And, when Bharata is crowned, her heart's desires would have been fulfilled. For my sake, Sumantra, please return to Ayodhyā."

To Guha, Rāma said: "Under the vow of asceticism, I shall not stay in inhabited forests. Let me depart." And before doing so, he obtained the milk that exudes from the banyan tree and matted his hair in the style of ascetics. Taking leave of Guha, Rāma asked Lakṣmaṇa to get into the boat first, then help Sītā to enter, and last of all he himself entered the boat. From then onwards this was the order in which they marched. Sītā offered a prayer to Gaṅgā for their safe sojourn in the forest and safe return to Ayodhyā. On reaching the other bank of Gaṅgā, in the Vatsa country, Rāma and Lakṣmaṇa killed four deer (or

-varāha, ṛṣya, pṛṣata and mahāruru—which together
herbs, made their meal.

53–54

That night they spent without Sumantra, the first night alone during their exile. Thoughts of Ayodhyā entered Rāma's mind. He said to Lakṣmaṇa: "This is our first night without Sumantra, I wonder what is happening in Ayodhyā. Surely, our father is tormented by grief. Perhaps, Kaikeyī is happily asleep. If Bharata has returned to Ayodhyā, maybe she might even take the king's life. Looking back at the events of the past few days, I begin to think that sensual pleasure is more powerful than wealth and dharma. Otherwise, how can the king banish his own son who has given no cause for offence? Yet, again, he who ignores his prosperity and dharma and devotes himself to sensual pleasures comes to grief soon, even as king Daśaratha has. Tonight I am thinking of the fate of our mothers. Surely, they are the hardest hit by this turn of events, and their grief is the worst. In her previous birth, my mother must have deprived mothers of their children; that is why she has to undergo this suffering now. Kausalyā's suffering is intolerable and great. I am really concerned on her behalf. Please return to Ayodhyā and look after our mothers; in the forest, I shall surely be able to take care of Sītā." Lakṣmaṇa's reply was emphatic and final: "Ayodhyā has surely been deprived of its light, in that you have come away. There is no use worrying over that, Rāma. But I will on no account leave you and return to Ayodhyā." Rāma accepted this; and from that moment onwards, they were three!

After spending the night under the big tree on a bed of grass prepared by Lakṣmaṇa; Rāma, Sītā and Lakṣmaṇa moved on. Soon they came to the confluence of the rivers Gaṅgā and Yamunā. Rāma noticed smoke rising at a distance and gladly announced: "Lakṣmaṇa, see, that is a clear indication that the sage Bharadvāja is in his hermitage, tending the sacred fire."

Bharadvāja welcomed them heartily. "I have been expecting you to come. I have heard of the happenings in Ayodhyā. This is a lovely place. You can spend the entire period of your exile here." But Rāma replied: "Certainly, this place is beautiful and holy. But, it is too close to the big cities, and the people of Ayodhyā, Kosala and other territories might often come here to see me or to see Sītā. Hence I feel we should not settle down here. Kindly suggest some other place." Conceding this argument, Bharadvāja further said: "At some distance from here is the sacred Citrakooṭa hill. One who looks at the summits of that hill enjoys prosperity and never falls into error. It is the abode of many sages. Take up your abode there." Rāma agreed to this proposal.

Ayodhyā 55–56

The sage Bharadvāja who frequented the Citrakooṭa hill, instructed Rāma in great detail on the way to reach there. He also offered special prayers for the safety of the three and for the success of their mission. Rāma bowed to the sage and said: "I shall follow your directions." He turned to Lakṣmaṇa and said: "Surely, we have earned a lot of merit in the past to deserve such affection from the sage."

They set about first to cross the river Yamunā. For this they had to prepare a raft with their own hands. They helped Sītā get on the raft and then jumped onto it. While they were in mid-stream, Sītā offered prayers to goddess Yamunā so that they could safely conclude their exile in fourteen years and return to Ayodhyā. On reaching the farther bank they left the raft and found the landmark that the sage had mentioned—a banyan tree. As instructed by the sage, Sītā offered prayers at the banyan tree, too.

They marched forward: Lakṣmaṇa leading the way, Sītā following him, and Rāma following Sītā. Whenever Sītā saw a lovely bush of wild flowers, she questioned Rāma about them; and often Lakṣmaṇa would gather and present her with a bouquet of wild flowers. After walking in this manner for some time, they again chose a large tree to spend the night under.

And, again, at dawn Rāma awoke and then awakened Lakṣmaṇa: "Listen to the sweet music of the birds, Lakṣmaṇa: night has passed and it is time to make a move." After their morning bath in the river Yamunā and prayers, they walked on towards Citrakooṭa. All along the way, Rāma kept pointing out to Sītā the beautiful flora and fauna of the forest. When they neared the Citrakooṭa hill, he pointed it out to Sītā and to Lakṣmaṇa; he announced joyously that there they would spend their exile sporting happily in the forest. Rāma said to Lakṣmaṇa: "It is a delightful hill, Lakṣmaṇa, with a variety of trees and creepers, and with plenty of fruits and roots. It thrills my very soul. And, many sages and holy men live here. I think we should live here."

They entered the hermitage of the sage Vālmīki who warmly welcomed them. At the command of Rāma, Lakṣmaṇa erected a hut in no time, with timber and thatch. Immediately thereafter, they performed the ceremony for the consecration of their hermitage, in order to prevent evil spirits haunting the newly constructed place and to ensure that the dwelling had the most sublime and spiritual atmosphere. Entering that hut afterwards, Rāma felt completely relieved of the unhappiness caused by the events of the preceding days.

Ayodhyā 57–58

As Sumantra drove the empty chariot into the city, the people wailed aloud once again, knowing that Rāma had indeed gone away. They despaired of ever seeing him again. They said: "Rāma's one all-absorbing thought always was: 'What is acceptable to the people, what is pleasing to them, and what will bring them happiness,' and he treated us like his own children." As he entered the palace, the consorts of the king expressed their grief once again: "Returning without Rāma, in what manner can Sumantra console the queen Kausalyā? Looking at the fate of Kausalyā, we conclude that it is as hard to give up one's life as it is to live it when assailed by misfortune."

When Sumantra entered the presence of the king and conveyed Rāma's salutations to him, the latter fainted anew. But, queen Kausalyā reassured him that he need have no reservations as Kaikeyī was not present there. Recovering consciousness, the king then bade Sumantra relate all the events and Rāma's messages in detail. His voice choked with tears, the king asked Sumantra: "How was it possible for Rāma, Lakṣmaṇa and Sītā, of royal descent, accustomed to being waited upon by servants and servant-maids, and to regal life in the palace, to adapt themselves to the hard life of ascetics? Sumantra, kindly tell me how Rāma sits, hunts, eats and lives now?"

After narrating the progress of the march of the three, Sumantra conveyed Rāma's messages. Firstly, Rāma wished that the venerable king's feet should be worshipped. Secondly, Rāma had this message for queen Kausalyā: "Be devoted to dharma. Maintain the sacred fire. Worship the feet of our lord the king considering him as god. In your relations with my other mothers, let not pride nor a false sense of dignity enter; and this even more so in the case of Kaikeyī of whom the king is especially fond. Regard Bharata as king: for though young in age, kings should be respected. This is political dharma." Rāma's message to Bharata specially concerned his attitude to the mothers: "Please regard queen Kausalyā as your own mother: she loves me dearly and is sure to feel my absence greatly." Sumantra said: "As he uttered these words, Rāma's eyes rained tears of grief."

Sumantra continued: "Lakṣmaṇa, however, was full of wrath. He was still bitterly against the banishment of Rāma; and asked, 'How can he who banishes Rāma be considered a father? How can he who exiled Rāma against the wishes of the people be considered king?' Sītā, however, was tongue-tied and her tearful face was turned all the time to Rāma, when he and Lakṣmaṇa spoke to me."

Ayodhyā 59–60

Sumantra continued: "After taking leave of Rāma, I turned back towards Ayodhyā. But my horses were unwilling to return without Rāma. So, I spent a couple of days with Guha. I hoped that Rāma would send for me to join him. But he did not. My heart laden with grief, I drove towards Ayodhyā. But, O king, Ayodhyā without Rāma is a body without soul. I found that the rivers, the groves and the forests, as also the living beings on the earth, in the sky and in the water—all behaved as if they were lifeless. As I drove through Ayodhyā, no one greeted me nor smiled at me. When they saw the empty chariot, people began to cover their faces and their eyes and cry. In this there was total unanimity: whether they were friendly, unfriendly or indifferent to Rāma, they all were grief-stricken."

Daśaratha wailed again: "Alas, I committed the greatest blunder of my life and reign. I acted impulsively to please my wife, whereas I should have taken the counsel of my preceptors and my ministers. If I had taken their counsel, this calamity might have been averted. Maybe it is the will of the gods. O Rāma, O Lakṣmaṇa, O Sītā! You do not know that I am dying of intense anguish, as a destitute and orphan. O Sumantra, will you not take me to where my beloved Rāma is?"

Looking at Kausalyā, the king described the ocean of grief in which he was sunk, in graphic terms. And while doing so, unable to bear the grief, he fainted again. Seeing this Kausalyā was terror-stricken and fell down. Looking at Sumantra, Kausalyā said: "Sumantra, kindly take me immediately to where Rāma and Lakṣmaṇa are. I cannot live here without them even for a moment."

The wise Sumantra calmly addressed the queen now: "Queen, please give up your sorrow, your delusion and the confusion caused by your unhappiness. Rāma has given up mental anguish; and he will surely live in the forest without the least sorrow. Even so, Lakṣmaṇa devoted as he is to Rāma and to his service, is earning great religious merit. Sītā's heart is wholly absorbed in Rāma. In fact, in the company of Rāma, she has begun to feel that she is sporting in a grove just outside Ayodhyā; and she does not feel the sorrow of exile at all. Therefore, even her physical body does not show signs of fatigue or the effects of inclement weather and the discomfort of forest life. She appears to be just the same celestial person that she was here. Oh, no, they do not deserve our grief, nor do you nor even the king deserve to be grieved for; whatever is happening now will be remembered by humanity for all time to come."

Ayodhyā 61–62

Stricken with great grief, the queen Kausalyā said thus to her husband: "You are indeed a glorious and righteous king; you are full of love and kindness. Yet, you failed to reflect for a moment on how your own sons and Sītā, your daughter-in-law, would be able to live in the forest. They were brought up in palaces; they have to live in a hut. They are accustomed to rich food; they have to live on ascetic fare. Their ears are used to listening to sweet music; they have to listen daily to the howling and roaring of wild animals in the forest. How could you expect Rāma who used to repose on soft beds, to sleep on grass mats, using his own arm as his pillow? Alas, I pity my own granite heart which is not shattered to a thousand pieces at the very thought of Rāma's exile to the forest. Alas, you are guilty of a great cruelty to Rāma in that you banished him from the kingdom. I doubt if even after the fourteen years of exile, Rāma will ascend to the throne. It is common knowledge that the brāhmaṇas will not eat the remnants of food given already to others; the pious people regard articles once used as unfit to be used again in a sacred rite. How, then, do you think that Rāma will accept the throne wrested from him, used by someone else, and then returned to him? Such a truthful son has been unjustly banished by you to the forest: it is hard to believe that you know what dharma means. Alas, I have been deprived of all support. It is said that the husband is a woman's first support, the second is her son, the third her relations—and she has no fourth support. Nay, by this unrighteous action, you have destroyed the kingdom, the people and the ministers, me and my son."

Hearing these harsh words, Daśaratha fell into a swoon again, uttering: "Rāma".

Stricken with grief, the king on regaining consciousness, folded his palms and said to Kausalyā: "Kausalyā, be pleased with me. Kindly do not utter harsh words to me." Full of remorse, Kausalyā drew Daśaratha's folded palms towards her head, placed them on her head, and said to him: "Bless me, lord. I am guilty, unforgivably guilty. That woman whose action forces her husband to bow to her is not praiseworthy either here or hereafter. Even though I know the course of dharma, I was temporarily robbed of my wits by great grief, and hence I said what I should not have said. Grief destroys courage, the wisdom that has been heard, and in fact everything: hence there is no enemy greater than grief. These five days without Rāma have been like five years to me; and this grief, therefore, built up to a climax. Terrible is this grief."

Ayodhyā 63

It was the sixth night after Rāma's departure to the forest. After his conversation with Kausalyā, the king slept for a while. He woke up at midnight and remembered his own past evil deed. And he narrated the following story to Kausalyā:

"Whatever a man does—whether it is good or evil—the fruit of that action he gains. He who does not realise the grave or light consequences of his own deeds at the very beginning—he indeed is immature and childish. What I am about to tell you happened before we were married when I was a young prince. I had learnt the art of shooting without seeing the target, with the help of sound emanating from the target.

"I had gone to the forest hunting. The sun had set. Night had fallen. I drove towards the bank of the river Sarayū. I wanted to bag a big buffalo or an elephant that night. It was dark; and in the silence of the forest I could hear what I thought was a sound made by an elephant. I could not see the elephant, but the sound was enough for me. I took aim and shot.

"At dawn I heard, again in the direction from which the sound had come, a human voice wailing terribly in agony: 'Who could have been interested in taking the life of an innocent ascetic? To whom have I caused the least offence? I came to this lonely place on the bank of the river, to fetch water to quench the thirst of my parents: and lo, I have been shot, and fatally wounded. The murderer can gain nothing by this evil action, but he will only reap evil fruits. I am not worried so much about the loss of my own life as about the future of my blind parents who are totally dependent upon me, and who have been looked after by me. Surely, when they know I am dead, they will give up their lives too. He is surely a fool who has by a foolish action brought about this triple murder.'

"Hearing this, I rushed to the scene. A young ascetic had been hit by me. He was filling his pot with water; and the sound made by water entering the pot had been mistaken by me as sound made by an elephant. I knelt penitently at his feet. He gazed at me with eyes afire with austerities and said: 'Go quickly to where my father is and seek his pardon; otherwise his wrath might destroy you. That path over there will lead you to where my parents live. Before you go, relieve me of this pain, by drawing out the missile lodged in my body, which is causing me great pain. Do not be afraid that you will thereby cause the death of a brāhmaṇa; for I was born of a vaiśya-father and śūdra-woman.' To relieve his distress I pulled the missile out; and in a moment he was dead."

Ayodhyā 64

King Daśaratha continued to narrate the story:

"Having committed the terrible deed, I reflected how best I could atone for it. Taking the path indicated by the dying youngster, I soon reached the hermitage occupied by the blind old couple. When the father heard my footsteps, he said: 'My beloved son, why have you taken so long to fetch wat are succour to the helpless, eyes to the blind, all our lif are centred in you: why don't you talk to me? My son, i I or your mother has given you offence, do not take it to heart: you are an ascetic, are you not?' Anxiety, fear, and remorse filled my heart. Struggling to give expression to what I felt at that moment, I said: 'Holy sir, I am not your son. I am a prince named Daśaratha. As a result of a sinful and ignorant action of mine, your son was fatally wounded by me. I am guilty of killing your son. Please command what I should do now.'

"Stupefied by grief, the aged ascetic replied: 'If you had yourself not come to me and confessed your wicked deed, your head would have broken into a million pieces. Moreover as you say, you committed this sin in ignorance, not knowingly. Otherwise, your whole family would have been destroyed. Now, take us to the place where our beloved son lies dead.'

"Thereupon, I led the aged blind couple to the place where the young ascetic lay dead. The old man touched the body of the son and wailed in terrible and heart-rending anguish. 'Who will attend to our needs as you did, beloved son?' wailed the old man, and recounted all that the young man used to do for him. He continued: 'Wait, my son: for soon we shall also follow you to the abode of death and there we shall pray to the god of death to bless us that you may continue to be with us and to serve us. May you be merged in the supreme being which is the goal of holy ones!' He then performed the funeral rites of his son whose spirit ascended to heaven. The father then said to me: 'Before I go, I have to pronounce this curse on you: since you brought about this grief born of separation from my son, you will also die of grief born of separation from your son.' Immediately he and his aged wife consigned themselves to the burning pyre, to enjoy the company of their son in heaven.

"I am suffering the fruits of that sin, Kausalyā."

Soon the king lost his sensations. "The grief caused by separation from my son is drying my life-forces," said the king. "O Rāma, have you really gone away? O Kausalyā, O Sumitrā, I cannot see anyone." Wailing thus, the king lost consciousness.

Ayodhyā 65–66

The next morning, the king's attendants gathered in the palace to awaken him with the usual music, panegyrics and benedictory verses from the scriptures. It was almost sunrise. The birds awoke hearing all this, but not the king, nor even the two queens Kausalyā and Sumitrā who were sleeping on the same couch.

The other consorts of the king thereupon entered the royal chamber and gently rocked the couch, in an effort to awaken the king and the queens. Even this did not do the trick. Upon their closer examination, they discovered that the king was not breathing. Seized with terror, they began to wail aloud. Hearing this lamentation, Kausalyā and Sumitrā, too, awoke. By the very fact that the queens were sleeping on the same couch with the king, they all concluded that the king had passed away in sleep. The lamentation of the queens was truly heart-rending. Kausalyā and Sumitrā uttered a loud cry 'O Lord' and fell down on the ground. The resplendent queens had lost all their lustre, now that they had lost their husband. There was uncontrollable and inconsolable weeping and wailing in the palace.

In uncontrollable and inconsolable grief and anguish, Kausalyā, looking at Kaikeyī who was also grief-stricken, gave vent to her bitter feelings: "Are you satisfied now, O Kaikeyī! You are the cause of the king's death. Now you have no more enemies: enjoy the sovereignty of the kingdom. How can a chaste woman survive the death of her husband? And yet in your greed, you have actually brought about his death as well as the destruction of our whole dynasty. You have brought misery and grief to king Janaka, to Sītā and to the whole family. Stricken with grief at what has been done to his daughters, king Janaka will surely perish. And Sumitrā and myself cannot survive the death of our husband."

The officials of the royal household, when they discovered the king's demise, prepared for what had to be done. They embalmed the king's body in a trough of oil and made the necessary preparations for the royal funeral. The funeral itself could not take place without the presence of the king's son; hence the embalming was resorted to. Looking at the embalmed body of the king Daśaratha, the widowed consorts lamented again and again at the cruelty of their fate—out of grief for the loss of their husband, and out of fear of what greater harm Kaikeyī had in store for them. They and the people of Ayodhyā were unanimous in their condemnation of Kaikeyī whose cruel act alone brought about the death of the king.

Ayodhyā 67–68

The next morning, the ministers of state as also the counsellors and sages assembled under the presidency of the sage Vasiṣṭha to deliberate on the immediate course of action. The ministers submitted to the assembly: "Unable to bear separation from his sons, Rāma and Lakṣmaṇa, king Daśaratha has ascended to heaven. Of his sons, Rāma and Lakṣmaṇa have gone to the forest; and Bharata and Śatrughna are in their uncle's house in the kingdom of the Kekayas. A king should immediately be nominated; for without a king, the kingdom will be destroyed. The evils of anarchy are well known to you all: the people of the kingdom cannot carry on their sacred and mundane affairs in peace, and neither righteousness nor normal trade and enjoyment of righteous pleasures is possible. Thieves and knaves will thrive; and wicked people will take the law into their own hands and assume the authority of rulers. All progress will be arrested, and no constructive activity will be undertaken. Law and order will come to an end. Justice will not prevail. Morality will be ignored. Neither religious rites nor public entertainment will take place. There will be fear and anxiety in the hearts of all people. In fact, even ascetics and sages will be reluctant to move about freely. When anarchy rules, no one can call anything his own; just as the big fish eats the small ones, the strong people will swallow the weak ones. What the eyes are to the body, the king is to the country. Embodying in himself virtue and nobility, the king is verily the father and mother of a kingdom. O sage Vasiṣṭha, pray decide what should be done now."

Vasiṣṭha said: "Bharata has already been nominated king. He is now in his uncle's house. Let swift messengers be despatched immediately to bring him back." The ministers and the counsellors heartily agreed to this proposal. Vasiṣṭha thereupon called upon a few chosen messengers to proceed immediately to Kekaya territory and to convey the following message to Bharata: "Greetings to you, O Bharata; the sages in Ayodhyā request you to return to that city at once, for an important task awaits you." Vasiṣṭha however warned them: "Do not tell Bharata of Rāma's exile nor of the king's death, nor of the misfortune suffered by the great dynasty."

The messengers left Ayodhyā almost immediately. Crossing the river Gaṅgā at Hastināpura, they rode farther west. They passed through Kurujāṅgala and Pāñcāla territories. They crossed the Ikṣumati river, went over the Sudāma mountain, to the Bahlika kingdom (Balkh), crossed the Vipāsa (Beas) river and other rivers and soon reached the city of Girivraja, the capital of the Kekaya kingdom.

Ayodhyā 69–70

Elsewhere, during the closing hours of that same night Bharata had a nightmare. As a consequence, the next day he was in no mood to enjoy himself. Seeing him depressed, his companions endeavoured their very best to distract him by surrounding him with music, dance and drama, fun and laughter; but Bharata did not pay much attention to these, absorbed as he was in brooding over his dream. When his friends questioned him, he narrated the essentials of his dream to them:

"Last night I had a most terrible dream. I saw my father falling down from a mountain peak into a pool of cow-dung. I saw him drink oil from his palms cupped as a receptacle. I also saw that the oceans had become dry; the moon had dropped onto earth; and everywhere the demons ruled. I saw the tusk of the royal elephant broken. I saw fierce fires instantly extinguished. Dark young women were hitting the king who was seated on an iron seat. The king, wearing crimson flowers, was driven in a southerly direction in a chariot borne by donkeys. An ugly demoness was laughing at the king. Such is the dream I saw last night, during the last quarter. Either the king, or I, or Rāma or Lakṣmaṇa will die. For, it is said that he who dreams of a chariot driven by donkeys will see the smoke rising from a funeral pyre. Having seen this ugly dream, I feel apprehensive. Though I see no immediate cause to fear, yet there is great fear in my heart. Hence I am unable to enjoy what would otherwise delight me."

At about the same time the messengers arrived from Ayodhyā. They quickly sought Bharata's presence and conveyed to him the message entrusted to them. Bharata for his part enquired in detail about the king, Rāma, Lakṣmaṇa, his mothers etc. To this enquiry the messengers gave an ambiguous and diplomatic answer: "All of them whose welfare you seek are well, O Bharata. The goddess of fortune is in your favour. Let there be no delay in your departure."

Bharata then sought the permission of his materna father who not only gave him permission, but loaded h presents (in return for the costly presents which the me from Ayodhyā had brought for the old man and his son, i.e. Bharata's uncle). But, Bharata was not made any happier by all the love, the affection and the costly presents bestowed upon him. In his heart there was an irrational fear, caused by the previous night's dream, and the mysterious haste displayed by the messengers from Ayodhyā.

When everything was ready, Bharata went into the inner apartments and took leave of his grandfather and his uncle. Accompanied by Śatrughna, the noble Bharata then ascended the chariot which sped towards Ayodhyā, escorted by a contingent of the Kekaya army.

Ayodhyā 71–72

From Girivraja (or Rajagriha), Bharata drove towards Ayodhyā, crossing the rivers Sudāma, Hṛādini, Śatadru (Sutlej) and Ailadhana; through the Aparaparvata Territory, Śalyakarṣana and the Mahāśaila hills: crossing the rivers Sarasvati and Gaṅgā, passing through the Vīramātsya territory; later he crossed the Yamunā and once again Gaṅgā at Prāgvaṭa—and on the seventh evening he reached Ayodhyā.

On entering Ayodhyā, Bharata was distressed to see the vast change. The city was in mourning. Nothing seemed to be right; there was no joy, no cheer, no auspicious sign anywhere. He questioned the charioteer: "Why is this so? I have heard of what a city looks like when the king is dead; and I see such scenes in Ayodhyā!"

He went straight to his father's apartment in the palace. Not finding him there, and mentally disturbed, he rushed to his own mother's apartment. There he saw his mother eagerly waiting for him. She rushed forward and with great joy embraced him and welcomed him. She questioned him about the travel; and he gave her a complete account of it. She enquired about her father and her brother; and he replied to her that they were well. Then he asked: "Where is father? He used to be in your apartment most of the time, reclining on that golden couch. I wish to bow down to him and touch his feet. Where is he?" Kaikeyī who was mentally unbalanced by greed, now told him (who did not know anything) what she knew—(the news that shocked him) as if it were something very pleasant. "Your father has gone to where everyone ultimately goes—to the other world," she said calmly. It struck Bharata like a thunderbolt and he fell down weeping. She tried to console him with the words: "Get up, pick yourself up, O king! Why are you lying down on the floor like this? People like you who are accepted by respectable society do not grieve like this!"

"I came hurriedly, thinking that the invitation meant either Rāma's coronation or the king's performance of a sacred rite. Alas! I do not see my father. Mother, tell me: what were father's last words?" Bharata asked. Kaikeyī replied: "He left his body wailing aloud the names of Rāma, Lakṣmaṇa, and Sītā, and said: 'Only they who are able to see them on their return from the forest are blessed.' " Even more shocked, Bharata asked: "Where is Rāma?" Kaikeyī replied: "He, with Lakṣmaṇa and Sītā, have gone to the forest." Deeply agitated, Bharata asked again: "For what crime has Rāma been exiled from the kingdom?" In answer to this vital question Kaikeyī narrated the whole story, and added: "My son, you know dharma, and you should now take the reins of the kingdom in your hands. It was for your sake, dear son, that I did all this. Do not grieve, do not worry, this kingdom is now dependent upon you. Perform the last rites of your father without delay and ascend the throne."

Ayodhyā 73–74

Kaikeyī's dreadful revelation of the truth sent her own son Bharata into a fit of uncontrollable rage, born of unutterable grief. He said: "What have I to do with the kingdom, grief-stricken as I am having been deprived of my father and my brother who is like a father to me? You have heaped upon me sorrow upon sorrow, by causing the death of my father and by having my brother sent to the forest. You are the exterminator of our dynasty. And, you say that you did all this for my sake. Surely, blinded by greed for political power, you failed to see in what love and reverence I hold Rāma. How can I take over the reins of government that he and he alone can hold? Remember, even if by some psychic or intellectual power I gain the ability to govern the country, yet, I will not ascend the throne; for I will never fulfil your wicked desire. In our dynasty it has always been that the eldest son ascended the throne. That noble tradition has been destroyed by you. However, I will not let that happen. I shall go to the forest, persuade Rāma to return to Ayodhyā, and either live in the forest as his substitute or come here and function as his servant.

"For this unpardonable sin, you deserve to go to hell. From now you have forfeited your right to speak to me—you who appear to be my mother, are in fact my enemy; you who are of despicable conduct, full of political greed, and killer of your own husband. You are unfit to call yourself the daughter of the noble king Aśvapati, my grandfather. You have earned eternal disrepute. What terrible hardships you have brought on mother Kausalyā! Don't you know that a son is born of every limb of oneself, and of one's own heart, and hence the most beloved of the mother? And, yet, incarnate cruelty that you are, you have deprived mother Kausalyā of her son. I have heard the following legend: Indra once saw the divine cow Surabhi weeping. When questioned by him Surabhi pointed to two bullocks which had fallen into a swoon on account of overwork, and said: 'Indra, I grieve to see my two sons lying in a swoon, because a thoughtless and wicked agriculturist who had yoked them to his plough has treated them with cruelty and merciless greed. Seeing my children thus overburdened with heavy loads and worked to exhaustion and great pain, I am filled with sorrow: there is no one who is as beloved as a son.' What immeasurable pain has been caused by you in the heart of mother Kausalyā! I cannot even endure the very thought of the great sin committed by you. You may enter the fire, or go to the forest, or hang yourself: or do what you like. I have resolved to go to the forest and bring Rāma back to the kingdom." Greatly shaken by the grief, Bharata fell down unconscious.

Ayodhyā 75–76

The ministers had gathered around Bharata in the meantime. Regaining consciousness, Bharata said: "I never desired the throne; nor did I advise the mother in this regard."

Hearing Bharata's voice, Kausalyā went to meet him; and at the same time Bharata, too, sought her presence. Bharata and Śatrughna saw that she had fainted on account of grief and caught hold of her feet. When she regained consciousness, she said to Bharata: "The kingdom is yours, Bharata, won for you by your mother. Great sorrow is mine. It would be better for me to go away to the forest where Rāma is." Folding his palms in salutation, Bharata humbly and tearfully said to her: "Mother, do you not know me, and my love for Rāma? Why then do you utter such harsh words? No, Rāma's exile is not my doing; in fact, I did not even know about it. I say on oath: if I am guilty of that offence let me suffer the fruits of all the sins mentioned in our scriptures. Let him who was responsible for Rāma's exile incur the sin of kicking a cow, of a master robbing his servant, of treason, of tyranny, of war crimes, of showing disrespect to elders, of betraying a friend, of blackmailing, of eating food without sharing with family and servants, of sleeping at dawn and at dusk, of arson, of adultery, of neglect of service of parents, of polluting water, of poisoning another, and of showing partiality while witnessing a dispute. Let him become slothful and inactive, ungrateful, shunned by all and hated. Let him be the abode of all the vices condemned in our scriptures: and let every kind of inauspiciousness and misfortune fall to his lot."

Kausalyā was deeply moved by Bharata's speech. Lovingly she said to him: "Child, enough: to one aggrieved by the loss of a son, you are adding your own grief. Luckily your heart has not swerved from the path of dharma; my child, you are devoted to truth and unto the divine realms you will ascend." She placed Bharata on her lap and consoled him.

The next morning, the sage Vasiṣṭha said to Bharata: "Enough of this grief, Bharata: let the funeral rites proceed." The king's body was taken out of the trough of oil. Bharata once again gave vent to his grief and lamented near the king's body. Vasiṣṭha once again said: "The king's funeral rites should be performed with a cool mind and without mental agitation." Thereupon the priests brought out the sacred fire which the king himself had diligently maintained in his house and with which his own funeral pyre would be kindled. When the funeral pyre was set ablaze, there were heart-rending cries by the women of the palace.

Ayodhyā 77–78

On the eleventh day, Bharata performed the necessary purificatory ceremony; on the twelfth he performed the appropriate ceremony for the peace of the departed soul he distributed lavish gifts to the brāhmaṇas and the the morning of the thirteenth day, once again Bharata the king when he went to the cremation ground i collect the ashes. Weeping uncontrollably, Bharata fell down unconscious. Śatrughna, too, fell down unconscious. When he regained consciousness, Śatrughna wailed aloud: "The ocean of grief generated by the wicked Mantharā, which took the shape of the two boons granted by my father, and which was infested with the crocodiles of Kaikeyī's greed, has swallowed us. Our beloved father used to look after us with great affection and love, and provided all our needs. Who will care for us now?" Hearing the two brothers lament like this, all the people of the palace also gave vent to their sorrow.

Seeing this, the sage Vasiṣṭha said to Bharata: "This is the thirteenth day; and the ceremonies connected with the funeral have to be done today. These three pairs of opposites (birth and death, joy and sorrow, gain and loss) are inevitable in the life of all beings: therefore, you should not behave like this." Hearing the admonition of the sage, the two princes got up and continued the rites connected with the thirteenth day of the mourning.

Later, Śatrughna said to Bharata: "Rāma indeed is the refuge of all beings in their sorrow: that Rāma who is endowed with all auspicious qualities has been exiled to the forest by a woman! What is even more strange is that the mighty Lakṣmaṇa tolerated all that happened and did not stop our father from committing this terrible injustice." Just as Śatrughna was saying this, the hunchbacked Mantharā entered the apartment. "This sinful woman is responsible for the whole tragedy," said Bharata and handing her over to Śatrughna: "Mete out the punishment she deserves." All her friends vanished from the apartment when Śatrughna grabbed Mantharā: they fled to the apartment of Kausalyā, for asylum! Unable to face Śatrughna's rage and rebuke, Kaikeyī sought her son's asylum! Thereupon Bharata said to Śatrughna: "Let us not kill these women, brother. I would myself have killed this sinful Kaikeyī, but for fear of thus offending the righteous and noble Rāma who may not approve of such action. Even if we kill this hunchback he would be displeased with us. Therefore, leave her alone."

Released from the grip of Śatrughna, Mantharā fled to the company of Kaikeyī who tried to console her.

Ayodhyā 79–80

The privy counsellors assembled together on the fourteenth day after the passing of king Daśaratha and said to Bharata: "Daśaratha is no more, and he sent Rāma and Lakṣmaṇa to the forest. Pray, be our king. There is no fault in this, as you have been nominated to the throne. Our kingdom is without a ruler, and that is not desirable." The articles needed for the coronation had already been made ready; and Bharata saw the people who had brought all these articles. With bowed head and joined palms, he went round these articles as a mark of veneration, and then spoke to the counsellors: "Men of culture and wisdom that you are, you should not make such a suggestion to me. Indeed, Rāma who is our elder brother shall be king. In his stead, I shall go to the forest and dwell there for fourteen years. Please get ready a contingent of our army with all the paraphernalia. I shall proceed to the forest, seek Rāma wherever he is, perform the installation ceremony there in the forest itself, and make him return to Ayodhyā. I shall in no circumstances fulfil the sinful desire of my so-called mother; I shall dwell in the forest, and Rāma will be king. Therefore, let our architects, engineers and workers proceed ahead, cutting a proper pathway for all of us to go to the forest."

The counsellors and others who heard this commendable decision of Bharata heartily approved of it and blessed him. And this in turn delighted the heart of Bharata. Engineers, artisans, architects and others had immediately been despatched to prepare the way for the army and other regalia to go to the forest.

This party consisted of geologists, wiremen, machinemen, architects, mechanical engineers, civil engineers, carpenters, water diviners, builders of bridges and tunnels, in addition to cooks, shoe-makers and domestic aids. These, along with the contingent of armed forces, appeared to be an ocean of humanity on the move. With lightning speed, they laid roads, levelled prominences, filled pits and potholes, planted trees where necessary, cut them down where they obstructed the path, dug wells, constructed dams and thus created lakes, and thus laid a first-class highway in no time, as it were. As they marched forward, they pitched their tents which were as numerous as the stars in the firmament. These camps had their own temples for worship and the performance of the religious rites, even during the march.

Built by experts, the highway looked extremely attractive and it was soon ready for use.

Ayodhyā 81–82

The next day, the palace officials who did not know of Bharata's decision were getting ready for the ceremonies connected with Bharata's coronation. The court musicians and panegyrists approached Bharata's palace and began to sing his praises and the glory of the dynasty. The musicians and the instrumentalists performed their morning duty: they did it for king Daśaratha before; they did it for Bharata now. Awakened by their noise, Bharata felt doubly distressed. He ordered them to stop. Turning to Śatrughna, Bharata expressed his distress in the following words: "Alas, what a terrible blunder has my mother committed! Daśaratha has gone to the other world; Rāma who is incarnate dharma has gone to the forest. I am drowned in the ocean of sorrow. And, the state is without a ruler."

In the royal court itself, the mighty sage Vasiṣṭha had taken his golden seat and was surrounded by his worthy disciples. He ordered the messengers of the court: "Please request the leaders of our community, and also Bharata and Śatrughna, along with their friends, to come to the court quickly. There is urgent business." The holy brāhmaṇas, the priests, the commanders of the army, the counsellors and others arrived promptly. As Bharata entered they cheered him, as they used to cheer Daśaratha.

Sage Vasiṣṭha voiced the feelings of the assembly in the following words addressed to Bharata: "My child, king Daśaratha has bequeathed this kingdom, with all its treasures, and its loyal subjects to you. Rāma, who had been commanded by the king to go to the forest, promptly obeyed his father's command. In the same manner, it is meet that you should ascend the throne. Ascend the throne which has thus been bestowed upon you both by your father and by your brother, and crown yourself king."

Bharata was greatly pained to hear this. In a faltering voice expressive of profound grief, he submitted: "How can a son of the king Daśaratha usurp the throne which rightfully belongs ɩther? Rāma is the elder and he is in every way superior . By usurping the throne I shall only gain eternal infamy and hell for myself and disgrace for the dynasty. This sin has been committed by my mother, but it does not please me. I salute Rāma standing here. I shall follow him and him only; and he alone is fit to be king. Holy sages, I have already given instructions for a contingent of the army and all our leaders to proceed with me to the forest where Rāma is. I shall persuade, nay force, Rāma to return. If, however, he refuses to return, I shall, like Lakṣmaṇa, stay with him in the forest. A beautiful road is already being paved for the joyous return of Rāma to Ayodhyā."

Ayodhyā 83–84

Soon the mighty river of devout humanity began to flow from Ayodhyā to the forest. Leaders of the community, the members of the royal court, the privy counsellors, the chief among the artisans of every type, members of the various guilds—carpenters, masons, cobblers, engineers, architects, artists, potters, weavers, goldsmiths and jewellers—physicians, washermen and tailors, musicians and dancers, formed part of this mighty expedition, led by nine thousand elephants richly caparisoned, sixty thousand chariots and men armed with various weapons, and a cavalry a hundred thousand strong. The people were saying to one another: "When shall we behold that Rāma who is the dispeller of the sorrow of the entire world, who is of the colour of the rain-bearing cloud, who has strong arms, who is firmly established in divinity, and who is of firm resolve? The moment we behold him our sorrows will vanish, just as the darkness of the world vanishes when the sun rises." Highly learned brāhmaṇas, resplendent with the lustre of deep meditation and spiritual attainments, followed Bharata in their own bullock-carts.

Soon they reached the bank of the holy Gaṅgā. Bharata ordered everybody to pitch tents and camp on the bank of the Gaṅgā for the night. This sea of humanity attracted the attention of Guha. He considered for a while who they might be. He could not fail to see Bharata who was standing in the waters of the Gaṅgā offering libations for the peace of the departed king. He deliberated: what could the motive of Bharata be in leading the vast army to the forest? "Perhaps, Bharata wants to kill Rāma and thus ensure his continued occupancy of the throne? Rāma is my Lord and also my friend." He said to his comrades: "We should diligently do what is in his interest. If Bharata is going to the forest to harm Rāma, we shall not let him cross the Gaṅgā. If, however, Bharata is favourably disposed to Rāma, then we shall gladly help him cross the river."

Taking some wild fruits and honey, Guha proceeded towards Bharata's tent. Sumantra who knew Guha already, saw him coming and immediately announced the event to Bharata: "Guha is in fact your dear friend and brother, as he is regarded as such by Rāma. It is good for you to see him and to befriend him. For, surely he knows where Rāma is." With great joy, Bharata had Guha brought into his tent immediately. With natural and spontaneous humility, Guha offered the fruits and honey to Bharata and lovingly said: "Though independent, we consider our principality as a suburb of Ayodhyā, Bharata. We welcome you. We do hope you will have a pleasant stay in this region."

Ayodhyā 85–86

The noble Bharata accepted Guha's hospitality with sincere gratitude. Then he questioned Guha: "Pray, tell me, by which route did my beloved brother proceed to the hermitage of Bharadvāja?" Guha replied at once: "Rest assured, Bharata, that my men will escort you through the forest. But, I wish to ask you a question; kindly give me a truthful answer. Are you or are you not pursuing the sinless Rāma with evil intention? The army that surrounds you raises this doubt in my mind."

Bharata felt greatly agitated to hear this question and he politely replied: "Brother, pray, be gracious to me and dismiss that thought. Rāma is my most esteemed elder brother whom I regard as a father to me. I tell you the truth: I am going to see Rāma and beg of him to return to Ayodhyā." Guha was greatly impressed by this revelation. Lovingly and joyously, Guha said to Bharata: "Blessed indeed art thou, O Bharata, and I see no one equal to you on this earth, in as much as you desire to renounce the kingdom that has come to you unsought. Your glory will be eternally sung in all the worlds, in as much as you wish to bring back Rāma and thus reverse his misfortune."

As they were speaking thus, the sun sank into the western horizon and darkness enveloped the earth. But, with his heart afire with grief, Bharata did not sleep. Oppressed by the weight of his sorrow, Bharata tossed about, unable to enjoy peace. Seeing this, however, Guha became utterly convinced of the noble intentions of Bharata.

To relieve him somewhat of his anguish, Guha revealed to him the events of the night when Rāma and Lakṣmaṇa along with Sītā slept on the same ground. Said Guha: "I tried to persuade Lakṣmaṇa to sleep, assuring him that I knew the forest very well and that I would guard all three of them against any harm. But he would not. 'How can we sleep, Guha,' said noble Lakṣmaṇa, 'when we see how this royal couple, Rāma and Sītā, sleep on bare ground with grass as their bed?' He then began brooding over the fate of Ayodhyā and the royal family. He said to me: 'Unable to bear separation from Rāma, surely the king will die. I do not think that either mother Kausalyā or my mother will survive this night: even if my mother lives expecting Śatrughna, mother Kausalyā will die. After completing the fourteen years of exile, Rāma and I will return to Ayodhyā, along with Sītā.' Talking about the glorious Rāma, we thus spent the night. The next day, wearing matted locks and clad in the bark of trees and skin of animals, with their weapons on their shoulders, the two heroes walked away with Sītā, with the gait of lordly elephants."

Ayodhyā 87–88

Guha's graphic description of the manner in which Rāma, Lakṣmaṇa and Sītā departed to the forest, made Bharata contemplate the feet of Rāma. Calmly he reflected for a while. They came alive in his consciousness. He visualised the royal family in coarse ascetic attire. Presently, he fainted! Seeing this, Śatrughna wailed aloud. Hearing this, the queens rushed to where Bharata lay. Mother Kausalyā lovingly lifted him with great tenderness. At her soothing touch, he woke up. She asked him: "Are you well, my son? On you now the lives of all of us and the people of Ayodhyā depend."

After reassuring Kausalyā that he was well, Bharata requested Guha: "Show me where my brother slept with Sītā. On what did he lie down, and what did he eat the night he spent here?" Guha replied: "I placed before the noble Rāma fruits and various delicious dishes which he politely returned saying, 'Friend, we do not accept gifts; we only know how to give.' He and Lakṣmaṇa subsisted only on the water of the holy Gaṅgā. Lakṣmaṇa then prepared a bed with grass, under yonder Ingudi tree, on which Rāma and Sītā slept, without showing the least discomfort."

In ecstasy mixed with intense grief, Bharata said: "Here, under this Ingudi tree, the noble Rāma spent the night with princess Sītā. These are the blessed blades of grass which touched Rāma's body. Accustomed to sleeping on soft beds, standing on floors paved with gold and precious stones, how could that noble prince and princess sleep on grass? He who was accustomed to be awakened by bards and musicians—how could he spend the night in this dense forest listening to the howls and roars of wild animals? It is unbelievable, and it appears untrue to me; it makes me feel that it is but a dream. Surely, even the gods are under the sway of adverse time which could make Rāma, the son of king Daśaratha sleep on the bare ground, and which could make Sītā, the daughter of king Janaka and the daughter-in-law of king Daśaratha sleep on the bare ground! Here, obviously the blessed Sītā slept; a few golden threads from her dress have got entangled in the grass here. Ah, the devout wife considers this grass-bed she shared with her husband most comfortable. Blessed is Lakṣmaṇa that he has gone with Rāma, to serve him. Ayodhyā is desolate, now that the king and Rāma have left it: even the enemies do not wish to invade Ayodhyā now, though it is left undefended! From now, I shall also wear matted locks and dress myself in the bark of trees. Rāma will return to Ayodhyā; and I shall take his place in the forest. If he does not return, I shall also stay with him as an ascetic and as his servant."

Ayodhyā 89–90

Bharata, Śatrughna, the queens and the priests and the entire entourage spent the night on the very spot where Rāma, Lakṣmaṇa and Sītā spent their night before leaving for Citrakooṭa. Early the next morning, Bharata got up and seeing Śatrughna still in bed, said to him: "Wake up, Śatrughna! It is high time we crossed the Gaṅgā. Please get Guha at once so that he may take us across the Gaṅgā." Śatrughna instantly replied: "I am not asleep, brother: I, too, am contemplating the glorious Rāma." At the same time Guha approached them and enquired of the princes if they had had a good night's rest. After an appropriate answer, Bharata continued: "Friend, we are eager to cross the Gaṅgā as soon as possible."

Within minutes, Guha brought together an armada of boats, big and small, several hundred in number, to transport the royal entourage across the holy river Gaṅgā. He himself brought a superb and carpeted boat for the princes and the queens. All of them entered the boats, which now began to cross the river. The elephants swam across with their mahouts. Many were the zealous citizens who swam across the Gaṅgā, some using empty pots to help them float and others depending on nothing but the strength of their arms. Reaching the other bank of the Gaṅgā, the party soon arrived at the forest near Prayāga (Allahabad).

Bharata allowed the entourage to camp in the forest and proceeded to the hermitage of Bharadvāja, accompanied by the sages and the priests alone. Bharadvāja welcomed them appropriately. He and Vasiṣṭha greeted each other with great reverence. They enquired of one another's welfare.

Bharadvāja intuitively knew the identity of Bharata and addressed him: "You ought to be in Ayodhyā, ruling the kingdom; what are you doing here? As a result of a plot engineered by a woman the noble Rāma has gone to the forest with his brother and his wife. I do hope that you do not wish to pursue him there and harm him." Bharata was greatly shaken by the words of the sage. In a pleading tone and tear-choked voice, he said "Lord, may such a thought not find a place in your holy mind. Whatever happened in Ayodhyā during my absence from there is totally contrary to the wishes of my heart. In fact, I am going to meet Rāma and beg him to return to Ayodhyā. And, I came here to find out where that noble prince is." Highly pleased, Bharadvāja reassured Bharata: "I knew your mind very well; but expressed the doubt in order to strengthen your resolve and manifest your glory. I also know where Rāma is: he is on the Citrakooṭa hill. However, spend the night here and depart tomorrow."

Bharata agreed to the sage's proposal.

Ayodhyā 91

The sage Bharadvāja offered the hospitality of the hermitage to the prince who politely replied: "Surely, the joyous way in which you received us here is more than enough hospitality." The sage, fully realising the prince's reluctance to impose himself and the royal entourage upon the hermit's hospitality, laughed heartily and said: "You are indeed noble, Bharata, in that you do not wish to take undue advantage of our hospitality. But, I would very much like to entertain and serve your army, too. Why did you leave the army and the other citizens who are accompanying you, at such a distance in the forest?" Bharata once again humbly and politely submitted: "Holy sir, I left them behind and came alone purposely! Kings and princes should always endeavour not to intrude upon the hermitages of ascetics. There is a large army and an even larger contingent of the citizens belonging to various strata of society and professions accompanying me on this pilgrimage. I did not want them to come near this peaceful hermitage and pollute the water and the earth, and damage the trees and huts."

Highly delighted with Bharata's thoughtfulness, the sage however asked the prince to let the army and the royal entourage enter the hermitage grounds and enjoy the sage's hospitality. While Bharata gave instructions accordingly, the sage retired into his own hut and after the necessary preliminary rituals entered into deep meditation and communion with the gods (forces) that control all natural phenomena. In that state of holy communion (samyama), the sage prayed: "May Viśvakarma (the lord of all actions) enable me to entertain my guests today. May Indra the chief of the gods, and the three guardian deities of the earth manifest themselves here and enable me to serve the guests properly. May all the rivers that flow on earth or in the celestial regions be present here in their subtle forms. May rivers of spirituous and non-spirituous liquors as also of pure water flow in this hermitage, for the pleasure of my guests. May the heavenly musicians and nymphs come to this hermitage to serve and entertain my royal guests. I also wish that 'trees' laden with wearing apparel and jewelry as also delicious fruits should appear in this hermitage. May there instantly be in this hermitage fragrant garlands, delicious drinks and food and meat."

The holy sage who was in a deep superconscious state of samādhi uttered the appropriate hymns to invoke the presence of the deities concerned. As he thus mentally prayed to these deities, with his palms joined in salutation, all the deities came there, one by one. Instantly a gentle and cool breeze blew over the place, robbing everyone of fatigue.

Ayodhyā 91

Soon the celestials appeared there. There was music and dancing everywhere. Bharata and his army looked on all this in sheer wonder. As they were looking, right in front of them, miles and miles of land instantly flattened out and a lovely lawn carpeted the land. Fruit trees appeared instantly everywhere. Beautiful mansions materialised everywhere, with stables for the animals of the royal entourage. In their midst, a royal palace materialised, garlands, buntings and other decorations hanging at all its entrances. Bharata entered that palace. Visualising Rāma seated on the royal throne, Bharata humbly went round it, bowing to Rāma seated on it, and took his place in the prime minister's chair.

After a little while, streams of milk and other beverages appeared. In that instant city there materialised hundreds of celestial men and women, as also the divine musicians who began to sing before Bharata. Others entertained him with their dance. In fact, even as members of Bharata's party were looking, the trees that were standing in the hermitage were transformed into musicians, drummers and dancers. Other trees instantly became royal servants—men and women. These servants said to the members of the armed forces: "Those of you who are accustomed to spirituous liquors, help yourselves to them; those of you who are hungry, help yourselves to milk and food; and those of you who wish to, eat the excellent meats and other food. Eat and drink according to your wish." These 'instant women' helped the soldiers bathe and get dressed. They helped to wash and feed the animals, too. Bewildered by all this, the animals did not recognise their masters and vice versa!

Bedazzled by what they experienced that evening, the soldiers said to one another: "We do not wish to go to Daṇḍaka forest, nor do we wish to return to Ayodhyā! May both Bharata and Rāma be blessed and may they be happy!" Delighted to witness the magic powers of the sage Bharadvāja, they said to one another; "This indeed is heaven." All of them picked up new and expensive garments from the trees. They saw in front of them gold and silver vessels full of the choicest delicacies and foodstuff of every sort. There were wells full of liquor and wine. There were innumerable gold plates for everyone to eat from. Every article of luxury had been provided, right down to ready-made toothpicks in their thousands, mirrors, combs and hair-brushes, shoes and wooden sandals, seats and beds. Thus the night passed. Early the next morning, the gods and the celestials took leave of the sage Bharadvāja and the hermitage looked as it was before. Bharata's men were wonderstruck by the marvellous demonstration of the sage's divine powers.

Ayodhyā 92–93

Bharata approached the sage Bharadvāja with great humility, joy and gratitude. The sage enquired: "Bharata, did you and your army and your entourage have a good night's rest and were all your needs supplied?" Bharata humbly submitted: "Even so, lord. I am eager to reach the presence of my brother. Pray, bless me, and tell me where he dwells now." The sage gave him full and detailed directions.

Acknowledging his gratitude, Bharata once again bowed to the sage. The noble queens also bowed to the sage. Bharata introduced them to the sage: "This, lord, is the eldest of the queens, Kausalyā whose beloved son is that foremost among men, Rāma. This is Sumitrā, the second queen, the mother of Lakṣmaṇa and Śatrughna. This third one is that cruel and extremely wicked queen Kaikeyī, my mother, who has brought this immeasurable unhappiness to all of us, and on account of whose terrible plot the king passed away and Rāma went to the forest." The sage Bharadvāja, endowed with omniscience, quickly interrupted and said: "Do not blame Kaikeyī, Bharata: for, surely, this exile of Rāma will be productive of great happiness to all. It is for the good of the gods, demons and the sages that Rāma has gone to the forest."

Bharata once again bowed to the sage; and immediately all of them proceeded towards Citrakooṭa hill. After thus travelling for some time, Bharata said to the sage Vasiṣṭha: "Holy one, I think we have come very close to the place that the sage Bharadvāja indicated. Here is the Citrakooṭa hill, and here is the river Mandākinī, too. And there lies the forest where surely Rāma dwells." From the elevated ground he was standing on, he pointed out to Śatrughna and said: "Look at this army and this entourage approaching the forest. Look at the dust they raise temporarily veiling the sky. The forest which was uninhabited and which was therefore silent, resounds with the noise produced by these people and these animals: it looks like Ayodhyā itself to me."

Bharata ordered the army to stop and despatched a few soldiers to scout round and try to find where Rāma's cottage stood. They saw smoke rising at some distance, and returning to Bharata, said: "Look at that smoke rising yonder: in this uninhabited forest, it is a sure sign of habitation. Surely, Rāma or some such ascetic lives there." Agreeing with their intelligence, Bharata ordered the army to halt there and decided to proceed alone, with just Sumantra and Dhṛti.

Ayodhyā 94–95

In the hermitage on the Citrakooṭa hill, Rāma, Lakṣmaṇa and Sītā had settled down. In fact, they had begun to love the simple, austere forest life. Often Rāma would roam the forest with Sītā, pointing out to her the various wonderful scenes signifying the wealth and the glory of the Citrakooṭa hill. He would say: "A single look at this pleasing and delightful mountain makes me forget the loss of the throne and even separation from our dear friends of Ayodhyā. I think that the mineral wealth of this hill is incalculable. Some of the peaks shine like silver, some are red, some yellowish; and here and there you can actually see precious gems sparkling—gems like topaz, crystal—with the colour of the Ketaka flower. Look at those beautiful birds with delightful plumage. Are not these deer beautiful, too: and what an extraordinary phenomenon it is—these leopards and tigers and bears are quite harmless. You can spend hours, days and years, looking at the infinite variety of trees found on the hill and in the forest. And, look at these men and women resembling celestials, sporting happily in the forest. Are not these cascades and waterfalls delightful; and do they not make you feel that this mountain is a living being? I will never taste sorrow if I live for a long, long time in this forest, of course, with you and Lakṣmaṇa. By coming away to this forest, I am happy that I have been able to fulfil father's pledge and I am happy, too, that Bharata has been installed on the throne. Moreover, I have heard it said that my forefathers felt that the forest-life is most conducive to freedom from the cycle of birth and death. And, in addition, the hill excels the capital of the heavenly kingdom in sheer beauty and wealth.

"Look at this holy river Mandākinī, Sītā. Look at those graceful swans. Look at the trees on both the banks of the river, showering flowers on the water. Holy sages and ascetics wearing matted locks on the crowns of their heads, with deer-skin and the bark of trees for their dress, bathe in this river every morning. There are others who pray to the sun, standing in the river. The waters of the holy river are pure and purifying, too. They are sparkling, clear, clean and holy. Come, come into the river along with me, and bathe in this holy river in which the sages and ascetics who have burnt all their impurities in the fire of their austerities also bathe.

"Sītā, revere the dwellers in this forest as you would the holy ones in Ayodhyā; regard this river as Sarayū. How happy I am to have Lakṣmaṇa and you, both of whom are devoted to me and joyously do my bidding."

Ayodhyā 96–97

On one occasion, when Rāma was sitting outside his hermitage with Sītā and Lakṣmaṇa, and pointing out to Sītā some wild fruits and explaining their qualities and use, he said: "Lakṣmaṇa, I hear tumultuous noise and I see a cloud of dust yonder. Please climb this tree and find out what is happening. Perhaps a royal party is out hunting in the forest." Lakṣmaṇa climbed the tree and looked; and he looked terrified! "There is a vast army surrounding this hill. It looks ominous. Let Sītā take shelter in that cave; and you had better arm yourself." Rāma asked again: "Can you not see whose army it is?"

Lakṣmaṇa could see whose army it was! And, he said angrily: "Ah, it is Bharata. Having got himself enthroned, he is obviously anxious to kill both of us and thus secure it forever. I can clearly see his personal ensign on the chariot. I can also see jubilant soldiers riding horses and elephants marching towards this hermitage. Come, quick, let us get ready for the fight. Ah, I am happy that today I shall see that treacherous Bharata who is the cause of all our hardship, who is the usurper of the throne of Ayodhyā. He will meet with his doom today, and at my hands. It is no sin to kill one who has committed a grievous sin, as Bharata has done. O Rāma, it is unwise to let a criminal go unpunished. If Kaikeyī has come, I shall kill her also. I shall rid this good earth of this dreadful fountain of sin. I shall destroy the entire army, and thus propitiate my weapons!"

Rāma who coolly listened to all this replied: "Lakṣmaṇa, I have vowed to fulfil father's promise. And my purpose will be defeated if we kill Bharata! Great ignominy will be ours. What shall we do with a throne thus tainted? Whatever I seek in this world (wealth, pleasure, dharma etc.,) is all for the sake of all of you. But I shall not seek sovereignty of the heaven by unrighteous means, Lakṣmaṇa. I fully believe that Bharata does not mean to harm us. He has surely heard about our exile and greatly distressed by the turn of events is coming to take us back to Ayodhyā possibly with the consent of our father. What makes you distrust him, Lakṣmaṇa? If it is for the sake of the throne that you are saying all this, I shall ask Bharata to let you rule the kingdom for all time to come! And I know he will not refuse." When Rāma said this, Lakṣmaṇa felt a great shame. Looking out again he saw the royal elephant coming forward, and announced: "The king is coming, too." But when Rāma saw that the royal (white) umbrella was not to be seen, he was worried. He asked Lakṣmaṇa to climb down.

Ayodhyā 98–99

After ordering the army and the royal entourage to camp on the outskirts of the forest, Bharata sent soldiers in different directions to look for Rāma's hermitage. He himself resolved to look for Rāma, if need be, throughout the forest. He said: "Till I see the noble Rāma, Lakṣmaṇa and Sītā, I cannot have peace of mind. How can I enjoy peace of mind till I lay my head at the feet of my beloved brother Rāma, the feet which bear the marks of royalty on them. Nay, I cannot enjoy peace of mind till that noble prince is installed on the throne which is his alone by birthright." After a while, he went up a tree to have a look around. From there he saw at a very short distance, smoke issuing from a hermitage. The very thought that it might be Rāma's hermitage sent a thrill of joy through his being.

He said to one of his aides: "Please get my mothers here: we have located Rāma's hermitage." As they were proceeding in the direction from which the smoke issued, Bharata saw various signs which confirmed his assumption: he saw the hut

at a distance, he saw pathways cleared, he saw c
saw petals of flowers on the ground (obviously
had dropped as they were being taken for wor
little strips of cloth tied to trees here and ther
serve as 'land-marks'. "Here and very soon I sh
lotus-like face of Rāma," he exclaimed in joy; but only for a moment, for the very next moment he was tormented by the thought that the noble prince who was born to rule the world, to enjoy sovereignty, to delight in regal pleasures, was sitting on the ground in a hut in a dense forest, subjecting his delicate limbs to severe hardship—all this on his (Bharata's) account. Describing all this again and again to his companions, Bharata shed tears.

He had reached the hermitage. From a distance he saw the gold-sheathed weapons of Rāma hanging outside the hut. He saw the ritual altar at which Rāma worshipped daily. And, soon, he saw Rāma himself seated on the ground on the outer verandah of the hut along with Sītā and Lakṣmaṇa. To see Rāma in the ascetic garb broke Bharata's heart. He saw that Rāma had matted locks gathered on top of his head. He saw that he was wearing bark and skins. He rushed towards Rāma's feet. He cried: "O my noble brother," but he could not say anything more. His throat was choked with tears. Tears flowed down the cheeks of Śatrughna. Rāma got up and embraced both of them; and tears rained from his eyes, too.

Ayodhyā 100

Seeing Bharata after a long time, Rāma was overwhelmed with joy. After repeatedly embracing him and kissing his forehead in tender affection, Rāma seated Bharata on his lap and began to enquire of his welfare and the welfare of everyone in Ayodhyā.

"I am happy to see you after a long time, Bharata: but why have you come to this dense and uninhabited forest? Why have you left father alone in the palace and come here? How can the old king endure your absence? I hope the king has survived the great tragedy that struck him. I hope, too, that he has not left this world. And, are you all right, Bharata? I hope you have not been cheated of your sovereignty, simple and pure-hearted that you are? Please also tell me: how is the venerable sage Vasiṣṭha? Do you honour and worship him, as

Everything Bharata should do to (and

you should, my beloved brother? How is my mother Kausalyā, and how is Sumitrā; how is our glorious mother Kaikeyī, I hope she is happy now.

"How are the priests of the royal household? Do you treat them with due respect and do they perform their religious duties properly? Do you honour the gods, our ancestors, the royal servants, the preceptors who are as worshipful as one's father, aged people, physicians and also the holy brāhmṇas? Are you looking after your own personal teacher, Sudhanvā who is well versed in warfare and knows the secret of missiles. And have you appointed the right type of counsellors to advise you? This is essential: for it is important to have ministers who will maintain strict secrecy, and this is the secret of victory. I hope you do not act without the advice of the ministers; and I also hope that you do not consult too many people. Again, I hope you do not proclaim your decisions before they are given effect to. Do you also ensure that the official secrets are not leaked out by untrustworthy officials?

"Do you realise that one wise man is more beneficial to the country than thousands of fools? Have you entrusted the most important offices to first-rate officers, secondary offices to mediocre officers and so on? Do the people have confidence in the ministers you have appointed? Do you have a brave, wise and able person as the chief of your army? For it is important to get rid of a physician whose treatment aggravates the suffering of the sick, a rebellious servant and a hero who is desirous of political power—he who does not get rid of these is himself destroyed. I hope that the servants of the state receive their wages at the appropriate time, promptly: or else the administrative machinery becomes inefficient."

Ayodhyā 100

Rāma continued:

"I hope you are vigilant, as a wise ruler should be, and have intelligence officers constantly watching the foremost functionaries in the state, they who are favourably disposed towards you and those who may not be so disposed. Especially they who have been hostile towards you and who may have later returned to your fold, should be carefully watched. I hope, Bharata, you do not encourage the worldly-minded brāhmaṇas who consider themselves learned but who are experts in destructive endeavour.

"Tell me, O Bharata, is Ayodhyā as impregnable as it has always been, and as its name implies? And, are the people of different groups and classes carrying on their respective professions diligently? Our kingdom has always been free from crime and violence, poverty and drought, and full of wealth of every kind, inhabited by cultured men and women with a keen sense of commonweal: is this tradition being maintained by you, my dear brother? Do the farmers and industrialists enjoy your special protection, so that the state of national economy may be sound? And, are the womenfolk in the kingdom properly looked after and guarded against all hardship and exploitation: and, what is equally important, I do hope there is no excessive reliance on them nor are they taken into your confidence in matters of national security.

"Brother, now tell me: are the forests in our territory well maintained? Are the cows and other animals properly taken care of? Do you ensure that your fort and other fortifications have adequate supplies of food and ammunition? I hope with all this you are able to balance your budget and you do not incur a deficit. And now something very important: have you ensured that law and order are strictly maintained in the state, that a thief does not go unpunished because of the greed of corrupt officials, that the courts of justice are totally impartial and that no innocent man is ever punished? For, the tears that fall from the eyes of an innocent man who is punished destroy the king's welfare.

"In your own person, O Bharata, do you strictly adhere to the code of righteous living? Are you regular in your prayers and religious practices? Pray, do not let dharma, material welfare and enjoyment of righteous pleasures, overlap one another. Each in its own good time, is a good rule. It is good to remember that the king himself should be the paragon of all the virtues which are expected of the people of the state. In addition to these, you should know how to deal with other kings and how to win the friendship of the men, women and children of the state. It is by ruling their kingdom according to dharma that our own forefathers have enjoyed life here and attained heaven hereafter."

Ayodhyā 101–102

Rāma then asked Bharata: "Now, please tell me, why have you come to the forest, abandoning your rightful place in Ayodhyā?"

Tearfully and with joined palms, Bharata replied: "Our father, the king, was driven by his wife, my mother, to commit the most terrible sin. But tormented by the grief caused by his separation from you, he ascended to heaven. My mother, herself, who is responsible for this despicable act will soon descend to hell. I am your humble servant, O Rāma: and pray, grant me this boon—return to Ayodhyā and be our king. This is the prayer of all our friends and relations, of all the people of our kingdom." Bharata fell at the feet of Rāma and touched them with his head.

Rāma lifted him up and fondly embracing him, said, with a cheerful countenance: "Bharata, my heart recoils from unrighteousness. Shall I set aside dharma for the sake of a kingdom? Be not disturbed, Bharata. I do not find any fault in you, in the least. I do not hold you responsible for what has happened. And, pray, do not blame your mother, either. The elders have freedom to do what they please with their wives and children and disciples. Hence, father, too, was quite justified in what he did. Whether he installed me on the throne or sent me to the forest—he had the right to do what he pleased. It is even so with our mothers, Bharata. We are bound to obey their commands. When our mother has commanded me to live in the forest, how can I go against it? Even so, you have been commanded to rule Ayodhyā; and you should obey, too."

Bharata replied: "Being the younger son ineligible to the throne, Rāma, I am not bound by this rule of conduct! In our dynasty it has always been that the throne passed from father to the eldest son. How can we violate this rule? The people speak of the king as a man: he who rules righteously leading the state to prosperity, they call a superman: but I think the king is truly a divinity. This will prove true if you install yourself on the throne."

Remembering king Daśaratha, Bharata said to Rāma: "Just after you had left Ayodhyā and even while I was in the Kekaya kingdom our father passed away. Come, brother, offer libations to him. For, they say that libations offered by dear ones prove of immeasurable good to the departed soul: and you were dear to father, who left this world thinking of you, and longing for you."

Ayodhyā 103

When Rāma was reminded that his father had passed away, he fainted. The three brothers and Sītā quickly sprinkled water on his face and body, and helped to revive him quickly. On regaining consciousness, Rāma expressed his grief: "The king has passed away; and you want me to return to Ayodhyā! What shall I do in Ayodhyā when the king has passed away; who will govern Ayodhyā now that the best among kings has passed away? Bharata, you and Śatrughna are truly blessed in that you were able to serve the king and perform his funeral rites. Even after the expiry of the fourteen years, I do not feel like returning to Ayodhyā, now that father is not there. Who will guide me, who will call me with affection, who will whisper endearing words in my ear when I have done something good?"

Then, they all went to the river Mandākinī. Standing in the water, Rāma offered libations of water for the peace of the departed soul: "May this water offered by me serve you, O king, who has joined our forefathers." He then offered the pulp of the Ingudi tree mixed with fruits: "Pray, accept this O king, for this is our food: indeed what food a man eats that indeed he offers to the gods, too."

After this, he returned to his hut along with his brothers and Sītā. The entire forest and the hillside resounded with the mourning of the princes. The members of Bharata's army and the royal entourage which had been stationed at some distance from the hermitage heard this heart-rending noise and were greatly distressed. At the same time, they surmised that Bharata had discovered the hermitage of Rāma. They ran towards the hermitage—from where the sound came. Some abandoned their vehicles and their mounts: and they ran on foot. Others who were older came in their vehicles and on horses and other animals.

Even from a distance they could see Rāma sitting outside his hut along with the brothers and Sītā. They had despaired of ever being able to set their eyes on him. And, they had, therefore, been mentally cursing the wicked Kaikeyī for being responsible for the banishment of Rāma. In total self-forgetful ecstasy they saw Rāma; their tear-bedimmed eyes feasted on ma, too, responded to their love. He greeted each one tely. It was a moving sight; though tears flowed freely.

104–105

The queens and the sage Vasiṣṭha then approached Rāma's hermitage. Kausalyā pointed out to Sumitrā the pathway which Lakṣmaṇa had made from the hermitage to the bank of the river. Kausalyā saw the Ingudi-pulp offering which Rāma had made to the departed soul of the king and lamented: "Lo, the mighty monarch has to be content with this poor offering: for his son, prince Rāma, who is born to rule, lives an ascetic life."

Rāma, when he saw them approaching the hut, ran forward and clasped their feet; after him Lakṣmaṇa bowed to them. Then Sītā followed suit. Kausalyā embraced Sītā and cried: "Seeing you endure such hardship, the fire of grief consumes me, O Sītā." Rāma bowed to the sage Vasiṣṭha. They all sat down, with Bharata seated just behind Rāma, with joined palms. All of them eagerly waited for whatever Bharata had to say.

Early the next morning, all of them assembled as before. Bharata said: "The kingdom has been bestowed upon me by my father and by my mother. It is mine. And, I hereby give it to you, O Rāma! No one can be its king except you. I am not your equal." The entire assemblage heartily approved.

But, Rāma replied: "The embodied being, Bharata, is not a free agent; he is driven to and fro by the end-result of his own action. However, everything in this world has destruction as its end, all exaltation has fall as its end, all meeting has separation as its end, and all living has death at the end. The clear recognition that a fruit has to fall and that a man has to die, frees one from fear. All this is natural and inevitable. One does not grieve over death any more than one grieves over the ripening and falling of a fruit! Grieve not for another, Bharata, be alert and see that life is passing whether you are sitting or moving. Unwise men do not perceive the ebbing away of life. Similarly, people do not perceive that time brings people together and separates them, even as logs of wood are brought together and separated in water. Perceiving all this clearly, one should diligently work out one's own true happiness: for such true happiness is indeed the goal of everyone.

"Our noble father who was devoted to righteousness has fulfilled his life's mission and has passed away. Mourning for him will not postpone our own death! Return to Ayodhyā and do what you should do; rule the kingdom. And, I too, shall do what I should do—live in the forest for fourteen years. This is the course of right action, O Bharata.

Ayodhyā 106–107

Bharata addressed Rāma once again: "O Rāma, there is none equal to you in the world. Knower of the self that you are, you do not lose your equanimity even in the midst of the greatest calamity. My mother has committed a terribly sinful deed, in my absence: though it is supposed to be for my sake, I dislike it. But for the fact that I honour the code which forbids a prince from killing a woman, I should have killed her. I hold her alone responsible and not our father: he was noble, with a great many noble deeds to his credit, he was aged, he was my father and so god himself to me, and above all he has passed away. Surely he would not have sanctioned this sin, if he had been in his senses. His action confirms the truth of an ancient saying, that one's mind gets muddled when death is near. As a worthy son of our father, it is proper for you to set aside this error committed by him. For, such has been declared to be the duty of a dutiful son: to rectify the errors of his father. If you do so, you will then have saved me, my mother as also my father from sin and calumny. Where is forest-life and where is kingship; where is matted locks and where is the royal function of protecting the people—pray, do not allow this incongruity in your conduct. It is a prince's duty to ascend the throne and righteously rule the kingdom: to run away from it and embrace an ascetic life is improper. If you are averse to pleasure, you can, even while ruling the kingdom, lead an ascetic life in Ayodhyā! O Rāma, I am junior and inferior to you in all respects: I cannot take your place. I have brought all the priests and ministers with me; let us consecrate you for the throne here and now. If, however, you do not concede, I shall also stay with you in the forest." Rāma, however, remained unmoved. The people, seeing this, were proud of Rāma for his firmness and were unhappy because he would not crown himself king. They applauded Bharata.

Rāma said: "I am in agreement with your arguments, Bharata. But there are other considerations. When father sought to marry your mother, he offered the kingdom itself as the price, which meant that her son or her nominee would be king. Moreover, you know how he had granted her two boons which she claimed now. We should guard the word which father has given. It is the sacred duty of a son. Because he saves his father from the hell known as 'put', the son is known as putra. You go to Ayodhyā; I shall go to Daṇḍaka forest. You rule the people; I shall rule the dwellers of the forest. You shall have the royal umbrella over your head; I shall find the shade of a tree. You have Śatrughna, and I have Lakṣmaṇa as a helpmate. Thus both of us will discharge our duty to our father."

Ayodhyā 108–109

A brāhmaṇa named Jābāli intervened in the dialogue. He said to Rāma: "It is proper that one should stick to one's word; but you should not have taken this improper vow in the first place. No one is related to anyone else in this world, O Rāma: everyone comes alone and goes alone. Only mad men think someone is his father or mother, etc. These relationships are temporary shelters which one invents and resorts to during the course of the journey of his life. Giving up this deluded idea that the king was your father, whose word you had to honour, etc., return to Ayodhyā and ascend the throne which is yours. Worrying over departed ancestors and endeavouring to please them is foolish, O Rāma: if by offering rice-balls in libations here, the departed ancestor can be satisfied, why does not one do so to satisfy the hunger of a relation travelling in distant lands? Rely on direct perception and do what you consider to be right; and do not depend upon heresay."

Rāma was annoyed that a brāhmaṇa could tender such heretical counsel. He rebuked the brāhmaṇa: "If I follow your advice I shall become a hypocrite. Though appearing to be good I shall in fact be the very opposite. If I do what I please or what I consider to be right, I shall be setting a bad example: and the people will copy my example. I shall not swerve from the path of truth: for truth alone is praiseworthy royal conduct. The kingdom and the whole earth are established in truth. People suspect, fear and shun the man who is untruthful and breaks his own promises. Truth alone is god in this world;

dharma is founded on truth; there is no religion higher than truth. Knowing this how can I swerve from the path of truth, O brāhmaṇa! I bear this truth on my head; the matted locks I carry because the holy ones do so, too. The ignorant man thinks evil, tells lies and indulges in wicked deeds. Thereby he loses all that is good and wholesome in this world. If I follow your advice, I shall also be guilty of this three-fold sin. Nay, I shall continue to dwell in the forest discharging my duty to father. Having come into this world of activity, one should engage oneself in right action. Fire, wind and soma share the fruits of man's action."

Jābāli thereupon said: "I am not an unbeliever, nor do I say what the unbelievers say, nor does unbelief exist. In accordance with the time, I have become a believer again; and in due course of time, I shall become an unbeliever. What I said has served its purpose: it expressed my and the people's eagerness that you should be king, and it has brought out your glory as a firm adherent to truth."

Ayodhyā 110–111

Seeing that Rāma was offended by Jābāli's arguments, the sage Vasiṣṭha intervened and said: "O Rāma, Jābāli knows very well what should be and should not be done in this world; but in his eagerness to make you return to Ayodhyā, he offered his arguments. I shall now narrate to you your own ancestry, from the Creator, his son Marīci whose son was Kaśyapa and whose son Vivasvān, the sun, founded the solar dynasty to which you belong. Manu was the son of Vivasvān and his son Ikṣvāku ruled Ayodhyā." Vasiṣṭha then mentioned all the ancestors of Rāma by name. The throne had invariably passed to the eldest son of the previous king. Vasiṣṭha said: "This tradition should not be violated by you." He continued: "Father, mother and preceptor—these three are the gurus of a person. Father only gives birth to him, whereas the preceptor gives him the highest wisdom and therefore he is called guru. By following my advice you will not be incurring sin."

Rāma was inflexible in his resolve. He submitted to the sage Vasiṣṭha: "The debt that a person owes to his father and mother is indeed great: for all the loving and tender service he has received from them, in feeding him, in putting him to sleep and in speaking sweet words to him. Such a father's command, that I should go to the forest, I will not falsify."

Bharata now sternly turned to Sumantra and commanded: "Prepare a bed of kuśa grass for me in front of this hut; I shall lie down there, not eating nor drinking anything, till Rāma returns to Ayodhyā." Sumantra looked at Rāma! Rāma said to Bharata: "Such a course of conduct is not appropriate for a prince! A brāhmaṇa can do so. No, Bharata, give up this impossible task and return to Ayodhyā." Bharata then turned to the people: "Why don't you talk Rāma out of his resolve?" And the spokesman of the people replied: "We have listened to both of you. What you say is right and noble; and we see that Rāma adheres to the truth and does not wish to transgress his father's command. Hence we are unable to say anything."

Bharata made one last attempt. He said: "All of you know that I did not covet the throne nor desire the banishment of Rāma. If Rāma insists on staying in the forest, I humbly offer myself as his substitute; let Rāma return to Ayodhyā." But Rāma replied: "Oh, no: a commitment entered into by our father, cannot be nullified by either you or me. And, to find a substitute would not be truthful adherence to that commitment. I shall fulfil my part, Bharata: and so should you fulfil your part."

Ayodhyā 112–113

The sages who had assembled on the grounds of Rāma's hermitage, and indeed the sages who were witnessing this divine event from their invisible realms, all of them lauded the righteous conduct of both the brothers. They now turned to Bharata and pleaded that he should accept Rāma's advice: "We, too, wish to see that Rāma fulfils the promise of his father made to Kaikeyī." Rāma felt greatly encouraged by this counsel of the sages and he sang their glories.

Bharata made one last attempt. He repeated the fundamental arguments: "O Rāma, you are equally obliged to adhere to the family tradition, to lend ear to the prayers of myself, and your mother. Moreover, I cannot rule the kingdom. All the people want that you should be their king." Once again Bharata fell down at the feet of Rāma and clasped them to his head. Once again Rāma put Bharata on his lap and affectionately said to him: "You are endowed with natural and genuine humility, Bharata, and with that you can rule the whole world. The moon may become bereft of light, the Himālayas may be bereft of snow, and the ocean may break its bounds but I will not dishonour the promise given by father. And this is my request to you: whatever might have been mother Kaikeyī's motives in doing what she did, you should not mind that but you should continue to treat her as your mother."

The sage Vasiṣṭha suggested a compromise! Rāma should make a gift of his wooden sandals to Bharata, which could be installed on the throne in Rāma's stead. Bharata at once placed the sandals in front of Rāma and prayed to him to bless them. When Rāma had done so, Bharata bowed to them and said: "The business of the state will be entrusted to these sandals, O Rāma; and, living on fruits and roots, I shall live outside Ayodhyā, eagerly looking forward to your return. If you do not return the day after the expiry of the fourteen years, I shall enter into the fire." Rāma agreed.

The brothers and the mothers took leave of Rāma with tearful eyes; and with tearful eyes Rāma re-entered his hut.

Reverently placing Rāma's sandals on his head, Bharata turned towards Ayodhyā. On the way, he met the sage Bharadvāja again and narrated to him all that happened in Citrakooṭa. The sage Bharadvāja was happy and happily pronounced the following words of blessing: "It is no wonder that all the noble qualities abide in you, O Bharata, even as water seeks lowly spots on earth. You are truly humble. Blessed is the father that has a son like you."

Ayodhyā 114–115

Bharata entered Ayodhyā which appeared to be completely devoid of life, of joy, of any sign of prosperity. It was a city in mourning; mourning for the late king Daśaratha, mourning for the exiled Rāma. Bharata sighed and said: "Surely, because my brother has left the city, it has lost all its splendour."

As soon as his mothers had entered their apartments, Bharata announced his decision: "I shall immediately proceed to Nandigrāma, and I shall dwell there enduring this great sorrow caused by my separation from Rāma." The counsellors agreed to the proposal. Sumantra had the chariot ready. All the preceptors, the counsellors, the heads of the administration, as also the army, accompanied Bharata to Nandigrāma. All the way to Nandigrāma, Bharata held Rāma's sandals devoutly on his head.

On arrival at Nandigrāma, Bharata announced again: "This kingdom has been given to me on trust by my brother who has also given me these precious sandals of his, which will attend to the welfare of the kingdom. I shall manage this kingdom as a trustee during the period of Rāma's absence, eagerly looking forward to the blessed day of his return to Ayodhyā. Immediately on his return I shall hand the reins of the kingdom to him and I shall rejoice when he wears these sandals on his feet once more. Thus even now I place the burdens of the state upon Rāma, upon his blessed sandals; and thus I absolve myself of the sin of usurping the throne."

The noble Bharata took up his residence in Nandigrāma, clad in bark with his matted locks gathered on the crown of his head. He himself held the royal umbrella over Rāma's sandals; and he offered all royal edicts to the sandals for approval before issuing them. He enthroned and crowned the sandals of Rāma, and, remaining subordinate to them carried on the administration of the kingdom. Whatever work had to be undertaken, whatever decisions had to be made, and whatever tribute had been received—Bharata offered all these to the sandals of Rāma at first and then took the necessary action.

Ayodhyā 116–117

One day, approaching an elderly hermit, Rāma humbly enquired: "Holy sir, I notice a certain restlessness amongst the holy men here. From their behaviour I infer that we are the cause of it. Pray, tell me: have I been guilty of actions unworthy of the honour of my family? Or, has my younger brother Lakṣmaṇa done something to annoy the sages? Or, may it be that the young lady Sītā has committed an act of indiscretion?"

The elderly sage quickly replied: "Oh, no, Rāma, nothing but the most exemplary conduct has been seen by all of us in you, Lakṣmaṇa and Sītā. But, it is true that there is some restlessness amongst us. It has been caused by a demon known as Khara who is the younger brother of Rāvaṇa. He is a cannibal. He has harassed the sages living in Janasthāna; and now he has turned his attention towards this place. We believe that he hates your presence here. And, as long as you are living here, so long these demons will harass the ascetics. They desecrate our altars and pollute the very atmosphere. Hence, we wish to leave this place and go elsewhere today. These demons do not like you, Rāma: and you will also do well to move from here." The hermits left Citrakooṭa.

Some time later, Rāma said to himself: "I shall also leave this place, but for other reasons. It was here I met Bharata, and my mothers and the citizens of Ayodhyā. The memory of that meeting lingers and disturbs the mental equilibrium. And, the elephants and the horses which accompanied Bharata have also polluted the place. It is better for us to move on." Deciding thus, Rāma, with Lakṣmaṇa and Sītā, left Citrakooṭa and went towards the Daṇḍaka forest.

Soon they reached the holy hermitage of the sage Atri who received them warmly. He called his celebrated wife Anasūyā and asked her to receive Sītā. Anasūyā thereupon took Sītā into the hut; Sītā bowed to the venerable lady who in turn blessed Sītā. Anasūyā said: "You have done the right thing, O Sītā, by following your noble husband, abandoning your relations and friends. That noble woman who loves her husband whether he lives in a city or in a forest, whether he is good or not so good, inherits the glorious worlds. Even if he is of bad conduct, lustful, and poor, for noble women the husband alone is supreme god. Serve your husband, noble Sītā, treating him as your god; and you will attain fame here and heaven hereafter."

Ayodhyā 118–119

Sītā rejoiced to hear the wholesome advice of Anasūyā. Sītā said: "I am beholden to you for your words of wisdom, worshipful lady! It is true, even as you have said, that a noble woman should treat her husband as god even if he is of evil disposition. How much more so, if he is as godly as Rāma is! Indeed, the way in which I should behave towards him has clearly been indicated to me by my mother-in-law: nay, even before my marriage, by my mother herself. What you have said has confirmed and reiterated their admonition: that except service of the husband, the woman has no other form of worship or asceticism. I remember too the lives of exemplars of this great principle—the great Sāvitrī, and Rohiṇī, and your self, too."

Anasūyā was pleased with these words uttered by Sītā and said: "Sītā, I have accumulated a lot of merit by my austerities. Please mention any boon of your choice: I shall give you whatever you want." What would Sītā want or ask for? She remained silent, after saying: "Your blessings are more than sufficient for me." Admiring her modesty and desirelessness, Anasūyā continued: "Well, then, I shall myself choose a boon for you! Here are divine garlands, dress, jewelry and cosmetic articles which will enhance the beauty of your limbs. These will enable you to enjoy unfading beauty and thus enhance the delight of your noble husband, Rāma."

Sītā humbly accepted the noble lady's gifts. Anasūyā then requested Sītā to narrate how she got married to Rāma. With great joy, Sītā told her the story of her immaculate birth, of her growth as the daughter of king Janaka, of the king's proclamation concerning her suitor, of the divine weapon of lord Śiva, of Rāma's visit to Mithilā along with Lakṣmaṇa and the sage Visvāmitra, of Rāma's prowess in firing the mighty weapon. "Then, my father immediately offered me in marriage to Rāma. He however, hesitated not knowing what his father's reaction would be! Soon his father also came, approved of the alliance, and thus I obtained the hand of Rāma," concluded Sītā.

Later, the hermits of the forest told Rāma: "Rāma, there are many demons in yonder forest. They are cannibals. They have many different forms. They drink blood. They eat ascetics and celibates who may be unclean or non-vigilant. Kindly destroy them, O Rāma. If you go along that path, you will be able to enter that dense forest."

Āraṇya Kāṇḍa
The Forest Life

Rāma entered the dense and fearsome forest named Daṇḍaka. Yet, in that forest they beheld the hermitages of sages who had made the forest their abode. Grass mats and deer-skin seats were found everywhere around each one of these hermitages. The little huts were yet very well maintained. The surroundings were clean. The altars for the performance of fire worship proclaimed the sanctity of the place. The ease with which birds and beasts played around the hermitages bore witness to the cosmic love that radiated from the hearts of the sages. The sages themselves filled the entire atmosphere with the auspicious sound of their chanting of the vedic hymns.

Rāma approached them with reverence and humility, with his weapons unloaded and sheathed. The sages, too, received Rāma, Lakṣmaṇa and Sītā with great joy and affection. After entertaining them with fruits, roots, etc., the sages lovingly and reverently said to Rāma: "You are our king, Rāma, whether you are in a city or in the forest; and we are fit to be protected by you. The king wielding the sceptre is worshipful in as much as he is regarded a part-manifestation of the Lord himself. We, hermits, have renounced violence and anger, and we are wholly devoted to the conquest of our mind and senses: hence it is for you to protect our person."

Rāma spent a night in the hermitage which was situated at the very entrance to that dense forest. The next morning, he took leave of the sages and proceeded on his way. The forest grew more and more formidable and awesome. Very soon, Rāma saw a terrible demon of indescribably ugly and terrifying form. This demon, too, saw Rāma, Lakṣmaṇa and

Sītā. He roared aloud. The monster sprang towards Sītā, took her, and after running away to a distance, said to Rāma and Lakṣmaṇa: "Hey you! What have you to do with this young woman—you who look like ascetics? You are a disgrace to the sacred orders of the ascetics. I shall take this woman away and marry her. I, the demon Virādha, shall destroy both of you sinners and drink your blood just now."

Sītā was sorely stricken with fear. Deeply distressed, Rāma said to Lakṣmaṇa: "What a tragedy, my dear Lakṣmaṇa, at the very commencement of our forest-life! Surely, mother Kaikeyī will be extremely pleased to hear that we have all been killed even before we settled down in the forest. To me there is nothing more tormenting than to see beloved Sītā touched by another man."

The brave Lakṣmaṇa consoled Rāma with the words: "Please do not worry, Rāma! In a few moments, the earth will drink this demon's blood."

Āraṇya 3–4

The monster roared again: "Hey you two! Tell me who you are, and where you are going." Rāma politely replied: "We are princes by birth, and we belong to the famous Ikṣvāku dynasty. Pray, tell us who you are and what you are doing in this forest."

The demon replied: "O noble king! I shall tell you who I am. My father is Jīva, and my mother Śatahradā. Here I am known as Virādha. I propitiated lord Brahmā the creator by my austerities and gained from him the boon that I shall be invulnerable to weapons and that I shall not die from broken limbs or injury. You can therefore not destroy me! Leave this woman and run away from here!"

Defying him, Rāma struck him with several missiles. Though pierced by them, he did not die. He, however, left Sītā and ran towards the brothers with a lance. Rāma broke the lance with his own missiles. But these missiles, however, had no power against Virādha: they struck him but when he yawned, they dropped to the ground! Virādha caught hold of Rāma and Lakṣmaṇa and lifting them up with one hand each, carried them away. Lakṣmaṇa tried to stop him. But, Rāma said: "Let him take us where he will: he is going in the same direction as we wish to go."

But Sītā was horrified. She shouted to the demon: "Pray, O best among demons! Take me and throw me to the wild animals; but leave the princes." Hearing this, Rāma and Lakṣmaṇa decided to dispose of the demon. Still sitting on his shoulders, the two princes each broke an arm. Virādha fell down; and they, now standing near him began hitting him with their fists. Rāma said to Lakṣmaṇa: "He is protected by his boon; we cannot kill him in this manner. Dig a pit in the ground. We shall bury him. and that is the only way in which he can meet with his end."

The monster Virādha now spoke: "O Rāma, I have been defeated by you, and my end is near. Due to the demoniacal quality of ignorance I did not recognise your glory. I was a celestial named Tumburu, but had incurred the displeasure of Kubera who cursed me, and so I became a demon. At my pleading he said: 'When Rāma kills you in a fight, you will return to heaven.' Released from that curse, I shall now return to heaven. Yonder lives the sage Śarabhaṅga; kindly go to see him, after burying me in that pit. For, this is the time-honoured way of dealing with demons." Lakṣmaṇa soon finished digging a huge pit into which they lowered the monster Virādha. Reunited with Sītā, the two princes proceeded on their course.

Āraṇya 5

Rāma then said to Lakṣmaṇa: "This is truly a dreadful forest and we have already had a foretaste of its true nature. Let us hurry to the hermitage of the sage Śarabhaṅga."

As he approached the hermitage, Rāma beheld a marvel. He saw a radiant space vehicle which stood without touching the earth. In it was the chief of the gods, Indra himself, shining with the resplendence of the sun. As Indra was talking to the sage Śarabhaṅga, angels and sages were serving him in many ways. Rāma pointed this marvel out to Lakṣmaṇa and said: "Lakṣmaṇa, see this wonder! Indra, the god of gods himself personally visiting the hermitage of the sage Śarabhaṅga. I have heard that he thus visits the sages' fire worship; but now I have seen it. Look at these celestials who have also come with him. All of them have the appearance of young men of twenty-five years of age: indeed, I have heard that the celestials are forever twenty-five years of age! Please stay here with Sītā, and I shall find out if it is in fact Indra." But, when Rāma went nearer the hermitage, Indra said to the sage: "Rāma is coming. This is, however, not the right occasion for me to see him. I shall see him after he has killed the wicked Rāvaṇa in battle. Rāma has to do a great many wonders here. I shall go now. And, you, too, move from here, to meet him." Indra's space vehicle rose into the sky.

Rāma then permitted Lakṣmaṇa and Sītā to accompany him, and all of them bowed to the sage Śarabhaṅga. Out of curiosity, Rāma enquired why Indra had visited the hermitage. The sage replied: "O Rāma, he came to take me away to the highest realm known as Brahma Loka which has been earned by my austerities. But, knowing that you were in the neighbourhood, I did not want to go to Brahma Loka without seeing you and without serving you as a guest should be served. Having seen you, I shall ascend to the higher regions one by one. I have earned them by dint of penance; and I humbly offer them to you today, O Rāma; please be gracious to accept them."

Deeply touched by the love and affection of the mighty sage, Rāma replied: "I can actually bring all those worlds to you, O sage; but kindly indicate a place in this forest for us to dwell." The sage replied: "Pray, O Rāma, go to the hermitage of the sage Sutīkṣṇa who will surely indicate where you can reside in this forest." After saying this, as Rāma was looking on, the sage kindled the sacred fire and entered into it. The fire consumed his physical body. The sage then shone with the lustre of fire and had the body of a young man of twenty-five years of age. He rose to the Brahma Loka, and was welcomed by the Creator.

Āraṇya 6–7

Soon after the ascension to heaven of the sage Śarabhaṅga, the sages and the ascetics of the neighbourhood called on Rāma. These sages belonged to different orders of ascetics. There were Vaikhānasas and Vālakhilyas who are said to have sprung from the nails and the hairs of the creator Brahmā. Other orders included, they who after they had eaten their single daily meal ensured that nothing was left for the next, they who drank solar and lunar rays, they who lived on powdered stone, or on leaves, they who used nothing but their own teeth to cut, powder or soften food, they who remained immersed in water, they who lay down with no bed, they who did not lie down at all, they who had no time for anything other than their spiritual practices, they who lived on water, they who lived on air, they who had only the sky for their roof, they who lay down on the altar, they who lived on tree-tops, they who wore only wet clothes, the self-controlled ones devoted to the repetition of the divine name, and they who surrounded themselves with fires with the blazing sun overhead. All were radiant with the lustre of self-realisation. They greeted Rāma and said to him: "Lord, the king appropriates a sixth of everyone's income; in return he should protect the people, treating them as his own children. If he does not he incurs sin. The king has a fourth share in the spiritual wealth earned by the sages; and in return he should protect them. It is in this spirit that we approach you, our king and protector. Here in this forest are diabolical beings that terrorise the sages and ascetics. Pray, protect us from them." Rāma graciously replied at once: "Indeed, I shall. It is surely for this purpose that my noble father sent me to the forest."

Taking leave of the sages, Rāma travelled onwards to the hermitage of the sage Sutīkṣṇa. The sage was serenely seated in the meditation posture. Rāma introduced himself to the sage. The sage graciously replied: "Rāma, I have been awaiting your arrival. I have heard everything from Indra who visited me just now to announce that I could now ascend to the higher worlds earned by my penance. On the strength of that penance I pray that the three of you may enjoy your life in the forest." Rāma thereupon requested the sage to indicate a suitable dwelling for him. The sage replied: "Stay in this hermitage itself. Except deer, you will have no trouble from any other creature." But Rāma submitted: "If I live here, it is possible that I might kill the deer, and this would be extremely displeasing to you. Hence I do not think I should settle down here."

Enjoying the hospitality of the sage Sutīkṣṇa, Rāma spent that night at the hermitage, along with Lakṣmaṇa and Sītā.

Āraṇya 8–9

Early the next morning, Rāma took leave of the sage Sutīkṣṇa: "Lord, we have spent a blissful night in your holy company, enjoying your hospitality. It is time we moved on before the sun gets too hot." Rāma, Lakṣmaṇa and Sītā bowed the sage who in turn lifted them up and embraced them, as a token of his blessing. He wished them well and requested them to return to his hermitage.

As they were marching into the depth of the forest, Sītā found an opportunity to lay her heart before Rāma. She said to him: "Lord, you are well acquainted with the bases of dharma, and do not stand in need of any instruction or admonition. However, I know that what appears to be a slight initial neglect often leads to gross violation of dharma. Adharma can only be avoided by one who is able to resist the painful effects of desire. These effects are three: the most formidable is falsehood in speech, and then adultery, and the third is unprovoked cruelty. Surely, you are incapable of the first two. I am, however, worried that you may succumb to the third. These ascetics have requested you to kill the demons who live in the Daṇḍaka forest, and you have agreed. Therefore, armed with your weapons and missiles, you are in a hurry to enter the terrible Daṇḍaka forest. I am not quite happy about it. You are armed, and it is possible that you might kill someone without seriously meaning to do so.

"Lord, I have heard the following story. In a certain forest lived an ascetic who was an extremely peaceful man of whom even birds and beasts were unafraid. Indra wanted to obstruct this holy man's penance. In the disguise of a warrior, Indra came to the ascetic and on some pretext left his sword with the ascetic with the request to guard it while the soldier was away. The ascetic was zealously guarding the sword and even took it with him when he wandered in the forest. To cut a long story short, after some time the ascetic began to wield the sword, forgetting his vow of non-violence. Keeping a lethal weapon with one is like playing with fire.

"I am anxious, Lord, that this should not happen to you. There is contradiction in an ascetic carrying a weapon; in one who wishes to lead a forest-life but behaves like a warrior. Handling a weapon perverts the mind. I am sure your parents will be delighted if we adhere to a life of dharma. And dharma is not for the pleasure-seeker. Dharma leads to prosperity; dharma itself gives great happiness; everything is gained by dharma, and the world is established in dharma. However, it demands iron will and self-control in order to preserve dharma."

Āraṇya 10

Rāma was delighted to hear that loving and righteous advice tendered by the tender-hearted Sītā. He replied:

"Surely, Sītā, you yourself are eager that no one in Daṇḍaka forest should be subjected to suffering. And that is my own wish, too. Sages and ascetics living in the forest came to me. As a prince I am their proper asylum. They sought refuge in me. When they sought my presence, I volunteered to serve them and help them in whatever way I could. They then narrated how they were being harassed in various ways by the cannibalistic demons that dwell in the forest. They are the holy brāhmaṇas who are fit to be worshipfully approached by us; yet they came to me, O Sītā, seeking my help. How could I refuse their prayer? Therefore, I granted their prayer. They were indeed capable of dealing with the demons themselves. They could destroy the demons by the power of their asceticism. However, such action on their part would be a violation of their vow of asceticism and would therefore destroy the fruits of their penance, as it were. Hence, they do not wish to undertake the task of punishing the wicked demons. Hence, again, it is my duty to undertake this task.

"Considering all this, I have given them my word that I shall protect them. And, now, having given them my word I cannot go back on it as long as I am alive. I can give up my life, give up Lakṣmaṇa and even you, my dear Sītā; but I cannot abandon the word I have given to anyone, especially to the holy brāhmaṇas, sages and ascetics. Have I made this clear to you, Sītā? As a prince, it is my duty to protect the people from evil-doers, and hence even without their request I should offer them such protection. Now these ascetics have actually requested for such protection, and I have promised to do so. There is therefore no going back on this promise at any cost. I shall, however, bear in mind the wise words which you have uttered on account of your great love for me. It is proper that you should so advise me, for you are really and truly my companion in dharma."

Thus speaking to each other, Rāma and Sītā proceeded towards the hermitages of the sages of the Daṇḍaka forest.

Araṇya 11

Rāma walked ahead; Sītā followed him; and behind them went Lakṣmaṇa. They admired the mountain peaks, the lakes, the trees, the flowers and the animals that they saw on their way. As they were thus walking, one evening they saw a large lake in which a large herd of elephants was bathing and playing and in which cranes and swans and other aquatic creatures lived free from fear, in utter delight. As Rāma came near that lake, he heard delightful music, issuing apparently from the lake itself. He could not see anyone in the neighbourhood. Puzzled at this extraordinary phenomenon, he asked a sage Dharmabhṛt who happened to be with the party at that time, to tell him more about the lake.

The sage narrated to Rāma the following story: "Rāma, this lake was actually created by a renowned ascetic purely by the power of his penance. That sage, known as Mandakarṇī, continued to perform his austerities in the lake, living on air, for a great number of years. Even the gods were perturbed: they thought that he wanted to usurp their powers. In order to divert his attention from his penance, the gods commissioned a select band of five apsaras (celestial nymphs). These nymphs came to this spot and plied their charms on the sage. The sage knew the truth and he fell in love with them, as it were, for the fulfilment of the purpose of the gods. He then created a huge palace within this very lake, in which he still lives along with those five nymphs. Hence this lake is known as Pancāpsara lake. The music that you heard is actually the music of these nymphs."

Rāma marvelled at the power of penance. Thus he wandered in the forest, visiting one hermitage after another, spending a few weeks in one, a few months in another, enjoying the company and the hospitality of the sages of the forest. As he was thus wandering happily in the forest along with Sītā and Lakṣmaṇa, ten years went by. Once again, he came to the hermitage of the sage Sutīkṣṇa and spent some months in his company.

One day Rāma said to Sutīkṣṇa: "Holy one, I have heard that the famous sage Agastya lives in this forest. Pray, tell me how we can reach that hermitage. I wish to meet him." Sutīkṣṇa replied: "In fact, Rāma, I was myself going to ask you to meet Agastya, along with Sītā and Lakṣmaṇa. Luckily, you have yourself expressed the same wish."

Sutīkṣṇa then explained to Rāma in great detail how to reach the hermitage of Agastya, and said: "If you wish to meet sage Agastya, better go today itself."

Āraṇya 11

Rāma, Lakṣmaṇa and Sītā reached a place surrounded by lofty mountains and dense forest. The pungent smell of pippali fruits confirmed that the site mentioned by Sutikṣṇa was close at hand. The hermitage of the brother of the sage Agastya was near.

At that stage, Rāma narrated the story of Agastya to Lakṣmaṇa: "There is an interesting story connected with the sage Agastya, Lakṣmaṇa, and I shall tell you. Two demons inhabited these parts in days of yore. They were Vātāpi and Ilvala. Ilvala disguised himself as a brāhmaṇa and spoke in a cultured dialect (sanskṛt). Thus he attracted the attention of the brāhmaṇas whom he invited to participate in the śrāddha rite for the propitiation of departed ancestors. He would nicely cook his own elder brother Vātāpi, disguised as a ram, and serve that meat to the brāhmaṇas, in accordance with the injunctions concerning the rite. When they had eaten that meat, he would call out: 'Vātāpi, come out.' Vātāpi would thereupon tear the bodies of the brāhmaṇas and emerge. The gods prayed to the sage Agastya to put an end to this atrocity. Agastya volunteered himself to eat in Ilvala's house. After the usual meal, Ilvala called 'Vātāpi, come out.' Agastya serenely said: 'How can Vātāpi come out; he has been digested by me!' The furious Ilvala thereupon attacked the sage Agastya who deprived him of his life by a mere look.

"Rid of them and of their kind, O Lakṣmaṇa, this southern country has prospered."

Soon they reached the hermitage of the brother of Agastya. Warmly received by him, Rāma spent that evening there. The next day, he said to Agastya's brother: "I wish to meet your illustrious brother." Taking leave of him, the three proceeded towards the hermitage of Agastya.

Rāma pointed out to Lakṣmaṇa: "See, O Lakṣmaṇa, this prosperous countryside. All this is due to the grace of the sage Agastya. Since he has rid the country of the demons, people live happily, free from fear. Even people of diabolical disposition have become peaceful and peace-loving. This is due to the grace of sage Agastya. Such is his spiritual power that no sinful man can live in the southern region now. On account of the sage's glory, again, the gods are easily pleased with the worshippers and grant the latter's noble desires." As he was saying this, they arrived at the hermitage of Agastya. And, Rāma sent Lakṣmaṇa to inform the sage of their arrival.

Āraṇya 12–13

Lakṣmaṇa humbly approached a disciple of the sage Agastya and announced: "Rāma, the son of the king Daśaratha has arrived here, along with his consort Sītā and me his brother and servant. He awaits the pleasure of the sage Agastya to meet him."

As Rāma entered the sanctuary, he saw there the sacred altars dedicated to the different gods who are invoked in the Vedic rites. The sage Agastya himself was coming forward to meet Rāma. Rāma, Lakṣmaṇa and Sītā bowed to the feet of the sage and stood with joined palms. The sage joyously enquired of their welfare and made them sit down, in order that he might offer them water to wash their hands and feet and food to eat. He said to Rāma: "This is the sacred duty of an ascetic, Rāma: he should offer worship to the sacred fire and then offer water and food to the guest: or else he incurs great sin, the fruit of which will be to eat his own flesh in the other world." Immediately after they had finished their meal, Agastya brought several rare weapons and missiles and presented them to Rāma: all of them had been fashioned by the celestial engineer Viśvakarma; and one had been used by lord Viṣṇu himself and another by Brahmā and yet another by Mahendra, etc. After explaining their glories, the sage gave them all to Rāma.

The sage then said to Rāma: "Rāma, I am delighted that you came here to see me. However, I see that all of you are extremely tired, obviously after a long journey. I see that Sītā needs some rest, too. I am thrilled that she accompanies you. Women are usually fickle-minded and they disown even a husband who has lost his fortune. They say that woman combines in herself the flippancy of lightning, the destructive sharpness of a weapon, and the speed of a bird. But, this your wife is free from all these blemishes; indeed she is praiseworthy and ranks with great women like Arundhatī."

Rāma was happy that he, his brother and also Sītā enjoyed the esteem of the mighty sage. He prayed: "Lord, kindly indicate a place where we can build a hermitage and spend the rest of the period of our exile." The sage Agastya thereupon replied: "Rāma, there is a place called Pañcavaṭī not far from here. That is the best place for you to settle down, to spend the balance of your exile. Of course, I know already all that happened in Ayodhyā, through intuition. I think that Sītā would feel happy to live in Pañcavaṭī, which is near the river Godāvarī. Living there, you can fulfil the promise given by your father and also offer protection to the weak and the helpless, the sages and the ascetics."

Āraṇya 14–15

Rāma, Lakṣmaṇa and Sītā were proceeding towards Pañcavaṭī. On the way they saw a huge vulture. Rāma's first thought was that it was a demon in disguise. The vulture said: "I am your father's friend!" Trusting the vulture's words, Rāma asked for details of its birth and ancestry.

The vulture said: "You know that Dakṣa Prajāpati had sixty daughters and the sage Kaśyapa married eight of them. One day Kaśyapa said to his wives: 'You will give birth to offspring who will be foremost in the three worlds.' Aditi, Diti, Danu and Kālaka listened attentively; the others were indifferent. As a result, the former four gave birth to powerful offspring who were superhuman. Aditi gave birth to thirty-three gods. Diti gave birth to demons. Danu gave birth to Aśvagrīva. And, Kālaka had Naraka and Kālikā. Of the others, men were born of Manu, and the sub-human species from the other wives of Kaśyapa. Tāmra's daughter was Sukī whose granddaughter was Vinatā who had two sons, Garuḍa and Aruṇa. My brother Sampāti and I are the sons of Aruṇa. I offer my services to you, O Rāma. If you will be pleased to accept them, I shall guard Sītā when you and Lakṣmaṇa may be away from your hermitage. As you have seen, this formidable forest is full of wild animals and demons, too."

Rāma accepted this new friendship. All of them now proceeded towards Pañcavaṭī in search of a suitable place for building a hermitage. Having arrived at Pañcavaṭī, identified by Rāma by the description which the sage Agastya had given, Rāma said to Lakṣmaṇa: "Pray, select a suitable place here for building the hermitage. It should have a charming forest, good water, firewood, flowers and holy grass." Lakṣmaṇa submitted: "Even if we live together for a hundred years, I shall continue to be your servant. Hence, Lord, you select the place and I shall do the needful." Rejoicing at Lakṣmaṇa's attitude, Rāma pointed to a suitable place, which satisfied all the requisites of a hermitage. Rāma said: "This is holy ground; this is charming; it is frequented by beasts and birds. We shall dwell here." Immediately Lakṣmaṇa set about building a hermitage for all of them to live in.

Rāma warmly embraced Lakṣmaṇa and said: "I am delighted by your good work and devoted service: and I embrace you in token of such admiration. Brother, you divine the wish of my heart, you are full of gratitude, you know dharma; with such a man as his son, father is not dead but is eternally alive."

Entering that hermitage, Rāma, Lakṣmaṇa and Sītā dwelt in it with great joy and happiness.

Āraṇya 16

Time rolled on. One day Lakṣmaṇa sought the presence of Rāma early in the morning and described what he had seen outside the hermitage. He said: "Winter, the season which you love most, has arrived, O Rāma. There is dry cold everywhere; the earth is covered with foodgrains. Water is uninviting; and fire is pleasant. The first fruits of the harvest have been brought in; and the agriculturists have duly offered some of it to the gods and the manes, and thus reaffirmed their indebtedness to them. The farmer who thus offers the first fruits to gods and manes is freed from sin.

"The sun moves in the southern hemisphere; and the north looks lustreless. Himālaya, the abode of snow, looks even more so! It is pleasant to take a walk even at noon. The shade of a tree which we loved in summer is unpleasant now. Early in the morning the earth, with its rich wheat and barley fields, is enveloped by mist. Even so, the rice crop. The sun, even when it rises, looks soft and cool like the moon. Even the elephants which approach the water, touch it with their trunk but pull the trunk quickly away on account of the coldness of the water.

"Rāma, my mind naturally thinks of our beloved brother Bharata. Even in this cold winter, he who could command the luxury of a king, prefers to sleep on the floor and live an ascetic life. Surely, he, too, would have got up early in the morning and has perhaps had a cold bath in the river Sarayū. What a noble man! I can even now picture him in front of me: with eyes like the petals of a lotus, dark brown in colour, slim and without an abdomen, as it were. He knows what dharma is. He speaks the truth. He is modest and self-controlled, always speaks pleasantly, is sweet-natured, with long arms and with all his enemies fully subdued. That noble Bharata has given up all his pleasures and is devoted to you. He has already won his place in heaven, Rāma. Though he lives in the city; yet, he has adopted the ascetic mode of life and follows you in spirit.

"We have heard it said that a son takes after his mother in nature: but in the case of Bharata this has proved false. I wonder how Kaikeyī, in spite of having our father as her husband, and Bharata as her son, has turned out to be so cruel."

When Lakṣmaṇa said this, Rāma stopped him, saying: "Do not speak ill of our mother Kaikeyī, Lakṣmaṇa. Talk only of our beloved Bharata. Even though I try not to think of Ayodhyā and our people there, when I think of Bharata, I wish to see him."

Āraṇya 17–18

After their bath and morning prayers, Rāma, Lakṣmaṇa and Sītā returned to their hermitage. As they were seated in their hut, there arrived upon the scene a dreadful demoness. She looked at Rāma and immediately fell in love with him! He had a handsome face; she had an ugly face. He had a slender waist; she had a huge abdomen. He had lovely large eyes; she had hideous eyes. He had lovely soft hair; she had red hair. He had a lovable form; she had a terrible form. He had a sweet voice; hers resembled the barking of a dog. He was young; she was haughty. He was able; her speech was crooked. He was of noble conduct; she was of evil conduct. He was beloved; she had a forbidding appearance. Such a demoness spoke to Rāma: "Who are you, young men; and what are both of you doing in this forest, with this lady?"

Rāma told her the whole truth about himself, Lakṣmaṇa and Sītā, about his banishment from the kingdom, etc. Then Rāma asked her: "O charming lady, now tell me who you are." At once the demoness replied: "Ah, Rāma! I shall tell you all about myself immediately. I am Śūrpaṇakhā, the sister of Rāvaṇa. I am sure you have heard of him. He has two other brothers, Kumbhakarṇa and Vibhīsaṇa. Two other brothers Khara and Dūsaṇa live in the neighbourhood here. The moment I saw you, I fell in love with you. What have you to do with this ugly, emaciated Sītā? Marry me. Both of us shall roam about this forest. Do not worry about Sītā or Lakṣmaṇa: I shall swallow them in a moment." But, Rāma smilingly said to her: "You see I have my wife with me here. Why do you not propose to my brother Lakṣmaṇa who has no wife here?" Sūrpaṇakhā did not mind that suggestion. She turned to Lakṣmaṇa and said: "It is all right. You please marry me and we shall roam about happily." She was tormented by passion.

Lakṣmaṇa said in a teasing mood: "O lady, you see that I am only the slave of Rāma and Sītā. Why do you choose to be the wife of a slave? You will only become a servant-maid. Persuade Rāma to send away that ugly wife of his and marry you." Sūrpaṇakhā turned to Rāma again. She said: "Unable to give up this wife of yours, Sītā, you turn down my offer. See, I shall at once swallow her. When she is gone you will marry me; and we shall roam about in this forest happily." So saying, she actually rushed towards Sītā. Rāma stopped her in time, and said to Lakṣmaṇa: "What are you doing, Lakṣmaṇa? It is not right to jest with cruel and unworthy people. Look at the plight of Sītā. She barely escaped with her life. Come, quickly deform this demoness and send her away.

Lakṣmaṇa drew his sword and quickly cut off the nose and the ears of Sūrpaṇakhā. Weeping and bleeding she ran away. She went to her brother Khara and fell down in front of him.

Āraṇya 19–20

The demon Khara was distressed to see his sister Śūrpaṇakhā fallen unconscious in front of him, bleeding profusely from the wounds to her nose and her ears inflicted by Lakṣmaṇa. Kneeling near her, Khara said in great anger: "Whose work is this? O my sister, you yourself are equal in prowess to the gods and demi-gods. Which foolish person has perpetrated this stupid action, thus inviting speedy death at my hands? Surely, not even Indra the god of gods would dare to offend me. Śūrpaṇakhā, regain consciousness and tell me who it is that has elected to die at my hands today."

Still dazed, Śūrpaṇakhā regained consciousness and said to Khara: "Today I saw in the forest two young, handsome, powerful men who had eyes resembling lotus petals, who were clad in bark of trees and deer-skin, who are living on fruits and roots like ascetics, who are devoted to self-control and austerities, and who are celibates: they are the sons of king Daśaratha, and are known as Rāma and Lakṣmaṇa. Along with them I also saw a beautiful young woman decked in jewels. And this is the result. Brother, you will do me a great favour if you have them killed: I wish to drink their blood."

Terribly enraged, Khara ordered fourteen of his demoniacal warriors: "Two men have dared to enter this Daṇḍaka forest. Go and kill them, and kill also the woman who is with them. Thus propitiate my sister. Let her drink the blood of those humans." The fourteen demons, accompanied by Śūrpaṇakhā, immediately proceeded to where Rāma lived. They saw Rāma. And, Rāma saw them, too. He said to Lakṣmaṇa: "Look after Sītā, Lakṣmaṇa; I shall quickly deal with these demons and return."

Rāma said to the demons: "We are ascetics who live here on fruits and roots. Why do you thus harass us? Also bear in mind that, requested by the sages and ascetics who are constantly tormented by you, we are here to kill sinners like you." The demons replied: "Having provoked our great leader Khara, you have surely forfeited your life. See, with these our weapons we shall kill you in no time." Saying so, they rushed towards Rāma with their lances and swords uplifted. Rāma cut those weapons down with his own missiles. Then he shot them with fourteen blunt missiles which pierced their hearts. They fell down dead.

Horrified to see this quick work, Śūpaṇakhā ran back to Khara.

Āraṇya 21–22

Seeing Śūrpaṇakhā rolling on the ground in front of him once more, Khara sharply demanded: "Why are you doing this to me? I have just now despatched the most formidable heroes of my army who will certainly kill those humans in no time. Those fourteen heroes are utterly faithful to me and are invincible in battle. Just have a little patience and give up this unnecessary emotionalism." Śūrpaṇakhā replied: "True, you sent those fourteen heroes with me a little while ago. But they are no more! With all their might they did attack Rāma and Lakṣmaṇa. They hurled their weapons with all their strength. But they are no more! With their hearts pierced by Rāma's missiles, they are lying dead. Having seen them thus lying dead and having seen the extraordinary prowess of Rāma, I have come again to you deeply distressed. If the demons of Daṇḍaka forest are to be saved in time, you should take some quick action. But, my own intelligence tells me that you have no strength to face Rāma. You think you are mighty, but in fact you are not. It is a disgrace and it is a great calamity if you are unable to deal with these human beings. They will surely and soon destroy all the demons, including you my brother."

Stung to the quick by her words, Khara said: "You will see how powerful I am. I account the human Rāma for nothing. By his own wicked deed in provoking me to battle he is as good as dead. I will instantly cut him down with my axe; and you will drink his blood." Śūrpaṇakhā was delighted with this assurance and began to praise him and inspire him. Khara then instructed his chief of staff Dūṣaṇa: "Order the fourteen thousand demons to get ready to march immediately. Bring my chariot, too, immediately. I wish to proceed at the head of the glorious Paulastya forces to destroy the humans who have dared to challenge us.

Soon the chariot, shining like the very sun, was brought and Khara ascended it. And, soon the mighty demoniacal army was ready, too. This army was equipped with all sorts of weapons—iron clubs, lances, maces. Preceded by this mighty army, Khara the demon of great prowess marched to where Rāma was, eager to fight the human enemy.

Āraṇya 23–24

The entire nature seemed to be against the de omens foreboding the destruction of the demons everywhere. Animals wailed. Fearful and evil-look were seen in the sky. The sun was surrounded by a red ring. A dreadful darkness prevailed on earth. People were confused and did not know one direction from another. There was an untimely eclipse of the sun. The earth trembled. There were dust-storms and hail-storms. Evil omens appeared on the person of Khara, too. His left arm throbbed. There was pain on his forehead. But, none of these had, however, the least effect upon him! He had great confidence in his own strength. He said: "I do not worry like weaklings: for I am strong. I can even shoot down the stars. I will not return from here without having killed Rāma, Lakṣmaṇa and Sītā. I am invincible, and I have never been defeated in battle by anyone. I shall propitiate my sister who has been disgraced by Rāma and Lakṣmaṇa." He roared as he marched towards Rāma's hermitage. Hearing this, the sages and the demi-gods prayed for Rāma's victory.

Khara was surrounded by twelve demons of great valour. Dūṣaṇa was accompanied by four great demons.

Rāma, too, noticed the evil omens and said to Lakṣmaṇa: "Look at these upheavals in nature which foretell the destruction of the demons, O Lakṣmaṇa. My missiles are getting excited at the prospect of being made proper use of today. I see that your face is radiant: and from that I infer that we shall be victorious. For, he whose face is lustreless on the eve of a battle shall be slain. Ah, Lakṣmaṇa, I can hear the tumult caused by the advancing forces of the demons. A wise man should take proper precautions against even a calamity which has not yet befallen him. I therefore wish that Sītā and you would take shelter in yonder cave, while I deal with these hordes of demons. I know that you are capable of killing all of them: but, this time I wish to do that myself. And, now please go." Lakṣmaṇa immediately left for the cave along with Sītā. Rāma was pleased with this implicit obedience.

Rāma readied his weapons and his missiles. The gods and the sages who were witnessing the scene blessed him. Some of them were worried: "How will Rāma who is single-handed be able to deal with fourteen thousand demons?" The demons were soon within sight. Rāma looked around and had a good

14,000

view of the demoniacal hordes. In anger, the charming countenance of Rāma took on the aspect of Rudra when he was about to destroy the ritual of Dakṣa.

Āraṇya 25

Khara and his mighty army reached the hermitage of Rāma. Khara saw Rāma standing with his weapon ready to fire. He commanded his charioteer: "Take my chariot right in front of Rāma himself." Going right up to Rāma, Khara began to attack Rāma with a volley of small fire. Having done so, the demon roared aloud. The followers of Khara, who were cruel by nature, began to hurl a number of conventional weapons at Rāma as also branches of trees and stones. In large numbers, the demons stampeded towards the hermitage in order to hit and to kill Rāma. Surrounded by them, Rāma looked like the great god Rudra surrounded by his own servants!

Rāma's body had sustained many injuries, but they were not serious. Yet, he resembled the setting sun whose lustre was partially hidden by the evening clouds. Seeing this the gods, the demi-gods and sages were worried. Greatly enraged by this sudden attack, Rāma wielded his revolving weapon, which released hundreds and thousands of missiles. These missiles were Nālikas (those which had a steel-point), Nārācas (wholly made of steel) and Vikarṇis (missiles with a barbed body). The demons fell like flies. Rāma's missiles cut down the conventional weapons of the demons. Hit by the missiles, the demons' skulls were broken, their sheilds and bows were torn away from them—and they fell like trees to the ground. They in turn hurled lances, and axes and other such weapons at him; but these were powerless against Rāma's weapons. Thus assailed by Rāma, the demons who survived retreated and ran to Khara for shelter.

Greatly perturbed that, single-handed, Rāma could kill thousands of the demons, Dūṣaṇa advanced towards Rāma. The retreating forces also returned to give battle to Rāma, hurling logs of wood and stones. Rāma roared aloud in triumph and used the most powerful Gandharva-missile which threw the demons into utter confusion. Immediately, he returned to his revolving weapon and discharged hundreds of missiles in all directions at the same time. Such was the effect of the Gandharva-missile and such was the speed with which Rāma discharged the missiles, that the demons did not see the missiles but only saw Rāma holding the weapon. Even he did not seem to be doing anything; the firing seemed to be automatic. And Rāma himself was hidden behind the fire by which even the sun was hidden.

The entire ground was strewn with the bodies of the dead demons. Their weapons had been broken; and even the stones hurled by them had been powdered. They had been utterly defeated.

Āraṇya 26

Distressed to see his men fall in their thousands, Dūṣaṇa commanded a battalion of specially chosen commandos to fight with and kill Rāma. They charged. The weapons they used were iron pikes, swords, slabs of stone and trees, and some arrows. Rāma intercepted and destroyed all these with his missiles.

Now Dūṣaṇa himself came forward. Rāma covered him with his missiles; but Dūṣaṇa returned the fire with equal effect. With extraordinary dexterity, however, Rāma destroyed Dūṣaṇa's weapon. At the same time, Rāma broke the head of Dūṣaṇa's charioteer and cut down the horses. Now both Rāma and Dūṣaṇa were without a chariot. Picking up a heavy weapon made of steel, gold and diamond and barbed wire, Dūṣaṇa rushed towards Rāma. With extraordinary accuracy Rāma cut off both the arms of Dūṣaṇa; and they fell down still holding the steel club.

The three commanders of Dūṣaṇa's forces now advanced to fight Rāma. One wielded a terrible looking pike, the other a scimitar, and the third an axe. Even as they were coming towards him, Rāma cut them down. Mahākapāla's skull was broken. With numerous missiles, Rāma overpowered (pramatha) Pramāthi. And he shot the eyes of Sthūlākṣa.

The demon Khara was mad with rage. He shouted at the remaining forces; "Look at this disgrace! Look how the mighty Dūṣaṇa has been slain by a puny human being! And yet all of you are just looking on. Come, attack this Rāma and destroy him at once."

The other demons rushed towards Rāma, and he quickly disposed of all of them, using missiles which resembled fire and which were adorned with gold and diamond. His missiles were never wasted. If there were a hundred demons; he used a hundred missiles. If there were a thousand demons he used a thousand missiles and destroyed them all.

Thus, single-handed, fighting as a foot-soldier, this human being, Rāma, killed fourteen thousand demons who were of terrible deeds. Only Khara and another demon known as Triśira survived.

Āraṇya 27–28

When Khara went forward to fight with Rāma, the demon Triśira approached him and sought permission to go instead. He said to Khara: "I swear that either I shall kill him or I shall be killed by him. I assure you that either you will return to Janasthāna, happy that I had killed Rāma, or, seeing that he has killed me, you will encounter Rāma yourself. But, let me go first." Khara approved of the idea.

The demon Triśira was very powerful and was quick to take the offensive. He hit Rāma on the forehead with his weapon. Though injured, Rāma took it as if he had been hit with flowers. He was greatly enraged. With his weapon Rāma discharged four missiles which had curved tips, and these took care of the horses. With eight missiles, he cut down the charioteer. As Triśira was jumping from the chariot, Rāma shot him in his heart and he was dead.

Khara came forward. He was endowed with very powerful weapons; and he had been instructed in the use of extremely powerful missiles, too. Sitting in his chariot, Khara discharged many missiles at Rāma. Correctly judging the strength of the enemy, Rāma also armed himself with a powerful weapon. Then began the most fierce battle between Rāma and Khara. The fire that emanated from both of them obscured the very sun that shone above. Khara used the missiles Nālikas, Nārācas and Vikarṇis towards Rāma. Rāma actually appeared to be fatigued and severely wounded. Taking advantage of this situation, Khara approached Rāma intent upon killing him. With first-class marksmanship, he knocked down Rāma's weapon with a single shot. When Rāma had thus been disarmed, Khara took immediate advantage of this and riddled Rāma with various missiles. The impact of these missiles was so great that the protective armour which Rāma had worn broke and fell down. Some of the missiles reached the vital parts of Rāma's body, too.

With irrepressible anger, Rāma now took up the 'weapon of Viṣṇu' that the sage Agastya had recently given him. Grasping it firmly, Rāma rushed at Khara and fired six times. With one shot he hit Khara's head, with two he hit his arms, and three he aimed at Khara's chest. At the same time, Rāma hit the chariot with one shot which broke the yoke, four shots were fired at the horses, and the sixth took care of the charioteer.

But the demon Khara was not slain yet. Deprived of his chariot, he jumped down and, mace in hand, he rushed towards Rāma.

Āraṇya 29–30

As Khara thus advanced, mace in hand, Rāma said to him: "O demon, you have to your credit immeasurable sin; the sin of tormenting and killing innocent hermits and ascetics. Even if one is the lord of the three worlds, such a sinner is fit to be shunned by all. You are about to reap the fruit of that sin. For, in this world the painful fruits of sins quickly follow, even as the results of having partaken of poisoned food. I consider that my father's real intention in sending me to the forest was to exterminate cruel and sinful demons like you. Soon I shall despatch you from this world. Soon, you will behold the same ascetics you tortured and killed: they will be going to heaven and you will be thrown into hell."

Khara made a suitable reply. He said: "You have so far killed only demons of ordinary strength. You, therefore, think that you are powerful! Do not boast. Real heroes and strong men do not boast. Their actions speak for them." After saying this, Khara immediately hurled that terrible mace at Rāma. Burning everything that was on its path, the mace neared Rāma. Rāma released an anti-missile missile which intercepted the mace and broke it.

Rāma asked Khara: "Is that all you can do? The mace has been destroyed. Now be ready to meet your own fate. When you have been laid to permanent sleep, this Daṇḍaka forest will once again become the resort of holy men who are the refuge of all the people of the world." Khara replied to Rāma: "I think because your end is near you do not know what to say and what not to say. During the last hour of their life, people lose their power of discrimination and do not know what to do and what not to do." However, with his mace destroyed by Rāma, Khara was unarmed. He looked around for a weapon to use. He uprooted a big tree and hurled it at Rāma. Rāma intercepted the tree with his missile. With a volley of a thousand shots, Rāma riddled the body of Khara. Even then the wicked demon did not die but came closer to Rāma. Rāma retreated two or three paces. He picked up the most fierce missile which the sage Agastya had given him. Hit by it, Khara fell down dead.

The sages sang Rāma's glory: "In just one hour and a half you have destroyed fourteen thousand dreadful demons. Wonderful is your strength." They said: "It was for this purpose alone that the sages Śarabhaṅga and Sutīkṣṇa cleverly suggested that you should dwell here. Freed from fear, the sages will practise austerities here." They blessed Rāma. Delighted to witness his exploits, Sītā embraced Rāma.

Āraṇya 31

One of the demons who had escaped earlier (Akampana) proceeded direct to Laṅkā and informed Rāvaṇa.

Surprised and angered, Rāvaṇa questioned Akampana: "Who dares to do such a foolish action? Which foolish being, human or superhuman, can afford to antagonise me? Not even Indra, nor Kubera the son of Viśrava, nor even the lord Viṣṇu himself, can be happy, after antagonising me! I am death unto death itself. Even the wind and the fire are afraid of me. Tell me truly: who perpetrated this crime?"

With trembling limbs, Akampana said: "Lord, it is the young son of king Daśaratha. It is Rāma who is so powerful that in front of him the demoniacal hordes fell in their hundreds and thousands. They were so terrified that in whichever direction they ran afraid to face him, they saw him in that direction! The missiles he discharged came towards the demons like fire-hooded snakes spitting fire." Rāvaṇa jumped up saying: "Oh, is that so? I shall immediately go to Janasthāna and kill that Rāma."

Akampana continued: "That is not so easy, Lord. You do not know the power of Rāma. You cannot conquer him in battle. He can break up the firmament and bring the stars, the moon and the planets down. And he can lift up the whole earth. Nay, Lord, he can destroy the entire creati everything anew. But I shall tell you how he can He has a most beautiful wife named Sītā. She e celestials in beauty: there is of course no mo beautiful as she is. If you can trick Rāma away her, you can bring about the death of Rāma. For, Rāma will not live without Sītā."

This plot appealed to Rāvaṇa. The next morning, Rāvaṇa got into his chariot and rode towards Janasthāna where he met the demon Mārīca. Rāvaṇa said to Mārīca: "Friend, my brother Khara and all the demons of Janasthāna have been killed by Rāma, the son of king Daśaratha. To take revenge, I have decided to abduct Sītā and thus bring about the death of Rāma. I need your help." Mārīca shuddered at the very thought. "O chief of demons, who has tendered you such destructive advice? Surely he is not your friend. He who has given you this advice and inspires you to abduct Sītā is your worst enemy: obviously, he wants you to pull out the fangs of a cobra he is afraid of! Pray, leave Rāma alone and do not provoke him. Pray, leave Sītā alone: enjoy the company of your own wives, and let Rāma enjoy the company of his wife, Sītā."

Rāvaṇa returned to Laṅkā.

Āraṇya 32–33

Śūrpaṇakhā witnessed the wholesale destruction of the demons of Janasthāna, including their supreme leader Khara. Stricken with terror, she ran to Laṅkā. There she saw her brother Rāvaṇa, the ruler of Laṅkā, seated with his ministers in a palace whose roof scraped the sky. Rāvaṇa had twenty arms, ten heads, was broad chested and endowed with all the physical qualifications of a monarch. He had previously fought with the gods, even with their chief Indra. He was well versed in the science of warfare and knew the use of the celestial missiles in battle. He had been hit by the gods, even by the discus (revolver) of lord Viṣṇu, but he did not die. For, he had performed breath-taking austerities for a period of ten thousand years, and offered his own heads in worship to Brahmā the creator and earned from him the boon that he would not be killed by any superhuman or subhuman agency (except by man). Emboldened by this boon, the demon had tormented the gods and particularly the sages.

Śūrpaṇakhā entered Rāvaṇa's presence, clearly displaying the physical deformity which Lakṣmaṇa had caused to her. She shouted at Rāvaṇa in open assembly: "Brother, you have become so thoroughly infatuated and addicted to sense-pleasure that you are unfit to be a king any longer. The people lose all respect for the king who is only interested in his own pleasure and neglects his royal duties. People turn away from the king who has no spies, who has lost touch with the people and whom they cannot see, and who is unable to do what is good for them. It is the employment of spies that makes the king 'far-sighted' for through these spies he sees quite far. You have failed to appoint proper spies to collect intelligence for you. Therefore, you do not know that fourteen thousand of your people have been slaughtered by a human being. Even Khara and Dūṣaṇa have been killed by Rāma. And, Rāma has assured the ascetics of Janasthāna which is your territory, that the demons shall not do them any harm. They are now protected by him. Yet, here you are; revelling in little pleasures!

"O brother, even a piece of wood, a clod of earth or just dust, has some use; but when a king falls from his position he is utterly useless. But that monarch who is vigilant, who has knowledge of everything, through his spies, who is self-controlled, who is full of gratitude and whose conduct is righteous—he rules for a long time. Wake up and act before you lose your sovereignty."

This made Rāvaṇa reflect.

Āraṇya 34–35

And, Rāvaṇa's anger was roused. He asked Śūrpaṇakhā: "Tell me, who is it that disfigured you thus? What do you think of Rāma? Why has he come to Daṇḍaka forest?"

Śūrpaṇakhā gave an exact and colourful description of the physical appearance of Rāma. She said: "Rāma is equal in charm to Cupid himself. At the same time, he is a formidable warrior. When he was fighting the demons of Janasthāna, I could not see what he was doing; I only saw the demons falling dead on the field. You can easily understand when I tell you that within an hour and a half he had killed fourteen thousand demons. He spared me, perhaps because he did not want to kill a woman. He has a brother called Lakṣmaṇa who is equally powerful. He is Rāma's right hand man and alter ego; Rāma's own life-force moving outside his body. Oh, you must see Sītā, Rāma's wife. I have not seen even a celestial nymph who could match her in beauty. He who has her for his wife, whom she fondly embraces, he shall indeed be the ruler of gods. She is a fit bride for you; and you are indeed the most suitable suitor for her. In fact, I wanted to bring that beautiful Sītā here so that you could marry her: but Lakṣmaṇa intervened and cruelly mutilated my body. If you could only look at her for a moment, you would immediately fall in love with her. If this proposal appeals to you, take some action quickly and get her here."

Rāvaṇa was instantly tempted. Immediately he ordered his amphibian vehicle to be got ready. This vehicle which was richly adorned with gold, could move freely wherever its owner willed. Its front part resembled mules with fiendish heads. Rāvaṇa took his seat in this vehicle and moved towards the seacoast. The coastline of Laṅkā was dotted with hermitages inhabited by sages and also celestial and semi-divine beings. It was also the pleasure resort of celestials and nymphs who went there to sport and to enjoy themselves. Driving at great speed through them, Rāvaṇa passed through caravan parks scattered with the space vehicles of the celestials. He also drove through dense forests of sandal trees, banana plantations and cocoanut palm groves. In those forests there were also spices and aromatic plants. Along the coast lay pearls and precious stones. He passed through cities which had an air of opulence.

Rāvaṇa crossed the ocean in his amphibian vehicle and reached the hermitage where Mārīca was living in ascetic garb, subsisting on a disciplined diet. Mārīca welcomed Rāvaṇa and questioned him about the purpose of his visit.

Āraṇya 36–37

Rāvaṇa said to Mārīca: "Listen, Mārīca. You know that fourteen thousand demons, including my brother Khara and the great warrior Triśira have been mercilessly killed by Rāma and Lakṣmaṇa who have now promised their protection to the ascetics of Daṇḍaka forest, thus flouting our authority. Driven out of his country by his angry father, obviously for a disgraceful action, this unrighteous and hard-hearted prince Rāma has killed the demons without any justification. And, they have even dared to disfigure my beloved sister Śūrpaṇakhā. I must immediately take some action to avenge the death of my brother and to restore our prestige and our authority. I need your help; kindly do not refuse this time.

"Disguising yourself as a golden deer of great beauty, roam near the hermitage of Rāma. Sītā would surely be attracted, and she would ask Rāma and Lakṣmaṇa to capture you. When they go after you, leaving Sītā alone in the hermitage, I shall easily abduct Sītā." Even as Rāvaṇa was unfolding this plot, Mārīca's mouth became dry and parched with fear. Trembling with fear, Mārīca said to Rāvaṇa:

"O king, one can easily get in this world a counsellor who tells you what is pleasing to you; but hard it is to find a wise counsellor who tells you the unpleasant truth which is good for you—and harder it is to find one who heeds such advice. Surely, your intelligence machine is faulty and therefore you have no idea of the prowess of Rāma. Else, you would not talk of abducting Sītā. I wonder: perhaps Sītā has come into this world to end your life, or perhaps there is to be great sorrow on account of Sītā, or perhaps maddened by lust, you are going to destroy yourself and the demons and Laṅkā itself. Oh, no, you were wrong in your estimation of Rāma. He is not wicked; he is righteousness incarnate. He is not cruel hearted; he is generous to a fault. He has not been disgraced and exiled from the kingdom. He is here to honour the promise his father had given his mother Kaikeyī, after joyously renouncing his kingdom.

"O king, when you entertain ideas of abducting Sītā you are surely playing with fire. Please remember: when you stand facing Rāma, you are standing face to face with your own death. Sītā is the beloved wife of Rāma, who is extremely powerful. Nay, give up this foolish idea. What will you gain by thus gambling with your sovereignty over the demons, and with your life itself? Please consult the noble Vibhīṣaṇa and your virtuous ministers before embarking upon such unwise projects. They will surely advise you against them."

Āraṇya 38–39

Mārīca continued: "I shall tell you of my own personal encounters with Rāma. Long ago, I was young and energetic, mighty and proud of my strength. I had the terrible form of a huge cloud. I used to be the terror of ascetics in the forest. I would desecrate their sacred rituals. Once the sage Viśvāmitra was about to perform a sacred rite. In order to protect it from our disturbance, he approached king Daśaratha and demanded the services of Rāma to guard the altar. Daśaratha pleaded that Rāma was too young to do so. Yet, Viśvāmitra assured the king that though young, Rāma was the only one capable of dealing with demons, and took Rāma to his hermitage.

"While the sacred rite was in progress, I went to the hermitage as usual. Seeing the young boy Rāma outside, I tried to enter. But Rāma aimed one missile at me, by which I was hurled a long distance, into the ocean! Rāma could do that even when he was no more than a child! How can we measure his present strength? And, how can you meet him in battle? Surely, if you decide to go ahead with your plot all of us will suffer. In this world, people suffer on account of others' sins, too, just as fish living in a pond infested with snakes suffer. It is a great sin to commit adultery. Desist from it and enjoy your own wives, O King.

"Hear of the second encounter I had with Rāma, more recently. I was roaming in the forest with a couple of other demons, molesting and killing ascetics and drinking their blood. During the course of our wandering we came to where Rāma lived at that time. Assuming the form of a deer, I rushed at Rāma, thinking that since he was living in the forest as an ascetic he would be powerless and weak. He took his weapon and discharged a couple of missiles at us. I had tasted the fruit of Rāma's wrath before: I fled and Rāma did not pursue me. The others were killed.

"Thus saved miraculously for the second time, I have abandoned cruelty and am now living here as an ascetic, practising yoga and self-control. I see Rāma alone in every tree, holding his weapon. The whole forest appears as Rāma to me. Even words which commence with the syllable 'ra'—like ratna, ratha—frighten me. He can easily kill all your soldiers and generals, O King; entertain no doubt about that. I know his prowess at first hand. If you antagonise him, many innocent people also will suffer. Rāma will surely exterminate the entire demon-race. If Rāma killed Khara, it was Khara's fault that he provoked Rāma and invited a fight. If you do not accept my advice O King, we shall all perish."

Āraṇya 40–41

Mārīca's advice was unpalatable to Rāvaṇa. He would not take it, even as one who wants to die will refuse to take a wholesome remedy. On the other hand, he severely reprimanded Mārīca. He said: "You advice is ill-conceived and useless. You cannot stop me from abducting Sītā who is dearer than life to Rāma and without whom Rāma would not live. What you have said would have been proper if I had asked you for counsel: I do not want your counsel now, I want implicit obedience to my command. I am sorry, Mārīca, that you do not know how to behave towards the king. You should speak to the king words which are not unfavourable, softly spoken, and beneficial and even then humbly and politely. Kings are like fire, Indra (king of gods), the moon, Yama (the god of death), and Varuna (the god of water). Therefore, the kings possess the fierceness of fire, the lordliness of Indra, the gentleness of the moon, the ruthlessness of Yama and the fluidity of water. Hence, one should behave cautiously with kings. I did not ask you for your counsel but I am asking you to do this job for me. If you do this, I shall bestow half the kingdom of Laṅkā upon you; if you refuse, I shall kill you just now. Better make up your mind to obey. Take the form of a golden deer and tempt Sītā. At her request surely Rāma would pursue you. After leading him away, shout: 'O Sītā, O Lakṣmaṇa'. Hearing this Lakṣmaṇa will also go in search of Rāma, leaving Sītā alone. At this time I shall easily take Sītā away. It may be true that this involves risk to your life; but death is certain if you disobey me."

In spite of this threat, Mārīca fearlessly advised Rāvaṇa again: "He who gave you this suggestion is a great sinner. It is the ministers' duty to give proper advice to the king: your ministers have failed in this duty and should be executed. When a king embarks upon evil his ministers should restrain him: your ministers have not done this. A minister who does this earns the grace of the Lord and through that wealth and happiness. If he does not do this, and the king pursues his evil way, everyone, including the ministers, suffer. Ministers who encourage their king to indulge in violence and evil, are themselves destroyed along with the king. For what the king does inevitably involves all his subjects who also suffer the consequences. If I do what you say, Rāma will surely and swiftly kill me; and soon after that he will kill you also. But then, I shall deem myself blessed and I shall have met my end at the hands of Rāma himself, which is preferable. If you take away Sītā to Laṅkā, rest assured that that is the end of yourself. Neither the demons, nor Laṅkā will survive."

Āraṇya 42

Rāvaṇa was determined, and Mārīca knew that there was no use arguing with him. Hence, after the last-minute attempt to avert the catastrophe, Mārīca said to Rāvaṇa: "What can I do when you are so wicked? I am ready to go to Rāma's āśrama. God help you!" Not minding the taunt, Rāvaṇa expressed his unabashed delight at Mārīca's consent. He applauded Mārīca and said: "That is the spirit, my friend: you are now the same old Mārīca that I knew. I guess you had been possessed by some evil spirit a few minutes ago, on account of which you had begun to preach a different gospel. Let us swiftly get into this vehicle and proceed to our destination. As soon as you have accomplished the purpose, you are free to go and to do what you please!"

Both of them got into the amphibian vehicle which behaved like an aerial car (for it was in fact a hovercraft), and quickly left the hermitage of Mārīca. Once again they passed forests, hills, rivers and cities: and soon they reached the neighbourhood of the hermitage of Rāma. They got down from that hovercraft which had been embellished with gold. Holding Mārīca by the hand, Rāvaṇa said to him: "Over there is the hermitage of Rāma, surrounded by banana plantations. Well, now, get going with the work for which we have come here." Immediately Mārīca transformed himself into an attractive deer. It was extraordinary, totally unlike any deer that inhabited the forest. It was unique. It dazzled like a huge gem stone. Each part of its body had a different colour. The colours had an unearthly brilliance and charm. Thus embellished by the colours of all the precious stones, the deer which was the demon Mārīca in disguise, roamed about near the hermitage of Rāma, nibbling at the grass now and then. At one time it came close to Sītā; then it ran away and joined the other deer grazing at a distance. It was very playful, jumping about and chasing its tail and spinning around. Sītā went out to gather flowers. She cast a glance at that extraordinary and unusual deer. As she did so, the deer too, sensing the accomplishment of the mission, came closer to her. Then it ran away, pretending to be afraid. Sītā marvelled at the very appearance of this unusual deer the like of which she had not seen before and which had the hue of jewels.

Āraṇya 43

From where she was gathering flowers, Sītā, filled with wonder to see that unusual deer, called out to Rāma: "Come quick and see, O Lord; come with your brother. Look at this extraordinary creature. I have never seen such a beautiful deer before." Rāma and Lakṣmaṇa looked at the deer, and Lakṣmaṇa's suspicions were aroused: "I am suspicious; I think it is the same demon Mārīca in disguise. I have heard that Mārīca could assume any form at will, and through such tricks he had brought death and destruction to many ascetics in this forest. Surely, this deer is not real: no one has heard of a deer with rainbow colours, each one of its limbs shining resplendent with the colour of a different gem! That itself should enable us to understand that it is a demon, not an animal."

Sītā interrupted Lakṣmaṇa's talk, and said: "Never mind, one thing is certain; this deer has captivated my mind. It is such a dear. I have not seen such an animal near our hermitage! There are many types of deer which roam about near the hermitage; this is just an extraordinary and unusual deer. It is superlative in all respects: its colour is lovely, its texture is lovely, and even its voice sounds delightful. It would be a wonderful feat if it could be caught alive. We could use it as a pet, to divert our minds. Later we could take it to Ayodhyā: and I am sure all your brothers and mothers would just adore it. If it is not possible to capture it alive, O Lord, then it can be killed, and I would love to have its skin. I know I am not behaving myself towards both of you: but I am helpless; I have lost my heart to that deer. I am terribly curious."

In fact, Rāma was curious, too! And so, he took Sītā's side and said to Lakṣmaṇa: "It is beautiful, Lakṣmaṇa. It is unusual. I have never seen a creature like this. And, princes do hunt animals and cherish their skins. By sporting and hunting kings acquire great wealth! People say that that is real wealth which one pursues without premeditation. So, let us try to get the deer or its skin. If, as you say, it is a demon in disguise, then surely it ought to be killed by me, just as Vātāpi who was tormenting and destroying sages and ascetics was justly killed by the sage Agastya. Vātāpi fooled the ascetics till he met the sage Agastya. This Mārīca, too, has fooled the ascetics so far: till coming to me today! The very beauty of his hide is his doom. And, you, Lakṣmaṇa, please guard Sītā with great vigilance, till I kill this deer with just one shot and bring the hide along with me."

Āraṇya 44–45

Rāma took his weapons and went after the strange deer. As soon as the deer saw him pursuing it, it started to run away. Now it disappeared, now it appeared to be very near, now it ran fast, now it seemed confused—thus it led Rāma far away from his hermitage. Rāma was fatigued, and needed to rest. As he was standing under a tree, intrigued by the actions of the mysterious deer, it came along with other deer and began to graze not far from him. When Rāma once again went for it, it ran away. Not wishing to go farther nor to waste more time, Rāma took his weapon and fitted the missile of Brahmā to it and fired. This missile pierced the illusory deer-mask and into the very heart of the demon. Mārīca uttered a loud cry, leapt high into the sky and then dropped dead onto the ground. As he fell, however, he remembered Rāvaṇa's instructions and, assuming the voice of Rāma cried aloud: "Hey Sītā; Hey Lakṣmaṇa."

Rāma saw the dreadful body of the demon. He knew now that Lakṣmaṇa was right. And, he was even more puzzled by the way in which the demon wailed aloud before dying. He was full of apprehension. He hastened towards the hermitage.

In the hermitage, both Sītā and Lakṣmaṇa heard the cry. Sītā believed it was Rāma's voice. She was panic-stricken. She said to Lakṣmaṇa: "Go, go quickly: your brother is in danger. And, I cannot live without him. My breath and my heart are both violently disturbed." Lakṣmaṇa remembered Rāma's admonition that he should stay with Sītā and not leave her alone. He said to her: "Pray, be not worried." Sītā grew suspicious and furious. She said to him: "Ah, I see the plot now! You have a wicked eye on me and so have been waiting for this to happen. What a terrible enemy of Rāma you are, pretending to be his brother!" Distressed to hear these words, Lakṣmaṇa replied: "No one in the three worlds can overpower Rāma, blessed lady! It was not his voice at all. These demons in the forest are capable of simulating the voice of anyone. Having killed that demon disguised as a deer, Rāma will soon be here. Fear not." His calmness even more annoyed Sītā, who literally flew into a rage. She said again: "Surely, you are the worst enemy that Rāma could have had. I know now that you have been following us, cleverly pretending to be Rāma's brother and friend. I know now that your real motive for doing so is either to get me or you are Bharata's accomplice. Ah, but you will not succeed. Presently, I shall give up my life. For I cannot live without Rāma." Cut to the quick by these terrible words, Lakṣmaṇa said: "You are worshipful to me: hence I cannot answer back. It is not surprising that women should behave in this manner: for they are easily led away from dharma; they are fickle and sharp-tongued. I cannot endure what you said just now. I shall go. The gods are witness to what took place here. May those gods protect you. But I doubt if when Rāma and I return, we shall find you." Bowing to her, Lakṣmaṇa left.

Āraṇya 46

Rāvaṇa was looking for this golden opportunity. He disguised himself as an ascetic, clad in ochre robes, carrying a shell water-pot, a staff and an umbrella, and approached Sītā who was still standing outside the cottage eagerly looking for Rāma's return. His very presence in that forest was inauspicious: and even the trees and the waters of the rivers were frightened of him, as it were. In a holy disguise, Rāvaṇa stood before Sītā: a deep well covered with grass; a death-trap.

Gazing at the noble Sītā, who had now withdrawn into the cottage and whose eyes were raining tears, Rāvaṇa came near her, and though his heart was filled with lust, he was chanting Vedic hymns. He said to Sītā in a soft, tender and affectionate tone: "O young lady! Pray, tell me, are you the goddess of fortune or the goddess of modesty, or the consort of Cupid himself?" Then Rāvaṇa described her incomparable beauty in utterly immodest terms, unworthy of an anchorite whose form he had assumed. He continued: "O charming lady! You have robbed me of my heart. I have not seen such a beautiful lady, neither a divine or a semi-divine being. Your extraordinary form and your youthfulness, and your living in

this forest, all these together agitate my mind. It i
that you should live in this forest. You should stay
In the forest monkeys, lions, tigers and other wild an
The forest is the natural habitat of demons who ro
You are living alone in this dreadful forest: are you not afraid, O fair lady? Pray, tell me, why are you living in this forest?"

Rāvaṇa was in the disguise of a brāhmaṇa. Therefore, Sītā offered him the worship and the hospitality that it was her duty to offer a brāhmaṇa. She made him sit down; she gave him water to wash his feet and his hands. Then she placed food in front of him.

Whatever she did only aggravated his lust and his desire to abduct her and take her away to Laṅkā.

Āraṇya 47–48

Sītā, then, proceeded to answer his enquiry concerning herself. He appeared to be a brāhmaṇa; and if his enquiry was not answered, he might get angry and curse her. Sītā said: "I am a daughter of the noble king Janaka; Sītā is my name. I am the beloved consort of Rāma. After our marriage, Rāma and I lived in the palace of Ayodhyā for twelve years." She then truthfully narrated all that took place just prior to Rāma's exile to the forest. She continued: "And so, when Rāma was twenty-five and I was eighteen, we left the palace and sought the forest-life. And so the three of us dwell in this forest. My husband, Rāma, will soon return to the hermitage gathering various animals and also wild fruits. Pray, tell me who you are, O brāhmaṇa, and what you are doing in this forest roaming all alone."

Rāvaṇa lost no time in revealing his true identity. He said: "I am not a brāhmaṇa, O Sītā: I am the lord of demons, Rāvaṇa. My very name strikes terror in the hearts of gods and men. The moment I saw you, I lost my heart to you; and I derive no pleasure from the company of my wives. Come with me, and be my queen, O Sītā. You will love Laṅkā. Laṅkā is my capital, it is surrounded by the ocean and it is situated on the top of a hill. There we shall live together, and you will enjoy your life, and never even once think of this wretched forest-life."

Sītā was furious to hear this. She said: "O demon-king! I have firmly resolved to follow Rāma who is equal to the god of gods, who is mighty and charming, and who is devoted to righteousness. If you entertain a desire for me, his wife, it is like tying yourself with a big stone and trying to swim across the ocean: you are doomed. Where are you and where is he: there is no comparison. You are like a jackal; he the lion. You are like base metal: he gold."

But Rāvaṇa would not give up his desire. He repeated: "Even the gods dare not stand before me, O Sītā! For fear of me even Kubera the god of wealth abandoned his space vehicle and ran away to Kailāsa. If the gods, headed by Indra, even sense I am angry, they flee. Even the forces of nature obey me. Laṅkā is enclosed by a strong wall; the houses are built of gold with gates of precious stones. Forget this Rāma, who lives like an ascetic, and come with me. He is not as strong as my little finger!" Sītā was terribly angered: "Surely you seek the destruction of all the demons, by behaving like this, O Rāvaṇa. It cannot be otherwise since they have such an unworthy king with no self-control. You may live after abducting Indra's wife, but not after abducting me, Rāma's wife.

Āraṇya 49–50

Rāvaṇa made his body enormously big and said to Sītā: "You do not realise what a mighty person I am. I can step out into space, and lift up the earth with my arms; I can drink up the waters of the oceans; and I can kill death itself. I can shoot a missile and bring the sun down. Look at the size of my body." As he expanded his form, Sītā turned her face away from him. He resumed his original form with ten heads and twenty arms. Again he spoke to Sītā: "Would you not like to be renowned in the three worlds? Then marry me. And, I promise I shall do nothing to displease you. Give up all thoughts of that mortal and unsuccessful Rāma."

Rāvaṇa did not wait for an answer. Seizing Sītā by her hair and lifting her up with his arm, he left the hermitage. Instantly the golden space vehicle appeared in front of him. He ascended it, along with Sītā. Sītā cried aloud: "O Rāma." As she was being carried away, she wailed aloud: "O Lakṣmaṇa, who is ever devoted to the elder brother, do you not know that I am being carried away by Rāvaṇa?" To Rāvaṇa, she said: "O vile demon, surely you will reap the fruits of your evil action: but they do not manifest immediately." She said as if to herself: "Surely, Kaikeyī would be happy today." She said to the trees, to the river Godāvarī, to the deities dwelling in the forest, to the animals and birds: "Pray, tell Rāma that I have been carried away by the wicked Rāvaṇa." She saw Jaṭāyu and cried aloud: "O Jaṭāyu! See, Rāvaṇa is carrying me away."

Hearing that cry, Jaṭāyu woke up. Jaṭāyu introduced himself to Rāvaṇa: "O Rāvaṇa, I am the king of vultures, Jaṭāyu. Pray, desist from this action unworthy of a king. Rāma, too, is a king; and his consort is worthy of our protection. A wise man should not indulge in such action as would disgrace him in the eyes of others. And, another's wife is as worthy of protection as one's own. The cultured and the common people often copy the behaviour of the king. If the king himself is guilty of unworthy behaviour what becomes of the people? If you persist in your wickedness, even the prosperity you enjoy will leave you soon.

"Therefore, let Sītā go. One should not get hold of a greater load than one can carry; one should not eat what he cannot digest. Who will indulge in an action which is painful and which does not promote righteousness, fame or permanent glory? I am sixty thousand years old and you are young. I warn you. If you do not give up Sītā, you will not be able to carry her away while I am alive and able to restrain you! I shall dash you down along with that space vehicle."

Āraṇya 51

Rāvaṇa could not brook this insult: he turned towards Jaṭāyu in great anger. Jaṭāyu hit the spacecraft and Rāvaṇa; Rāvaṇa hit Jaṭāyu back with terrible ferocity. This aerial combat between Rāvaṇa and Jaṭāyu looked like the collision of two mountains endowed with wings. Rāvaṇa used all the conventional missiles, the Nālikas, the Nārācas and the Vikarṇis. The powerful eagle shrugged them off. Jaṭāyu tore open the canopy of the spacecraft and inflicted wounds on Rāvaṇa himself.

In great anger, Jaṭāyu grabbed Rāvaṇa's weapon (a cannon) and broke it with his claws. Rāvaṇa took up a more formidable weapon which literally sent a shower of missiles. Against these Jaṭāyu used his own wings as an effective shield. Pouncing upon this weapon, too, Jaṭāyu destroyed it with his claws. Jaṭāyu also tore open Rāvaṇa's armour. Nay, Jaṭāyu even damaged the gold-plated propellers of Rāvaṇa's spacecraft, which had the appearance of demons, and thus crippled the craft which would take its occupant wherever he desired and which emitted fire. With his powerful beak, Jaṭāyu broke the neck of Rāvaṇa's pilot.

With the spacecraft thus rendered temporarily useless, Rāvaṇa jumped out of it, still holding Sītā with his powerful arm. While Rāvaṇa was still above the ground, Jaṭāyu again challenged him: "O wicked one, even now you are unwilling to turn away from evil. Surely, you have resolved to bring about the destruction of the entire race of demons. Unknowingly or wantonly, you are swallowing poison which would certainly kill you and your relations. Rāma and Lakṣmaṇa will not tolerate this sinful act of yours: and you cannot stand before them on the battlefield. The manner in which you are doing this unworthy act is despicable: you are behaving like a thief not like a hero." Jaṭāyu swooped on Rāvaṇa and violently tore at his body.

Then there ensued a hand-to-hand fight between the two. Rāvaṇa hit Jaṭāyu with his fist; but Jaṭāyu tore Rāvaṇa's arms away. However, new ones sprang up instantly. Rāvaṇa hit Jaṭāyu and kicked him. After some time, Rāvaṇa drew his sword and cut off the wings of Jaṭāyu. When the wings were thus cut, Jaṭāyu fell, dying. Looking at the fallen Jaṭāyu, Sītā ran towards him in great anguish, as she would to the side of a fallen relation. In inconsolable grief, Sītā began to wail aloud.

Āraṇya 52–53

As Sītā was thus wailing near the body of Jaṭāyu, Rāvaṇa came towards her. Looking at him with utter contempt, Sītā said: "I see dreadful omens, O Rāvaṇa. Dreams as also the sight and the cries of birds and beasts are clear indicators of the shape of things to come. But you do not notice them! Alas, here is Jaṭāyu, my father-in-law's friend who is dying on my account. O Rāma, O Lakṣmaṇa, save me, protect me!"

Once again Rāvaṇa grabbed her and got into the spacecraft which had been made airworthy again. The Creator, the gods and the celestials who witnessed this, exclaimed: "Bravo, our purpose is surely accomplished." Even the sages of the Daṇḍaka forest inwardly felt happy at the thought, "Now that Sītā has been touched by this wicked demon, the end of Rāvaṇa and all the demons is near." As she was carried away by Rāvaṇa, Sītā was wailing aloud: "O Rāma, O Lakṣmaṇa."

Placed on the lap of Rāvaṇa, Sītā was utterly miserable. Her countenance was full of sorrow and anguish. The petals of the flowers that dropped from her head fell and covered the body of Rāvaṇa for a while. She was of beautiful golden complexion; and he was of dark colour. Her being seated on his lap looked like an elephant wearing a golden sash, or the moon shining in the midst of a dark cloud, or a streak of lightning seen in a dense dark cloud.

The spacecraft streaked through the sky as fast as a meteor would. On the earth below, trees shook as if to reassure Sītā: "Do not be afraid", the waterfalls looked as if mountains were shedding tears, and people said to one another, "Surely, dharma has come to an end, as Rāvaṇa is carrying Sītā away."

Once again Sītā rebuked Rāvaṇa: "You ought to feel ashamed of yourself, O Rāvaṇa. You boast of your prowess; but you are stealing me away! You have not won me in a duel, which would be considered heroic. Alas, for a long, long time to come, people will recount your ignominy, and this unworthy and unrighteous act of yours will be remembered by the people. You are taking me and flying at such speed: hence no one can do anything to stop you. If only you had the courage to stop for a few moments, you would find yourself dead. My lord Rāma and his brother Lakṃaṇa will not spare you. Leave me alone, O demon! But, you are in no mood to listen to what is good for your own welfare. Even as, one who has reached death's door loves only harmful objects. Rāma will soon find out where I am and ere long you will be transported to the world of the dead."

Rāvaṇa flew along, though now and then he trembled in fear.

Āraṇya 54–55

The spacecraft was flying over hills and forests and was approaching the ocean. At that time, Sītā beheld on the ground below, five strong vānaras seated and watching the craft with curiosity. Quickly, Sītā took off the stole she had around her shoulders and, removing all her jewels and putting them in that stole, bundled them all up and threw the bundle into the midst of the vānaras, in the hope that should Rāma chance to come there they would give him a clue to her whereabouts.

Rāvaṇa did not notice this but flew on. And now the craft, which shot through space at great speed, was over the ocean; a little while after that, Rāvaṇa entered Laṅkā along with his captive Sītā. Entering his own apartments, Rāvaṇa placed Sītā in them, entrusting her care to some of his chief female attendants. He said to them: "Take great care of Sītā. Let no male approach these apartments without my express permission. And, take great care to let Sītā have whatever she wants and asks for. Any neglect on your part means instant death."

Rāvaṇa was returning to his own apartments: on the way he was still considering what more could be done to ensure the fulfilment of his ambition. He sent for eight of the most ferocious demons and instructed them thus: "Proceed at once to Janasthāna. It was ruled by my brother Khara; but it has now been devastated by Rāma. I am filled with rage to think that a mere human being could thus kill Khara, Dūṣaṇa and all their forces. Never mind: I shall put an end to Rāma soon. Keep an eye on him and keep me informed of his movements. You are free to bring about the destruction of Rāma." And, the demons immediately left.

Rāvaṇa returned to where Sītā was and compelled her to inspect the apartments. The palace stood on pillars of ivory, gold, crystal and silver and was studded with diamonds. The floor, the walls, the stairways—everything was made of gold and diamonds. Then again he said to Sītā: "Here at this place there are over a thousand demons ever ready to do my bidding. Their services and the entire Laṅkā I place at your feet. My life I offer to you; you are to me more valuable than my life. You will have under your command even the many good women whom I have married. Be my wife. Laṅkā is surrounded by the ocean, eight hundred miles on all sides. It is unapproachable to anybody; least of all to Rāma. Forget the weakling Rāma. Do not worry about the scriptural definitions of righteousness: we shall also get married in accordance with demoniacal wedding procedure. Youth is fleeting. Let us get married soon and enjoy life."

Āraṇya 56

Placing a blade of grass between Rāvaṇa and herself, Sītā said: "O demon! Rāma, the son of king Daśaratha, is my lord, the only one I adore. He and his brother Lakṣmaṇa will surely put an end to your life. If they had seen you lay your hands on me, they would have killed you on the spot, even as they laid Khara to eternal rest. It may be that you cannot be killed by demons and gods; but you cannot escape being killed at the hands of Rāma and Lakṣmaṇa. Rāvaṇa, you are doomed, beyond doubt. You have already lost your life, your good fortune, your very soul and your senses, and on account of your evil deeds Laṅkā has attained widowhood. Though you do not perceive this, death is knocking at your door, O Rāvaṇa. O sinner, you cannot under any circumstances lay your hands on me. You may bind this body, or you may destroy it: it is after all insentient matter, and I do not consider it worth preserving, nor even life worth living—not in order to live a life which will earn disrepute for me."

Rāvaṇa found himself helpless. Hence, he resorted to threat. He said: "I warn you, Sītā. I give you twelve months in which to make up your mind to accept me as your husband. If within that time you do not so decide, my cooks will cut you up easily for my breakfast." He had nothing more to say to her. He turned to the female attendants surrounding her and ordered them: "Take this Sītā away to the Aśoka grove. Keep her there. Use every method of persuasion that you know of to make her yield to my desire. Guard her vigilantly. Take her and break her will as you would tame a wild elephant."

The demonesses thereupon took Sītā away and confined her to the Aśoka grove, over which they themselves mounted guard day and night. Sītā did not find any peace of mind there, and stricken with fear and grief, she constantly thought of Rāma and Lakṣmaṇa.

It is said that at the same time, the creator Brahmā felt perturbed at the plight of Sītā. He spoke to Indra, the chief of gods: "Sītā is in the Aśoka grove. Pining for her husband, she may kill herself. Hence, go reassure her, and give her the celestial food to sustain herself till Rāma arrives in Laṅkā." Indra, thereupon, appeared before Sītā. In order to assure her of his identity he showed that his feet did not touch the ground and his eyes did not wink. He gave her the celestial food, saying: "Eat this, and you will never feel hunger or thirst, nor will fatigue overpower you." While Indra was thus talking to Sītā, the goddess of sleep (Nidrā) had overpowered the demonesses.

Āraṇya 57–58

Mārīca, the demon who had disguised himself as a unique deer, had been slain. But Rāma was intrigued and puzzled by the way in which Mārīca died, after crying: "O Sītā, O Lakṣmaṇa." Rāma sensed a deep and vicious plot. Hence he made haste to return to his hermitage. At the same time, he saw many evil omens. This aggravated his anxiety. He thought: "If Lakṣmaṇa heard that voice, he might rush to my aid, leaving Sītā alone. The demons surely wish to harm Sītā; and this might well have been a plot to achieve that purpose."

As he was thus brooding and proceeding towards his hermitage, he saw Lakṣmaṇa coming towards him. The distressed Rāma met the distressed Lakṣmaṇa; the sorrowing Rāma saw the sorrowful Lakṣmaṇa. Rāma caught hold of Lakṣmaṇa's arm and asked him, in an urgent tone: "O Lakṣmaṇa, why have you left Sītā alone and come? My mind is full of anxiety and terrible apprehension. When I see all these evil omens around us, I fear that something terrible has happened to Sītā. Surely Sītā has been stolen, killed or abducted."

Lakṣmaṇa's silence and grief-stricken countenance added fuel to the fire of anxiety in Rāma's heart. He asked again: "Is all well with Sītā? Where is my Sītā, the life of my life, without whom I cannot live even for an hour? Oh, what has happened to her? Alas, Kaikeyī's desire has been fulfilled today. If I am deprived of Sītā, I shall surely die. What more could Kaikeyī wish for? If, when I enter my hermitage, I do not find Sītā alive, how shall I live? Tell me, Lakṣmaṇa; speak. Surely, when that demon cried: 'O Lakṣmaṇa' in my voice, you were afraid that something had happened to me. Surely, Sītā also heard that cry and in a state of terrible mental agony, sent you to me. It is a painful thing that thus Sītā has been left alone; the demons who were waiting for an opportunity to hit back have been given that opportunity. The demons were sore distressed by my killing of the demon Khara. I am sure that they have done some great harm to Sītā, in the absence of both of us. What can I do now? How can I face this terrible calamity?"

Still, Lakṣmaṇa could not utter a word concerning what had happened. Both of them arrived near their hermitage. Everything that they saw reminded them of Sītā.

Āraṇya 59–60

And, once again before actually reaching the hermitage, and full of apprehension on account of Sītā, Rāma said to Lakṣmaṇa: "Lakṣmaṇa, you should not have come away like this, leaving Sītā alone in the hermitage. I had entrusted her to your care." When Rāma said this again and again, Lakṣmaṇa replied: "I have not come to you, leaving Sītā alone, just because I heard the demon Mārīca cry: 'O Lakṣmaṇa, O Sītā' in your voice. I did so only upon being literally driven by Sītā to do so. When she heard the cry, she immediately felt distressed and asked me to go to your help. I tried to calm her saying: 'It is not Rāma's voice; it is unthinkable that Rāma, who is capable of protecting even the gods, would utter the words, 'save me.' She, however, misunderstood my attitude. She said something very harsh, something very strange, something which I hate even to repeat. She said: 'Either you are an agent of Bharata or you have unworthy intentions towards me and therefore you are happy that Rāma is in distress and do not rush to his help'. It is only then that I had to leave."

In his anxiety for Sītā, Rāma was unimpressed by this argument. He said to Lakṣmaṇa: "Swayed by an angry woman's words, you failed to carry out my words; I am not highly pleased with what you have done, O Lakṣmaṇa."

Rāma rushed into their hermitage. But he could find no trace of Sītā in it. Confused and distressed beyond measure, Rāma said to himself, as he continued to search for Sītā: "Where is Sītā? Alas, she could have been eaten by the demons. Or, taken away by someone. Or, she is hidden somewhere. Or, she has gone to the forest." The search was fruitless. His anguish broke its bounds. Not finding her, he was completely overcome by grief and he began to behave as if he were mad.

Unable to restrain himself, he asked the trees and the birds and the animals of the forest; "Where is my beloved Sītā?" The eyes of the deer, the trunk of the elephant, the boughs of trees, the flowers—all these reminded Rāma of Sītā. "Surely, you know where my beloved Sītā is. Surely, you have a message from her. Won't you tell me? Won't you assuage the pain in my heart?" Thus Rāma wailed. He thought he saw Sītā at a distance and going up to 'her', he said: "My beloved, do not run away. Why are you hiding yourself behind those trees? Will you not speak to me?" Then he said to himself: "Surely it was not Sītā. Ah, she has been eaten by the demons. Did I leave her alone in the hermitage only to be eaten by the demons?" Thus lamenting, Rāma roamed awhile and ran around awhile.

Āraṇya 61–62

Again Rāma returned to the hermitage, and, seeing it empty, gave way to grief again. He asked Lakṣmaṇa: "Where has my beloved Sītā gone, O Lakṣmaṇa? Or, has she actually been carried away by someone?" Again, imagining that it was all fun and a big joke which Sītā was playing, he said: "Enough of this fun, Sītā; come out. See, even the deer are stricken with grief because they do not see you." Turning to Lakṣmaṇa again, he said: "Lakṣmaṇa, I cannot live without my Sītā. I shall soon join my father in the other world. But, he may be annoyed with me and say: 'I told you to live in the forest for fourteen years; how have you come here before that period?' Ah Sītā, do not forsake me."

Lakṣmaṇa tried to console him: "Grieve not, O Rāma. Surely, you know that Sītā is fond of the forest and the caves on the mountainside. She must have gone to these caves. Let us look for her in the forest. That is the proper thing to do; not to grieve."

These brave words took Rāma's grief away. Filled with zeal and eagerness, Rāma along with Lakṣmaṇa, began to comb the forest. Rāma was distressed: "Lakṣmaṇa, this is strange; I do not find Sītā anywhere." But Lakṣmaṇa continued to console Rāma: "Fear not, brother; you will surely recover the noble Sītā soon."

But this time, these words were less meaningful to Rāma. He was overcome by grief, and he lamented: "Where shall we find Sītā, O Lakṣmaṇa, and when? We have looked for her everywhere in the forest and on the hills, but we do not find her." Lamenting thus, stricken with grief, with his intelligence and his heart robbed by the loss of Sītā, Rāma frequently sighed in anguish, muttering: "Ah my beloved".

Suddenly, he thought he saw her, hiding herself behind the banana trees, and now behind the karnikara trees. And, he said to 'her': "My beloved, I see you behind the banana trees! Ah, now I see you behind the karnikara tree: my dear, enough, enough of this play: for your fun aggravates my anguish. I know you are fond of such play; but pray, stop this and come to me now."

When Rāma realised that it was only his hallucination, he turned to Lakṣmaṇa once more and lamented: "I am certain now that some demon has killed my beloved Sītā. How can I return to Ayodhyā without Sītā? How can I face Janaka, her father? Oh, no: Lakṣmaṇa, even heaven is useless without Sītā; I shall continue to stay in the forest; you can return to Ayodhyā. And you can tell Bharata that he should continue to rule the country."

Āraṇya 63–64

Rāma was inconsolable and even infected the brave Lakṣmaṇa. Shedding tears profusely, Rāma continued to speak to Lakṣmaṇa who had also fallen a prey to grief by this time: "No one in this whole world is guilty of as many misdeeds as I am, O Lakṣmaṇa: and that is why I am being visited by sorrow upon sorrow, grief upon grief, breaking my heart and dementing me. I lost my kingdom, and I was torn away from my relations and friends. I got reconciled to this misfortune. But then I lost my father. I was separated from my mother. Coming to this hermitage, I was getting reconciled to that misfortune. But I could not remain at peace with myself for long. Now this terrible misfortune, the worst of all, has visited me.

"Alas, how bitterly Sītā would have cried while she was carried away by some demon. May be she was injured; may be her lovely body was covered with blood. Why is it that when she was subjected to such suffering, my body did not split into pieces? I fear that the demon must have cut open Sītā's neck and drunk her blood. How terribly she must have suffered when she was dragged by the demons.

"Lakṣmaṇa, this river Godāvarī was her favourite resort. Do you remember how she used to come and sitting on this slab of stone talk to us and laugh? Probably she came to the river Godāvarī in order to gather lotuses? But, no: she would never go alone to these places.

"O sun! You know what people do and what people do not do. You know what is true and what is false. You are a witness to all these. Pray, tell me, where has my beloved Sītā gone. For, I have been robbed of everything by this grief. O wind! You know everything in this world, for you are everywhere. Pray, tell me, in which direction did Sītā go?"

Rāma said: "See, Lakṣmaṇa, if Sītā is somewhere near the river Godāvarī." Lakṣmaṇa came back and reported that he could not find her. Rāma himself went to the river and asked the river: "O Godāvarī, pray tell me, where has my beloved Sītā gone?" But the river did not reply. It was as if, afraid of the anger of Rāvaṇa, Godāvarī kept silent.

Rāma was disappointed. He asked the deer and the other animals of the forest: "Where is Sītā? Pray, tell me in which direction has Sītā been taken away." He then observed the deer and the animals; all of them turned southwards and some of them even moved southwards. Rāma then said to Lakṣmaṇa: "O Lakṣmaṇa, see, they are all indicating that Sītā has been taken in a southerly direction."

Āraṇya 64

Lakṣmaṇa, too, saw the animals' behaviour as sure signs indicating that Sītā had been borne away in a southerly direction, and suggested to Rāma that they should also proceed in that direction. As they were thus proceeding, they saw petals of flowers fallen on the ground. Rāma recognised them and said to Lakṣmaṇa: "Look here, Lakṣmaṇa, these are petals from the flowers that I had given to Sītā. Surely, in their eagerness to please me, the sun, the wind and the earth, have contrived to keep these flowers fresh."

They walked further on. Rāma saw footprints on the ground. Two of them he immediately recognised as those of Sītā. The other two were big—obviously the footprints of a demon. Bits and pieces of gold were strewn on the ground. Lo and behold, Rāma also saw blood which he concluded was Sītā's blood: he wailed again: "Alas, at this spot, the demon killed Sītā to eat her flesh." He also saw evidence of a fight: and he said: "Perhaps there were two demons fighting for the flesh of Sītā."

Rāma saw on the ground pieces of a broken weapon, an armour of gold, a broken canopy, and the propellers and other parts of a spacecraft. He also saw lying dead, one who had the appearance of the pilot of the craft. From these he concluded that two demons had fought for the flesh of Sītā, before one carried her away. He said to Lakṣmaṇa: "The demons have earned my unquenchable hate and wrath. I shall destroy all of them. Nay, I shall destroy all the powers that be who refuse to return Sītā to me. Look at the irony of fate, Lakṣmaṇa: we adhere to dharma, but dharma could not protect Sītā who has been abducted in this forest! When these powers that govern the universe witness Sītā being eaten by the demons, without doing anything to stop it, who is there to do what is pleasing to us? I think our meekness is misunderstood to be weakness. We are full of self-control, compassion and devoted to the welfare of all beings: and yet these virtues have become as good as vices in us now. I shall set aside all these virtues and the universe shall witness my supreme glory which will bring about the destruction of all creatures, including the demons. If Sītā is not immediately brought back to me, I shall destroy the three worlds—the gods, the demons and other creatures will perish, becoming targets of my most powerful missiles. When I take up my weapon in anger, O Lakṣmaṇa, no one can confront me, even as no one can evade old age and death."

Āraṇya 65–66

Seeing the world-destroying mood of Rāma, Lakṣmaṇa endeavoured to console him. He said to Rāma:

"Rāma, pray, do not go against your nature. Charm in the moon, brilliance in the sun, motion in the air, and endurance in the earth—these are their essential nature: in you all these are found and in addition, eternal glory. Your nature cannot desert you; even the sun, the moon and the earth cannot abandon their nature! Moreover, being king, you cannot punish all the created beings for the sin of one person. Gentle and peaceful monarchs match punishment to crime: and, over and above this, you are the refuge of all beings and their goal. I shall without fail find out the real criminal who has abducted Sītā; I shall find out whose armour and weapons these are. And you shall mete out just punishment to the sinner. Oh, no, no god will seek to displease you, O Rāma: Nor these trees, mountains and rivers. I am sure they will all eagerly aid us in our search for Sītā. Of course, if Sītā cannot be recovered through peaceful means, we shall consider other means.

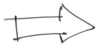

"Whom does not misfortune visit in this world, O Rāma? And, misfortune departs from man as quickly as it visits him. Hence, pray, regain your composure. If you who are endowed with divine intelligence betray lack of endurance in the face of this misfortune, what will others do in similar circumstances?

"King Nahuṣa, who was as powerful as Indra, was beset with misfortune. The sage Vasiṣṭha, our family preceptor, had a hundred sons and lost all of them on one day! Earth is tormented by volcanic eruptions, and earthquakes. The sun and the moon are afflicted by eclipses. Misfortune strikes the great ones and even the gods.

"For, in this world people perform actions whose results are not obvious; and these actions which may be good or evil, bear their own fruits. Of course, these fruits are evanescent. People who are endowed with enlightened intelligence know what is good and what is not good. People like you do not grieve over misfortunes and do not get deluded by them.

"Why am I telling you all this, O Rāma? Who in this world is wiser than you? However, since, as is natural, grief seems to veil wisdom, I am saying all this. All this I learnt only from you: I am only repeating what you yourself taught me earlier. Therefore, O Rāma, know your enemy and fight him."

Āraṇya 67–68

Rāma then asked Lakṣmaṇa: "O Lakṣmaṇa, tell me, what should we do now?" Lakṣmaṇa replied: "Surely, we should search this forest for Sītā."

This advice appealed to Rāma. Immediately he fixed the bayonet to his weapon and with a look of anger on his face, set out to search for Sītā. Within a very short time and distance, both Rāma and Lakṣmaṇa chanced upon Jaṭāyu, seriously and mortally wounded and heavily bleeding. Seeing that enormous vulture lying on the ground, Rāma's first thought was: "Surely, this is the one that has swallowed Sītā." He rushed forward with fixed bayonet.

Looking at Rāma thus rushing towards him, and rightly inferring Rāma's mood, Jaṭāyu said in a feeble voice: "Sītā has been taken away by Rāvaṇa. I tried to intervene. I battled with the mighty Rāvaṇa. I broke his armour, his canopy, the propellers and some parts of his spacecraft. I killed his pilot. I even inflicted injuries on his person. But he cut off my wings and thus grounded me." When Rāma heard that the vulture had news of Sītā, he threw his weapon away and kneeling down near the vulture embraced it.

Rāma said to Lakṣmaṇa: "An additional calamity to endure, O Lakṣmaṇa. Is there really no end to my misfortune? My misfortune plagues even this noble creature, a friend of my father's." Rāma requested more information from Jaṭāyu concerning Sītā, and also concerning Rāvaṇa. Jaṭāyu replied: "Taking Sītā with him, the demon flew away in his craft, leaving a mysterious storm and cloud behind him. I was mortally wounded by him. Ah, my senses are growing dim. I feel life ebbing away, Rāma. Yet, I assure you, you will recover Sītā." Soon Jaṭāyu lay lifeless. Nay, it was his body, for he himself ascended to heaven. Grief-stricken afresh, Rāma said to Lakṣmaṇa: "Jaṭāyu lived a very long life; and yet has had to lay down his life today. Death, no one in this world can escape. And what a noble end! What a great service this noble vulture has rendered to me! Pious and noble souls are found even amongst subhuman creatures, O Lakṣmaṇa. Today I have forgotten all my previous misfortunes: I am extremely tormented by the loss of this dear friend who has sacrificed his life for my sake. I shall myself cremate it, so that it may reach the highest realms."

Rāma himself performed the funeral rites, reciting those Vedic mantras which one recites during the cremation of one's own close relations. After this, Rāma and Lakṣmaṇa proceeded on their journey in search of Sītā.

Āraṇya 69

Proceeding in a south-westerly direction, Rāma and Lakṣmaṇa reached a dense, deep and untrodden forest. This was the Krauñca forest. Then they proceeded in an easterly direction and got out of that forest. They went past the hermitage of the sage Mātaṅga. The forest adjoining this hermitage was even more fearful than all the previous ones they had passed through. And there they saw a huge cave which had never seen the light of the sun or of the moon. Near this cave, they saw a demoness, most frightful to look at. She had a belly that protruded to a great length, her teeth were sharp, her skin was hard and she was eating the wild animals of the forest. When she saw them approaching, she quickly pounced upon Lakṣmaṇa and began to drag him away saying, "Come, let us enjoy." She said to Lakṣmaṇa: "I am Ayomukhi. I love you; and surely you realise that I am worthy of you. With me you can roam this forest and enjoy life." Quickly he did to her what he had already done to Śūrpaṇakhā.

The brothers proceeded further and into an even denser forest which was difficult to enter. Apprehending trouble, Lakṣmaṇa said to Rāma: "Keep your weapon in readiness, O Rāma: I see many evil omens, though there is also a good omen which portends success to us." Even as he was saying this, there was great tumult ahead of them. Soon they saw a terrible looking and unusual demon.

That demon had a broad chest, it had an enormous body, but it had no head and no neck, and it had its mouth in its belly. He spoke like thunder. He had only one eye on his forehead which was on his chest. He was endowed with long arms by which he drew his prey to himself! He blocked the path of Rāma and Lakṣmaṇa. And, when they came near him, he caught hold of them, even though they tried to retrace their steps. His name was Kabandha.

In Kabandha's vice-like grip, the two brothers could not do anything. Rāma braved the ordeal. Lakṣmaṇa, however, was distressed. He said to Rāma: "I am finished, O Rāma. Let my life be offered in sacrifice to this demon; and pray, escape from his grip and go forth to find Sītā. And, then, regaining your kingdom, may you rule for ever." And this time Rāma consoled him and restored his self-confidence. Kabandha said to them: "I was extremely hungry. Surely, you have walked into my hands in order to appease my hunger." Rāma was stricken with grief once again, and he said: "Surely, Time and Death do not spare any one. Before we recover from one tragedy, we are overtaken by another."

Āraṇya 70–71

Kabandha asked them: "Pray, tell me who you are—you have come to me at the right time to appease my hunger." Lakṣmaṇa thereupon said to Rāma: "Rāma, obviously this demon's strength is in his arms. Let us quickly cut them off. He is unarmed; and hence it is not proper for us to kill him."

Kabandha was annoyed by this conversation between Rāma and Lakṣmaṇa. And, so, without wasting any more time, he got ready to devour them. As he drew them nearer to his mouth in order to do so, Rāma and Lakṣmaṇa, who knew what to do where and when, quickly cut off the demon's arms with their swords. The demon fell down on the ground giving a mighty roar. Once again, he looked at the princes and questioned: "Who are you?" Lakṣmaṇa told him who they were and what brought them to the forest; in turn he asked the demon: "Who are you?"

Kabandha narrated his biography, in the following words: "In my previous life I possessed a gigantic and radiant form which rivalled the sun and the moon. I was very powerful. Power-drunk, I used to harass the sages and even the gods.

"And, I propitiated the creator Brahmā and obtained from him the boon of a very long life. Intoxicated further with this boon, I even picked a quarrel with Indra, the king of the gods. Using his mighty weapon, the thunderbolt, Indra struck me, deprived me of my legs, head and mouth which had all been pushed into my torso. When I pleaded that he could have killed me instead, he said he did not want to go against the boon of the Creator. When I prayed, 'With this form how can I find my food?', Indra bestowed exceptionally long arms upon me.

"With this form, I once attacked the sage Sthūlaśira; and he cursed me: 'Continue to remain in this form!' I begged of him to modify his curse so that this dreadful state might come to an end. He blessed me: 'When Rāma and Lakṣmaṇa come here and cut off your hands, you will be released from this form.' By the very fact that you have cut off my arms, I know that you are Rāma. Please perform my cremation: and then I shall be able to help you in any manner you wish me to."

Rāma at once thought of Sītā! He asked Kabandha: "Pray, tell me where Sītā is. I hear she has been abducted by Rāvaṇa. I do not know who he is, what he looks like and where he is. Pray, tell me all this." But the demon repeated: "I have no power to divine the answers to your questions. Before being cremated by you, I have no knowledge of the answers to your questions concerning Sītā."

Āraṇya 72–73

Helped by Lakṣmaṇa Rāma personally cremated the demon Kabandha. As the funeral pyre was lit, the uncouth body of Kabandha seemed to melt away in the fire. From that fire there emerged a radiant being clad in spotless attire and adorned by precious jewels. Stationed in space in his ethereal body, this divine being, said to Rāma:

"O Rāma, I shall now reveal to you the way in which you will surely find Sītā. In this world, when one is faced with a calamity, there are the six ways of overcoming it: and one of them is to cultivate the friendship of one in similar predicament. Without such a friend you will not succeed in your mission of recovering Sītā. I shall tell you where and how to find such a friend. There is a vānara known as Sugrīva whose brother Vāli has driven him out of the kingdom. Sugrīva will help you in your task. At the same time, surely he can be helped in his ambition to regain his lost kingdom. Thus you can be of mutual help. However, even if you are unable to help him in his work, he will certainly help you in yours. Sugrīva dwells on the Ṛṣyamūka hill. He is very clever, and knows everything in this world. He is also highly cultured and true to his word. He has a large band of vānaras under him, with whose help Sītā can easily be discovered. If necessary, he will send the vānara hosts to invade Laṅkā and, after destroying the demons, bring Sītā back to you." The transformed Kabandha then described the route to the Ṛṣyamūka hill in great detail. He said: "Proceeding in a westerly direction, from hill to hill, from forest to forest, you will come to the Pampā lake whose waters are clear and free from weed. You will find beautiful swans and fish in the lake. You will feed them, and you will drink the waters of the lake. Later you will meet the vānaras, who also come to the lake. Rāma, in days of yore, the sage Mātaṅga lived in that region. His disciples used to serve him by bringing foodstuff from the forest. Drops of sweat that fell from their bodies watered the plants in the forest whose blossoms, therefore, do not fade nor die. The sage is no more; and even his disciples have cast off their physical bodies. But, one aged lady-disciple of the sage is still alive. She is Śabarī who is eagerly awaiting your visit, after which she will ascend to heaven. That forest is known as Mātaṅgavana. To the east of this Mātaṅgavana is the Ṛṣyamūka hill. It is steep and is difficult to ascend. However, it has its own special reward for the hero who ascends it: his dreams come true. Rāma, when you reach this hill, you will surely give up your grief. Sugrīva dwells in a cave on the side of this mountain."

Āraṇya 74–75

Rāma and Lakṣmaṇa followed the directions of Kabandha. They reached the western shore of the Pampā lake. There they saw the beautiful hermitage of the ascetic Śabarī.

When Śabarī saw them, she welcomed them with great respect and devotion. She bowed to their feet. She worshipped Rāma. Rāma enquired after her welfare and the fruition of her spiritual practices.

Filled with the highest devotion, Śabarī replied to Rāma: "I have now reached the perfection of my austerities, for I have beheld you. Today my birth has borne its fruit; the worship I have offered my preceptors has been endowed with meaning. I shall attain to heaven, too, O Rāma, now that I have seen you. My eyes have beheld you; my heart has been purified; and I shall ascend to the worlds of eternal life, by your grace."

She continued: "When you had just arrived at the Citrakooṭa hill, the other disciples of the sage Mātaṅga ascended to heaven. They said to me: 'Soon Rāma and Lakṣmaṇa will come here; stay here till then and worship them. You can then join us.' I lay before you, O Rāma, the best fruits of this forest. Pray accept them and bless me." After accepting her hospitality, Rāma requested her to show him the objects associated with the sage Mātaṅga and his disciples. Śabarī thereupon showed them round the forest named after Mātaṅga, the place where they practised their austerities and shed their bodies, the altar at which they worshipped, the confluence of the seven oceans, the dress of the bark of trees left behind by them (and which had not faded), and the flowers which remained fresh. After thus showing them round, Śabarī offered her body into the sacred fire and, discarding her physical body, assumed a resplendent astral body and ascended to heaven.

Rāma then said to Lakṣmaṇa: "Lakṣmaṇa, we have seen the holy hermitage of these holy sages, full of wonder; we have seen the blessed animals that roam this place freely; we have seen the seven seas; and we have offered libations for our ancestors, too. I feel that all our past evil actions have been atoned and that our misfortune has come to an end."

Leaving that hermitage of Śabarī they went towards the Ṛṣyamūka hill, after passing near the Mātaṅgasara lake which is a subsidiary lake to Paṁpā, and which was full of alligators and turtles, and which, with its many coloured lotuses and lilies looked like a beautiful carpet. Having reached the hill, Rāma said to Lakṣmaṇa: "Please go and look for Sugrīva."

Kiṣkindhā Kāṇḍa Rāma's Stay in Kiṣkindhā

Spring was upon the earth. Life sprang up from the earth. It was the time for new manifestation, new growth, new birth. Love was in the air. Love stirred in the hearts of all beings.

Spring entered Rāma through the avenues of his senses. Everything that he saw, everything that he heard, everything he smelt and everything that he touched, reminded him of his beloved Sītā. Memory of Sītā renewed his grief. And, thus, he lamented the loss of Sītā:

"Look at this beautiful Paṁpā lake, O Lakṣmaṇa: how it sparkles like a huge gem. And look at these trees laden with flowers. Soothing to the eyes, they agitate my mind and renew my grief. I think of the ascetic life that Bharata is leading there in Ayodhyā, because of me, and I think of Sītā. The whole ground is carpeted with lovely flowers of many hues. The trees are laden with flowers of their own and of the creepers that entwine them.

"See here, Lakṣmaṇa, these Karṇikāra trees do not look like trees any more. With the colourful blossoms on them, they make me feel that they are noble men clad in yellow robes and decked with ornaments. With all this, however, my heart is heavy. This spring which has brought joy and song to birds and beasts, only intensifies my sorrow, as I have been separated from my beloved Sītā. And, Cupid who brings love and pleasure to beings only aggravates my grief. When these birds and beasts used to chirp or cry, Sītā used to be delighted and she would seek my company to share the delight. See, O Lakṣmaṇa, how male birds and even the bees, when they are united with mates utter delightful sounds expressing their joy. All entering through the avenues of my senses, awaken love in me.

"I am afraid, O Lakṣmaṇa, that this extremely pleasant season, spring, might consume me with grief, for I have been deprived of the company of Sītā. Sītā who is out of my sight, and spring which is here—both together burn me. Strange it is that even the pleasant breeze is scorching me with sorrow. The male peacock dancing with the peahen seems to be mocking at me! See, Lakṣmaṇa, how this peahen approaches her mate so fondly: love is common to all beings; sub-human beings, too. My beloved Sītā too would come to me like that, had she not been abducted by the demon."

Kiṣkindhā 1

"Surely, it is spring now where my Sītā lives. When even I am tormented by the coming of spring and the absence of Sītā, how will she be able to enjoy spring or to avoid being tormented by spring? I am beginning to feel more and more convinced, O Lakṣmaṇa, that scorched by the fire of separation from me, Sītā cannot live. Sītā and I are eternally united with each other—she in me and I in her.

"But no. Look at that crow. It used to cry foreboding the abduction of Sītā. Now it seems to me that it is conveying the joyous message that I will soon be re-united with my beloved.

"On the other hand, when I see that Aśoka tree shaking in the wind and shedding its flowers, it looks as if it is shaking its fists at me and threatening me. Look at this placid and beautiful Pampā lake, literally covered with lilies and lotuses which are also beautifully reflected on the water. But it does not cause me any joy; for I do not have Sītā with me.

"What a strange power that love possesses! It powerfully revives the memory of the beloved who has gone away and who is inaccessible. I can surely cope with the sorrow in me caused by separation from Sītā: but this spring season makes this sorrow impossible to bear. Whatever was enjoyable with Sītā becomes insufferable without her!

"Everything here and now reminds me of Sītā. The lotus reminds me of Sītā's lotus-like eyes. The soothing and cool breeze reminds me of Sītā's breath.

"Surely, the Ṛṣyamūka hill is rich in minerals; even the dust that rises from it seems to be many coloured, suggesting mineral dust. All the trees are in full bloom. And, the creepers entwining the trees suggest lovers in embrace. Look at the wind; it is having a very good time. It blows from tree to tree, from forest to forest, enjoying the aroma and the sweetness of the different blossoms.

"It looks as if the trees vie with one another, in a spirit of healthy competition, in clothing themselves with richer and richer garments of lovely flowers. And as the wind blows over them, it seems to me that each tree is boasting about its own supremacy over the others—nodding its head in self-assertion.

"This place is so beautiful, O Lakṣmaṇa, that if only Sītā were with me here, I would not even think of the pleasures of the lord of heaven."

Kiṣkindhā 1

"Look at those two deer, O Lakṣmaṇa: the male and the female deer, how they sport happily on that mountain. Alas, I have lost my beloved Sītā. I can be happy only when I am reunited with Sītā. Life is unbearable without Sītā; but I know that when I regain Sītā I shall regain zest for life and joy, too. I am worried about Sītā: she must be suffering terribly on account of her separation from me.

"I am also worried about what I can do when I return to Ayodhyā upon completion of the fourteen years: how shall I face king Janaka and what shall I tell him when he enquires of Sītā? And, what shall I tell my mother Kausalyā when she lovingly enquires about her beloved daughter-in-law?

"How dreadful it is, O Lakṣmaṇa, that she who insisted upon following me in my adversity has been taken away from me! How terrible it is that she who wanted to be with me, to serve me even during my exile, has thus been abducted and I was not able to prevent it! Where is Sītā, O Lakṣmaṇa? When will I hear her sweet speech?

"O Lakṣmaṇa, go to Ayodhyā and rejoin the noble Bharata. Forget me. I cannot live without Sītā."

The noble and wise Lakṣmaṇa said to Rāma: "Abandon this sorrow caused by your separation from Sītā, O Rāma! Even a dry wick gets ignited when it is smeared with a lot of gum. Even so, a cool mind is agitated by too much of sneha (affection or gum). Surely, wherever he may be, Rāvaṇa cannot live, if he does not give up Sītā immediately. Even if he goes to the nether world, even if he hides himself in the womb of Diti (the mother of the demons), I shall kill him and rescue Sītā.

"Maintain the auspicious state of mind which is your own nature: a lost object is not retrieved except by effort! Hence, we should cultivate enthusiasm. Enthusiasm is the greatest power. For a man endowed with enthusiasm nothing in this world is impossible of achievement. A man endowed with enthusiasm does not despair in action. We shall regain Sītā by recourse to enthusiastic action, O Rāma. Give up this sorrow born of affection which has unfortunately veiled your own supreme glory."

Thus encouraged by Lakṣmaṇa, Rāma regained his composure and both of them began to ascend the Ṛṣyamūka hill. One day Sugrīva saw two mighty men coming up that hill, and greatly frightened, took refuge in the hermitage of the sage Mātaṅga.

Kiṣkindhā 2–3

When Sugrīva saw the two mighty heroes, Rāma and Lakṣmaṇa, he apprehended danger: he was afraid that they had been sent by his elder brother to kill him. He said as much to his ministers. Surrounded by his ministers, Sugrīva kept constantly moving from one hill to another, in an attempt to avoid a confrontation with the visitors.

Seeing Sugrīva thus agitated, one of his ministers, Hanumān said to him: "Pray, give up this irrational fear. We are still on the Malaya (Ṛṣyamūka) hill which is inaccessible to Vāli. And I do not see Vāli anywhere here. A king like you should not allow his mind to be perturbed. We should watch the actions and gestures of others and know what goes on in their mind! That indeed is wise statesmanship, O King!"

Hanumān's speech appealed to the heart of Sugrīva. He then said to Hanumān: "It is natural, O Hanumān, for one who sees such mighty warriors as these, to be apprehensive. Kings, like Vāli, when they wish to destroy their enemies, resort to many deceptive means: hence kings should not be trusted. We cannot place any reliance on their appearance, either, O Hanumān; for enemies destroy others, often assuming a disguise. Vāli is shrewd; and we should also resort to a shrewd plan to foil his attempt to destroy me. O Hanumān, pleas disguise yourself and go to them; and for my sak who they are, with the help of their gestures and w you praise me."

Hanumān disguised himself as a mendicant and humbly approached the two princes. After bowing to them, he asked them: "You look like royal sages or gods, but you are clad like ascetics. Pray, tell me who you are and what you are doing here. You have powerful arms like princes; yet, they are not adorned with ornaments! Yet, your weapons are excellent and richly covered with gold and precious stones. I shall tell you who I am. A great leader of the jungle folk (vānaras) named Sugrīva lives here, having been driven out of his kingdom by his cruel brother Vāli. I am Hanumān, his minister. Sugrīva seeks your friendship. I, too, am a vānara though disguised as a mendicant."

Rāma greatly admired the speech of Hanumān, and said to Lakṣmaṇa: "Surely, Lakṣmaṇa, no one who is not a master of the three Vedas can speak like him. There is not a single fault in his language, mode of expression, choice of words or gestures. I am greatly impressed by it. Pray, give him a suitable reply." Lakṣmaṇa then said to Hanumān: "We have indeed heard of the noble Sugrīva already, O vānara! We would also love to meet Sugrīva and cultivate his friendship for mutual benefit."

Kiṣkindhā 4–5

Hanumān was delighted to hear Lakṣmaṇa's words. He asked Rāma: "Pray, tell me why you are here in this forest and in what way we may help you."

Lakṣmaṇa gave a full and detailed account up to the abduction of Sītā. He added: "We do not know where the demon who has thus abducted Sītā lives and what his powers are. And, not long ago we met the demon Danu (another name for Kabandha) who, while he was ascending to the higher worlds, vouched to us the knowledge, that Sugrīva would help us find the demon who had taken Sītā away. We have therefore come here at his bidding. This is an extraordinary event, O Hanumān! He who is the refuge of the whole world seeks the refuge of Sugrīva. He whose gratification brings about the gratification of all, seeks the grace of Sugrīva, the chief of the vānaras. Sugrīva should help accomplish Rāma's purpose, O Hanumān."

Hanumān was even more delighted by this speech. He said: "It is our good fortune that both of you who have mastered your mind and senses have come here. Sugrīva, too, needs your help. Deprived of his wife and his kingdom by his brother Vāli, Sugrīva lives here in exile in great fear. And Sugrīva will surely render all possible help to Rāma."

Hanumān shed the disguise of a mendicant and escorted the princes to the presence of Sugrīva. Hanumān acquainted Sugrīva with the identity of Rāma and Lakṣmaṇa, and announced: "O King, receive Rāma and Lakṣmaṇa with due honour and make friendship with them."

Welcoming Rāma and Lakṣmaṇa, Sugrīva then said to them: "I have heard everything from Hanumān. If my friendship is acceptable to you, here is my hand!" Hearing this, Rāma grasped the hand of Sugrīva in his own hand; and he embraced Sugrīva in genuine affection and friendship. Hanumān then kindled the sacred fire which bore witness to this new and significant alliance. Going round the fire, Sugrīva said to Rāma: "You are now my beloved friend; and from now on we shall share our joys and sorrows."

When they had all been seated, after this ceremony, Sugrīva said to Rāma: "My brother Vāli has deprived me of my kingdom, and even my wife has been taken away by him, O Rāma. I live here on this hill which is difficult of access to Vāli. But I live in great and constant fear. Kindly ensure, O Rāma, that this cause of my fear may be removed." Rāma immediately said: "Look at these missiles of mine, O Sugrīva! I shall soon kill that wicked Vāli."

Kiṣkindhā 6–7

Sugrīva said to Rāma: "O Rāma, Hanumān has told me all about the purpose for which you have come here. I do not know where Rāvaṇa lives nor what his powers are. But I shall soon find out. Let Rāvaṇa be on this earth or in the nether world: he will not escape! Please rest assured. Incidentally, I remember something which happened not long ago. I believe it was Sītā who was being carried away by a demon who was obviously Rāvaṇa. That lady saw us sitting on this hill and threw a bundle which fell near us. She was wailing aloud: 'O

Rāma, O Lakṣmaṇa.' The bundle contained some jewels which we have preserved."

Rāma was impatient to see the bundle of jewels! When Sugrīva brought it, Rāma, looking at it, began to wail aloud once again. He said to Lakṣmaṇa: "See, O Lakṣmaṇa, look at this garment of Sītā's with the jewels she was wearing at the time Rāvaṇa abducted her, and which she has thrown down. It is lucky that she dropped them on soft ground; they are intact." Looking at them, Lakṣmaṇa said: "I do not recognise the ornaments worn by Sītā on her head or on her body; but I do recognise the ornaments that adorned her feet for I noticed them every day as I bowed to her." Once again Rāma asked Sugrīva: "O Sugrīva, where does this demon live, who has abducted Sītā causing such unhappiness to me, and bringing destruction, through me, to the whole race of demons?"

Once again, Sugrīva said: "I do not know where he lives, O Rāma. But do not worry yourself. I promise that I shall do the needful to bring Sītā to you; give up sorrow. Abandon weakness of mind, O Rāma. See, I have also been deprived of my kingdom and my wife. Though I belong to a primitive jungle tribe, I do not grieve: it does not behove you, belonging to a civilised princely family, to grieve and to lose heart. I pray to you with folded palms: regain manliness and do not let sorrow enter your heart. For, there is no happiness for those who worry and grieve; and they are robbed of their energy, too. Hence you should not grieve. Even living becomes doubtful in the case of one who has yielded to sorrow. Give up sorrow and be brave, O Rāma. Please do not think I am preaching! I am only mentioning this for your own good, as a friend that I am."

Thus encouraged by Sugrīva, Rāma immediately regained his composure. He said to Sugrīva: "My friend, do what a true friend should do to relieve one of his grief! Such friendship as exists between us is indeed rare in this world nowadays, O Sugrīva. I have never uttered a lie: nor shall I ever be guilty of falsehood. I shall accomplish your purpose."

Kiṣkindhā 8

Sugrīva was supremely happy to hear Rāma's words. He said: "O Rāma, with your friendship and with your help, one can gain heaven itself, not to speak of one's own kingdom. I shall also be able to render some help to you, though right now I am unable to bring this home to you, on account of the misfortune into which I have fallen. Your friendship is of immeasurable value to me. Your friendship will raise me in the estimation of my people. Good people relinquish all sense of private ownership when they cultivate the friendship of other good people: gold, silver and even precious jewels they hold in common, without feeling, 'This is mine, not yours'. Such indeed shall be our friendship. Again, for the sake of one's friends one abandons wealth, pleasure and even one's country."

Rāma entirely agreed with Sugrīva's declaration of the characteristics of friendship. Cutting down one of the trees standing nearby, Sugrīva enabled all of them to have seats. After they had all sat down, Sugrīva once again submitted to Rāma: "O Rāma, driven out of my kingdom and deprived of my wife, I am living in sorrow and fear. I pray to you to relieve me of my distress." Rāma replied: "Surely, O Sugrīva, helpful service is the fruit of friendship, and harm comes out of enmity; I shall immediately kill that sinner who has robbed you of your wife. Don't you see these powerful missiles which I possess? They will soon rob Vāli of his life!"

Delighted with this assurance, Sugrīva applauded Rāma, and submitted again: "O Rāma, I am stricken with sorrow: and you are the sole refuge of those who are grief-stricken. And, regarding you as my dear friend, I take refuge in you, and worry you like this." As he said this, his eyes filled with tears. He wiped them and endeavoured to regain his composure. And he continued: "O Rāma, Vāli is a mighty vānara. He not only usurped my throne, but threw me out of the kingdom after insulting me. Then he seized my wife and also incarcerated my relations. He is always plotting to kill me. That was the reason why I was stricken with fear when I first saw you two coming here. These few vānaras are the only companions I have. But, now that you have become my friend, I am sure my sorrow has come to an end. For in joy and sorrow, friends are the only resort of friends."

Rāma then asked Sugrīva: "Kindly tell me the whole story. How did you happen to incur the displeasure of Vāli and why did he usurp your kingdom and seize your wife?"

Kiṣkindhā 9–10

Sugrīva said: "Vāli is my elder brother. He is exce strong. Father was very fond of him. And I loved h When father died, naturally Vāli was installed on the throne of our territory known as Kiṣkindhā.

"Vāli had an enemy known as Māyāvī, the son of Māyā. One day Māyāvī came to our territory and challenged Vāli to a duel. The womenfolk of the court and even I endeavoured to hold Vāli back from accepting this challenge: we wished to prevent bloodshed. But Vāli would not hear us.

"When Vāli came out to fight Māyāvī, the latter suddenly got frightened and he began to run. Vāli followed him; so did I. The demon Māyāvī entered a terrible cavern underground. Vālī followed him, after instructing me: 'Stay at the mouth of this cavern, Sugrīva, while I pursue this demon and kill him.' I pleaded that he should take me with him also; but Vāli refused.

"I waited for a year at the mouth of this cavern. I heard terrible noises inside. But, Vāli did not return. Blood gushed out of that cavern. I could not hear Vāli's roar. I surmised that he had been killed by the demon. Heart-broken I returned to the kingdom. The ministers who somehow came to know the truth, installed me on the throne.

"Some time later, Vāli returned to the kingdom. I greeted him but he did not take any notice of me. He was filled with rage. I humbly said to him: 'I feel that we are all fortunate in that you have returned to us alive. Here is your throne: pray take it. With troubled mind, I spent a year at the entrance to the cavern. I saw blood; and thought that you had been killed. Out of fear and sorrow I closed the cavern with a big rock and returned. The ministers insisted on installing me on the throne, as they did not wish to endanger the security of the state by leaving it without a ruler. I did not desire it. Pray forgive me. You are the ever adored king and I am as I was before.'

"But, however much I pleaded with him, he refused to listen to me. He was furious. He accused me unjustly. He said: 'I had asked you to stay at the mouth of the cavern. I killed the demon Māyāvī and, trying to come out of the cavern, I did not even know the way, because you had covered the cavern with a rock. I kicked the stone off and have come here.

Only to see that you have become king!' In great anger he drove me out of the kingdom with just one piece of cloth. And I have sought asylum on this hill which for another reason is out of bounds for Vāli."

Rāma repeated his pledge: "Your sorrow will end soon, as soon as I behold the sinful Vāli who has seized your wife."

Kiṣkindhā 11

Sugrīva said: "Surely Rāma, when you are roused to anger you can destroy even the worlds with your missiles, as the sun could at the close of the epoch. However, listen attentively while I describe the powers of Vāli, and then please do the needful.

"There once was a demon named Dundubhi who had the appearance of a buffalo. He too was extremely powerful. One day he went to the ocean itself and standing on the shore challenged the ocean to a fight! The ocean said to him: 'Pray, do not worry me! I am not your equal in might. But I shall tell you who might be able to take up your challenge. It is the father-in-law of lord Śiva himself. It is Himavān. Kindly go to him and have a trial of strength.'

"Dundubhi lost no time in approaching Himavān. He began to shatter the mountain-peaks and destroy the hills. Tormented in this fashion, Himavān said to Dundubhi: 'Kindly do not torment me like this, O Dundubhi. I am not well versed in battle, for I am an abode of ascetics. I shall, however, tell you who is your equal in strength and heroism, so that you could challenge him to a duel. It is Vāli, the son of Indra, who dwells in the Kiṣkindhā territory. If you wish to meet your match and fight, he is the one you should approach quickly.'

"Dundubhi went to Kiṣkindhā. He lost no time in making his presence felt. He shook the earth, ravaged the forest and roared aloud. Vāli challenged Dundubhi to a fight. As Vāli emerged from the palace he was surrounded by a number of ladies, and he also appeared to be intoxicated. Dundubhi declined to fight him, saying: 'Enjoy yourself tonight, Vāli, and come back to me tomorrow. You are boasting in front of women, and you are intoxicated. It is unethical to fight and kill a person who is intoxicated or who has a broken limb, who is unarmed or who is emaciated. It is equal to the killing of an unborn child. You are drunk and your mind is befuddled with passion.

So, enjoy yourself today and take leave of your friends and relations and your kingdom! You will see them no more.'

"But Vāli would not be put off! He grabbed the demon, lifted him up, whirled him around and dashed him on the ground. Vāli hit Dundubhi with his fists and feet. The demon was dead. However, while Vāli kicked the demon and hurled him to a distance of four miles, blood from the demon fell in the vicinity of the hermitage of the sage Mātaṅga."

Kiṣkindhā 11

"When the sage Mātaṅga found that the vicinity of his hermitage had been desecrated by the blood and that the trees in the neighbourhood had either been destroyed or defoliated, he was annoyed. He knew that it was the work of the jungle folk (vānaras). He came out of his hermitage and saw the vānaras. He uttered a curse: 'He who killed this demon-buffalo (Dundubhi) and who caused blood to fall in the vicinity of the hermitage and he who is responsible for the destruction of this forest which I have nourished like my own child, shall no longer enter this forest; if he does, he will instantly die. Nor shall his companions enter this forest; if they do, they will instantly become rocks and remain petrified for thousands of years. Today is the last day that they will have access to this forest; if they do not leave this forest now, they will be petrified tomorrow.' Hearing this curse and this ultimatum, the vānaras ran to Vāli and in answer to his enquiry, informed him of the curse and the ultimatum. Vāli himself went to the sage and apologised with his palms joined: but the sage would not listen to him.

"From that time, this forest is out of bounds to Vāli and his companions; and therefore it is safe for me to dwell in it. Hence, I have taken refuge in this place. There you see, O Rāma, the huge skeletal remains of the mighty Dundubhi. And, these are the trees that Vāli would shake with his bare hands and defoliate! Such are his powers and such is his strength."

Lakṣmaṇa was amused at this narration which clearly expressed Sugrīva's anxiety and his uncertainty of the outcome of Rāma's encounter with Vāli. He asked Sugrīva: "Well, well, tell me how you can be convinced of Rāma's prowess?" Sugrīva suggested: "Vāli kicked Dundubhi and the demon flew four miles and landed here. If Rāma could kick the skeleton and throw it to a distance of three hundred yards, I should be convinced. O Rāma, I do not belittle your might nor do I frighten you; but having seen Vāli's prowess, I am faint-hearted."

Rāma went towards the skeleton, lifted it up with his toe and tossed it to a distance of eighty miles. Sugrīva was greatly impressed. But a doubt entered his mind: Vāli kicked the full body of Dundubhi, whereas Rāma tossed only the dry bones! Hence, Sugrīva suggested another test: "O Rāma, Vāli could cut these trees down with a single missile from his weapon. Can you also do so? I am sure you can; yet I want to see you do so. Even as the sun is the foremost of radiant beings, the Himālayas the foremost of mountains, and the lion is the foremost of animals, even so you are the foremost among men."

Kiṣkindhā 12

Hearing the words of Sugrīva, Rāma playfully readied his weapon, fixed a missile to it and fired it. This gold-plated missile pierced the big trees, pierced the mountain itself and the whole earth, and, the wonder of wonders, returned to Rāma. Seeing this, Sugrīva bowed to Rāma and said to him with his palms joined in salutation: "O Rāma, you are indeed supreme and can kill even the god of heaven, Indra. I have no doubt about this. My sorrow has now gone, and I am supremely happy, having got you who are equal to the gods as my friend. O Rāma, make haste and destroy my enemy who lives in the form of a brother."

Rāma, too, was eager to do so. He said to all of them: "Let us go." And they moved towards Kiṣkindhā where Vāli lived. Roaring and shouting, Sugrīva challenged Vāli to come out. Vāli, who was of undoubtedly superior strength, was surprised at this effrontery and came out to meet the challenge of Sugrīva. Quickly they joined hands in a duel.

The two brothers, Vāli and Sugrīva, struck each other and kicked each other. The fighting was fierce. Rāma, Lakṣmaṇa and the others watched this terrible fighting from behind trees which stood at a distance. Though Rāma stood with his weapon in readiness to shoot the most deadly missile, he did not shoot because he could not make out who Vāli was and who Sugrīva was! They resembled each other so much that Rāma was undecided. Naturally, Sugrīva was severely wounded, and he flew from the place and rushed up the Ṛṣyamūka hill. Vāli chased him right up to the foot of the hill and then withdrew.

Rāma sought the presence of Sugrīva immediately. Sugrīva was terribly disappointed and disheartened. He said to Rāma: "O Rāma, you have let me down terribly. You could have told me earlier that you did not want to kill Vāli, and I would not have ventured to go to him." Rāma explained: "I could not make out who was who! I did not want to discharge the missile, lest I should kill you. To kill one to whom I have given asylum would be a great sin. Please go again. But this time wear something to distinguish you from Vāli! In this way I may know who is who when both of you close in on each other to fight the duel." At Rāma's instruction, Lakṣmaṇa gathered some wild flowers known as Gajapuṣpi, made a garland of it and put this garland around the neck of Sugrīva. All of them went to Kiṣkindhā once more.

Kiṣkindhā 13–14

Sugrīva led the way. Lakṣmaṇa followed close on his heels. Then came Rāma himself. Behind him were Hanumān, and the other companions of Sugrīva. They proceeded towards Kiṣkindhā. They saw numerous trees laden heavily with flowers. They passed by mountains and caves. They beheld wild animals and birds. They saw many deer roaming the forests. And they saw elephants, too.

Then they entered a charming grove which interested Rāma. Sensing that it was of special significance, Rāma asked Sugrīva to relate to him any story which might be connected with it. Sugrīva then narrated the following story to Rāma: "O Rāma, this hermitage is the abode of the seven sages known collectively as the Saptajana. They were highly self-controlled sages who remained forever suspended with their heads down, and who lay down on water. They ate once in seven days. After thus performing austerities for seven thousand years they ascended to heaven with their bodies. No wild animal or bird dares to visit this grove; and divine fragrance as well as celestial music issues from this place all the time. They who devoutly bow to these seven sages here do not suffer any physical ailment, O Rāma. Hence, it behoves you and Lakṣmaṇa too, to bow down to the sages here and receive their blessings." Rāma and Lakṣmaṇa did so.

Armed with their weapons and their missiles, Rāma, Lakṣmaṇa and the vānaras entered Kiṣkindhā. Sugrīva was itching for a fight. He said to Rāma: "O Rāma, we have reached Kiṣkindhā where Vāli dwells. Pray, be sure to destroy him this time." Rāma reassured him with these words: "O Sugrīva, you have been garlanded by Lakṣmaṇa with these Gajapuṣpi flowers which shine around your neck, distinguishing you from Vāli. Let me see him once and he will immediately fall dead. The end of your misfortune, the end of your fear and grief is near, O Sugrīva. If I fail to fulfil my promise to you, then you can accuse me. I do not boast lest there should be transgression of dharma; but I tell you in truth that I shall fulfil my promise today. Go forth and roar aloud. This will surely attract the attention of Vāli who will then come out to accept your challenge, for heroes do not brook a challenge without returning the courtesy."

Sugrīva advanced towards the palace of Vāli and roared. This sound was so powerful and heart-rending that the birds and the beasts were scattered by it. This further encouraged Sugrīva who ran closer to Vāli's abode yelling all the time!

Kiṣkindhā 15–16

Hearing Sugrīva's yelling once again, Vāli was terribly annoyed. His vanity was hurt. His anger was roused. And, therefore, his radiance was eclipsed as it were. Vāli, the mighty hero of immeasurable strength could not tolerate this insult to his valour. He rushed out of his apartment.

Tārā, his wife, however, intervened and politely said to him: "Lord, I wish you would not rush out to meet Sugrīva like this. It is better to reflect over this new development and take stock of the situation and then fight if necessary after some time. Sugrīva was badly wounded and made to flee a little while ago. He has now returned. Surely, he has someone to help him. Sugrīva is clever. He would not trust an ally whose strength he has not carefully tested. This should be considered.

"Moreover, I heard a little while ago a rumour in the countryside. This rumour was confirmed by your son Aṅgada who had the intelligence reports brought in by the spies. Rāma and Lakṣmaṇa, the sons of Daśaratha, have arrived in this territory. Rāma and Sugrīva have entered into a friendship.

Rāma is mighty, and he is also the abode of dharma. Therefore, I consider that hostility with Rāma is unwise. I am advising you out of affection, not because I find fault with you, O Lord. Let there be no enmity between you and your brother Sugrīva, but let there be forbearance, and let there be friendship with Rāma, too. Let Sugrīva be prince regent and let love be restored between you brothers. Surely, your brother deserves your love and affection."

This wise counsel did not please Vāli who had reached the end of his life-span. He said sternly to Tārā: "Thank you for your advice. You have done your job. You have shown me enough affection. Now you may return home. I shall return after subduing the arrogant Sugrīva. I cannot tolerate his insulting behaviour." Tārā could only invoke the blessings of God on Vāli.

The two mighty brothers immediately joined in the fiercest battle. Vāli hit Sugrīva; and Sugrīva vomited blood profusely. Sugrīva hit Vāli with a big tree: and Vāli reeled under the impact. However, soon Vāli got the upper hand and began to belabour Sugrīva with all his might. Thus tormented, Sugrīva continued to fight, looking around, as if seeking help.

Rāma knew that the time had come for him to intervene. He fixed a dreadful missile to his weapon and fired it. The missile, when fired, left the weapon with the sound of thunder and struck the chest of Vāli. Hit by this missile, Vāli, the mighty warrior who was radiant with valour, fell.

Kiṣkindhā 17

But, Vāli did not die. He wore a celestial chain which had been given to him by Indra, the chief of the gods, and which preserved his life-force, radiance and charm. But the missile of Rāma, with which he had been hit, had illumined his path to heaven and had brought him to the supreme state.

Rāma and Lakṣmaṇa went forward to where he lay on the ground. Looking at them, and in courteous words but harsh tone, Vāli addressed Rāma: "Born of the great emperor Daśaratha, O Rāma, you have committed an unrighteous act. You shot me while I was fighting someone else; you shot me from a place of hiding. People glorify you that you are righteous, devoted to truth, compassionate, etc. I thought all this was true. So, though Tārā my wife had heard that you were here as an ally of Sugrīva, I fought with him. No one would expect you to strike me in an unchivalrous manner.

"Rāma, I have given you no offence at all: I did not encroach upon your territory, nor invade your capital nor did I commit an act of aggression against you. Yet, you sought to kill me, while I was fighting another person! Yet, again, you appear in the disguise of a righteous person, wearing a matted lock and deer-skin and bark of trees. Peaceful negotiation, charity, forgiveness, dharma, truth, firmness, valour, and also the punishment of criminals—these are the qualities of kings. We are primitive jungle folk living like animals on fruits and roots. People usually fight for land, gold and beautiful women; but we have none of these here! Yet, you have sought to kill me, for no apparent reason. Having perpetrated this crime of indiscriminate killing, what will you tell the holy men concerning yourself? Neither my skin nor my flesh is of any use either. Five animals endowed with claws are allowed to be eaten by brāhmaṇas and kṣatriyas (princes and warriors): they are the rhinoceros, the porcupine, the iguana, the hare, and the turtle. But people do not even touch my skin or my flesh, and the meat from my body is forbidden; and yet I, who am endowed with five fingers and toes, have been killed. You have transgressed the bounds of dharma; you have broken the code of morality.

"My wife Tārā did tell me about your arrival here, and of your friendship with Sugrīva to achieve your mission. Had you told me of your misfortune, I would have brought your wife back in no time! I would have roped Rāvaṇa alive and brought him to you. I suppose my end is near; no one can escape death. But, what is your justification for bringing about my end?"

Kiṣkindhā 18

Rāma replied:

"You do not know dharma, or worldly affairs, or the laws governing enjoyment, nor the people's behaviour in different conditions and circumstances: and yet you blame me. The whole earth belongs to the kings descended from Manu and therefore my forefather Ikṣvāku. The present ruler in the dynasty of the Ikṣvāku is my noble brother Bharata. He is the supreme monarch of the whole earth: and I derive my mandate from him, to ensure that all the subjects of that noble emperor observe the laws of virtue.

"I consider that you are the worst among sinners. I shall tell you why. According to the code of righteousness, one's elder brother, father and one's teacher are to be treated as one's father. In the same way, one's younger brother, son and disciple should be regarded as one's son. Yet, here you are: you are living with your younger brother's wife who is like a daughter to you! Dharma is extremely subtle and difficult to understand; and the conduct of the virtuous is difficult to understand; only the Self dwelling in the hearts of all knows what is right and what is wrong. The first and foremost reason why I struck you down was: you are living in sin with your younger brother's wife, and I as a representative of the emperor consider it my duty to mete out this punishment to you. There is in connection with this the well known commandment: 'By undergoing the just punishment meted out by the king, the criminal is purified and goes to heaven. If the criminal goes unpunished, the king is guilty of the crime.' Even mighty ones have been thus punished: and others have carried out expiatory actions to get rid of sins.

"Secondly, Sugrīva is my friend, even as Lakṣmaṇa is. I have given him my word of honour that his kingdom and his wife shall be restored to him. It is my duty therefore to honour this promise.

"You might ask, why I did not fight directly with you and kill you. I say: people kill wild animals or animals which serve as meat from a place of hiding or without any provocation. Hence, it was right on my part to kill you whether you were fighting with me or not, for you are of the same species as forest-dwelling animals. Thus relieved of your sin by accepting the rightful punishment, you will ascend to heaven, O vānara."

Vāli retracted his accusation and apologised for the harsh words he had uttered. He then begged of Rāma: "Pray, let Aṅgada be properly looked after. I know that he (Sugrīva) who has your guidance will rule efficiently and justly. But my only anxiety concerns my son Aṅgada." Rāma reassured him in this regard.

Kiṣkindhā 19–20

When the mighty Vāli fell, the vānaras fled. When Tārā heard the shocking news, she ran to where he was. She saw aras and questioned them: "Why are you vānaras abandoning the mighty king whom you accom-' The vānaras quickly warned Tārā: "Pray, dear t go near where the king's body lies now. Vāli your son Aṅgada is alive. It is better to protect deadly missiles of that mighty Rāma whose valour we have witnessed. Ah, with his missiles he powdered rocks and trees: his missiles are like lightning and have the power of lightning. We have never seen or heard of such missiles. Let us quickly return and guard Kiṣkindhā: any moment now, the victorious Sugrīva along with Hanumān and others might storm the territory."

The noble Tārā was not afraid. She said: "Nay, I shall go to where my blessed husband lies. I have lost him: what shall I do with the kingdom or with Aṅgada?" Soon she saw Vāli fallen on the ground—the same Vāli whose valour rivalled that of the king of heaven, Indra. She saw Rāma and Lakṣmaṇa and also Sugrīva standing nearby.

Tārā collapsed by the side of Vāli's body and lamented: "Lord, why do you not speak to me today? Why have you abandoned me? Surely, the earth is dearer to you than me, O ruler of the earth, and hence today you have abandoned me and you embrace the earth with your limbs. O mighty hero, you have paid the penalty for living with Sugrīva's wife. Nay, I do not find fault with you, nor accuse you. Time alone is your killer: your time had come and therefore you who could not be subdued by anyone in the world have been trapped by Sugrīva. I have never known sorrow, lovingly protected as I was by you: but now I shall have to live as a miserable widow. Your son Aṅgada: who knows what his fate will be now? Ah, well, Rāma has fulfilled the promise he had given to Sugrīva, to kill you and to restore his kingdom and his wife to him. Sugrīva will surely be happy and will rejoice. Brushing aside my warning counsel, you rushed to meet with your own end, O Lord. What shall we, your devoted wives, do now?" All the wives of Vāli joined in the lament. They all prayed to the departed Vāli: "Lord, if we had done anything to incur your displeasure, kindly forgive us." They devoutly touched his feet and shed profuse tears.

Tārā who was thus lamenting the death of Vāli, along with the other wives of the hero, resolved to fast unto death at the very place where Vāli was slain.

Kiṣkindhā 21–22

The wise Hanumān said to Tārā: "O noble lady, after leaving this world, every being gets the due reward for the good and evil actions performed here. One who should be pitied grieves for another. Who should grieve for whom—the dead or the living—when physical life is like a bubble here! Therefore, turn your mind away from this fruitless grief and apply it to the protection of Aṅgada and to the performance of the funeral of the departed hero. Vāli has discharged his duty in this world and he has surely reached the blessed state of righteous monarchs. It is now your turn to discharge the duties allotted to you, O Queen! Let Aṅgada be crowned king and let the funeral rites be performed for Vāli."

However, Tārā was inconsolable. She replied: "A hundred Aṅgadas will not equal in my eyes one Vāli, my dearly beloved lord. You may all go your way: my place is here, where my lord fell."

Of course, Vāli was not dead, for he still wore the golden chain which protected his vital force. He opened his eyes and looked at Sugrīva and said: "Brother, do not blame me for whatever happened. I think that we were not meant to be happy together: hence all this came to be. I shall soon quit this body and this world. I wish that you should be king after me. Pray, listen to my requests and accede to them. First and foremost: kindly look after my son Aṅgada. He is equal in valour and might to me. He has had a comfortable life: let him not be subjected to unhappiness. Secondly, do not disregard the counsel of Tārā. She is never wrong. Thirdly, get busy to accomplish the purpose of Rāma. Not to do so would be breach of trust and might well cost you your very life. Lastly: I shall give you this divine golden chain as my parting gift. Wear this. Its lustre and its protecting power might wane as soon as I die. So let me transfer it to you even before." Vāli took off that chain and gave it to Sugrīva. He knew death was near.

Finally, he said to his son Aṅgada: "My child, consider well the time and place before doing anything. Endure the pleasant and the unpleasant, happiness and unhappiness. Be obedient to Sugrīva. Do not take undue advantage of Sugrīva, as you could of me. Be friendly with his friends and treat his enemies as yours. However, avoid excessive affection and hate towards all: both these are evil; tread the middle path."

Vāli's soul left his body. All the vānaras lamented aloud. They recounted his mighty exploits, particularly his encounter with the celestial named Golabha who fought for fifteen years but was slain by Vāli. Tārā collapsed near the body of Vāli.

Kiṣkindhā 23–24

Tārā again wailed: "Ah great hero! Your body is completely covered with blood and mud; and the presence of the missile which has pierced your heart also prevents me from embracing your body. Fate is in Sugrīva's favour now. Hence, he is victorious. My own sorrow makes me feel that a girl should never be given in marriage to a hero, for sooner or later she has to suffer this agony of separation from him. She may be wealthy and have many sons; yet, she is a widow. I pleaded with you to desist from this fight; you did not like my plea; I could not prevent you from fighting. Now that you are dead, we are all dead."

When Sugrīva saw all this, he was terribly shaken. He approached Rāma and said in a voice choked with grief: "O Rāma, indeed you have shown superhuman valour and might: and you have slain the powerful Vāli. But, now that he is dead, my heart turns away from the kingdom. On account of great anger and hate I wanted the death of my brother; now that he is dead, my heart is tormented with grief. He would never kill me. Even when he could have, he would merely tell me: 'Go away and don't do this again.' But I have been the cause of his death. He was noble; I am ignoble. He was virtuous; I am sinful. Who will absolve me of this sin, O Rāma? I do not deserve the esteem of the people; I do not deserve the throne; how can I, O Rāma, after I have committed this terrible sin which is unrighteous and which is destructive to the whole race? Grant me leave, O Rāma: let me enter into the fire. The other vānaras will surely fulfil your mission and find Sītā for you." These words caused great sorrow and concern to Rāma.

At the same time Tārā beheld Rāma and moved towards him. She said: "Your glory is immeasurable, O Rāma. You are an embodiment of dharma. I have just one prayer to offer you. Please grant it. In the same manner in which you killed my husband, kill me, too, so that I may rejoin him. You know the pangs of separation from one's own wife; let my husband not suffer them. You will not sin by killing me, a woman: for I am but the other half of my husband. Such is the declaration of the Vedic texts, that wife is identical with the husband."

Dissuading her from the wish to die, Rāma said to her: "O heroine, do not allow the mind to entertain such wrong thoughts. The universe has been created by the Lord who has so ordained that happiness and unhappiness should be inseparable from the world. This is the universal law. Therefore give up this grief which is unworthy of the wives of heroes." This appeased Tārā.

Kiṣkindhā 25

Rāma addressed all of them:

"A show of grief does not promote but does impede the progress of the departed soul to its own freedom. Yet, it is good to observe traditional mourning. You have shed enough tears. Now let the funeral rites be duly undertaken.

"Niyati (Time or the inner controller of things or the law of cosmic motion) is the sole cause of everything in this world. And this mysterious force alone is the instrument of action, too. It is this law of cosmic motion that prompts all activities. No one does anything in this world; no one prompts any one to do anything either; all beings manifest their nature, and nature is rooted in the eternal law or Time which alone is the inner prompter. Time does not transcend itself; strictly adhering to its nature, it does not transgress its own bounds. Time (or the law of motion) has no friend nor relation, it is not prompted by motives nor does it seek to overpower anyone: it has no relationships at all, and it is not subject to anyone's will. Yet, the intelligent and wise man can easily discern the changes brought about by time: and one can see that dharma, worldly prosperity and enjoyment are all attained by one in course of time.

"Vāli has fulfilled his duty and has reached the highest abode. It is good that all of you should give up your grief and organise the funeral. It is good to do it at the proper time."

Lakṣmaṇa took charge of the funeral operations. Under his directions, the different vānaras got all the necessary articles together, including a lovely palanquin in which to carry Vāli's body to the crematorium. One of the vānaras rushed into a huge cave and immediately emerged with the palanquin. Sugrīva and Aṅgada lifted up Vāli's body and placed it on the palanquin. The body was then carried to the crematorium. Vānaras preceded the palanquin, paving the way with jewels instead of the usual flower petals. All the vānara-women wailed aloud: and their lament made it look as if the whole forest were mourning the hero.

The body was lowered at the spot chosen for the cremation. Once again, Tārā fell upon the body of her lord and wailed inconsolably, placing his head on her lap. Then, they placed the body on the pyre. Aṅgada offered fire to the pyre in accordance with the tradition and humbly went round the burning pyre.

After the cremation, all the vānaras bathed in the river, offered libations to the departed soul and returned to their homes. Sugrīva approached Rāma.

Kiṣkindhā 26–27

Hanumān said to Rāma: "By your grace, O Rāma, Sugrīva has gained this kingdom of Kiṣkindhā. When you permit him, he will triumphantly enter the territory and be crowned king. Rāma, you will love the Kiṣkindhā territory." Rāma quickly replied to him: "I shall not enter Kiṣkindhā, O Hanumān. My father's command implies that I should not enter a village or a town. Let Sugrīva be crowned immediately." And to Sugrīva, Rāma said: "As soon as you are yourself crowned, install Aṅgada on the throne, too, as the crown prince. I see that the rainy season has just commenced; and it will last four months. It is unsuitable for the work that lies before us. Hence, you can spend those four months in Kiṣkindhā devoting that period to the affairs of the state; and I shall spend that period here in a cave. But, soon after the rainy season, please take quick steps to destroy Rāvaṇa and bring Sītā back to me."

Sugrīva entered Kiṣkindhā. The vānaras cheered him and welcomed him. The leaders of the vānaras gathered all the articles needed to crown him king. They kindled the sacred fire to the accompaniment of Vedic chants. They crowned him king. In accordance with the commands of Rāma, Sugrīva installed Aṅgada on the throne as crown prince. Sugrīva sought the presence of Rāma again and conveyed to him the news of the coronation and, having regained Ruma his wife, he re-entered his apartments in Kiṣkindhā.

Rāma and Lakṣmaṇa took up their abode on the nearby mount Praśravaṇa. They selected a cave on the mountainside, which was spacious and also well ventilated. On the northern side, there was a lovely mountain whose peak looked like a cloud. On the southern side there was another mountain which was snow-capped. And, there was a river flowing nearby. The cave was not far from Kiṣkindhā, either: they could actually listen to the music and the sound of the drums which issued from Kiṣkindhā as the happy vānaras danced expressing their joy. However, Rāma did not find happiness there, without Sītā, who was dearer to him than his very life.

When Rāma expressed his grief, Lakṣmaṇa tried to console him, and added: "I am merely reviving your own power and wisdom but not teaching you." Rāma replied: "I have thrown off this grief which is an obstacle to all undertakings. I am eagerly awaiting the arrival of winter when Rāvaṇa will be conquered and Sītā regained. I am sure Sugrīva will do this for me. A hero rewards help with reciprocity; the ungrateful man who does not repay the debt he owes is shunned by good men."

Kiṣkindhā 28

The rainy season had set in. To assuage the pain of separation from Sītā, Rāma described poetically the beauty and the grandeur of the season. He said to Lakṣmaṇa:

"Behold, O Lakṣmaṇa, the onset of the monsoon. That season is upon us during which nothing can be done to recover Sītā. The sky which received water-vapour from the oceans, held it there for nine months, as it were, is now delivering water! Black clouds are stacked up: and they look like steps—and it looks as though one could ascend these steps and garland the sun! The evening clouds are red and you can at the same time see white clouds around them: it looks as if somebody's bleeding wounds have been dressed in white bandage. The earth is both hot and wet with streams of water: it reminds me of Sītā who is burning with anguish and weeping for me. The mountains appear like religious students: the dark clouds are like deer-skin around the waist, the streams like the sacred thread, and the sound coming from the caves is like OM. Look at that lightning surrounded by dark cloud: like Sītā struggling in the grip of Rāvaṇa.

"Those trees laden with flowers and the others dripping with water, as if they were shedding tears, awaken in me love for Sītā. Cows and bulls seeking each other's company make me long for Sītā. Listen to this jungle orchestra, O Lakṣmaṇa: the bees playing stringed instruments, the frogs vocalising the drum-beats, and the rain-bearing clouds playing the drums. And look at these peacocks dancing merrily. Clouds obscure the sun throughout the day so that one can only surmise that the sun has set by the behaviour of the birds and the beasts. The torrential rains have put an end to the hostility of the rival kings and also to the movement of traffic on the roads.

"Elsewhere: in Ayodhyā, Bharata must have completed all the preparations for the rainy season and must now be observing the vows connected with this season. Sarayū is probably in flood. In Kiṣkindhā, Sugrīva is enjoying life, having recovered his wife and his kingdom. But my grief is boundless; the monsoon season seems endless; Rāvaṇa is a terrible enemy difficult to overcome: thus everything appears to me. I hope Sugrīva, after resting for some time, offers to help me of his own accord. That indeed is the characteristic of a true friend. I hope he does not prove to be ungrateful. Because of the difficulties involved in undertaking expeditions during the rainy season, I did not press him to undertake the task immediately. I am eagerly awaiting the pleasure of Sugrīva and the end of the rains."

Lakṣmaṇa reassured Rāma that Sugrīva would indeed fulfil his pledge and thus consoled Rāma.

Kiṣkindhā 29

The rainy season had departed. The skies were clear. Lightning and thunderclouds had ceased. But Hanumān saw that king Sugrīva was engrossed in the enjoyment of the pleasures of the senses and had forgotten his duty, the due performance of which would earn for him both earthly good fortune and dharma. Indeed, he even neglected the affairs of the state, which he had delegated to his ministers, and had isolated himself from the people: he had entirely given himself up to sense-indulgence. There was no threat to his sovereignty, now that Vāli had been killed, thanks to the prowess of Rāma. But Hanumān saw the danger of unrighteousness, of neglecting duty.

Hanumān knew the art of persuasion and the use of words. Humbly and gently he approached Sugrīva, and by singing his praises pleased him, brought delight to his mind. Then, in the following words, he brought home to the king what was beneficial, truthful and appropriate, in words wisely portraying a mixture of displeasure and pleasure, and bearing the stamp of trustworthiness and certainty:

"O King, you have regained your kingdom and your wife. Your work has thus been accomplished. Now, the work of your friend remains. In this world, O King, he who renders timely help to his friends prospers; his fame grows and his power grows, too. That king to whom his treasury, his armed forces, his friends and himself are of equal importance rules over a mighty kingdom. Hence, one should abandon everything and serve one's friends; else, one invites disaster. Again, such service must be timely: spectacular service rendered to a friend after the time for such service has passed defeats its purpose. Therefore, pray, let Rāma's work be undertaken and ways and means adopted to discover and recover Sītā. Rāma does not remind you of his mission, though surely he is anxious to have it accomplished soon, because he is in your hands now. Moreover, we should not forget that Rāma is powerful and capable enough to destroy even gods and demi-gods, let alone demons: yet, he is waiting to see if you will fulfil your promise. Service of Rāma is good in itself: and even if he had done nothing for you, it would have been praiseworthy to serve him. How much more so when he has rendered inestimable service to you! Hence, pray, command the vānaras to search for Sītā. We shall all of us obey your command and shall not rest till Sītā is found."

Sugrīva commended this advice and commanded that all the vānaras be quickly summoned to Kiṣkindhā. He decreed: "Anyone who does not turn up within fifteen days from now will lose his life." Thus general conscription was ordered by Sugrīva.

Kiṣkindhā 30

Dwelling in the cave, along with Lakṣmaṇa, Rāma was counting the days of the rainy season. Each day seemed interminable, as long as one whole year, on account of his separation from Sītā. He noticed at last that the rainy season had really and truly come to an end. Winter was fast approaching. Sugrīva ought to have been busy sending vānaras out to look for Sītā.

Rāma thought: "While we were together in the hermitage, Sītā used to love the way the crane cried out to its mate: she had the sweet voice of the crane! How does she find any joy now? The aśana tree is in full bloom here, and it reminds me of her; when she perceives the aśana tree in full bloom, what will she do when she is unable to see me? That lovely Sītā whose voice was as sweet as the swans', used to wake up every morning listening to the swans: how does she besport herself now? How miserable she will be, now that she is without me, when she sees the cakravaka birds flying together in pairs, reminding her of me and my love for her? I do not find any delight while roaming the forest, the banks of the rivers or lakes, without her, my beloved Sītā. With her love and longing for me greatly intensified by the onset of early winter, she is surely tormented on account of her separation from me."

Lakṣmaṇa, who had gone out to fetch fruits, returned and saw Rāma seated with a grief-stricken countenance. This was not new: and he knew what was bothering his brother. Lakṣmaṇa said to Rāma: "O noble one! Why do you thus yield to passion, thus denying your own vigour? Grief robs you of the equanimity of your mind. Can you not drive this grief away by means of yoga? Pray, regain composure and peace of mind, and thus regain your inner strength, by means of the practice of yoga (kriyā yoga) and the attainment of the yoga of samādhi; you will then enjoy the ability to do what needs to be done. Do not worry about Sītā: for she cannot be kept away from you by anyone in the three worlds! No doubt, we should do whatever is necessary, and this we should do with extraordinary efficiency and diligence; and even this ought to be done without becoming anxious about the outcome."

Kiṣkindhā 30

Rāma said to Lakṣmaṇa: "Look, O Lakṣmaṇa, the rainy season has come to an end. Indra, the god of thunderstorm, has completed his work and has now retired. The clouds have brought their work to a successful conclusion and they are resting, too. The winds that tossed the rain-clouds here and there and made them empty themselves have ceased. The rumbling and the thundering that filled the sky have yielded to utter silence. The mountain-peaks and the forests shine brilliantly, having been thoroughly washed by the rains.

"The sound of cascading water, the croaking of frogs and the cries of peacocks have ceased. Snakes are coming out of their holes. The roads have been washed clean of mud; and they are once again passable, thus inviting kings to march over them. The waters of the rivers and the lakes are pellucid and clear. Cupid, the god of love, is once again roaming the world ready to awaken passion in the hearts of men and women.

"Now is the time for kings to undertake expeditions against their enemies. And this is the time that had been agreed upon for Sugrīva to send vānaras out in search of Sītā. Yet, I do not see any sign of Sugrīva. The four months of the rainy season have passed; to me they looked like a hundred years, grief-stricken as I was on account of my separation from Sītā. But, Sugrīva has not shown grace towards me. I think that he is neglecting me, feeling that I am 'a destitute, exiled from the kingdom, outwitted by Rāvaṇa, far from home, poor, tormented by passion,' and that I am completely dependent upon him. He himself volunteered to begin the search for Sītā as soon as the rainy season came to an end: now he has completely forgotten, the fool. I think you had better go and tell him: 'That ungrateful man who receives favours from his friends promising to reciprocate, and then fails to honour the promise is most wicked. He is a hero, indeed, who fulfils his promise, whether it looks good or not good. Or, do you wish to provoke me to use my missile once more, as I did in order to kill Vāli?' Now that his own purpose has been accomplished, Sugrīva conveniently forgets his own promise. He has obviously given himself up to the enjoyment of sensual pleasures. Surely, he does not realise what would happen if my anger were roused and directed against him! Better go and tell him: 'The road that Vāli took on his way out of this world is not closed; beware.' Tell him that I shall destroy him and all his people. Say whatever you think is necessary to make him undertake the search for Sītā immediately."

Lakṣmaṇa saw that Rāma was angry; and his own anger towards Sugrīva was fully aroused.

Kiṣkindhā 31

Rāma's anger and grief roused Lakṣmaṇa's fury! He said: "It is wicked of Sugrīva thus to ignore his promise, Rāma. And such wicked people should not be entrusted with the kingdom. I shall send him this very day to the abode of death where he shall behold his brother Vāli. We can then ask Aṅgada to send out vānaras to search for Sītā."

Rāma pacified Lakṣmaṇa with the words: "Noble men like you do not contemplate such a sinful action, O Lakṣmaṇa! The man who destroys anger is a hero, the best among men. Pray, deal with Sugrīva as a friend should be dealt with. Lovingly point out to him the urgency of the matter and the righteousness of the cause."

Lakṣmaṇa, who always did as he was told to do, thereupon considered what he had to say to Sugrīva, the latter's possible reaction and the further approach to him: Lakṣmaṇa was as wise as the guru himself. Yet, full of the anger generated by his brother's anger caused by his love of Sītā, he left for Kiṣkindhā. At his approach, the vānaras who were roaming the forest of Kiṣkindhā were frightened: they sensed his anger and knew the danger of encountering him. Quickly they grabbed whatever rocks and trees they could lay their hands on, ready to defend themselves. Lakṣmaṇa's rage grew worse. Seeing this, the vānaras dispersed and ran to where Sugrīva was.

The leader of the vānaras tried to gain Sugrīva's ear to convey the news of Lakṣmaṇa's arrival. But Sugrīva was too heavily drunk to be able to pay any attention to anything. The ministers of Sugrīva could not decide upon the proper course of action and therefore ordered all the vānaras to defend Kiṣkindhā against Lakṣmaṇa. They rushed back to where Lakṣmaṇa was. Aṅgada went forward to meet Lakṣmaṇa and ascertain the cause of his fury. Still furious, Lakṣmaṇa commanded Aṅgada to announce him to Sugrīva at once.

Aṅgada sized up the situation and returned to the palace and caught hold of the feet of both his uncle and his wife Ruma. Sugrīva was still inebriated. Then all the frightened vānaras yelled in fear outside the palace. This made Sugrīva return to sobriety.

Some of his ministers then submitted: "Rāma and Lakṣmaṇa who are devoted to truth and who wear human appearance are fit to be rulers, though they have given you your kingdom. Lakṣmaṇa stands at your door; and hence the frightened vānaras yell: Do as Rāma did to you, and in good time, O king; and fulfil your promise to him."

Kiṣkindhā 32–33

Sugrīva said: "I have not insulted Rāma nor Lakṣmaṇa. I have not done anything to offend them. Why is then Lakṣmaṇa angry with me?" Hanumān very politely submitted to Sugrīva: "I think the reason is obvious, O King. You had promised to organise the search for Sītā as soon as the rainy season came to an end; the rainy season is at an end, but the search has not started yet. You are unaware of the passage of time. Lakṣmaṇa has surely come to remind you of this! I think it is best for you to offer your apologies to him and immediately implement your promise."

Aṅgada requested Lakṣmaṇa to enter the palace. The palace which had seven enclosures, each with its own gate, showed signs of superaffluence.

Lakṣmaṇa, who possessed an unblemished character, did not enter Sugrīva's own inner apartments: still fuming with rage, he stood alone outside. Sugrīva heard the rattle of Lakṣmaṇa's weapon, and knew that he was there as Aṅgada had said. He said to Tārā: "Pray, go and find out the cause of Lakṣmaṇa's wrath. Surely, he would not behave unbecomingly with you. And then come and tell me the truth."

Tārā approached Lakṣmaṇa and asked: "Kindly tell me the reason why you are angry with us." Lakṣmaṇa was pleased with Tārā's conciliatory approach and said: "Sugrīva is immersed in the enjoyment of sensual pleasures and has lost sight of his promise to us. He is drunk and is never sober. Such drinking is contrary to dharma and the attainment of one's welfare. Drinking is an obstacle to dharma, to material welfare and even to enjoyment of righteous pleasures. Ingratitude is inimical to dharma; and the loss of a friend is inimical to material welfare. And Sugrīva is inviting these two by his neglect of his obligation to Rāma."

Tārā quickly informed Lakṣmaṇa: "In fact, O Lakṣmaṇa, Sugrīva has already taken steps towards the fulfilment of his promise to Rāma. Vānaras have already begun to arrive here in obedience to his command. Yet, I know that he has been negligent. I know the reason for this, too: you do not know the power of lust though you know how powerful anger is. A man subject to lust is unaware of the time and the place, of dharma or of material welfare. Even sages have succumbed to lust; how then do you expect a vānara who is uncultured to overcome it? Pray, come in and meet Sugrīva." Lakṣmaṇa entered and saw Sugrīva seated on his couch with his wife Ruma in his arms. This enraged him further.

Kiṣkindhā 34–35

Profoundly shocked to see Lakṣmaṇa blazing with anger, Sugrīva regained his sobriety. Followed by his queens and others, he humbly approached Lakṣmaṇa with joined palms.

Lakṣmaṇa said, still burning with anger: "A righteous king is honoured by all. The unrighteous king who makes false promises is shunned by all. It is said that one who promises to give a horse and does not fulfil that promise suffers the sin of killing a hundred horses. Disregarding one's own promise is suicide, O Sugrīva. One who promises to help a friend in return for help received, and goes back upon this promise is sinful and fit to be executed. And there is no atonement prescribed for ingratitude. Though the holy ones have prescribed an atonement for even the killing of a cow, for drinking liquor, and for transgressing a vow, they have none for ingratitude. Ingratitude is unpardonable sin. You are an ungrateful vānara, who has forgotten his promise and who is engaged, on the contrary, in the indulgence of the senses. Shame! Whereas you should be busy in the service of Rāma, you are lost in sense-indulgence. Do you also wish to go the way Vāli went, a target for Rāma's blazing missile? You have not tasted the power of Rāma's missiles, and that is why you are behaving like this."

Tārā came forward to answer on behalf of Sugrīva: she said, "O Lakṣmaṇa, kindly do not speak thus to Sugrīva. He does not deserve those harsh words uttered by you, nor is he culpable of the accusations you have made. Sugrīva has not forgotten the debt he owes to the gallant Rāma. It is true that having been deprived of sensual pleasures for such a long time, he has fallen into their trap. We are told that the sage Viśvāmitra spent ten years with the nymph Ghṛtācī as if they were a single day! Sensual pleasure has that power to dull one's perceptions. Surely, lust is very powerful. But, you should not blame Sugrīva without first ascertaining the truth and you should not get so angry. Noble men like you do not let anger rise in them without fully comprehending the facts. I am quite certain that Sugrīva will renounce his kingdom, wealth, his wife Ruma, me and even Aṅgada, in order to do what pleases Rāma. He will surely kill Rāvaṇa and restore Sītā to Rāma. Vāli used to tell us that there are a thousand billion, three hundred and ninety-nine thousand and six hundred demons, in Laṅkā. All these have to be killed before Rāvaṇa can be killed and Sītā rescued. All this cannot be done without proper help and suitable organisation. Sugrīva has already ordered all the vānaras to report to him soon. All the other tribes in this forest are also to report to him soon. Pray, therefore, give up your anger."

Kiṣkindhā 36–37

Hearing the humble and polite submission of Tārā, Lakṣmaṇa felt pacified and gratified. He nodded. Sugrīva said to Lakṣmaṇa: "Whatever I have today, O Lakṣmaṇa, I owe to the grace of Rāma. I cannot repay the debt I owe him. Nor does he stand in need of my humble services. By his own prowess, he can kill Rāvaṇa and regain Sītā; I consider it a blessing that he allows me to assist him in this endeavour. I have not forgotten that with just one missile he pierced the seven giant trees, the yonder mountain and the earth, too! I pray that if I have done anything wrong in my dealing with both of you, out of love or out of neglect, I may be forgiven."

Pleased with Sugrīva's demeanour and words, Lakṣmaṇa said: "In you, O Sugrīva, my brother has an excellent friend and helper. You have a pure heart. You are surely fit to be the ruler of the vānaras. With your help, Rāma will surely destroy Rāvaṇa and regain Sītā. For you are a peer to Rāma himself in energy and strength. Pray, forgive the harsh words I uttered a few moments ago, on account of my sorrow and impatience."

Sugrīva now turned to Hanumān and ordered: "Quickly get the vānaras from the following mountain-ranges: Mahendra, Himālaya, Vindhyā, Kailāsa and Mandara. Get the vānaras who are black in colour and who have the strength of elephants, who live on the Añjana hill and who can run like wind. Also, other vānaras dwelling on the eastern and western mountains, on the Padma, the Mahāśaila, Meru, Dhūmra and also the Mahāruṇa mountains. If they disobey my order or delay in coming here, they will lose their lives. Let swift messengers be despatched at once."

This was immediately carried out. All the vānaras who had been commanded by Sugrīva thus came to Kiṣkindhā quickly. Vast hordes of vānaras moved towards Kiṣkindhā. Thirty million vānaras of black colour, a hundred million vānaras of golden colour from the western mountain, millions of vānaras of the colour of the lion's mane from the Kailāsa mountain ranges, millions more from the Himālayan ranges, more from the Vindhyās, and countless vānaras from the shores of 'the ocean of milk' and a distant continent known as Tamālavana—all of them arrived in Kiṣkindhā, bearing various presents to king Sugrīva. Some of them halted at the site of a sacred rite performed earlier to propitiate lord Śiva; here they ate ethereal fruits and roots which had the power to free one from hunger for a month! They said to Sugrīva: "Vānaras from all the mountains and the forests are here." Pleased with them, Sugrīva accepted their offerings.

Kiṣkindhā 38–39

Sugrīva was happy. With the help of the vānaras that had arrived, Rāma's mission was as good as accomplished. Lakṣmaṇa said to Sugrīva: "Let us go to Rāma." Sugrīva agreed enthusiastically and ordered his body-guards to fetch his excellent vehicle. Soon this vehicle which was plated in gold and had a lovely white hood arrived. Lakṣmaṇa ascended it along with Sugrīva.

Surrounded by just the leaders of the vānara-hordes, Sugrīva sought the presence of Rāma. Seeing Rāma at distance, Sugrīva descended from the vehicle and stood humbly with his palms joined in salutation. All the vānara leaders did likewise, too. Rāma saw in front of him what looked like an ocean of vānaras. He was highly pleased.

Sugrīva fell at the feet of Rāma; and Rāma lovingly lifted him up and embraced him. Rāma then lovingly and gently addressed Sugrīva: "There is a time for acquiring religious merit, dharma, O Sugrīva. And, there is a time for working for material prosperity and for the enjoyment of sensual pleasures. But, one who neglects dharma and worldly duties and is engrossed in sense-indulgence wakes up too late, like the man who sleeps on the branches of a tree and wakes up after falling from it. Now is the time for taking the necessary steps to search for Sītā."

Sugrīva repeated what he had said to Lakṣmaṇa already: "Whatever I have today I owe to you, O Rāma. How can I forget the debt I owe you? One who thus forgets the debt he owes a friend is a vile sinner. You see these vānaras: they are the leaders of vānaras. They have come from all over the world, bringing with them countless vānaras, in order to fight Rāvaṇa, and to bring back Sītā." Rāma was supremely delighted. He said again: "You are my best friend, O Sugrīva: and with your help I shall get rid of all my enemies."

As they were thus conversing with each other, there was a great tumult. Raising a cloud of dust, all the vānaras marched towards where Rāma was. Millions upon millions of vānaras of every description, of every colour and stature, belonging to the various tribes of jungle folk, were there.

Sugrīva introduced them to Rāma. Standing with his palms joined in salutation to Rāma, Sugrīva said: "Let these vānara armies be comfortably stationed on the sides of the mountains and in the forests; and let the commanders of the forces bring me correct information concerning their number and strength."

Kiṣkindhā 40

Later, Sugrīva submitted to Rāma: "Countless vānaras have arrived, each tribe with its own leaders. All of them are endowed with terrible strength and courage. They await your orders: they are your army." Rāma replied: "I think that the first task is to find out whether Sītā is still alive or not, where she is and where is that land where Rāvaṇa lives. You are more qualified than I am to commission these vānara leaders with appropriate tasks in this connection. You know what is in my mind, and you know what is to be done: and you are, to me, next only to Lakṣmaṇa in your understanding of the mission and in your wisdom concerning the right manner in which it is to be carried out."

Overjoyed at the confidence that Rāma placed in him, Sugrīva called upon Vinata, a tribal leader, to conduct the search in the "eastern region". In his briefing of Vinata, Sugrīva said: "Go to the eastern region of the earth, O Vinata, and hly search for the abode of Rāvaṇa and the whereabouts Cross the several mighty rivers, Gaṅgā, Yamunā, Sarayū ers. Make an intense search in the great territories of ɔrahmamāla, Videha, Kosala and others, too. Search the territories of the golden-coloured Kirāṭas. Go to the Yavadvīpa; go beyond this to the mountain Śiśira. Go over to the other shore where you will find the Red Sea. Look for Sītā in the forests in the neighbourhood and on the hillsides. Search all the islands in this region.

"When you cross the Red Sea, you will come to an island which is inhabited by an unusual type of demon. They are called Mandehas and they remain suspended from the sides of the mountains. Every morning they are burnt by the resplendence of the sun and of the sages offering prayers; they fall into the water, regain their life and their vitality and get back to the mountainside where they hang upside down again. When you go beyond this, you will see an ocean which is white, which looks like the ocean of milk. In the middle of this ocean, you will see a white mountain called Ṛṣabha. Beyond that ocean you will come to a fresh-water ocean. In the subterranean regions of that ocean you will find a terrible fire raging which is known as Vadavāmukha. To the south of the northern shore of this ocean you will find a big mountain with golden lustre. In front of that you will see a thousand-hooded serpent, white like the moon, clad, as it were, in a blue garment: it is the support of the earth. Then you will see the mountain that represents the eastern extremity of the earth. Beyond that, and inaccessible, is utter darkness. Search up to this point for Sītā. And, report to me in a month."

Kiṣkindhā 41

To search for Sītā in the southern region, Sugrīva handpicked the best of the vānaras. Nīla, son of Agni, Hanumān, the son of Vāyu, the supremely mighty Jāmbavān (son of the grandfather), and many other mighty vānaras were chosen to constitute this party. He appointed Aṅgada, the son of Vāli, and the prince regent himself as the commander of the vānara forces that constituted this search party.

In his briefing, Sugrīva specially mentioned those places which were difficult of access. He said: "Start with the Vindhya mountains, and the plains of the rivers Narmadā, Kṛṣṇā Godāvarī, and Varadā. Thoroughly search the regions of Mekhala, Utkala, Vidarbha, Vaṅga, Kaliṅga, Āndhra, Cola, Pāṇḍya and Kerala. Then proceed to the Malaya mountains, with the blessings of the sage Agastya whom you will see there.

"Proceed from there to the golden gated city of the Pāṇḍyas whose city walls are studded with precious stones. Between the city and the hermitage of Agastya is the Mahendra mountain which is full of gold, and which Agastya sank into the ocean. Indra himself visits this mountain every fortnight.

"Beyond this is the inaccessible island which is eight hundred miles wide: it is inaccessible to human beings. Search this island carefully. Surely that is the territory of the powerful Rāvaṇa who deserves to be killed. Before you leave that territory make sure that Sītā is not there: do not leave anything in doubt.

"Eight hundred miles beyond that island in the ocean is the partly submerged island Puṣpitaka with its high mountains resembling gold and silver. One hundred and twelve miles beyond Puṣpitaka is the mountain Sūryavān, beyond that Vaidyuta, and beyond that the mountain Kuñjara where the sage Agastya has a hermitage which is eighty miles broad, eighty miles high, made of gold and precious gems. There exists the abode of serpents known as Bhogavatī. Search this most dreadful place carefully. Search the mountain beyond this, known as Riṣabha.

"Beyond that is the world of the manes: do not go there. Wherever you go search for Sītā carefully. Whoever returns first in a month and says Sītā has been discovered will enjoy luxuries equal to mine, for he will be most dear to me."

Kiṣkindhā 42

After the vānaras had been despatched in the southerly direction, Sugrīva turned to Suṣena who had the complexion and appearance of a cloud. Suṣena was the father of Tārā, the father-in-law of the king, and had great prowess. Sugrīva spoke to him, and to the other vānara leaders, among them the vānara named Mārīca and the group of vānaras named Mārīcas (who were the sons of the sage Marīci):

"Proceed in the westerly direction, over the Saurāṣṭra and the Candracitra territories, as also Bahlika and Kukṣi. Search all these territories for Sītā. Then go to the confluence of the

Sindhu river with the ocean. You will find a big mountain there, named Somagiri which has a hundred peaks. On the hillsides in the delightful forests dwell winged lions which carry away huge fish and also elephants. Search these forests carefully.

"When you come to the seashore, you will behold a mountain with a golden peak of eight hundred miles, known as the Pariyatra mountain. A tribe of celestials dwells there: they are powerful. Hence, do not provoke them by disturbing the forest. But search for Sītā there. Near that mountain but in the ocean you will find another mountain named Vajra, which dazzles like diamond and other precious gems. Look well in its caves for Sītā.

"In a quarter of the ocean there stands the mountain Cakravān: Viśvakarma established there the Sahasrāra Cakra, a wheel with a thousand spokes (or a revolver with a thousand chambers). Once lord Viṣṇu killed the demons Pañcajana and Hayagrīva and took the conch from the former and the cakra from the latter. There is also the huge mountain known as Varāha, five hundred and twelve miles long, on which is the golden city of Prāgjyotiṣapura, the abode of the demon Naraka. Beyond that is a mountain made of gold entirely, named Megha, on which Indra the god of heaven was crowned by the gods. Beyond that are sixty thousand golden hills, with the mount Meru on which the sage Merusāvarṇi dwells. Bow to him and ask him about Sītā. But do not proceed beyond this point.

"Do not tarry longer than a month. Along with you, O heroes, my own father-in-law is sent. This father-in-law of mine is a mighty warrior; you should all obey him. Surely, you are commanders of your own forces; but all of you should treat him as your supreme authority. Thus should you go west in search of Sītā. When Sītā is found and is restored to Rāma, we shall have fulfilled our duty. In your expedition, if you find it expedient to engage yourselves in other activities, please do so!"

Kiṣkindhā 43

After Suṣena had departed with his search-party in the westerly direction Sugrīva turned to another mighty vānara named Śatabalī. He said to Śatabalī:

"Followed by a large horde of the vānaras and by your own counsellors who are all descendants of the sun, proceed northward, O mighty vānara! And let a diligent and thorough search for Sītā be carried out by all of you. When we have recovered Sītā and handed her to Rāma, we shall have accomplished the greatest task of our life. His life alone is fruitful who accomplishes the service of one in need, even if the latter has rendered him no service: how much more vital it is when it is rendered in return for a great service!

"Proceed to the land of the mlecchas, the pulindas, the surasenas, the prasthalas, the bharatas, the kurus and the mādras, the kāmbojas and the yavanas, all lying to the north of here. Search there and search in the Himālayan mountains. Go on to the hermitage of the sage Soma, beyond which is the Kāla mountain. Search in the caves for Sītā. Beyond that is the Sudarśana mountain; beyond that Devasakha: search there.

"Beyond that is a desolate stretch of land devoid of mountains, rivers and trees. Get over this quickly. You will see the mount Kailāsa. Beyond the Krauñca mountain is the mountain known as Maināka. When you go over this, you will see the hermitage of siddhas. You will also see women with the faces of horses. Near that you will see the lake Vaikhānasa. Beyond this lake the very sky is illumined by the lustre of the sages who dwell there. Proceed in that direction. You will come across the river Śailoda. On the banks of that river is the territory known as Uttara Kuru. The trees there are laden with flowers and fruits, some of which look like precious stones! From the trees the men and women living there obtain dresses, beds and jewelries. They are very fortunate men and women, and they live there enjoying themselves. No one is unhappy there; and every day they grow in qualities that please the mind. Beyond that is the golden mountain known as Somagiri. They who have reached the world of Indra, the world of Brahmā and the celestial world see that mountain. Even when the sun does not shine there, the whole place is illumined by the shining mountain! Lord Viṣṇu, lord Śiva and Brahmā live there, surrounded by sages. Do not venture into that region. But search all the other territories. And endeavour your very best to find Sītā."

Kiṣkindhā 44–45

Sugrīva was certain that Hanumān alone was capable of accomplishing the task! Hence, though he had employed millions of vānaras to form the search-party, he had a special message for Hanumān. Sugrīva said to Hanumān: "O Hanumān, I do not see any obstruction to you either on land, or in the air or on water, nay not even in heaven. You know all the beings in the three worlds and you know their strength and their weakness, too. One who is equal to you in strength and lustre has not been born in this world, O Hanumān! Hence, you alone should devise a plan for the discovery of Sītā. In you alone is there the strength, the might and the intelligence as well as right judgement."

Rāma was delighted to hear this. He took off his signet ring, giving it to Hanumān with these words: "O Hanumān, please take this ring with you. When you show this to Sītā, she will readily recognise that you have come from me at my request. Your enthusiasm and application to the allotted task, your strength and your valour as also Sugrīva's estimation of you—all these together convince me that you will meet with success. O Hanumān! I depend upon you. You are endowed with great strength. Please do all that is necessary to find Sītā."

Having received their respective commissions, all the vānara hordes led by their respective leaders, departed in their allotted directions. And, Rāma and Lakṣmaṇa returned to their abode in the cave on the Praśravaṇa hill.

As the vānara hordes marched in their respective directions, they enthusiastically shouted: "I will find Sītā." "I shall kill Rāvaṇa." "I can go even to the nether worlds, to find Sītā." "I can cross the ocean, to search for Sītā." "I can cross a mighty ocean, in order to find Sītā." "No one can obstruct my path, and live."

Great was their enthusiasm. Great was their eagerness to achieve the mission of Rāma.

Kiṣkindhā 46–47

While Sugrīva was thus instructing the leaders of the search-party, Rāma was amazed at the detailed and accurate knowledge of the geography of the world which Sugrīva possessed. Out of admiration and curiosity, he asked Sugrīva how he came to know world geography so well and so thoroughly.

Sugrīva replied: "O Rāma, you know how Māyāvi, the son of Dundubhi, challenged my elder brother Vāli, how Vāli chased him into the cave, how I waited outside the cave for a whole year for Vāli to emerge after killing the demon. How I saw blood issue from the cave and how I thereby concluded that Vāli had been killed. You also know that thereafter I returned to Kiṣkindhā and was installed on the throne by the ministers. Vāli returned after some time, having pushed the stone away from the mouth of the cave where I had placed it, and even though I apologised and begged of him to ascend the throne, Vāli was greatly enraged and he pursued me, intent on killing me.

"Then I began to run for my life, O Rāma. I went to the easternmost quarter of the earth, and found that Vāli still pursued me. I then similarly ran in the four directions. During that flight, I saw every part of the earth, which of course appeared like the footprint of a calf. It was during that period that I acquired an intimate and detailed knowledge of the earth. When I returned to Kiṣkindhā, perplexed and unable to decide what to do, Hanumān said to me: 'I now remember that Vāli incurred the displeasure of the sage Mātaṅga who cursed him and forbade him from ever setting foot on the Riṣyamūka hill; if we go there, Vāli will not pursue you.' And I quickly came to the Riṣyamūka hill where I continued to live till recently."

The vānaras who had gone in different directions conducted a diligent search following Sugrīva's instructions. They searched everywhere. They left nothing undone, no place unsearched. But they had no success. At the end of one month from the date they left Kiṣkindhā, they returned to Kiṣkindhā in dejection and despair. They reported to Sugrīva: "O King, we have searched everywhere. When we saw a powerful person, suspecting him to be Rāvaṇa we pursued him, challenged him and even killed him. But we could not find Sītā. But surely, Hanumān will attain success. He has gone in the direction in which Sītā had been taken."

Kiṣkindhā 48, 49, 50

Aṅgada, Hanumān and others went in the southerly direction. They thoroughly searched the region of the Vindhya mountains. Though they searched everywhere for Sītā, they could not find her. In course of time, they reached an utterly desolate region where nothing grew, and there were no birds nor beasts to be seen. In that region there once lived a great sage named Kaṇḍu who was a great ascetic and full of spiritual power. It so happened that during their residence in that region, his son who was just ten years of age, died. The sage was furious and pronounced a terrible curse on the land that could not support the boy's life! And, so it became desolate.

The vānaras went deep into a terrible forest. They saw an awesome demon there. Aṅgada thought that it was Rāvaṇa and in a fierce battle killed him. But, alas, Sītā could not be found. The vānaras' morale was very low. Enthusiasm was at a low ebb.

Aṅgada said to them: "Pray, friends, do not yield to grief, despair, lethargy and inaction. Enthusiasm which knows no despair, efficiency, a mind that is not overcome by lethargy or dejection—these are the aids to the achievement of one's purpose. We should continue our search without the least relaxation of effort. Surely, if you strive earnestly, the fruit of your action is assured. It is also good to remember what our king Sugrīva's displeasure means and what a terrible disappointment to Rāma it would be." The vānara Gandhamādana applauded Aṅgada's exhortation.

All the vānaras, thereupon, went up the Silver Mountain (Rajata Parvatam) to search for Sītā. But they could not find her. They retraced their steps, exhausted and worn out with fatigue.

As they were exploring the caves on the south-western side of the mountain, they discovered an inaccessible cave known as Rikṣabilam, guarded by a demon. They were hungry and thirsty and they saw that the cave contained plants, trees, birds and geese, from which they inferred that there was water in the cave. The cave was very large and very deep. They penetrated deep into the cave and after some time, they found a spot that was clear and visible. Holding on to each other they went towards the clear spot, with great hope and joy.

In that region, they saw gold, precious gems and stones, luxurious apartments and palaces. Amazed to see all these, they went further; and not far they beheld a radiant ascetic woman, clad in bark and deer-skin. Approaching that woman with humility Hanumān asked: "O holy lady, who are you, what is this cave-dwelling and whose are these precious jewels?"

Kiṣkindhā 51, 52, 53

In response to Hanumān's enquiry concerning the cave and herself, the ascetic replied: "O mighty vānara, there was a great magician known as Maya, by whom this cave was built. He was a great builder for the demons in days of yore. He did great penance and thus propitiated Brahmā the creator; and Brahmā transferred to Maya the vast wealth of the sage Śukra. Having obtained what he wanted to, Maya gave himself to the enjoyment of sensual pleasures with the celestial nymph Hema. When he had thus been weakened, Indra wielded his deadly missile and killed him: and Indra appointed Hema to inherit the vast fortune that Maya possessed. I am Swayamprabhā, the daughter of the sage Merusāvarṇi: and I guard the palace of Hema, who is my dear friend. Pray, appease your hunger and slake your thirst, with these fruits and drinks; and then tell me who you all are."

After refreshing himself and all the vānaras, Hanumān narrated to Swayamprabhā the story of Rāma up to the point of his meeting with Sugrīva, and how they were all in search of Rāma's consort Sītā. He concluded: "While we were thoroughly exhausted and fatigued and were tormented by hunger and thirst, we saw aquatic birds fly out of this cave and surmised that there would be water inside. You have saved our lives by your hospitality; pray, tell us what we can do to repay the debt we owe you." Swayamprabhā replied politely: "I am an ascetic, and do not stand in need of anyone's service." Hanumān said again: "Pray, tell us how to get out of here! For we are in a great hurry and we have already exceeded the time allotted to us." Swayamprabhā appreciated their difficulty and asked all of them to close their eyes; and in the twinkling of an eye, they were all out of the cave. Swayamprabhā pointed to Hanumān: "That way lies the Praśravaṇa mountain and in the opposite direction is the ocean." She returned to her cave.

All the vānaras assembled to deliberate the next step. They were greatly worried: for, they had already exceeded the time limit set by Sugrīva, even when they were in the cave. If they returned later than expected and moreover without any news of Sītā, Sugrīva would surely have them all executed. Aṅgada said: "Death is certain for us if we return to Sugrīva after the lapse of the time limit set by him and without any news of Sītā. It is therefore better that we sit down here and fast unto death. In fact I was crowned prince not by Sugrīva but by Rāma. And, Sugrīva who has no great love for me, might take this opportunity to have me killed." All the vānaras agreed: "We have surely offended Sugrīva and it is not wise nor safe to go to him now. Let us continue to look for Sītā and return to Sugrīva after we get some news; or we shall seek to enter the abode of Death."

Kiṣkindhā 54–55

A leader of the vānaras suggested that they should all take refuge in the cave to escape the wrath of king Sugrīva. Aṅgada did not turn this suggestion down. And, Hanumān saw in this the birth of a plot which might lead to a fight between Sugrīva and Aṅgada. Aṅgada was highly intelligent and was a past-master in the art of politics. Hanumān who was wise, thereupon used the third of the four political devices in dealing with an opponent: he created differences of opinion among the vārana-chiefs. He then said to Aṅgada: "You are truly a great hero and very strong. But the vānaras are fickle minded and may not be loyal to you. None of these leaders of the vānaras, not even I, will turn their backs upon Sugrīva and follow you. You are antagonising a very powerful hero, which is unwise. And, the worst of all, you think that this cave is safe sanctuary: it is not. Even Indra broke into it and killed Maya. Lakṣmaṇa's missiles will shatter the whole cave in no time. All the vānaras will very soon abandon you, for lack of supplies of food and other amenities. This plan which has been suggested is fraught with great danger. I think it is wiser to return to Kiṣkindhā and beg of Sugrīva to forgive the delay. He is a righteous person and will not harm you."

Aṅgada retorted in fury: "Whom do you call righteous? Sugrīva? He who seduced his elder brother's wife who is like his own mother? He who blocked his own brother's exit from a cave? He who completely forgot the good done to him by Rāma, when he had achieved his purpose and was enjoying himself? Do not forget that it was for fear of Lakṣmaṇa's anger that he sent out all of us to search for Sītā, not because he thought it was a righteous cause! Do you think that Sugrīva will tolerate me as prince—I who am the son of his enemy Vāli? It may be that he will not openly kill me or harm me publicly. He will surely devise some secret punishment for me; And it is better to die now than to submit to solitary confinement. No, I am not coming. You may return. Salute him on my behalf and tell him everything. Then tell my mother and also queen Rumā."

Saying so, Aṅgada fell down. All the vānaras followed suit and decided to fast unto death. In despair and utter dejection, they even cursed the day on which Rāma and Sugrīva met each other. They were talking loudly about Rāma's banishment, the loss of Sītā, the death of Jaṭāyu, Rāma's killing of Vāli and so on. Even as they were talking, a great danger hovered over their heads.

Kiṣkindhā 56, 57, 58

The sound, the gust of wind and dust preceded the arrival near the cave of a huge vulture. The vānaras who were seated on a flat surface outside the cave saw the vulture perched on a big rock. The vulture was known as Sampāti and was the brother of Jaṭāyu. It said to itself: "Surely, unseen providence is in control of the whole world. By that benign providence it has been decreed that my food should thus arrive at my very door, as it were. As and when each one of these vānaras dies I shall eat the flesh." The vānaras, however, heard this and were greatly disturbed.

With a mind agitated by intense fear, Aṅgada said to Hanumān: "Death has come to us, disguised as a vulture. But, then, did not the noble Jaṭāyu give up his life in the service of Rāma. Even so we shall die in his service. Jaṭāyu suffered martyrdom while actually trying to help Sītā; but we, unfortunately, have not been able to find where she is."

Sampāti heard this. His mind was now disturbed. He asked: "Who is there who mentioned the name of my dearly beloved brother Jaṭāyu? I have not heard from him or of him for a very long time. Hearing of his murder my whole being is shaken. How did it happen?"

Even after this, the vānaras were sceptical: however, they helped Sampāti get down from the rock. Aṅgada then related the whole story of Rāma, including his friendship with Sugrīva and the killing of Vāli. He concluded: "We were sent in search of Sītā. We cannot find her. And the time-limit set by Sugrīva has expired. Afraid to face him, we have decided to fast unto death, lying here."

Sampāti said: "Jaṭāyu was my brother. Both of us flew to the abode of Indra when the latter had killed the demon Vṛtra. Jaṭāyu was about to faint, while we were near the sun. And I shielded him. By the heat of the sun my wings were burnt and I fell down here. Though wingless and powerless, I shall help you in my own way, O vānaras, for the sake of Rāma. Some time ago, I saw a beautiful lady being carried away by Rāvaṇa: she was crying: 'O Rāma, O Lakṣmaṇa'. He dwells in Laṅkā, an island eight hundred miles from here. There, I can actually see Rāvaṇa and also Sītā living in Laṅkā, on account of the strength of my vision. I can also see through intuition that you will find Sītā before returning to Kiṣkindhā. Now, take me to the seaside so that I can offer libations for the peace of my brother's soul." The vānaras gladly obliged Sampāti.

Kiṣkindhā 59–60

Jāmbavān who heard Sampāti mention that he had seen Sītā, approached Sampāti and asked: "Pray, tell me in detail where Sītā is and who has seen her?" Sampāti replied:

"Indeed, my son Supārśva had an even more direct encounter with Rāvaṇa and Sītā than I had. I shall narrate the story to you in detail. Please listen.

"I told you that in a foolhardy attempt to fly to the sun, my wings got burnt. I fell down wingless on this mountain. Just as the celestials are excessively lustful, snakes possess terrible anger, deer are easily frightened, and we vultures are voracious eaters. How could I appease insatiable hunger when I had no wings? My son Supārśva volunteered to supply me with food regularly. One day, recently, he failed to appear at the usual time, and I was tormented by hunger. When I took him to task for that lapse, he narrated what had happened that day. He said: 'I was looking for some meat to bring to you for your meal. At that time I saw a big demon flying away with a lady in his arms. I stopped him wishing to bring both of them for your meal today. But he begged of me to let him go: who could deny such a request? So I let him go. Later, some of the sages in the region exclaimed: "By sheer luck has Sītā escaped alive today." After they had flown away, I went on looking in that direction for a considerable time, and I saw that lady dropping ornaments on the hills. I was delayed by all this, O father!' It was from my son Supārśva that I heard about the abduction of Sītā in the first place. I could not challenge and kill Rāvaṇa, because I had neither wings nor the strength for it. But I shall render service to Rāma in my own way.

There lived on this mountain a great sage named Niśākara. On the day that Jaṭāyu and I flew towards the sun and on which my wings had been completely burnt, I fell down here. I remained unconscious for some time. Later I regained consciousness. With great difficulty I reached the hermitage of the sage, as I was eager to see him. After some time I saw him coming to the hermitage, surrounded by bears, deer, tigers, lions and snakes! When he entered the hermitage, they returned to the forest. He merely greeted me and went in. But soon he came back to where I was and said: 'Are you not Sampāti? Was not Jaṭāyu your brother? Both of you used to come here in human forms, to salute me. Ah, I recognise you. But tell me: who has burnt your wings and why have they been burnt?"

Kiṣkindhā 61, 62, 63

Sampāti continued: "My physical condition and the loss of wings and vitality prevented me from giving a complete account of our misadventure. However, I said to the sage: 'Determined to pursue the sun, we flew towards it. We soared high into the sky. From there we looked at the earth: the cities looked like cart-wheels! We heard strange noises in the space. The mountains on earth looked like pebbles; the rivers looked like strings which bound the earth! The Himālaya and the Vindhyā appeared to be elephants bathing in a pond. And our sense of sight was playing tricks with us. It looked as if the earth were on fire. We then concentrated on the sun to get our bearings right. It looked as big as the earth. Jaṭāyu decided to return. I followed him. I tried to shield him against the fierce rays of the sun; and my wings were burnt. Jaṭāyu fell in Janasthāna, I think. I am here on the Vindhyā. What shall I do now? I have lost everything. My heart seeks death which I shall meet by jumping off a peak.'

"The sage, however, contemplated for a while and said: 'Do not despair. You will get back your wings, sight, life force and strength. A prediction have I heard: soon the earth will be ruled by king Daśaratha whose son Rāma will go to the forest in obedience to his father's will, and there Rāma will lose his wife Sītā in search of whom he will send vānaras. When you inform the vānaras where Sītā is kept in captivity, you will gain new wings. In fact, I can make your wings grow now: but it is better you get them after rendering a great service to Rāma.' Soon afterwards, the sage left this world.

"I have impatiently been waiting for you all, all these hundreds of years. I have often thought of committing suicide; but I have abandoned the idea every time, knowing that I have an important mission in life. I even scolded my son the other day for his having let Rāvaṇa get away with Sītā; but I myself could not pursue Rāvaṇa."

As Sampāti was speaking thus, new wings sprouted from his sides, even as the vānaras were looking on. The vānaras were delighted. Sampāti continued: "It is by the grace of the sage Niśākara that I have regained these wings, O vānaras. And, the sprouting of these wings is positive proof that you will be successful in finding Sītā."

Sampāti flew away, in an attempt to see if he could still fly! The vānaras had abandoned the idea of fasting unto death. They had regained their enthusiasm and their morale. They set out once again in search of Sītā.

Kiṣkindhā 64–65

Sampāti's words inspired confidence in the vānaras, but that enthusiasm lasted only till they actually faced the ocean itself. They reached the northern shore of the southern ocean, and stopped there. When they saw the extent of the ocean, their hearts sank. All of them wailed with one voice: "How can we get beyond this and search for Sītā?"

Aṅgada said to them: "Do not despair, O vānaras! He who yields to despondency is robbed of his strength and valour, and he does not reach his goal." Upon hearing this, all the vānaras surrounded Aṅgada, awaiting his plan. He continued: "Who can cross this ocean? Who will fulfil the wish of Sugrīva? Surely, it is by the grace of that vānara who is able to cross this ocean that we shall all be able to return home and behold our wives and children: it is by his grace that Rāma and Lakṣmaṇa can experience great joy." No one answered. Aṅgada said again: "Surely, you know that you have immeasurable strength. No one can obstruct your path. Come on, speak up. Let me hear how far each one of you can go."

One by one the mightiest amongst the vānaras answered: "I can go eighty miles." "I can go double that distance." "I can cover treble that distance." And so on till Jambavān's turn came. He said: "In days of yore I had great strength and I could easily have gone across and returned. But on account of my great age I have grown weak. Once upon a time when lord Viṣṇu assumed the gigantic form (to measure the whole earth with one foot, and the sky with the other) I went round him. But now, alas, I am incapable of crossing this little ocean."

Aṅgada himself declared: "I can surely cross this ocean and go to Laṅkā. But I am not sure if I can make the return journey. And, if I do not return, my going to Laṅkā would have been in vain." But Jambavān intervened and said: "Oh, no: you should not undertake this task. When an expedition is organised the commander himself should not participate in it. You are the very root of this whole expedition. And, the wise say that one should always protect the root; for so long as the root is preserved one can always expect to reap the harvest. You are our respected leader, and you should therefore not risk your own life in this venture."

Aṅgada said: "If no one else can cross the ocean and I should not, then we are all doomed to die here. What shall we do?" Jambavān, however, had other ideas: he said: "O prince, there is someone amongst us who can do this."

Kiṣkindhā 66–67

Jambavān said to Hanumān: "What about you, O mighty hero? Why don't you speak up? Your might is equal to that of Sugrīva, nay even to that of Rāma and Lakṣmaṇa; and yet you are quiet.

"I shall remind you of your birth and your ancestry. There once was a nymph called Puñjikasthalā. She was once cursed by a sage as a result of which she was reborn as Añjanā, the daughter of a vānara chief called Kuñjara. Añjanā married Kesari. This nymph who had the body of a human woman was once resting on the top of a hill. It is said that the wind-god, by whom her clothes had been blown up revealing her attractive legs, fell in love with her. Her body was, as it were, embraced by the wind-god. But she was furious and exclaimed: 'Who dares to violate my chastity?' The wind-god replied: 'Nay, I shall not violate you, O vānara lady! However, since as wind I have entered your body, you will bear a child who will vie with me in power.'

"Añjanā gave birth to you, O Hanumān! When you were a baby, you once saw the sun in the sky. You thought it was a fruit, and jumped up to pluck it from the sky. But, Indra struck you down with his thunderbolt and you fell down. Your left chin was broken; and hence you came to be known as hanu-man. It is said that when you were thus injured, the wind-god was angered; there was no movement of wind in the world. The frightened gods propitiated the wind-god; and Brahmā the creator then gave you the boon of invincibility in battle. When Indra come to know that you did not die on being hit by the thunderbolt, he conferred a boon on you, that you will die only when you wish to.

"There is no one equal to you in strength or in the ability to cross this ocean, nay, an ocean far wider than this. All others are despondent; the mission surely depends upon you."

When his glory was thus sung and he was reminded of his own power, Hanumān grew in stature, as it were. Seeing him thus filled with enthusiasm, the other vānaras jumped for joy. Hanumān grew in size; and shook his tail in great delight. He said: "Of course I can cross this ocean! With the strength of my arms I can push this ocean away. Stirred by my legs, the ocean will overflow its bounds. I can break up mountains. I can leap into the sky and sail along. I am equal to the wind-god in strength and valour. No one is equal to me other than Garuḍa of divine origin. I can even lift up the island of Laṅkā and carry it away."

Greatly inspired by Hanumān's words, the vānaras exclaimed with one voice: "Bravo, O Hanumān. You have saved us all. We shall pray for the success of your mission, standing on one leg till you return." Hanumān ascended the mountain, ready to leap.

Sundara Kāṇḍa
Beautiful Exploits of Hanumān

Hanumān was preparing to jump into the ocean and to cross the ocean to go to Laṅkā. Before undertaking this momentous and vital adventure, he offered prayers to the sun-god, to Indra, to the wind-god, to the Creator and to the elements. He turned to the east and offered his salutations to the wind-god, his own divine parent. He turned his face now to the south, in order to proceed on his great mission.

As he stood there, with his whole being swelling with enthusiasm, fervour and determination, and as he pressed his foot on the mountain before taking off from there, the whole mountain shook. And the shock caused the trees to shed their flowers, birds and beasts to leave their sheltered abodes, subterranean water to gush forth, and even the pleasure-loving celestials and the peace-loving ascetics to leave the mountain resorts, to fly into the sky and watch Hanumān's adventure from there. Giving proof of their scientific skill and knowledge, these celestials and sages remained hovering over the hill, eager to witness Hanumān's departure to Laṅkā. They said to one another: "This mighty Hanumān who is the god-child of the wind-god himself, will swiftly cross this ocean; for he desires to cross the ocean in order to achieve the mission of Rāma and the mission of the vānaras."

Hanumān crouched on the mountain, ready to go. He tensed his body in an effort to muster all the energy that he had. He held his breath in his heart and thus charged himself with even more energy.

He said to the vānaras who surrounded him: "I shall proceed to Laṅkā with the speed of the missile discharged by Rāma. If I do not find Sītā there, I shall with the same speed go to the heaven to search for her. And, if I do not see her even there, I shall get hold of Rāvaṇa, bind him and bring him over to the presence of Rāma. I shall definitely return with success. If it is difficult to bind Rāvaṇa and bring him, I shall uproot Laṅkā itself and bring it to Rāma."

After thus reassuring the vānaras, Hanumān took to the sky. The big trees that stood on the mountain were violently drawn into the slip-stream. Some of these trees flew behind Hanumān; others fell into the ocean; and yet others shed their blossoms on the hill tops, where they lay as a colourful carpet, and on the surface of the ocean where they looked like stars in the blue sky.

Sundara 1

The mighty Hanumān was on his way to Laṅkā. He flew in the southerly direction, with his arms outstretched. One moment it looked as if he would soon drink the ocean; at another as if he desired to drink the blue sky itself. He followed the course of wind, his eyes blazing like fire, like lightning.

Hanumān flying in the air with his tail coiled up behind looked like a meteor with its tail flying from north to the south. His shadow was cast on the surface of the ocean: this made it appear as if there were a big ship on the ocean. As he flew over the surface of the ocean, the wind generated by his motion greatly agitated the ocean. He actually dashed the surface of the ocean with his powerful chest. Thus the sea was churned by him as he flew over it. Huge waves arose in his wake with water billowing high into fine spray which looked like clouds. Flying thus in the sky, without any visible support, Hanumān appeared to be a winged mountain.

Hanumān was engaged in the mission of Rāma: hence the sun did not scorch him. Rāma was a descendant of the solar dynasty. The sages who were present there in their ethereal forms showered their blessings upon him.

Sāgara, the deity presiding over the ocean, bethought to himself: "In days of yore, Rāma's ancestors, the sons of king Sāgara, rendered an invaluable service to me. And it therefore behoves me to render some service to this messenger of Rāma who is engaged in the service of Rāma. I should see that Hanumān does not tire himself and thus fail in his mission. I should arrange for him to have some rest before he proceeds further."

Thus resolved, Sāgara summoned the deity presiding over the mountain named Maināka which had been submerged in the ocean, and said to Maināka: "O Maināka, Indra the chief of gods has established you here in order to prevent the denizens from the subterranean regions from coming up. You have the power to extend yourself on all sides. Pray, rise up and offer a seat to Hanumān who is engaged on an important mission on behalf of Rāma, so that he can refresh himself before proceeding further."

Sundara 1

Readily agreeing to this request, the mountain Maināka rose from the bed of the ocean. As Hanumān flew towards Laṅkā he saw this mountain actually emerge from the ocean and come into his view. However, he considered that it was an obstacle to his progress towards Laṅkā, an obstruction on his path, to be quickly overcome. Hanumān actually flew almost touching the peak of the mountain and by the force of the motion, the peak was actually broken.

Assuming a human-form the deity presiding over the Maināka mountain addressed Hanumān who was still flying: "O Hanumān, pray accept my hospitality. Rest a while on my peak. Refresh yourself. The ocean was extended by the sons of king Sāgara, an ancestor of Rāma. Hence the deity presiding over the ocean wishes to return the service as a token of gratitude: thus to show one's gratitude is the eternal dharma. With this end in view, the ocean-god has commanded me to rise to the surface and offer you a resting place. It is our tradition to welcome and to honour guests, even if they are ordinary men; how much more important it is that we should thus honour men like you! There is yet another reason why I plead that you should accept my hospitality! In ancient times, all the mountains were endowed with wings. They used to fly around and land where they liked; thus, they terrorised sages and other beings. In answer to their prayer, Indra the chief of gods, wielded his thunderbolt and clipped off the wings of the mountains. As Indra was about to strike me, the wind-god bore me violently away and hid me in the ocean—so that I escaped Indra's wrath. I owe a debt of gratitude to the wind-god who is your god-father. Pray, allow me to discharge that debt by entertaining you."

Hanumān replied politely: "Indeed, I accept your hospitality, in spirit. Time is passing; and I am on an urgent mission. Moreover, I have promised not to rest till my task is accomplished. Hence, forgive my rudeness and discourtesy: I have to be on my way." As a token acceptance of Maināka's hospitality, Hanumān touched the mountain with his hand and was soon on his way. The gods and the sages who witnessed this scene were greatly impressed with Maināka's gesture of goodwill and Hanumān's unflagging zeal and determination. Indra, highly pleased with the Maināka mountain, conferred upon it the boon of fearlessness.

Sundara 1

The gods and the sages overseeing Hanumān's flight to Laṅkā had witnessed his first feat of strength when he took off from the Mahendra mountain, and his second feat of strength and enthusiasm when he declined even to rest and insisted on the accomplishment of the mission. They were eager to assure themselves still more conclusively of his ability to fulfil the task he had undertaken.

The gods and the sages now approached Surasā (mother of the Nāgas) and said to her: "Here is Hanumān, the god-child of the wind-god, who is flying across the ocean. Pray, obstruct his path just a short while. Assume a terrible demoniacal form, with the body as big as a mountain, with terrible looking teeth and eyes, and mouth as wide as space. We wish to ascertain Hanumān's strength. And we therefore wish to see whether when he is confronted by you, he triumphs over you or becomes despondent."

In obedience to their command, Surasā assumed a terrible form and confronted Hanumān with her mouth wide open. She said to him, as he approached her mouth while flying in the air: "Ah, fate has decreed that you should serve as my food today! Enter my mouth and I shall eat you up."

Hanumān replied: "O lady, I am on an important mission. Rāma, the son of king Daśaratha, came to the forest to honour his father's promise. While he was in the forest with his wife,

Sītā, and his brother, Sītā was abducted by Rāvaṇa, the ruler of Laṅkā. I am going to Laṅkā to find her whereabouts. Do not obstruct my path now. Let me go. If the gods have ordained that I should enter your mouth, I promise that as soon as I discover Sītā and inform Rāma of her whereabouts, I shall come back and enter your mouth."

But, Surasā could not be put off. She repeated: "No one can escape me; and it has been decreed that you shall enter my mouth." She opened her mouth wide. Hanumān, by his yogic power, made himself minute, quickly entered her mouth and as quickly got out! He then said to her: "O lady, let me now proceed. I have fulfilled your wish and honoured the gods' decree: I have entered your mouth! Salutations to you! I shall go to where Sītā is kept in captivity."

Surasā abandoned her demoniacal form and resumed her own form which was pleasant to look at. She blessed Hanumān: "Go! You will surely find Sītā and re-unite her with Rāma." The gods and the sages were thrilled to witness this third triumph of Hanumān.

Sundara 1

Hanumān continued to fly towards Laṅkā, along the aerial route which contains rain-bearing clouds, along which birds course, where the masters of music move about, and along which aerial cars which resemble lions, elephants, tigers, birds and snakes, fly—the sky which is also the abode of holy men and women with an abundant store of meritorious deeds, which serves as a canopy created by the creator Brahmā to protect living beings on earth, and which is adorned with planets, the moon, the sun and the stars.

As he flew onwards, he left behind him a black trail which resembled black clouds, and also trails which were red, yellow and white. He often flew through cloud-formations.

A demoness called Simhikā saw Hanumān flying fearlessly in the sky and made up her mind to attack him. She said to herself: "I am hungry. Today I shall swallow this big creature and shall appease my hunger for some time." She caught hold of the shadow cast by Hanumān on the surface of the ocean. Immediately, Hanumān's progress was arrested and he was violently pulled down. He wondered: "How is it that suddenly I am dragged down helplessly?" He looked around and saw demoness Simhikā. He remembered the description ugrīva had given of her and knew it was Simhikā doubt.

umān stretched his body and the demoness opened he outh wide. He saw her mouth and her inner vital organs through it. In the twinkling of an eye, he reduced himself to a minute size and dropped into her mouth. He disappeared into that wide mouth. The gods and the sages witnessing this were horrified. But with his adamantine nails he tore open the vital parts of the demoness and quickly emerged from her body. Thus, with the help of good luck, firmness and dexterity Hanumān triumphed over this demoness. The gods applauded this feat and said: "He in whom are found (as in you) these four virtues (firmness, vision, wisdom and dexterity) does not despair in any undertaking."

Hanumān had nearly covered the eight hundred miles, to his destination. At a short distance he saw the shore of Laṅkā. He saw thick forests. He saw the mountains known as Lamba. And he saw the capital city Laṅkā built on the mountains. Not wishing to arouse suspicion, he softly landed on the Lamba mountains which were rich in groves of Ketaka Uddalaka and cocoanut trees.

Sundara 2

Though Hanumān had crossed the sea, covering a distance of eight hundred miles, he felt not the least fatigue nor exhaustion. Having landed on the mountain range close to the shore of the ocean, Hanumān roamed the forests for some time. In them he saw trees of various kinds, bearing flowers and fruits. He saw the city of Laṅkā situated on the top of a hill, surrounded by wide moats and guarded by security forces of demons. He approached the northern gate to the city and quietly surveyed it. That gate was guarded by the most ferocious looking demons armed to the teeth with the most powerful weapons. Standing there, he thought of Rāvaṇa, the abductor of Sītā.

Hanumān thought: "Even if the vānara forces do come here, of what use would that be? For Rāvaṇa's Laṅkā cannot be conquered even by the gods. Only four of us can cross the ocean and come here—Aṅgada, Nīla, Sugrīva and myself. And that is totally useless. One cannot negotiate with these demons and win them over by peaceful means. Anyhow, I shall first find out if Sītā is alive or not, and only then consider the next step."

In order to find out where Sītā was kept in captivity, he had to enter Laṅkā. The wise Hanumān considered that aspect of his mission. He thought: "Surely, I must be very careful, cautious and vigilant. If I am not, I might ruin the whole mission. An undertaking even after it has been carefully deliberated and decided upon will fail if it is mishandled by an ignorant or inefficient messenger. Therefore I should consider well what should be done and with due regard to all the pros and cons, I should vigilantly ensure that I do nothing which ought not to be done. I should enter the city in such a way that my presence and my movements are not detected; and I see that Rāvaṇa's security forces are so very efficient that it will not be easy to escape detection."

Thus resolved, Hanumān reduced himself to a small size, to the size of a cat as it were, and when darkness had fallen, proceeded towards the city. Even from a distance he could see the affluence that the city enjoyed. It had buildings of many storeys. It had archways made of gold. It was brilliantly lit and tastefully decorated. The city was of unimaginable beauty and glory. When Hanumān saw it, he was filled with a mixture of feelings, feelings of despondence, and joy—joy at the prospect of seeing Sītā, and despondency at the thought of the difficulty involved in it.

Unnoticed by the guards, Hanumān entered the gateway.

Sundara 3

Hanumān was still contemplating the difficulties of the imminent campaign for the recovery of Sītā. Conquering Laṅkā by force seemed to him to be out of the question. He thought: "Possibly only Kumuda, Aṅgada, Suṣena, Mainda, Dvivida, Sugrīva, Kuśaparva, Jāmbavān and myself may be in a position to cross the ocean and come here. However, in spite of the heavy odds against such a campaign, there is the immeasurable prowess of Rāma and Lakṣmaṇa: surely they can destroy the demons without any difficulty whatsoever."

As he was entering the city, he was intercepted by Laṅkā, the guardian of the city. She questioned him: "Who are you, O vānara? This city of Laṅkā cannot be entered by you!"

Hanumān was in no mood to reveal his identity: and he questioned her, in his turn: "Who are you, O lady? And why do you obstruct my path?" Laṅkā replied: "At the command of the mighty Rāvaṇa, I guard this city. No one can ignore me and enter this city: and you, O vānara, will soon enter into eternal sleep, slain at my hands!"

Hanumān said to her: "I have come as a visitor to this city, to see what is to be seen here. When I have seen what I wish to see, I shall duly return to where I have come from. Pray, let me proceed." But Laṅkā continued to say: "You cannot enter without overpowering me or winning my permission," and actually hit Hanumān on his chest with her hand.

Hanumān's anger was aroused. Yet, he controlled himself: for he did not consider it right to kill a woman! He clenched his fist and struck Laṅkā. She fell down, and then revealed: "Compose yourself, O vānara! Do not kill me. The truly strong ones do not violate the code of chivalry, and they do not kill a woman. I am Laṅkā, and he who has conquered me has conquered Laṅkā. That was what Brahmā the creator once said: 'When a vānara overpowers you, know that then the demons have cause for great fear.' I am sure that this prophecy refers to you, O vānara! I realise now that the inevitable destruction of the demons of Laṅkā has entered the territory in the form of Sītā who has been forcibly brought here by Rāvaṇa. Go, enter the city: and surely you will find Sītā and accomplish all that you desire to accomplish."

Sundara 4–5

Hanumān did not enter the city through the heavily guarded main gate, but climbed over the wall. Then he came to the main road and proceeded towards his destination—the abode of Rāvaṇa. On the way Hanumān saw the beautiful mansions from which issued the sound of music, and the sound of the citizens' rejoicing. He saw, too, prosperous looking mansions of different designs calculated to bring happiness and greater prosperity to the owners of the mansions. He heard the shouts of wrestling champions. Here and there he heard bards and others singing the glories of Rāvaṇa, and he noticed that these bards were surrounded by citizens in large numbers, blocking the road.

Right in the heart of the city, Hanumān saw in the main square numerous spies of Rāvaṇa: and these spies looked like holy men, with matted hair, or with shaven heads, clad in the hides of cows or in nothing at all. In their hands they carried all sorts of weapons, right from a few blades of grass to maces and sticks. They were of different shapes and sizes and of different appearance and complexions. Hanumān also saw the garrison with a hundred thousand soldiers right in front of the inner apartments of Rāvaṇa.

Hanumān approached the palace of Rāvaṇa himself. This was a truly heavenly abode. Within the compound of the palace and around the building there were numerous horses, chariots, and also aeroplanes. The palace was built of solid and pure gold and the inside was decorated with many precious stones, fragrant with incense and sandalwood which had been sprinkled everywhere: Hanumān entered the palace.

It was nearly midnight. The moon shone brilliantly overhead. From the palace wafted the strains of stringed musical instruments; good-natured women were asleep with their husbands; the violent night-stalkers also emerged from their dwellings to amuse themselves. In some quarters, Hanumān noticed wrestlers training themselves. In some others, women were applying various cosmetic articles to themselves. Some other women were sporting with their husbands. Others whose husbands were away looked unhappy and pale, though they were still beautiful. Hanumān saw all these: but he did not see Sītā anywhere.

Not seeing Sītā, the beloved wife of Rāma, Hanumān felt greatly distressed and unhappy and he became moody and dejected.

Sundara 6, 7, 8

Hanumān was greatly impressed by the beauty and the grandeur of Rāvaṇa's palace which he considered to be the crowning glory of Laṅkā itself. He did not all at once enter Rāvaṇa's inner apartments. First he surveyed the palaces of the other members of the royal family and the leaders of the demons, like Prahasta. He surveyed the palaces of Rāvaṇa's brothers Kumbhakarṇa and Vibhīṣaṇa, as also that of Rāvaṇa's son Indrajit. He was greatly impressed by the unmistakable signs of prosperity that greeted him everywhere. After thus looking at the palaces of all these heroes, Hanumān reached the abode of Rāvaṇa himself.

Rāvaṇa's own inner apartments were guarded by terrible looking demons, holding the most powerful weapons in their hands. Rāvaṇa's own private palace was surrounded by more armed forces; and even these garrisons were embellished by gold and diamonds. Hanumān entered the palace and saw within it palanquins, couches, gardens and art galleries, special chambers for enjoying sexual pleasures and others for indulging in other pastimes during the day., There were also special altars for the performance of sacred rituals. The whole palace was resplendent on account of the light emitted by precious stones which were found everywhere. Everywhere the couches, the seats and the dining vessels were of gold; and the floor of the whole palace was fragrant with the smell of wine and liquor. In fact Hanumān thought that the palace looked like heaven on earth, resplendent with the wealth of precious gems, and fragrant with the scent of a variety of flowers which covered its dome making it look like a flower-covered hill.

There were swimming pools with lotuses and lilies. In one of them there was the carved figure of a lordly elephant offering worship to Lakṣmī, the goddess of wealth.

Right in the centre of the palace stood the best of all aeroplanes, known as Puṣpaka. It had been painted with many colours and provided with numerous precious gems. It was decorated with lovely figures of snakes, birds, and horses fashioned of gems, silver and coral. Every part of that aeroplane had been carefully engineered, only the very best materials had been used, and it had special features which even the vehicles of the gods did not have—in fact, in it had been brought together only special features! Rāvaṇa had acquired it after great austerities and effort.

Hanumān saw all this. But, he did not see Sītā anywhere!

Sundara 9

Hanumān ascended the aeroplane Puṣpaka from which he could easily look into the inner apartments of Rāvaṇa! As he stood on the aeroplane, he smelt the extraordinary odour emanating from Rāvaṇa's dining room—the odour of wines and liquors, the smell of excellent food. The smell was appetising and Hanumān thought the food should be nourishing. And, he saw at the same time the beautiful hall of Rāvaṇa which had crystal floors, with inlaid figures made of ivory, pearls, diamonds, corals, silver and gold. The hall was resplendent with pillars of gems. There was on the floor, a carpet of extraordinary beauty and design. On the walls were murals of several countries' landscapes. This hall thus provided all the five senses with the objects for their utmost gratification! A soft light illumined this hall.

On the carpet beautiful women lay asleep. With their mouths and their eyes closed, they had fallen asleep, after drinking and dancing, and from their bodies issued the sweet fragrance of lotuses. Rāvaṇa, sleeping there surrounded by these beautiful women, looked like the moon surrounded by the stars in the night sky. They were all asleep in beautiful disorder. Some were using their own arms as the pillow, others used the different parts of yet others' bodies as their pillow. Their hair was in disarray. Their dress was in disarray, too. But none of these conditions diminished the beauty of their forms. From the breath of all the women there issued the smell of liquor.

These women had come from different grades of society. Some of them were the daughters of royal sages, others those of brāhmaṇas, yet others were the daughters of gandharvas (celestial artists), and, of course, some were the daughters of demons: and all of them had voluntarily sought Rāvaṇa, for they loved him. Some he had won by his valour; others had become infatuated with him. None of these women had been carried away by Rāvaṇa against their wish. None of them had been married before. None of them had desire for another man. Rāvaṇa had never before abducted any woman, except Sītā.

Hanumān thought for a moment: Rāvaṇa would indeed have been a good man if he had thus got Sītā too, to be his wife: that is, before she had married Rāma and if he had been able to win her by his valour or by his charm. But, Hanumān contemplated further: by abducting the wife of Rāma, Rāvaṇa had certainly committed a highly unworthy action.

Sundara 10–11

In the centre of that hall, Hanumān saw the most beautiful and the most luxurious bed: it was celestial in its appearance, built entirely of crystal and decked with gems. The lord of the demons, Rāvaṇa himself was asleep on it. The sight of this demon was at first revolting to Hanumān; so he turned his face away from Rāvaṇa. But then he turned his gaze again to Rāvaṇa. He saw that the two arms of Rāvaṇa were strong and powerful, and they were adorned with resplendent jewelry. His face, his chest, in fact his whole body was strong and radiant. His limbs shone like the lightning.

Around this bed were others on which the consorts of Rāvaṇa were asleep. Many of them had obviously been entertaining the demon with their music; and they had fallen asleep with the musical instruments in their arms. On yet another bed was asleep the most charming of all the women in that hall: she surpassed all the others in beauty, in youth and in adornment. For a moment Hanumān thought it was Sītā: and the very thought that he had seen Sītā delighted him.

But that thought did not last long. Hanumān realised: "It cannot be. For, separated from Rāma, Sītā will not sleep, nor will she enjoy herself, adorn herself or drink anything. Nor will Sītā ever dwell with another man, even if he be a celestial: for truly there is none equal to Rāma." He turned away from the hall, since he did not see Sītā there.

Next, Hanumān searched the dining hall and the kitchen: there he saw varieties of meats and other delicacies, condiments and a variety of drinks. The dining hall floor had been strewn with drinking vessels, fruits and even anklets and armlets which had obviously fallen from their wearers as they were drinking and getting intoxicated.

While he was thus inspecting the palace and searching for Sītā, a thought flashed in Hanumān's mind: was he guilty of transgressing the bounds of morality, in as much as he was gazing at the wives of others, while they were asleep with their ornaments and clothes in disarray? But, he consoled himself with the thought: "True, I have seen all these women in Rāvaṇa's apartment. But, no lustful thought has entered my mind! The mind alone is the cause of good and evil actions performed by the senses; but my mind is devoted to and established in righteousness. Where else can I look for Sītā, except among the womenfolk in Rāvaṇa's palace: shall I look for a lost woman among a herd of deer? I have looked for Sītā in this place with a pure mind; but she is not to be seen."

Sundara 12–13

Hanumān had searched the whole palace of Rāvaṇa. But he could not find Sītā. He reflected: "I shall not yield to despair. For, it has been well said that perseverance alone is the secret of prosperity and great happiness; perseverance alone keeps all things going, and crowns all activities with success. I shall search those places which I have not yet searched." He then began to search for Sītā in other parts of the palace. He saw many, many other women, but not Sītā.

Hanumān then searched for Sītā outside the palace. Yet, he could not find her. Once again dejection gripped him. He thought: "Sītā is to be found nowhere; yet Sampāti did say that he saw Rāvaṇa and he saw Sītā, too. Perhaps it was mistaken identity. It may be that slipping from the control of Rāvaṇa, Sītā dropped her body into the sea. Or, it may be she died of shock. Or, perhaps when she did not yield to him, Rāvaṇa killed her and ate her flesh. But it is impossible that she had consented to be Rāvaṇa's consort. Whether she is lost, or she has perished or has died, how can I inform Rāma about it? On the other hand, to inform Rāma and not to inform Rāma—both these appear to be objectionable. What shall I do now?" He also reflected on the consequence of his returning to Kiṣkindhā with no news of Sītā. He felt certain that: "When Rāma hears the bad news from me, he will give up his life. So will Lakṣmaṇa. And then their brothers and mothers in Ayodhyā. Nor could Sugrīva live after Rāma departs from this world. He will be followed to the other world by all the vānaras of Kiṣkindhā. What a terrible calamity will strike Ayodhyā and Kiṣkindhā if I return without news of Sītā's safety!" He resolved: "It is good that I should not return to Kiṣkindhā. Like an ascetic I shall live under a tree here. Or, I can commit suicide by jumping into the sea. However, the wise ones say that suicide is the root of many evils, and that if one lives one is sure to find what one seeks."

The consciousness of his extraordinary strength suddenly seized Hanumān! He sprang up and said to himself: "I shall at once kill this demon Rāvaṇa. Even if I cannot find Sītā, I shall have avenged her abduction by killing her abductor. Or, I shall kidnap him and take him to Rāma." Then he thought of a few places in Laṅkā he had not yet searched; one of them was Aśoka-grove. He resolved to go there. Before doing so, he offered a prayer: "Salutations to Rāma and Lakṣmaṇa; salutations to Sītā, the daughter of Janaka. Salutations to Rudra, Indra, Yama, the wind-god, to the moon, fire, and the Maruts." He turned round in all directions and invoked the blessings of all. He knew he needed them for he felt that demons of superhuman strength were guarding the Aśoka-grove.

Sundara 14–15

Hanumān then climbed the palace wall and jumped into the Aśoka-grove. It was most beautiful and enchanting, with trees and creepers of innumerable types.

In that grove, Hanumān also saw the bird sanctuary, the ponds and artificial swimming pools hemmed by flights of steps which had been paved with expensive precious and semi-precious stones. He also saw a hill with a waterfall flowing from its side. Not far from there, he saw a unique Aśoka or Simśapā tree which was golden in its appearance. The area around this tree was covered with trees which had golden leaves and blossoms, giving the appearance that they were ablaze.

Climbing up that unique Simśapā tree, Hanumān felt certain that he would soon see Sītā. He reasoned: "Sītā was fond of the forests and groves, according to Rāma. Hence, she will doubtless come to this yonder lotus-pond. Rāma did say that she was fond of roaming the forest: surely, then, she would wish to roam this grove, too. It is almost certain that the grief-stricken Sītā would come here to offer her evening prayers. If she is still alive, I shall surely see her today."

Seated on that Aśoka or Simśapā tree, Hanumān surveyed the whole of the grove. He was enthralled by the beauty of the grove, of the trees, and of the blossoms which were so colourful that it appeared as if the whole place were afire. There were numerous other trees, too, all of which were delightful to look at. While he was thus surveying the scene, he saw a magnificent temple, not far from him. This temple had a hall of a thousand pillars, and looked like the Kailāsa. The temple had been painted white. It had steps carved out of coral. And its platforms were all made of pure gold.

And, then, Hanumān saw a radiant woman with an ascetic appearance. She was surrounded by demonesses who were apparently guarding her. She was radiant though her garments were soiled. She was beautiful in form, though emaciated through sorrow, hunger and austerity. Hanumān felt certain that it was Sītā, and that it was the same lady whom he had momentarily seen over the Ṛṣymūka hill. She was seated on the ground. And, she was frequently sighing, surely on account of her separation from Rāma. With great difficulty, Hanumān recognised her as Sītā: and in this he was helped only by the graphic and vivid description that Rāma had given him.

Looking at her, thus pining for Rāma, and recollecting Rāma's love for her, Hanumān marvelled at the patience of Rāma in that he could live without Sītā even for a short while.

Sundara 16–17

Hanumān contemplated the divine form of Sītā for a few minutes; and he once again gave way to dejection. He reflected: "If even Sītā who is highly esteemed by the noble and humble Lakṣmaṇa, and who is the beloved of Rāma himself, could be subjected to such sorrow, indeed one should conclude that Time is all-powerful. Surely, Sītā is utterly confident in the ability of Rāma and Lakṣmaṇa to rescue her; and hence she is tranquil even in this misfortune. Only Rāma deserves to be her husband, and she to be Rāma's consort." How great was Rāma's love for Sītā! And, what an extraordinary person Sītā was! Hanumān continued to 'weigh' her in his own mind's balance: "It was for the sake of Sītā that thousands of demons in the Daṇḍaka forest were killed by Rāma. It was for her sake alone that Rāma killed Vāli and Kabandha. Khara, Dūṣaṇa, Triśira—so many of these demons met their end because of her. And, why not: she is such a special person that if, for her sake, Rāma turned the whole world upside down it would be proper. For, she was of extraordinary birth, she is of extraordinary beauty and she is of extraordinary character. She is unexcelled in every way. And, what an extraordinary love she has for Rāma, in that she patiently endures all sorts of hardships living, as she does, as a captive in Laṅkā. Again, Rāma pines for her and is eagerly waiting to see her, to regain her. Here she is, constantly thinking of Rāma: she does not see either these demonesses guarding her, nor the trees, flowers or fruits, but with her heart centred in Rāma, she sees him alone constantly." He was now certain that that lady was in fact Sītā.

The moon had risen. The sky was clear and the moonlight enabled Hanumān to see Sītā clearly. He saw the demonesses guarding Sītā. They were hideous-looking and deformed in various parts of their bodies. Their lips, breasts and bellies were disproportionately large and hanging. Some were very tall; others were very short. They were mostly dark-complexioned. Some of them had ears, etc., that made them look like animals. They were querulous, noisy, and fond of flesh and liquor. They had smeared their bodies with meat and blood; and they ate meat and blood. Their very sight was revolting and frightening. There in their midst was Sītā.

Sītā's dress and her appearance reflected her grief. At the foot of the tree whose name, Aśoka, meant free of sorrow, was seated Sītā immersed in an ocean of sorrow, surrounded by these terrible demonesses! It was only her confidence in the prowess and the valour of her lord Rāma that sustained her life. Hanumān mentally prostrated to Rāma, to Lakṣmaṇa and to Sītā and hid himself among the branches of the tree.

Sundara 18, 19, 20

Night was drawing to a close. In his palace, Rāvaṇa was being awakened by the Vedic recitation of brāhmaṇa-demons who were well versed in the Vedas and other scriptural texts, and also by musicians and bards who sang his praises. Even before he had time to adorn himself properly, Rāvaṇa thought of Sītā and longed intensely to see her. Quickly adorning himself with the best of ornaments and clad in splendid garments, he entered the Aśoka-grove, accompanied by a hundred chosen women who carried golden torches, fans, cushions and other articles. They were still under the influence of alcohol: and Rāvaṇa, though mighty and powerful, was under the influence of passion for Sītā.

Hanumān recognised the person he had seen asleep in the palace the previous night.

Seeing him coming in her direction, the frightened Sītā shielded her torso with her legs and hands, and began to weep bitterly. Pining for Rāma, distressed on account of her spearation from him and stricken with grief, the most beautiful and radiant Sītā resembled eclipsed fame, neglected faith, enfeebled understanding, forlorn hope, ruined prospect, disregarded command, and obstructed worship; eclipsed moon, decimated army, fuelless flame, river in drought. She was constantly engaged in the prayer that Rāma might soon triumph over Rāvaṇa and rescue her.

Rāvaṇa appeared to be chivalrous in his approach to Sītā, and his words were meaningful and sweet: he said to Sītā, "Pray, do not be afraid of me, O charming lady! It is natural for a demon to enjoy others' wives and abduct them forcibly; it is the demon's own dharma. But, I shall not violate you against your wishes. For, I want to win your love; I want to win your esteem. I have enough strength to restrain myself. Yet, it breaks my heart to see you suffer like this; to see you, a princess, dressed like this in tattered and dirty garments. You are born to apply the most delightful cosmetic articles, to wear royal attire, and to adorn yourself with the most expensive jewels. You are young, youthful: this is the time to enjoy yourself, for youth is passing. There is none in the three worlds who is as beautiful as you are, O princess: for, having fashioned you, the Creator has retired. You are so beautiful that no one in the three worlds—not even Brahmā the creator—could but be overcome by passion. When you accept me, all that I have will become yours. Even my chief wives will become your servants. Let me warn you: no one in the three worlds is my match in strength and valour. Rāma, even if he is alive, does not even know where you are: he has no hope of regaining you. Give up this foolish idea of yours. Let me behold you appropriately dressed and adorned. And, let us enjoy life to your heart's content."

Sundara 21–22

Rāvaṇa's words were extremely painful to the grief-stricken Sītā. She placed a blade of grass in front of her, unwilling even to speak to Rāvaṇa directly, and said: "You cannot aspire for me any more than a sinful man can aspire for perfection! I will not do what is unworthy in the eyes of a chaste wife. Surely, you do not know dharma, nor do you obviously listen to the advice of wise counsellors. Set an example to your subjects, O demon: and consort with your own wives; desire for others' wives will lead to infamy. The world rejoices at the death of a wicked man: even so it will, soon, on your death. But do not desire for me. You cannot win me by offering me power or wealth: for I am inseparable from Rāma even as light from the sun. He is the abode of righteousness, of dharma; take me back to him and beg his pardon. He loves those who seek his refuge. If you do not, you will surely come to grief: for no power on earth can save you from Rāma's weapon. His missiles will surely destroy the entire Laṅkā. In fact, if you had not stolen me in the absence of Rāma and Lakṣmaṇa, you would not be alive today: you could not face them, you coward!"

Rāvaṇa's anger was roused, and he replied: "Normally, women respond to a pleasant approach by a man. But you seem to be different, O Sītā. You rouse my anger; but my desire for you subdues that anger. My love for you prevents me from killing you straight away; though you deserve to be executed, for all the insulting and impudent words you utter. Well, I had fixed one year as the time-limit for you to make up your mind. Ten months have elapsed since then. You have two more months in which to decide to accede to my wish. If you fail to do so, my cooks will prepare a nice meal of your flesh for me to eat."

But, Sītā remained unmoved. She said to Rāvaṇa: "You are prattling, O wicked demon: I can by my own spiritual energy reduce you to ashes: but I do not do so on account of the fact that I have not been so ordered by Rāma and I do not want to waste my own spiritual powers."

The terrible demon was greatly enraged by these words of Sītā. He threatened her: "Wait, I shall destroy you just now." But he did not do so. However, he said to the demonesses guarding Sītā: "Use all your powers to persuade Sītā to consent to my proposal." Immediately, Rāvaṇa's consorts embraced him and pleaded: "Why don't you enjoy our company, giving up your desire for Sītā? For, a man who seeks the company of one who has no love for him comes to grief, and he who seeks the company of one who loves him enjoys life." Hearing this and laughing aloud, Rāvaṇa walked away.

Sundara 23–24

After Rāvaṇa had left the grove, the demonesses said: "How is it that you do not value Rāvaṇa's hand? Perhaps you do not know who he is. Of the six Prajāpatis who were the sons of the creator himself, Pulastya is the fourth; of Pulastya was the sage Viśrava born, and he was equal to Pulastya himself in glory. And this Rāvaṇa is the son of Viśrava. He is known as

Rāvaṇa because he makes his enemies cry. It is a great honour to accept his proposal. Moreover, this Rāvaṇa worsted in battle the thirty-three deities presiding over the universe. Hence he is superior even to the gods. And, what is most important: he surely loves you so much that he is prepared to abandon his own favourite wives and give you all his love."

Sītā was deeply pained by these words uttered by the demonesses. She said: "Enough of this vulgar and sinful advice. A human being should not become the wife of a demon. But, even that is irrelevant. I shall not under any circumstance abandon my husband and seek another." The demonesses were enraged and began to threaten Sītā. And, Hanumān was witnessing all this.

The demonesses said again: "You have shown enough affection to the unworthy Rāma. Excess of anything is undesirable and leads to undesirable result. You have so far conformed to the human rules of conduct. It is high time that you abandoned that code, abandoned the human Rāma and consented to be Rāvaṇa's wife. We have so far put up with the rude and harsh words you have uttered; and we have so far offered you loving and wholesome advice, intent as we are on your welfare. But you seem to be too stupid to see the truth. You have been brought here by Rāvaṇa; you have crossed the ocean. Others cannot cross the ocean and come to your rescue. We tell you this, O Sītā: even Indra cannot rescue you from here. Therefore, please do as we tell you, in your interest. Enough of your weeping. Give up this sorrow which is destructive. Abandon this wretched life. Attain love and pleasure. Make haste, O Sītā: for youth, especially of women, is but momentary and passes quickly. Make up your mind to become Rāvaṇa's wife. If, however, you are obstinate, we shall ourselves tear your body and eat your heart."

Other demonesses took up the cue and began to threaten Sītā. They said: "When I first saw this lovely woman brought into Laṅkā by Rāvaṇa the desire arose in me that I should eat her liver and spleen, her breasts and her heart. I am waiting for that day . . . . What is the delay? Let us report to the king that she died and he will surely ask us to eat her flesh! . . . . We should divide her flesh equally and eat it, there should be no quarrel amongst us . . . . After the meal, we shall dance in front of the goddess Bhadrakāli."

Sundara 25–26

In utter despair, Sītā gave vent to her grief by thinking aloud: "The wise ones have rightly said that untimely death is not attained here either by man or a woman. Hence though I am suffering intolerable anguish on account of my separation from my beloved husband, I am unable to give up my life. This grief is slowly eating me. I can neither live nor can I die. Surely, this is the bitter fruit of some dreadful sin committed in a past birth. I am surrounded by these demonesses: and how can Rāma reach me here? Fie upon human birth, and fie upon the state of dependence upon others, as a result of which I cannot even give up my life.

"What a terrible misfortune it was that even though I was living under the protection of Rāma and Lakṣmaṇa, I was abducted by Rāvaṇa, in their absence. Even more terrible it is that having been separated from my beloved husband I am confined here surrounded by these terrible demonesses. And, the worst part of it is: in spite of all these misfortunes, my heart does not burst with anguish thus letting me die. Of course, I shall never allow Rāvaṇa to touch me, so long as I am alive.

"I wonder why Rāma has not taken steps to come to my aid. For my sake he killed thousands of demons while we were in the forest. True I am on an island; but Rāma's missiles have no difficulty crossing oceans and finding their target. Surely, he does not know where I am. Alas, even Jaṭāyu who could have informed Rāma of what had happened was killed by Rāvaṇa. If only he knew I was here, Rāma would have destroyed Laṅkā and dried up the ocean with his missiles. All the demonesses of Laṅkā would weep then, as I am weeping now; all the demons would be killed by Rāma. Laṅkā would be one huge crematorium.

"I see all sorts of evil portents. I shall be re-united with Rāma. He will come. He will destroy all these demons. If only Rāma comes to know where I am, Laṅkā will be turned desolate by him, burnt by his terrible missiles. On the other hand, the time is fast running out: the time limit that Rāvaṇa had fixed for me to decide. Two more months: and I shall be cut into pieces for Rāvaṇa's meal. May it be that Rāma himself is no more, having succumbed to grief on account of my separation? Or, may it be that he has turned an ascetic? Usually, people who love each other forget each other when they are separated; but not so Rāma whose love is eternal. Blessed indeed are the holy sages who have reached enlightenment and to whom the pleasant and the unpleasant are non-different. I salute the holy ones. And, fallen into this terrible misfortune, I shall presently give up my life."

Sundara 27

Hearing the words of Sītā, some of the demonesses grew terribly angry. They threatened: "We shall go and report all this to Rāvaṇa; and then we shall be able to eat you at once." Another demoness named Trijaṭā just then woke up from her slumber and announced: "Forget all this talk about eating Sītā, O foolish ones! I have just now dreamt a dream which forewarns that a terrible calamity awaits all of you." The demonesses asked: "Tell us what the dream was."

Trijaṭā narrated her dream in great detail: "I saw in my dream Rāma and Lakṣmaṇa, riding a white space vehicle. Sītā was sitting on a white mountain, clad in shining white robes. Rāma and Sītā were re-united. Rāma and Lakṣmaṇa then got on a huge elephant which Sītā, too, mounted. Sītā held out her arms and her hands touched the sun and the moon. Rāma, Lakṣmaṇa and Sītā later mounted the Puṣpaka space vehicle and flew away in a northerly direction. From all these I conclude that Rāma is divine and invincible.

"Listen to me further. In another dream I saw Rāvaṇa. His head had been shaven. He was covered with oil. He wore crimson clothes. He was drunk. He had fallen from the Puṣpaka space vehicle. Later, I saw him dressed in black but smeared in a red pigment and dragged by a woman riding a vehicle drawn by donkeys. He fell down from the donkey. He was prattling like a mad man. Then he entered a place which was terribly dark and foul-smelling. Later a dark woman with body covered in mud, bound Rāvaṇa's neck and dragged him away in a southerly direction. I saw Kumbhakarṇa as also the sons of Rāvaṇa in that dream; all of them undergoing the same or similar treatment. Only Vibhīṣaṇa's luck was different. He was clad in white garment, with white garlands, and had a royal white umbrella held over his head.

"I also saw in that dream that the whole of Laṅkā had been pushed into the sea, utterly destroyed and ruined. I also saw a rather strange dream. I saw Laṅkā burning furiously: though Laṅkā is protected by Rāvaṇa who is mighty and powerful, a vānara was able to set Laṅkā ablaze, because the vānara was a servant of Rāma.

Hanuman

"I see a clear warning in these dreams, O foolish women! Enough of your cruelty to Sītā; I think it is better to please her and win her favour. I am convinced that Sītā will surely achieve her purpose and her desire to be re-united with Rāma."

Hearing this, Sītā felt happy and said: "If this comes true, I shall certainly protect all of you."

Sundara 28, 29, 30

But, the demonesses did not pay heed to Trijaṭā. And, Sītā thought:

"Truly have the wise ones declared that death never comes to a person before the appointed time. My time has come. Rāvaṇa has said definitely that if I do not agree to him I will be put to death. Since I can never, never love him, it is certain that I shall be executed. Hence, I am condemned already. I shall, therefore, incur no blame if I voluntarily end my life today. O Rāma! O Lakṣmaṇa! O Sumitrā! O Kausalyā! O Mother! Caught helplessly and brought to this dreadful place, I am about to perish. Surely it was my own 'bad-time' that approached me in the form of that golden deer, and I, a foolish woman sent the two princes in search of it. Maybe, they were killed by some demon. Or, maybe they are alive and do not know where I am.

"Alas, whatever virtue I practised and the devotion with which I served my own lord and husband, all these have come to naught; I shall presently abandon this ill-fated life of mine. O Rāma, after you complete the fourteen-year term of exile, you will return to Ayodhyā and enjoy life with the queens you might marry. But, I who loved you and whose heart is forever fastened to you, shall soon be no more.

"How shall I end this life? I have no weapon; nor will anyone here give me a weapon or poison to end my life. Ah, I shall use this string with which my hair has been tied and hang myself from this tree."

Thinking aloud in this manner, Sītā contemplated the feet of Rāma and got ready to execute herself. At the same time, however, she noticed many auspicious omens which dissuaded her from her wish to end her life. Her left eye, left arm and left thigh throbbed. Her heart was gladdened, her sorrow left her for the moment, her despair abated, and she became calm and radiant once again.

Hanumān, sitting on the tree, watched all this. He thought: "If I meet Sītā in the midst of these demonesses, it would be disastrous. In fact, she might get frightened and cry and before I could make the announcement concerning Rāma, I might be caught. I can fight all the demons here; but then I might be too weak to fly back. I could speak to her in the dialect of the brāhmaṇa; but she might suspect a vānara speaking sanskrit to be Rāvaṇa himself! To speak to Sītā now seems to be risky; yet, if I do not, she might commit suicide. If one does not act with due regard to place and time, the contrary results ensue. I shall sing the glories of Rāma softly and thus win Sītā's confidence. Then I shall deliver Rāma's message to her in a manner which will evoke her confidence."

Sundara 31, 32, 33

After deep deliberation, Hanumān decided upon the safest and the wisest course! Softly, sweetly, clearly and in cultured accents, he narrated the story of Rāma. He said: "A descendant of the noble Ikṣvāku was the emperor Daśaratha, who was a royal sage in as much as he was devoted to asceticism and righteousness, while yet ruling his kingdom. His eldest son Rāma was equally powerful, glorious and righteous. To honour his father's promise to his step-mother, Rāma went to the Daṇḍaka forest along with his brother Lakṣmaṇa, and his wife Sītā. There, Rāma killed thousands of demons. A demon disguised as a deer tricked Rāma and Lakṣmaṇa away, and at that time, the wicked Rāvaṇa abducted Sītā. Rāma went searching for her; and while so wandering the forest cultivated the friendship of the vānara Sugrīva. Sugrīva commissioned millions of vānaras to search for Sītā. Endowed with extraordinary energy, I crossed the ocean; and blessed I am that I am able to behold that Sītā."

Sītā was supremely delighted to hear that speech. She looked up and down, around and everywhere, and saw the vānara Hanumān. But, seeing the vānara seated on the tree, Sītā was frightened and suspicious. She cried aloud: "O Rāma, O Lakṣmaṇa." She was terror-stricken as the vānara approached her; but she was pleasantly surprised to see that he came humbly and worshipfully. She thought: "Am I dreaming? I hope not; it forebodes ill to dream of a vānara. Nay, I am not dreaming. Maybe, this is hallucination. I have constantly been thinking of Rāma. I have constantly uttered his name, and talked about him. Since my whole being is absorbed in him, I am imagining all this. But, I have reasoned out all this carefully within myself; yet, this being here is not only clearly seen by me, but it talks to me, too! I pray to the gods, may what I have just heard be true."

With his palms joined together in salutation over his head, Hanumān humbly approached Sītā and asked: "Who are you, O lady? Are you indeed the wife of that blessed Rāma?"

Highly pleased with this question, Sītā thereupon related her whole story: "I am the daughter-in-law of king Daśaratha, and the daughter of king Janaka. I am the wife of Rāma. We lived happily in Ayodhyā for twelve years. But when Rāma was about to be crowned, his step-mother Kaikeyī demanded the boon from her husband that Rāma should be banished to the forest. The king swooned on hearing this; but Rāma took it upon himself to fulfil that promise. I followed him; and Lakṣmaṇa, too, came with us. One day when they were away, Rāvaṇa forcibly carried me and brought me here. He has given me two more months to live; after which I shall meet my end."

Sundara 34–35

Once again bowing down to Sītā, Hanumān said to her: "O divine lady, I am a messenger sent by Rāma. He, as also his brother Lakṣmaṇa, send their greetings and hope that you are alive and well." Sītā rejoiced and thought to herself: "Surely, there is a lot of truth in the old adage: 'Happiness is bound to come to the man who lives, even though after a long time.' " But, as Hanumān came near her, she grew suspicious and would not even look at him: she thought, and said to him: "O Rāvaṇa! Previously you assumed the disguise of a mendicant and abducted me. Now, you have come to torment me in the guise of a vānara! Pray, leave me alone." But, on the other hand, she reasoned to herself: "No this cannot be; for on seeing this vānara, my heart rejoices."

Hanumān, however, reassured her: "O blessed Sītā, I am a messenger sent by Rāma who will very soon kill these demons and rescue you from their captivity. Rāma and Lakṣmaṇa constantly think of you. So does king Sugrīva whose minister Hanumān, I am. Endowed with extraordinary energy I crossed the sea. I am not what you suspect me to be!"

At her request, Hanumān recounted the glories of Rāma: "Rāma is equal to the gods in beauty, charm and wisdom. He is the protector of all living beings, of his own people, of his work and of his dharma; he is the protector of people of different occupations, of good conduct, and he himself adheres to good conduct and makes others do so, too. He is mighty, friendly, well-versed in scriptures and devoted to the holy ones. He is endowed with all the characteristics of the best among men, which are: broad shoulders, strong arms, powerful neck, lovely face, reddish eyes, deep voice, dark-brown coloured skin; he has firm chest, wrist and fist; he has long eyebrows, arms and scrotum; he has symmetrical locks, testicles and knees; he has strong bulging chest, abdomen and rim of the navel; reddish in the corner of his eyes, nails, palms and soles; he is soft in his glans, the lines of his feet and hair; he has deep voice, gait and navel; three folds adorn the skin of his neck and his abdomen; the arch of his feet, the lines on his soles, and the nipples are deep; he has short generative organ, neck, back and shanks; three spirals adorn the hair on his head; there are four lines at the root of his thumb; and four lines on his forehead; he is four cubits tall; the four pairs of his limbs (cheeks, arms, shanks and knees) are symmetrical; even so the other fourteen pairs of limbs; his limbs are long. He is excellent in every way. Lakṣmaṇa, Rāma's brother, is also full of charm and excellences."

Sundara 35–36

Hanumān then narrated in great detail all that had happened. He mentioned in particular how Rāma was moved to tears when Hanumān showed him the pieces of jewelry that Sītā had dropped on the hill. He concluded that narrative by affirming: "I shall certainly attain the glory of having seen you first; and Rāma too will soon come here to take you back." He also revealed to Sītā his own identity: "Kesari, my father, lived on the mountain known as Malayavān. Once he went to the Gokarṇa mountain at the command of the sages to fight and to kill a demon named Sāmbasadana who tormented the people. I was born of the wind-god and my mother Añjanā. I tell you again, O divine lady, that I am a vānara, and I am a messenger sent by Rāma; here, behold the ring which has been inscribed with the name of Rāma. Whatever might have been the cause of your suffering captivity, it has almost come to an end."

When she saw the signet ring, Sītā felt the presence of Rāma himself; she was filled with joy. Her attitude to Hanumān, too, immediately and dramatically changed. She exclaimed: "You are heroic, capable, and wise, too, O best among vānaras. What a remarkable feat you have accomplished by crossing this vast ocean, a distance of eight hundred miles. Surely, you are not an ordinary vānara in that you are not afraid of even Rāvaṇa. I am delighted to hear that Rāma and Lakṣmaṇa are well. But why has he not rescued me yet: he could dry up the ocean, in fact he could even destroy the whole earth with his missiles if he wanted to. Perhaps, they had to wait for the propitious moment, and that moment which would mean the end of my suffering has not yet arrived.

"O Hanumān, tell me more about Rāma. Does he continue to rely on both self-effort and divine agency in all that he undertakes? Tell me, O Hanumān, does he still love me as before? And, I also hope that, pining for me, he does not waste away. And also tell me: how will Rāma rescue me from here. Will Bharata send an army? When he renounced the throne and when he took me to the forest, he displayed extraordinary firmness: is he still as firm in his resolves? Oh, I know that he loves me more than anyone else in this world."

Hanumān replied: "You will soon behold Rāma, O Sītā! Stricken with grief on account of his separation from you, Rāma does not eat meat, nor drink wine; he does not even wish to ward off flies and mosquitoes that assail him. He thinks of you constantly. He hardly sleeps; and if he does, he wakes up calling out 'Ah Sītā'. When he sees a fruit or flower, he thinks of you." Hearing the glories of Rāma, Sītā was rid of sorrow; hearing of his grief, Sītā grew equally sorrowful.

Sundara 37

Sītā replied to Hanumān: "Your description of Rāma's love for me comes to me like nectar mixed with poison. In whatever condition one may be, whether one is enjoying unlimited power and prosperity or one is in dreadful misery, the end of one's action drags a man as if he were tied with a rope. Look at the way in which Rāma, Lakṣmaṇa and I have been subjected to sorrow: surely, no one can overcome destiny. I wonder when the time will come when I shall be united with Rāma once again. Rāvaṇa gave me one year, of which ten months have passed and only two are left. At the end of those two months, Rāvaṇa will surely kill me. There is no alternative. For, he does not fancy the thought of taking me back to Rāma. In fact, such a course was suggested by Rāvaṇa's own brother Vibhiṣaṇa: so his own daughter Kalā told me. But Rāvaṇa turns a deaf ear upon such wise counsel."

Hanumān said to Sītā: "I am sure that Rāma will soon arrive here, with an army of forest-dwellers and other tribes, as soon as I inform him of your whereabouts. But, O divine lady, I have another idea. You can rejoin your husband this very day. I can enable you to end this sorrow instantly. Pray, do not hesitate; get on my back, and seek union (yogam) with Rāma now. I have the power to carry you, or even Laṅkā, Rāvaṇa and everything in it! No one will be able to pursue me or to overcome me. What a great triumph it will be if I return to Kiṣkindhā with you on my back!"

For a moment Sītā was thrilled at this prospect. But she remarked almost in jest: "You are speaking truly like a vānara, an ignorant tribesman. You are so small: and you think you can carry me over the ocean!" Hanumān, thereupon, showed Sītā his real form. Seeing him stand like a mountain in front of her, Sītā felt sure that his confidence was justified, but said to him: "O mighty Hanumān, I am convinced that you can do as you say. But I do not think it is proper for me to go with you. You may proceed at great speed; but I may slip and fall into the ocean. If I go with you, the demons will suspect our relationship and give it an immoral twist. Moreover, many demons will pursue you: how will you, unarmed as you are, deal with them and at the same time protect me? I might once again fall into their hands. I agree you have the power to fight them: but if you kill them all, it will rob Rāma of the glory of killing them and rescuing me. Surely, when Rāma and Lakṣmaṇa come here with you, they will destroy the demons and liberate me. I am devoted to Rāma; and I will not of my own accord touch the body of another man. Therefore, O

Hanumān, enable Rāma and Lakṣmaṇa to come here with greatest expedition."

Sundara 38

Hanumān, the wise vānara, was highly impressed and thoroughly convinced of the propriety of Sītā's arguments. He applauded them, and prayed: "If you feel you should not come, pray, give me a token which I might take back with me and which Rāma might recognise."

This suggestion revived old memories and moved Sītā to tears. She said to Hanumān: "I shall give you the best token. Please remind my glorious husband of a delightful episode in our forest-life which only he and I know. This happened when we were living near Citrakooṭa hill. We had finished our bath; and we had had a lot of fun playing in water, Rāma was sitting on my lap. A crow began to worry me. I kept it away threatening it with stones. It hid itself. When I was getting dressed and when my skirt slipped a little, the crow attacked me again: but I defended myself angrily. Looking at this Rāma laughed, while sweetly pacifying me.

"Both of us were tired. I slept on Rāma's lap for sometime. Later Rāma slept with his head resting on my lap. The crow (who was Indra's son in disguise) attacked me again and began to inflict wounds on my body. A few drops of blood trickled from my chest and fell on Rāma who awoke. Seeing the vicious crow perched on a nearby tree, Rāma picked up the missile named after the creator and hurled it at the crow. That crow flew round to the three worlds but found no asylum anywhere else.

"Eventually it sought refuge with Rāma himself. Rāma was instantly pacified. Yet, the missile could not be neutralised. The crow sacrificed its right eye and saved its life." As she was narrating the story, Sītā felt the presence of Rāma and addressed him: "O Rāma, you were ready to use the Brahmā-missile towards a mere crow for my sake; why do you suffer my abduction with patience? Though I have you as my lord and master, yet I live here like a destitute! Have you no compassion for me: it was from you I learnt that compassion is the greatest virtue!" She said to Hanumān again: "No power on earth can confront Rāma. It is only my ill-luck that prevents them from coming to my rescue."

Hanumān explained: "It was only ignorance of your whereabouts that has caused this delay, O divine lady. Now that we know where you are, the destruction of the demons is at hand." Sītā said: "The fulfilment of this mission depends upon you; with your aid, Rāma will surely succeed in his mission. But, please tell Rāma that I shall be alive only for a month more." Then as a further token, Sītā took off a precious jewel from her person and gave it to Hanumān. Receiving that jewel, and with Sītā's blessings Hanumān was ready to depart.

Sundara 39–40

Once again Sītā reminded Hanumān: "I had kept with me this jewel which was to me the very presence of Rāma. Whenever I looked at it, it was as if Rāma were with me. It will remind Rāma of me, of my mother and of king Daśaratha. Pray, tell Rāma all that you have seen here, how I live, how I pine for him and how I remain alive only in the hope of seeing him again. Say all this in such a way that Rāma will rescue me alive; and thus shall you have earned the merit of using the power of speech aright. What, when and how Rāma does now depends entirely upon what and how you say to him when you meet him." Hanumān reassured her.

But, fear and doubt haunted Sītā who said: "I am haunted by a doubt, O Hanumān. How will the hordes of the hill-tribes cross the ocean and come here? Of course it will be glorious if Rāma kills Rāvaṇa and his demon followers and returns with me to Ayodhyā. But, how do you think this can be achieved?"

To reassure her, Hanumān said: "It is easy for us vānaras, O divine lady. The vānaras are very powerful. They have often gone round the world along the aerial routes. Sugrīva's army consists of vānaras equal to me and far superior to me: in fact none in that army is inferior to me in power. Surely, it is obvious that no wise leader will send a superior hero as a messenger; only inferior ones are sent as messengers. Have no misgivings, O Sītā. I shall myself carry Rāma and Lakṣmaṇa on my back and bring them here. The rest of the work is easy."

Once again Sītā said to Hanumān as he was about to depart: "Pray, give that jewel to Rāma; it is something I have cherished and considered a most precious memento. Also remind him:

once when the auspicious mark on my forehead had got wiped out, he himself applied it once again and laughed. Remind him of the story of the crow which I have already narrated to you. And, please do not forget to tell him that I can keep myself alive here—and that, too, only for his sake—only for a month more."

And, once again, Hanumān said to Sītā: "I swear that even as you are constantly thinking of him, Rāma, too is constantly thinking of you, O Sītā. And there will be no delay at all in his arrival here."

Sītā felt unhappy when Hanumān got ready to leave and put in the last word: "You have the best tokens of my love for Rāma. Pray, tell him everything in detail. Ensure that Rāma is able to end my agony in the shortest possible time."

Sundara 41–42

Hanumān took leave of Sītā, but did noι leave Laṅkā. He thought: "The time has come for a showdown of military strength. With the demons you cannot negotiate; you cannot win wealthy and prosperous enemies with tempting baits of gifts; nor can you sow seeds of discord among the powerful: hence a show of strength alone seems to be appropriate. Before leaving Laṅkā I should give these demons a foretaste of our strength; only then will these demons adopt a respectable attitude when we face them in battle. Moreover, success comes to one only if one utilises the opportunity afforded by an expedition to accomplish not only the principal objective, but several secondary ones. Surely, there are many paths to success in a venture; and one who knows many ways of reaching his goal is assured of success. I see that this is Rāvaṇa's own pleasure-grove, and it is rich and beautiful. I shall destroy it. This will surely provoke Rāvaṇa who might come here with his army. And that would give me an opportunity to estimate his strength and to give him an indication of what he could expect from us."

With devasting suddenness, Hanumān unleashed his energy and began to destroy the Aśoka-grove. Birds and beasts ran in all directions out of fear. The demonesses took to their heels. Some of them, who were guarding Sītā, and who were asleep, woke up and seeing this vānara, demanded of Sītā: "Who is this?" Sītā replied: "How do I know who it is? Only a snake knows where a snake's legs are! I, too, am frightened, not knowing who he is: I, too, think that he is perhaps a demon."

All the demonesses ran to Rāvaṇa's presence and reported the matter. They said: "A vānara who is powerful and terrible to look at has devastated the Aśoka-grove, O lord! Some of us saw him speak to Sītā. But Sītā does not reveal his identity. We do not know who he is. He may be a messenger from Indra or Kubera or Rāma himself, come to find out where Sītā is. It is also significant that though this vānara destroyed the whole of the Aśoka-grove, he did not touch the area where Sītā is, nor the Simśapa tree under which she is confined."

Rāvaṇa was enraged. Immediately he ordered a number of slaves (kiṅkaras) to go to the Aśoka-grove and capture Hanumān. They went armed with all sorts of crude weapons. They assailed him. Hanumān gave out a battle-cry: "Victory to Rāma, to Lakṣmaṇa, and to the king Sugrīva! I am Rāma's servant and messenger, Hanumān by name, who destroys all his enemies. Not a thousand Rāvaṇas are equal to me in might! I shall destroy Laṅkā, bow to Sītā and return." The army of slaves was soon disposed of! And, the demons who witnessed this battle reported the tragedy to Rāvaṇa.

Sundara 43, 44, 45

The Aśoka-grove had been destroyed; and the slaves had been killed. But Hanumān was not satisfied. He turned his attention to an important monument, heavily guarded by Rāvaṇa's soldiers. Stretching himself tall, and swelling with enthusiasm, Hanumān climbed up that monument and began breaking it, filling the whole of Laṅkā with that sound. He shouted triumphantly from the top of that monument: "Victory to Rāma! Victory to Lakṣmaṇa! Victory to Sugrīva who is protected by Rāma! I am Hanumān, the messenger of Rāma. Even a thousand Rāvaṇas cannot stand before me in battle. I shall destroy Laṅkā, bow to Sītā and return."

Seeing him and hearing this, a hundred demons posted to guard the monument rushed towards him with iron maces, clubs and other such weapons. The mighty Hanumān shook the monument; the pillars broke loose and their clash sparked off a blaze; Hanumān killed the demons with a pillar. Once again Hanumān proclaimed: "There are thousands of vānaras even more powerful than I am. Sugrīva will soon arrive here, surrounded by them, for your destruction. Then there will neither be a Laṅkā, nor all of you, nor even Rāvaṇa, who has earned the enmity of Rāma.

All this was duly reported by the demons to Rāvaṇa. At his command, a mighty demon named Jambumālī came to fight and to capture Hanumān. The duel was terrible. Jambumālī hit Hanumān with various weapons and wounded him. The bleeding vānara looked beautiful even then. Hanumān lifted a huge rock and threw it at Jambumālī who broke it with his missiles. Hanumān picked up an iron mace from the field and hurled it at Jambumālī with great force. Jambumālī was dead.

Rāvaṇa then sent the seven sons of his ministers. They were adepts in aerial combat. Their bombers thundered and roared as they arrived on the scene. They began to shoot at Hanumān even before they reached him. Hanumān, too, flew into the sky and successfully dodged the shots.

This was followed by a fierce hand-to-hand fight. None of the seven heroes could stand before Hanumān. Within a very short space of time, he killed all of them. The whole place was strewn with shattered remains of the planes and the dead bodies of the slain demons. Blood flowed freely, like a river. The cries of the wounded filled Laṅkā.

Hanumān stood triumphantly in the archway to the grove.

Sundara 46

Next, Rāvaṇa sent five mighty warriors who were commanders of his army to deal with the vānara. They were Virūpākṣa, Yūpākṣa, Durdhara, Praghasa and Bhāsakarṇa. He cautioned them in the following words:

"Go with a sizeable army. Be vigilant and do whatever may be necessary, having due regard to the place and time. I do not think we are dealing with a vānara. I have considered all that this vānara has done, and I have to come to the conclusion that he is a mighty being endowed with extraordinary prowess. It is quite possible that the gods, our enemies, have bred a specially powerful being to kill us. You have so far defeated all sorts of beings—gods, sages, demons and demigods. And I have known several mighty vānaras—Vāli, Sugrīva, Jāmbavān, Nīla, Dvivida etc. But none of them has the prowess that this vānara has. Strive your utmost, therefore, to take him prisoner. I know you are capable of dealing with any being on earth—even the gods and demi-gods. But be vigilant and protect yourselves: for in a war success is unpredictable."

The five commanders proceeded towards the Aśoka-grove. They saw there the mighty Hanumān, shining like the sun just risen; they could see that he was excellent and great in every respect—very fast-moving, exceptionally courageous, exceedingly strong, very wise, fired with supreme enthusiasm, and endowed with a very strong body. As soon as they saw him, all of them fired at him simultaneously. Hanumān was injured: but the injuries appeared to be flowers crowning his head.

Hanumān flew; and he was pursued by Durdhara. In the course of this aerial combat, when Durdhara was flying at a low altitude, Hanumān dived right on Durdhara's aircraft, like lightning hitting a mountain. The aircraft crashed; Durdhara was dead.

Hanumān continued to course through the air. Virūpākṣa and Yūpākṣa took off in their aircraft and began to fire at Hanumān. Suddenly, Hanumān landed in the grove, pursued by the demons. And, before they could reach the ground, he pulled out a big tree and hit their crafts with it. Both these demons were killed.

Praghasa and Bhāsakarṇa attacked Hanumān. They used a spear and a dart and engaged in hand-to-hand fighting. Hanumān fended their attacks off, picked up a huge rock which looked like a mountain-peak and threw it at them. And, that was their end.

Sundara 47

Rāvaṇa was worried. When the death of the mighty commanders at the hands of the vānara was reported to him, he looked round and then gazed at his young son, Akṣa. Akṣa was young, but even then he was fierce and aggressive. Akṣa took his father's gaze to be a question and sprang to his feet, eager to fight. Not a word was exchanged between father and son, but they understood each other very well.

Akṣa jumped into his aircraft. This was an extraordinary craft. It had been acquired after great effort and great sacrifice. It was plated in pure gold. It had turrets of precious stones. It had eight engines and, propelled by them, it was capable of attaining the speed of the mind! It could not be assailed by even gods and demons. As it coursed through the air, it looked like lightning. It was equipped with eight gun-turrets for firing missiles, pointed in the eight directions. All the parts of this craft were held firmly together by cords of pure gold.

Hanumān was surprised to see Akṣa. As they stood facing each other, emitting terrible fire as it were, everyone who witnessed this combat trembled with fear. Aiming accurately, Akṣa fired three shots which wounded Hanumān's head.

For a moment Hanumān reeled. But, when he realised that it was Rāvaṇa's own son that he was facing, his enthusiasm returned to him. Even as Hanumān continued to look at Akṣa in great fury, the latter continued to fire. Hanumān roared fiercely. He flew. Akṣa followed him in hot pursuit, firing his missiles all the time. Hanumān dodged all of them with great dexterity.

Hanumān thought: "He looks like a boy, but his deeds are not those of a boy. At first I thought I should not kill this little boy. Surely, he is a brilliant child. But, he is powerful and can fight with even gods and demons. If he is disregarded, he will overpower me; hence I shall kill him. A spreading bush-fire should not be ignored."

Having thus made up his mind, Hanumān fired at the eight engines and silenced them. With his craft thus shattered in its vulnerable parts, Akṣa fell down with the craft. Akṣa took up his sword and rushed towards Hanumān. Hanumān caught hold of the legs of Akṣa, whirled him in the air and dashed him on the ground. He was dead.

Sundara 48

The death of Akṣa at the hands of Hanumān was surely a severe blow to Rāvaṇa who, however, did not show his grief. He turned to his other son Indrajit of matchless valour. He said to Indrajit: "My son, you have fought even the gods and won a victory over Indra. In all respects you are my equal. When you join a battle, I feel confident of victory. Now, this vānara has killed all our slaves, as also Jambumālī, and the sons of our ministers, and even your brother Akṣa. I think you should tackle him. It is no use taking a big army; for the men panic or get killed. Even ordinary missiles and weapons do not seem to have any effect on this vānara: but I know you will use whatever missile is called for with due consideration to time and place. It may be said that it is unwise for me to send you, my eldest son: yet that is the dharma of a king. You too should learn military tactics and acquire proficiency in war by winning victories over enemies."

That was enough for Indrajit who set out to where Hanumān was. His own aircraft resembled Garuḍa, the divine bird, and was equally swift. It had four engines each like a tiger, which were all equipped with sharp 'teeth'. Indrajit, whose prowess was equal to that of Indra, boarded this craft and proceeded with incredible speed.

Hanumān felt happy when he saw Indrajit himself coming. In fact, the firmament was crowded with gods and demi-gods who were eager to witness this battle. Hanumān, too, began to fly. He successfully evaded all the missiles of Indrajit.

Indrajit realised that Hanumān could not be killed. He decided to take him prisoner. Even for this purpose, he had to use the most powerful missile, the one dedicated to Brahmā the creator. Hit by this, Hanumān fell down: it did not kill him but only bound him, incapacitated him. Hanumān enjoyed such a boon from Brahmā himself that even that missile would affect him only for an hour or so. Yet, he thought to himself: "I do not have the power to break the bonds of this supreme missile; I should honour the missile and allow myself to be bound by it." Moreover, he said to himself: "Even this is good; for surely I shall be able to meet Rāvaṇa face to face."

Seeing him fallen, the demons crowded round him, hit him, and tied him with ropes. This freed Hanumān from the missile's effect at once: for such is the law, that spiritual power does not co-exist with physical power. Yet, Hanumān remained docile. They dragged him to the presence of Rāvaṇa.

Sundara 49, 50, 51

Hanumān gazed at the resplendent Rāvaṇa who was excellent in every way. Rāvaṇa was seated on a crystal throne which was inlaid with jewels and had the most expensive covering. Hanumān looked at him and thought: "What charm, what heroism, what nobility of being, and what splendour; Rāvaṇa is wonderfully endowed with all the excellences. If only he were not devoted to unrighteousness, he could well be the ruler of heaven, nay even of its ruler."

Rāvaṇa was struck by the majesty of Hanumān's appearance and the strength which was evident. He commanded his ministers to ascertain the purpose of his visit to Laṅkā and why he had laid the Aśoka-grove to waste. The ministers addressed their questions to Hanumān and cautioned him: "Tell us the truth, and you will be released. If you utter flasehood, you will not live!"

Hanumān replied: "I am not a messenger of the gods or demi-gods. But I am a messenger from Sugrīva. As I wished to meet Rāvaṇa in person, I pulled down the trees in his pet grove. And, when the demons attacked me, I killed them in self-defence."

Turning to Rāvaṇa himself, Hanumān said: "I have a message from Sugrīva. You know Sugrīva and he is like a brother to you." Hanumān then narrated the story of Rāma's birth and exile, the loss of Sītā in the forest, Rāma's friendship with Sugrīva, and the search for Sītā organised by Sugrīva.

"O King! I tell you what is good in the past, present and future. Accept my advice. Restore Sītā to Rāma. A glorious king like you should not stoop to such unrighteous conduct and abduct another's wife. No one in the three worlds can face the terrible power of Rāma and his brother Lakṣmaṇa: Rāma killed the mighty Vāli with just one shot. I have done a difficult task: I have discovered the whereabouts of Sītā. Soon, Rāma will complete this task.

"You cannot persuade Sītā to accept you, any more than a virulent poison can be digested. Listen to me, and do not forfeit the fruits of merits acquired by you in your previous birth. Sītā is surely the terrible Kālarātri who has been brought here for your own destruction. Restore her to Rāma. Else, you will see Laṅkā burning and all the demons killed. No one, not even you, not even Indra the god of gods can escape Rāma's wrath. Rāma can destroy all the worlds and create them again! I am a humble servant of Rāma and his messenger: what I have said to you is the truth, listen to me."

Sundara 52–53

Rāvaṇa was furious with uncontrollable rage on hearing Hanumān's words. He ordered Hanumān's immediate execution. However, Rāvaṇa's brother Vibhīṣaṇa intervened and counselled Rāvaṇa as follows:

"O mighty King! If even you can be overpowered by anger, then surely knowledge of scriptures is a useless burden. Be composed; and let proper punishment be meted out to this vānara after due deliberation.

"The scriptures forbid the killing of a messenger or an ambassador. For, he is merely advocating his master's cause and he is entirely dependent upon his master. Yet, it is also true that this vānara has destroyed the grove and killed many of your soldiers.

"The proper punishment for such crimes is mutilation of the body, flogging, shaving the head and branding—disgrace which is worse than death. They who sent this messenger here, however, deserve the death penalty. And, if you kill this vānara then the episode might come to an end there, because no one else on the enemy's side will be able to cross the ocean and come here, and you will not be able to destroy your enemy."

The mighty Rāvaṇa appreciated the counsel and accepted it with his intelligence. He modified his order: "They say that the tail is the most important ornament of a vānara; set fire to it. Let this vānara return afterwards. With his tail ablaze take him round the city so that he and his comrades might know that such mischief as he has been guilty of will not go unpunished in Laṅkā."

The demons bound Hanumān, soaked his tail in oil and set it ablaze. Hanumān thought: "For the sake of Rāma's cause I shall endure even this. When they drag me around the city, I shall be able to take a better note of its military strength and gather more military information. It is good that I see Laṅkā in daylight, too." The demons dragged Hanumān around the city. They announced him as Rāma's spy. Some of the demonesses went to Sītā and informed her of Hanumān's predicament. Sītā prayed to the god of fire: "If I have been faithful to my husband and if I have served my husband; if I have performed any austerities at all, O God, be cool to Hanumān." An icy cold wind began to blow.

Hanumān, too, was intrigued to see that the fire did not burn him nor hurt him. He concluded: "Surely, Sītā's grace, Rāma's glory, and the friendship of wind and fire, have mitigated the heat; and fire does not affect me." Hanumān quickly freed himself from the bonds, picked up an iron mace and killed the demons guarding the city. And he began to inspect Laṅkā once more, with his tail ablaze.

Sundara 54–55

Hanumān reflected again: "I have destroyed the Aśoka-grove, killed the demons and met Rāvaṇa. I have done all that I wanted to do except the destruction of the fortress of Rāva ṇa. What more can I do here, before I return to Rāma?" He thought: "My tail is burning; with it I shall burn down the houses of the chiefs of Laṅkā."

Hanumān flew up and set ablaze, one after the other, all the houses of the foremost among the warriors of Laṅkā. Flying over Laṅkā, Hanumān thundered along like a cloud at the time of cosmic destruction. A fierce wind spread the fire. All the state houses were ablaze. Molten metals like gold etc., flowed from the houses carrying precious stones which had adorned the doors and the walls. The demons ran from the buildings thoroughly confused and frightened.

The entire city of Laṅkā was burnt down by Hanumān. The terrified demons and demonesses said to one another: "Surely he is the chief of the gods; or maybe he is Death itself. Or perhaps he is the embodiment of the power of lord Viṣṇu himself." Everywhere there was weeping and wailing. Tongues of fire reached the sky. The whole mountain on which the city stood was afire. As Hanumān stood on the shore of the ocean and quenched the fire on his own tail, the gods and the sages sang his glories and praised him for his exploits.

Hanumān's joy did not last long. A question arose in his heart: "What about Sītā? Was she also consumed by the fire?" Hanumān said to himself: "What a dreadful tragedy it is that blinded by anger I have unwittingly destroyed Sītā herself! What sin does man not commit while in the influence of anger; he might even kill his own guru and insult holy men! Surely, he who is able to subdue his anger by patience, he alone is Man. No doubt Sītā has been consumed by this fire. What shall I do now? Surely, it is wiser for me to jump into this ocean and perish, too. For, if Rāma hears of Sītā having been burnt in the fire, he will die; so will Lakṣmaṇa, Sugrīva and all the people in Ayodhyā. What a dreadful sequel to my anger!"

But, Hanumān experienced auspicious omens. And, he reflected: "But, surely, Sītā cannot be consumed by this fire. Fire does not burn fire! No doubt it was Rāma's grace and Sītā's power that ordained that the fire did not burn me! I am sure that on account of her austerities, truthfulness and chastity, Sītā is immune to the effects of fire. At the same time, the demi-gods and sages who were roaming the sky announced: "Hanumān has indeed burnt the whole of Laṅkā; but Sītā is safe." Delighted to hear this, Hanumān got ready to return to Rāma.

Sundara 56–57

Hanumān wished to make sure that Sītā was in fact safe and well. He went to the Aśoka-grove to see her: he said: "I am supremely blessed that you are safe, O divine lady!" Knowing that he was about to depart, Sītā felt unhappy: and in a manner characteristic of women, she repeated her own misgivings concerning the power of the vānaras to cross the ocean, and the likelihood of Rāvaṇa putting an end to her life before she could rejoin her lord. And, she reiterated that she should not escape along with Hanumān, but that Hanumān should do everything in such a way that Rāma destroyed the demons and attained glory and regained her.

Hanumān too once again reassured the noble Sītā that all would be well and that soon she would find Rāma in Laṅkā and that her sorrow would soon come to an end. After receiving Sītā's blessings, Hanumān went up the mountain named Ariṣṭa, ready to take off, for he was eager to behold Rāma and he was delighted that the mission had been accomplished. Hanumān, the god-son of the wind-god, flew northwards like a huge cloud floating in space. It looked as if as he took off the mountain sank into the bowels of the earth; trees shook and rocks flew from hill tops. A terrible roar was heard in his wake.

Hanumān swiftly flew across the ocean and once again he beheld the Mahendra mountain at a distance. He let out a terrific roar, which filled the entire space. The vānara friends of Hanumān were eagerly awaiting his return on the Mahendra mountain. When they heard the mighty roar, they knew that he was returning after successfully completing his mission and they were delighted, eager as they were to see him again. Jāmbavān, the tribal leader, assured all the vānara hordes that the very sound of the roar indicated success of the mission! All the vānaras rushed to the nearby trees, broke the branches and the twigs, wrapped their own garments around these thus improvising flags, and excitedly waved these flags. This was their way of welcoming their hero.

Hanumān landed on a hillside strip. He was warmly received by the leaders of the vānara tribes, who worshipped him. He in turn worshipped the elders. And then he announced: "Sītā has been seen." Afterwards, he took Aṅgada aside and narrated in detail how he saw Sītā in the Aśoka-grove, how she had grown emaciated with grief and anxiety, and how she longed for Rāma day and night.

Aṅgada complimented Hanumān on his achievement: "No one is equal to you, O Hanumān! You have saved our lives. And, through your grace and help alone can Rāma recover Sītā."

Sundara 58–59

Jāmbavān now questioned Hanumān: "Pray tell us everything in detail. How did you discover that noble lady Sītā? How does she live? What is the strength of Rāvaṇa? Tell us: what should we report to Rāma when we meet him and what we should not inform him about."

Hanumān narrated the entire story of his historic adventure: he told them how he met with the obstacles on his flight over the ocean, the Maināka-episode, the Surasa-episode and also the Simhikā-episode. He told them of his encounter with the lady Laṅkā, his entry into Laṅkā and the search and the eventual discovery of Sītā in the Aśoka-grove. He told them how Rāvaṇa entered the grove, fell at the feet of Sītā and begged her to accept him, and how, when spurned by her, he would have struck her dead, but for the intervention of his wife Maṇḍodari. He told them of Sītā's grief and Trijaṭā's dream, of the clever way in which he gained Sītā's confidence, and how she told him a couple of intimate episodes in her life with Rāma and also gave him the jewel as a token of their meeting.

Hanumān then narrated in graphic detail the story of the destruction of the Aśoka-grove, and the subsequent destruction of the mighty demons sent by Rāvaṇa, and how he was bound by the Brahmā-missile used by Indrajit. He gave a full description of his meeting with Rāvaṇa, of Rāvaṇa's anger, of Vibhīṣaṇa's counsel, and the setting ablaze of Laṅkā. Hanumān concluded: "Everywhere in Laṅkā I have proclaimed, 'Victory to Rāma. Victory to Lakṣmaṇa. Victory to king Sugrīva', and everywhere I have announced that I was only a little messenger of Rāma. I have of course been able to do all this only by the grace of Rāma, your blessings and as my humble service to king Sugrīva."

Hanumān continued: "Sītā is truly worshipful and a glorious woman. By her power of chastity she could indeed reduce Rāvaṇa to ashes; since he has not been so reduced, I infer that he too has a vast store of merits earned by austerities and penance. But I am also confident that by our combined strength we can deal with Rāvaṇa and his forces. I can deal with Rāvaṇa myself, if all of you approve of it! Who on earth can face the mighty Jāmbavān, or Aṅgada, or Nīla, or Mainda or Dvivida? Whatever we decide to do must be done quickly, for Sītā's condition is indeed pitiable. She is clad in that one piece of cloth with which she was borne away by Rāvaṇa. She sleeps on the bare ground. Indeed, she is the picture of grief. She was, however, happy to hear of the alliance of Rāma and Sugrīva. Her devotion to Rāma is unshakeable. She could easily curse Rāvaṇa and bring about his destruction; but in the destruction of the powerful Rāvaṇa, Rāma has to play his part as an instrument."

Sundara 60–61

Aṅgada's enthusiasm was greatly roused, when he heard Hanumān extol the mighty strength of the vānaras that constituted the search party under the leadership of himself. He declared spiritedly: "As a matter of fact, the two vānaras Mainda and Dvivida who have earned the boon of invincibility in battle, from Brahmā himself, are capable of conquering Laṅkā. And, I am aware, too, that single-handed I can kill Rāvaṇa and conquer Laṅkā: and when you are all with me, the task is made much easier. I, therefore, feel that we should not go to Rāma and tamely report to him that Sītā has been seen and that she has, however, not been recovered. We have such strength, heroism and valour assembled here. We should not return to Kiṣkindhā before fully accomplishing Rāma's mission. You have already heard from Hanumān that he has burnt Laṅkā and that the foremost among the commanders and warriors of Rāvaṇa's army have already been killed by him. Very little remains to be done by all of us together. I therefore suggest that we ourselves should go to Laṅkā, kill all the remaining heroes, and recovering Sītā, should see Rāma with Sugrīva and Lakṣmaṇa. And then we shall place Sītā between Rāma and Lakṣmaṇa."

Jāmbavān intervened and said: "I do not think that your proposal is wise, O Aṅgada. We were sent out by king Sugrīva with the express command to search for Sītā and find out where she is. And, that mission has fully and satisfactorily been accomplished by Hanumān. We have no authority to fight with Rāvaṇa and to recover Sītā on our own strength. It may not be pleasing to Rāma to learn that we vānaras fought with the demons and recovered Sītā. Rāma has vowed that he would himself recover Sītā. We should certainly help him in this mission but we should not substitute for him. And, that will enable us to witness the extraordinary prowess of Rāma. Let us, therefore, return to Rāma straightaway and report the whole matter to him. We shall then reach a decision as to the next step."

Everyone, including Aṅgada, applauded and accepted this wise counsel.

On the way, they came to a grove known as Madhuvana, famous for its sweet honey. The vānaras gave themselves up to play. They teased each other, they pulled each other, they slapped each other in fun: they were hilarious. They obtained the permission of the elders in the party to take some honey from that grove. Having obtained the permission, however, they began almost to ruin the grove! Seeing this, the guard Dadhimukha protested. He even hit some of the vānaras. But the vānaras soon overpowered Dadhimukha, intoxicated as they were; and they continued to devastate the grove.

Sundara 62–63

Hanumān heartily encouraged them in their consumption of the honey and the devastations of the grove! He said: "I shall keep all intruders away; drink the honey to your heart's content." Aṅgada said to Hanumān: "Truly, to celebrate your victory, O Hanumān, we would do your bidding even if it were unworthy: with what great joy we should obey you when your command is so palatable!!" Brushing the guards aside, the vānaras entered the Madhuvana in vast numbers and denuded it of fruits and honeycombs. They drank the honey to their hearts' content; they got drunk. They played with one another, using the wax as balls.

The guards who had been overpowered and ignored, went to Dadhimukha with the complaint: "Encouraged by Hanumān, the vānaras have destroyed the Madhuvana; and we too have been nicely beaten and shown the path of the gods!" Once again Dadhimukha went to where the vānaras were revelling. Seeing him, the vānaras rushed forward to attack him. Aṅgada himself attacked Dadhimukha. Aṅgada was completely drunk and did not show the least mercy towards Dadhimukha even though the latter was related to Sugrīva. Aṅgada beat him up and threw him on the ground.

Surrounded by the guards, Dadhimukha immediately went to Sugrīva to report the matter. As soon as he entered the presence of Sugrīva, Dadhimukha fell on his face and saluted the king. Sugrīva questioned him as to what had happened. Dadhimukha related the facts; he said: "Madhuvana, which had so long been zealously guarded by you, by Vāli and even by your father, has completely been destroyed, O King, by the vānaras!" As he was thus complaining to Sugrīva, Lakṣmaṇa who was also present, questioned Sugrīva: "What does he say?"

Sugrīva replied to Lakṣmaṇa: "O Lakṣmaṇa, this vānara who has been appointed to guard the Madhuvana is complaining that the vānaras whom we have sent in the southerly direction for the search of Sītā have entered the Madhuvana and destroyed it. This makes me feel that the purpose has been accomplished. Otherwise they would not behave in this manner. Surely, Sītā has been seen, and that, too, by none other than Hanumān himself. That particular party consists of the very best among the vānaras—with Jāmbavān, Aṅgada and Hanumān; and hence I was sure that they would not fail. I infer from their action that they have returned from Laṅkā after having seen Sītā."

Turning to Dadhimukha, Sugrīva said: "Even the misdeeds of one who has accomplished his purpose have to be put up with; hence, continue to guard the Madhuvana. Go there and ask the vānaras to come here immediately. Rāma, Lakṣmaṇa and myself are very eager to see them all at once."

Sundara 64–65

Dadhimukha returned to Madhuvana. He approached Aṅgada humbly and apologetically. The vānaras, too, had become sober in the meantime. Dadhimukha said to Aṅgada: "O Prince, I do realise that all of you are fatigued having travelled afar; surely you need to nourish and refresh yourselves. Pray, let all the vānaras eat and drink the fruits of this grove to their hearts' content. You are the crown prince; and you are our lord and the owner of this grove. I reported your arrival here to your uncle Sugrīva. The king asked me to request you to proceed to his presence quickly as they are all eagerly awaiting you."

Aṅgada turned to the vānaras: "O vānaras, I believe that the news of our arrival has reached the ears of Rāma, too. From the way in which Dadhimukha narrates the king's orders, it appears as though all of them rejoice to hear of our return. I suggest it is time we returned. But, I shall do nothing against your wishes. Though I am the crown prince, I have no right to impose my wishes upon you; but I shall abide by your wishes."

The vānaras replied: "O Prince, who other than you would have uttered such words? In this world a man who enjoys some little power is intoxicated with it and thinks 'I am everything'. We, too, wish to proceed immediately to the presence of Sugrīva; and we await your command to do so."

Aṅgada thereupon said: "Let us go." And, the party turned towards Kiṣkindhā. Sugrīva noticed Aṅgada ready to land, and pointing him out to Rāma said: "It is certain that Sītā has been found, and that it was Hanumān who discovered her whereabouts. With Hanumān, Jāmbavān, Aṅgada and other heroes in this search party, it is impossible that the mission has failed. Moreover, they would not have dared to devastate Madhuvana if they had failed. Hence, O Rāma, take heart. Your sorrow is nearing its end."

There was great tumult in the air as the vānara forces began to arrive. Aṅgada landed close to Sugrīva. He, Hanumān and the other leaders now approached Sugrīva with hands joined in salutations. Rāma was supremely delighted to hear from Hanumān, "Sītā has been seen." Lakṣmaṇa gazed with pride and gratitude at Sugrīva. Rāma gazed with supreme affection at Hanumān.

Rāma then questioned Hanumān and the latter narrated in great detail how he crossed the ocean and how he went into Laṅkā and saw Sītā seated at the foot of the Siṁśapa tree. He assured Rāma that Sītā was constantly thinking of him and him alone. Hanumān realised that Rāma and Lakṣmaṇa had absolute confidence in him and narrated all the events that took place in Laṅkā, and handed to Rāma the jewel that Sītā had given him.

Sundara 66, 67, 68

The sight of that jewel revived the memories of Rāma and even so his grief. He burst into tears. Fondly gazing at it, he said: "My father-in-law presented this to Sītā on the occasion of our wedding. It was actually given by him to my father who then fastened it to Sītā's hair. Hence when I look at this I am reminded of my father, my father-in-law, and it is as if I have seen Sītā. O Hanumān, kindly narrate to me in detail all that she said to you: for when I hear of what she said, it soothes my heart."

Hanumān thereupon narrated in great detail the dialogue between him and Sītā. He also repeated to Rāma the story of the crow which she had told him as a token of their meeting. He said: "Sītā wishes me to ask you; 'You are such an adept in the use of the most powerful missiles, why then are you not rescuing me from the captivity of Rāvaṇa?' She also prays again and again: 'If you have any affection for me, kindly come soon and take me back, for I shall not be able to live for more than a month.' "

Hanumān then told Rāma how he had offered to carry Sītā away on his own back so that she could be reunited with Rāma immediately, and that Sītā had declined saying it would be adharma. Hanumān said: "She politely turned down the offer saying: 'It is not dharma, O Hanumān: when I was abducted in the forest, Rāvaṇa touched my body; but then I was helpless and so how could I prevent it?' And, she asked me to do whatever would be necessary for you to defeat Rāvaṇa in open combat and recover her."

Hanumān said further: "Having accomplished my mission, I was in a hurry to return to you. Sītā again pleaded with me to inform you of her sad plight and to urge you to go to Laṅkā quickly. She further said: 'I do not wish that Rāma should take me away from here as Rāvaṇa took me away stealthily from the forest; that is not worthy of Rāma." She then began to entertain doubts about our ability to cross the formidable ocean. I reassured her that in Sugrīva's army there are hundreds and thousands of great heroes far more powerful than I am, who could easily cross the ocean and fight the demons, conquer Rāvaṇa and rescue her. I even told her that in Sugrīva's army there is none inferior to me, and in support of this I said: 'Who would send the greatest hero as a messenger; the wise ruler would only send a third-rate hero as a messenger.' I assured her that you would soon invade Laṅkā, and in open combat kill Rāvaṇa and recover her honourably. Thus did I console the noble Sītā and she derived great consolation from my assurances."

Yuddha Kāṇḍa
The Great War

Rāma said: "A great and extremely rare feat has been accomplished by you, O Hanumān, and a great service rendered to Sugrīva, the king. In this world there are three types of servants. The best of them carries out the work allotted to him by the master, and goes even farther and, creatively anticipating the master's wishes, fulfills them, too. The mediocre servant does not, though capable, do anything more than what the master commanded him to do. And the worst of servants is he who, though capable, does not even carry out the master's wishes. You, O Hanumān, are the very best; you did a lot more than what king Sugrīva had asked you to do, and yet did not do anything which the master would have been displeased about. By finding out the whereabouts of Sītā, you have truly given a new lease of life to Lakṣmaṇa and to me, and to the whole dynasty of the Raghus. What can I give you as a reward? At the present moment, I can give you only this, my warm embrace." So saying Rāma warmly embraced Hanumān who was thrilled.

Rāma turned to Sugrīva and said: "Sītā has been found but not yet recovered. In order to do so we have to cross this formidable ocean. How can we accomplish this task?" Sensing Rāma's deep concern, Sugrīva endeavoured to reassure him: "Pray, do not entertain any misgivings, O Rāma. We shall soon cross the ocean, kill Rāvaṇa and recover Sītā. Grief and despair are the forerunners of failure. The vānara forces are already excited by the prospect of a fight with the demons; and they are ready to jump into the fire for your sake. We should now explore ways and means of building a bridge across the ocean.

But, give up grief which robs one of valour; when a ruler yields to grief and despair, he becomes inactive. An inactive ruler is useless; and people fear only the brave."

Rāma regained his self-confidence and said: "I can easily cross the sea by the power of my austerity, by building a bridge or by drying up the ocean!" In answer to his query, Hanumān said: "Laṅkā has four gates equipped with drawbridges, and is surrounded by a dreadful moat. It enjoys fourfold protection: a river circles it, it is set on a hill, it is surrounded by thick forests, and it is heavily fortified, with walls and moats. Each gate is guarded by hundreds of thousands of demons; and there is a huge pile of weapons at each gate. These weapons are six feet long and can fire a hundred rounds at the same time, killing hundreds simultaneously. The drawbridges are cleverly operated by engines, and they are gold-plated as a further protection against rust and enemy-attack. However, I have damaged these drawbridges and filled the moats with their debris. As for crossing the sea, just a handful of the foremost among the vānara leaders will accomplish the task: it may even be unnecessary to take the whole army."

Yuddha 4–5

Hanumān's account of Sītā's predicament and his 'intelligence report' concerning the military strength of the enemy inspired Rāma to take a quick decision. He declared: "I shall immediately invade Laṅkā and destroy it! This is an auspicious hour and today is auspicious for military ventures. O Sugrīva, order the army to march. O Nīla, let the army march by that route on which plenty of food is available. If the demons discover our preparation for invasion, they might try to poison the fruits and roots; extreme care and vigilance are necessary. Some of the vānaras should go ahead and conduct a careful reconnaissance: there may be demons waiting en route to ambush our army."

The king Sugrīva and the commander-in-chief of the tribal forces, Nīla, issued quick instructions for the army to march.

The army crossed rivers and lakes and passed mountains and forests. All the soldiers were highly enthusiastic and were eager to fight, and to recover Sītā; they marched without resting anywhere. And all their actions and every movement of their limbs gave some indication of their prowess.

When they reached the Mahendra mountain, Rāma went up to the peak of the mountain. From there he beheld the vast ocean. Surveying it from where he stood, he said to the vānara-chiefs: "O Sugrīva, we have now reached the shores of this ocean; the problem which we faced earlier now confronts us. Let the vānara armies be comfortably settled on the shore and then let us devise ways and means of crossing this ocean. At the same time, pray ensure that all possible precautions are taken against enemy infiltration and sabotage."

The army settled down on the sea-shore: it looked as if it were another ocean, only brown-coloured. The noise of the vānaras drowned the roar of the ocean. And, the leaders of the vānara forces settled down, looking at the vast ocean to consider ways of crossing it.

Rāma grieved for Sītā. He said to Lakṣmaṇa: "O Lakṣmaṇa, people say that as time fades away, grief fades away, too. But in my case it grows worse with the passage of time. Oh, when will I behold my beloved? When will I hold her face in my hands and kiss it? When will I closely embrace my Sītā, her full, firm breasts pressing my chest? The thought that the time-limit set by her for her recovery is slipping away causes me unbearable agony, O Lakṣmaṇa." Lakṣmaṇa comforted him suitably.

Yuddha 6, 7, 8

In Laṅkā, a worried Rāvaṇa called an assembly of his counsellors and commanders. He said to them: "An impossible task has been accomplished; an impregnable city has been penetrated; the indestructible has been destroyed and mighty heroes have been killed. And, all this by a simple vānara. Pray, consider what ought to be done and advise me. Three types of statesman have been described by the wise. The best among these is one who commences his ventures after consultation with his ministers and with the blessings of god. The middling is one who consults only himself, decides the right course of action and carries it out according to his own decision. The worst is one who fails to consider what is right and what is wrong, who ignores the divine, and who says: 'I will do it'. In the same manner, consultation itself can be divided into three categories. The best consultation is one in which the counsellors reach unanimous agreement which is in accord with the scriptures. Where there is a lot of argument and counter-argument before unanimity is reached is regarded as a mediocre consultation. Where each counsellor adheres to his own view and where no unanimity is reached—such a consultation is the worst. Pray, consider among yourselves the best course of action."

Inspite of this elaborate briefing, the demons impetuously jumped up, each brandishing a weapon like an iron club, javelin, sword or spear, and exclaimed: "Lord, what need is there for you to be afraid of Rāma? You conquered many gods, demi-gods and demons. Rāma is not equal to any of them, let alone claiming equality with you! One Indrajit alone will be able to deal with Rāma and his mighty army! Pray, send him at once, and that will be the end of your enemies."

In similar strain, the commanders of the demons spoke. Prahastha said: "We were literally taken unawares by Hanumān. If we had been prepared, we could have easily disposed of him." Durmukha said: "However, we should not take this lying down. I shall myself go and destroy the vānara army." Vajradamṣṭra said: "But, why think too much of Hanumān? Think of Rāma, our real enemy. I shall go alone and kill him with my iron mace. I also suggest a simple tactic by which the entire vānara army may be killed. A contingent of the most terrible demons should approach Rāma disguised as human beings, and say to him: 'We come from Bharata to help you'. At an opportune moment, they should fight the vānara army and destroy it." Kumbhakarṇa's son Nikumbha said: "None of you need worry: I shall immediately go over there and kill Rāma single-handed." And Vajrahanu said: "I shall myself go and swallow Rāma and return."

Yuddha 9, 10, 11

The demons who had thus counselled Rāvaṇa were impatient to prove their boast and to show their mettle; they stood up with their own weapons raised, shouting: We shall immediately kill Rāma, Sugrīva, Lakṣmaṇa as also that vānara Hanumān who devastated the city of Laṅkā." Vibhīṣaṇa rose from his seat, restrained the demons, and said to Rāvaṇa:

"There are occasions when one should resort to violence and there are occasions when it is unwise to resort to violence, brother. It is unwise of you even to hope to vanquish in battle

Rāma who is a master of himself and has the support of the divine. All of you have already had a foretaste of the strength, the valour and the intelligence of Hanumān: it is rash to assume that we can face him in battle. The worst error in military strategy is underestimation of enemy-strength.

"And, there is the other extremely important consideration. For what offence do you wish to fight and to kill Rāma? In fact, you are guilty of abducting his wife. If you say you did so as revenge for Rāma's killing of Khara and others, even that is not proper: Rāma killed Khara in self-defence, only when the latter attacked him.

"Abandon this unrighteous action, before Rāma's might and the strength of the vānara hordes destroys you. Give up hate which destroys happiness as well as dharma; and adhere to dharma which increases joy and fame; hand over Sītā to Rāma and let us live with our children and relations." Rāvaṇa did not reply, but retired to his own apartments.

The next morning, Vibhīṣaṇa once again sought the presence of his brother Rāvaṇa, and said: "Since the day you brought Sītā to Laṅkā, there has been a succession of evil portents which spell the destruction of Laṅkā and its inhabitants. Before the evil destiny which these evil omens portend overtakes us, it is good to make amends; and hence I appeal to you to restore Sītā to Rāma." Rāvaṇa abruptly dismissed Vibhīṣaṇa, curtly telling him: "I am not afraid of Rāma, and I will not give up Sītā."

Passion for Sītā and the disaffection of his own people had begun to tell upon Rāvaṇa's health, and he was becoming emaciated day by day. He had resolved upon war. He mounted his richly-decked chariot and surrounded by the commanders went to the council chamber. He then commanded his messengers to convene an emergency meeting of his council, for, he said, "I have extremely urgent matters to discuss."

Yuddha 12–13

Rāvaṇa addressed the assembly. At the very commencement, he ordered the commander-in-chief Prahasta: "Pray, ensure immediately that the defence of the city of Laṅkā is impregnable and that all the arms of the defence forces are well placed and equipped." This order was immediately carried out.

Rāvaṇa continued his address to the council: "Sometime ago, I abducted Sītā, the beloved wife of Rāma, and brought her from the Daṇḍaka forest to Laṅkā; she is the most beautiful woman I have seen so far. I have endeavoured to persuade her to accept my hand and my love; but she has so far spurned them. She had asked for a year in which to make up her mind and I granted this.

"Now I understand that her husband Rāma is preparing to invade Laṅkā along with a formidable army of vānaras. I do not know if they will all be able to cross the ocean. On the other hand, you all know what havoc was wrought by one of the vānaras who had come here as but a messenger. And, we do not know what steps the enemy might take to accomplish his purpose. On the other hand, so long as I have your whole-hearted support, I do not fear anyone on earth, let alone the human being Rāma. Only the other day you enabled me to attain victory over the gods. May I therefore suggest that we should now discuss ways and means of achieving my aim: Rāma and Lakṣmaṇa should be killed and Sītā should not be returned from Laṅkā."

Kumbhakarṇa was filled with anger and retorted: "Why did you not consult us before you went to Daṇḍaka and abducted Sītā? He who does today what ought to have been done earlier, and he who does earlier what ought to be done later—he does not know the course of right action. He who engages himself in right action does not regret nor repent, O Rāvaṇa. However, you have now called us for consultations and wish to fight Rāma. We shall all stand by you and destroy Rāma. Fear not."

Mahāpārśva, another demon leader, said: "Achieve your purpose by force, O King! Seduce Sītā by force; and then there is nothing to be afraid of. We shall deal with Rāma suitably." Rāvaṇa said in answer to this: "Alas, I cannot do that. Listen to a misadventure of mine. Once upon a time, a celestial nymph was thus seduced by me. She was Puñjikasthala; and she reported my conduct to Brahmā the creator who thereupon cursed me: 'If you thus forcibly seduce any other woman from now on, your head will burst into a hundred pieces.' Hence I am not able to force Sītā to accept my love. Yet, I am confident that I will kill Rāma and then Sītā will have no choice but to accept me."

Yuddha 14, 15, 16

Vibhīṣaṇa spoke: "Before the terrible vānaras invade and destroy Laṅkā, before Rāma's missiles take your life, restore Sītā to Rāma."

Prahastha intervened and said: "How silly! We have no fear even from the gods! And, none whatsoever from Rāma."

Vibhīṣaṇa continued: "You are all mistaken in your estimation of the power of Rāma. None of you will be able to withstand his missiles. Those of you who encourage the king in his evil action are indeed his enemies. They who have enjoyed the king's favours have the duty to restrain him, if necessary by force, from unrighteous and self-destructive actions. He indeed is a real minister who counsels what is good for the master, having fully considered his own and the enemy's strength, and the possibilities of increase or decrease or steady maintenance of such strength."

Indrajit, Rāvaṇa's son, leapt to his feet and said: "Uncle, you are a disgrace to the race of demons. Such cowardice as you have betrayed is unworthy of even mortals, much less of us demons. Uncle Vibhīṣaṇa is utterly weak and timid, and there is no heroism nor prowess in him. I defeated even Indra, the god of gods; should I be afraid of the mortal Rāma? The least among the demons can look after Rāma; there is no cause for fear."

Vibhīṣaṇa continued: "You are but a young lad, Indrajit: and you speak like one. Unfortunately, however, you are bragging your way to death. I repeat, the only wise course is for us to restore Sītā to Rāma, along with wealth and jewels."

Rāvaṇa was greatly enraged to hear this repeated advice of Vibhīṣaṇa. He said: "One may live with an enemy or a venomous snake, but not with a hypocritical friend who is devoted to the enemy. Indeed, O Vibhīṣaṇa, one's own worst enemy is a close relative who is guided by his own self-interest. Such a kinsman is hostile to even a righteous king and is ever intent on bringing about his downfall. Wealth exists in the cow; from kinsman only fear flows; women are noted for fickleness; and the brāhmaṇa for austerities. It seems to be natural, my brother, that you do not like that I should prosper. I have shown you all my affection; but I realise that affection bestowed upon the hostile is fruitless and can even be dangerous. If what you said had been said by someone else, I would have had him executed: but, what shall I do with you, traitor!"

Vibhīṣaṇa replied: "They at whose door death knocks do not heed good counsel. In this world, O King, there are many who utter pleasant words; but very rare indeed is one who proffers unpleasant but wholesome advice, and rare is one who listens to such advice. Forgive the offence I have given you. Save yourself. May all be well with you."

Yuddha 17–18

Having spoken his mind to Rāvaṇa, Vibhīṣaṇa immediately flew to where Rāma was, accompanied by four of his devoted demons. When the vānaras saw that a demon was flying towards their camp, they were alarmed and sought Sugrīva's permission to shoot him down. While still airborne, Vibhīṣaṇa announced his identity and his intention: "I am the brother of Rāvaṇa who has sought his own doom by having abducted Sītā. I have abandoned my wife and children and I seek Rāma's asylum. Pray, inform Rāma, the refuge of the whole world, that Vibhīṣaṇa seeks his refuge."

All the vānaras sought Rāma's presence. Sugrīva opened the discussion, with the words: "He is from the enemy; he is an enemy. He may be a spy. He may be an infiltrator. In any case he is suspect. Give us leave to kill him, O Rāma." Rāma sought the advice of the vānara-leaders.

Others advised cautious investigation. Hanumān, however, differed from them all and said: "Vibhīṣaṇa has rejected his unrighteous brother and sought you, O Rāma. He should be accepted. None of the other courses suggested is feasible. If he is an enemy and a spy he cannot so easily be discovered as such by our spying or by our interrogation. His face is calm and tranquil, and his demeanour humble and pure: there is no suspicion in my mind."

While Rāma approved of this, Sugrīva cautioned him: "He has betrayed his own brother; whom else would he not betray?"

Rāma, while appreciating the wisdom of these words, said: "Kinsmen are normally friendly to oneself; but in the case of rulers, however, the reverse is true! His own kinsmen and the rulers of neighbouring states are the king's worst enemies. In this light you can understand why Vibhīṣaṇa has abandoned his brother and come here. In this world all brothers are not like Bharata, all sons are not like me, nor friends like you!

"We have heard how a dove offered hospitality to a hunter, its own enemy: are we worse than that dove that we are reluctant to accept Vibhīṣaṇa? Even so have the sages declared: 'Even an enemy seeking one's refuge should be protected at all costs'. Failure in the protection of refugees is a terrible sin, indeed. This is my firm vow: if one seeks my refuge just once and says: 'I am yours', him I shall protect from all fear. Hence, I have granted asylum to whoever has come, whether it is Vibhīṣaṇa or Rāvaṇa himself! Bring them to me."

Sugrīva was delighted. "We shall now regard Vibhīṣaṇa as one of us," Sugrīva declared.

Yuddha 19–20

Vibhīṣaṇa, having obtained the vānaras' permission to land, circled above the field and landed. Along with his four companions Vibhīṣaṇa fell at the feet of Rāma.

Rāma asked him, at once: "Pray, tell me truthfully, what is the strength of the demons and their weakness, too." Vibhīṣaṇa replied: "Rāvaṇa has a boon from Brahmā the creator that he shall not be killed by the gods, demons, demi-gods, snakes and birds. Kumbhakarṇa, his brother, is possessed of terrible might. Rāvaṇa's army chief, Prahasta, is also a mighty hero. So, too, is Indrajit, Rāvaṇa's son, who has magic powers, too. Rāvaṇa has millions of demons who constitute his army."

Undaunted, Rāma declared: "I shall kill Rāvaṇa along with his commander-in-chief and others; and I shall crown you king—this I promise."

Rāma decided to seal this friendship immediately. He asked Lakṣmaṇa to fetch water from the ocean: "And with that water, crown Vibhīṣaṇa king of Laṅkā: for he has earned my pleasure." Lakṣmaṇa promptly brought the water, and as the astonished vānaras were looking on, Vibhīṣaṇa was consecrated king of Laṅkā.

Vibhīṣaṇa advised them: "The deity presiding over the ocean is indebted to Rāma: it was Rāma's forefather who rendered a great service to the ocean. Hence, I suggest that Rāma should propitiate that deity and ask for a way to cross the ocean." Rāma accepted that advice and took up his seat near the ocean.

A spy named Sārdūla had surveyed the strength of the vānara forces and reported the concentration of the troops on the sea-shore to Rāvaṇa. Greatly disturbed by this report, Rāvaṇa summoned Śuka and said: "Go at once to the other shore and say to Sugrīva: 'You are like a brother to me. What offence have I caused you in that you wish to invade Laṅkā along with your army?' "

Assuming the form of a bird, Śuka immediately arrived at Sugrīva's camp and delivered Rāvaṇa's message. The vānaras began to assail Śuka but were restrained by Rāma. Sugrīva replied: "Tell Rāvaṇa; 'I am neither your friend nor benefactor. You have antagonised Rāma and hence you deserve the same treatment as was meted out to Vāli! You boast of your prowess. Why then did you kill the aged Jaṭāyu? Why did you not take Sītā away in the presence of Rāma? Nay, your life has come to an end!' " As the bird was about to fly away, Aṅgada said: "It is not a messenger; it is a spy which should be killed!" As the vānaras seized the bird, it appealed to Rāma who requested the vānaras to release it alive, saying: "It is but a messenger of Rāvaṇa and should not be killed." It was however kept in protective custody.

Yuddha 21–(22)

On a grass mat with his arm alone as his pillow, Rāma reclined, vowing to propitiate the god of the ocean and thus to secure his help to cross over to Laṅkā. The arm that had gifted thousands of cows, the arm that had been adorned by unguents and ornaments, the arm that Sītā had used as her pillow, the arm whose strength inspired fear in the enemy-hearts—that arm was the sole support for the head of Rāma, the ascetic, as he lay down on the sea-shore praying to the god of the ocean to show his grace. Rāma resolved: "I should now cross this ocean; or I shall dry up the ocean."

He lay there for three days and nights, without any sign of the ocean-god's pleasure. Rāma was seized with impatience and anger. He said to Lakṣmaṇa: "Here is an example, O Lakṣmaṇa, of how the wicked misinterpret the noble man's virtue: they think it is his weakness! The world respects only the man who is loud and noisy, vain and aggressive! Neither fame nor victory is won by a peaceful approach, O Lakṣmaṇa. See what I do now. Bring my weapon and bring the missiles.

I shall dry up the ocean so that the vānaras may walk to Laṅkā."

Rāma got hold of his formidable weapon and took a few terrible missiles and discharged them at the ocean. These caused such a violent commotion that they whipped tidal waves of huge proportions. The creatures of the ocean, the huge snakes and other deep-sea creatures were disturbed and distressed. Mountainous waves rose in the sea. There was a terrifying roar from the ocean. Even Lakṣmaṇa was frightened.

Rāma looked at the ocean and said in great anger: "I shall dry up the entire ocean! Utterly deprived of your essence, O ocean, only a sand-bed will remain." He took the most powerful missile endowed with the powers of the Creator himself and hurled it at the ocean. The effect of this was unimaginable and beyond description. Mountains began to shake. There was an earthquake. There was dense darkness everywhere. The course of the sun, the moon and the planets was disturbed. The sky was illumined as if by the sudden appearance of thousands of meteors. Accompanied by deafening thunderclaps, the sky shone with lightning. Gale-force winds swept the surface of the earth and the ocean. Even the peaks of mountains were dislodged.

Living beings everywhere cried in agony. The waters of the ocean were stirred up so suddenly and with such force that it appeared as though the ocean would overstep its bounds and submerge the land.

Yuddha 22–23

The deity presiding over the ocean then rose from the ocean and meekly approached Rāma. To Rāma who was standing burning with anger, his weapon ready to discharge the most deadly missile, the Ocean said:

"Rāma, everything in nature is governed by the immutable law which alone determines the inherent characteristic of every element in nature. In accordance with that law, it is natural for the ocean to be unfathomable and impassable. Yet, I shall suggest a way out, and I shall indicate the path by which the vānaras will be able to go over to Laṅkā."

Rāma asked the Ocean: "Against whom shall I direct this unfailing missile which has been readied for the purpose of drying the ocean?" And the Ocean pointed to the well-known

Drumakulya inhabited by sinners: directed to this spot, Rāma's missile dried up the ocean there, and, in order to compensate for this action, Rāma blessed that piece of land: "You will be fertile and you will be full of fruit-bearing trees."

The Ocean said: "Rāma, here is Nala who is the son of the great Viśvakarma (the architect of all). Let him construct a bridge across these waters, for he is as good as his father. I shall gladly support that bridge."

Nala at once voluntarily offered: "What the Ocean has said is indeed true. I shall construct the bridge across these waters: and I am as proficient as my father. Actually, the Ocean owes a debt of gratitude to Rāma, for a great service was rendered by Rāma's ancestors to the Ocean. Yet, it was not gratitude that inspired the Ocean to give way; fear did it! The ungrateful man in this world recognises only punishment, not love or affection."

At Rāma's command, thousands of vānaras got ready for the mighty undertaking. They cut down logs of wood; they rolled away huge rocks and stones. They threw all these into the ocean which was greatly agitated by this. Some of the vānaras held a plumbline so that the rocks could be placed in a straight line. With the help of the vānaras of immeasurable strength and mighty deeds, Nala put up the bridge across the ocean, using logs of wood, rocks and stones. The eight hundred mile long bridge took five days to build. Celestial beings (devas or beings of light) and Gandharvas (celestial musicians) watched this marvellous feat.

As soon as the bridge was completed, Vibhīṣaṇa stood guard at the southern (Laṅkā) end, to prevent sabotage by the enemy. Sugrīva then said to Rāma: "Let Hanumān take you and let Aṅgada take Lakṣmaṇa, to Laṅkā." They were ready to depart.

Yuddha 24–25

Soon Rāma was on the other side of the ocean. He beheld Laṅkā, shining with decorations; and his heart sought Sītā. It would not be long before he recovered her. Rāma said to Lakṣmaṇa: "Look, O Lakṣmaṇa, the beautiful city on the hill which was constructed in days of yore by the architect Viśvakarma. With its multi-storeyed buildings, gardens and grove, it shows all the signs of extreme affluence."

Rāma then asked Sugrīva: "Order the release of the messenger of Rāvaṇa, Śuka who had come to us in the disguise of a bird." As soon as he was released, Śuka returned to Rāvaṇa's palace, and reported to Rāvaṇa: "I went to Sugrīva and gave him your message. But, the vānaras caught hold of me and would have killed me, but for Rāma's timely intervention. They have built a bridge and have crossed the formidable ocean with the vānara army. Rāma with his deadly weapon and missiles is here. Only two courses are open to you now: either restore Sītā to Rāma or fight."

Rāvaṇa declared with great vehemence: "I will not give up Sītā, even if I have to fight with the gods and demi-gods and demons. Oh, I am eagerly waiting to shoot Rāma and see him bleeding. Rāma has no idea of my might and that is why he is foolish enough to ask for a fight."

At the same time, Rāvaṇa was anxious within himself; and he called upon two demons, Śuka and Sāraṇa and said to them: "Effectively mask your identity and penetrate into the enemy's army. Ascertain its strength and report everything in detail. I could not believe it when I was told that they had built a bridge across the ocean; but now there is no doubt that they are ready to fight. Hence it is good that we should have a correct account of their strength."

The demons disguised themselves as vānaras and stealthily entered the vānara forces. Seeing the vastness of the army, they were bewildered and could not estimate the number and the strength. Vibhīṣaṇa apprehended the two spies. He took them to Rāma and said to him: "Here are two demon-spies, O Rāma: they deserve to be executed." Rāma said to them: "Have you seen everything, O demons? Then go back to Rāvaṇa and report to him. If you have not seen everything, I shall gladly ask Vibhīṣaṇa to show you, so that you can present a full and complete account of our strength to Rāvaṇa." Thus released by Rāma, they went to Rāvaṇa and Sāraṇa said to him: "O King, I was caught by Vibhīṣaṇa, but it was Rāma who saved my life. He asked me to convey to you the message that he would invade Laṅkā and destroy it tomorrow itself. Enough of this hostility with Rāma, O King, pray; make peace with him."

Yuddha 26–27

Rāvaṇa said sternly to Sāraṇa: "You are frightened, coward! But I will not give up Sītā even if I have to fight the very gods, demi-gods and demons of the whole world." Immediately, Rāvaṇa went up the palace which was a white house with golden domes, and which had the height of several palmyrah trees placed one on top of another, (or, which had many storeys). From there he saw the whole country covered by the vānara forces.

Rāvaṇa thereupon commanded Sāraṇa: "Come here and point out to me who is who in this army. Who are the commanders and what is their strength?"

Sāraṇa replied: "That powerful vānara standing at the head of the army, by whose shouts Laṅkā shakes, is Nīla. That hero who paces the ground with great fury is Aṅgada, Vāli's son. Behind him is Nala, the builder of the bridge. That white vānara Śveta is a big organiser and is Sugrīva's military adviser. There stands Kumuda. And there is Caṇḍa, surrounded by countless vānaras. Even so is Rambha yonder surrounded by countless vānaras. That fearless vānara is Śarabha, who has an equally vast army. Those two mighty vānaras are Panaśa and Vinata. That Krodhana is a mighty commander. Undaunted and fearless even of death, there Gavaya stands at the head of a huge force. Even the commanders of this mighty army cannot be counted: and they are all intrepid heroes. They are all utterly dedicated to the cause of Rāma, and determined to win.

"There stands another leader, Hara, who is followed by numerous commanders of the army. And, there is Dhūmra, the leader of another tribe. Yet another tribe is led by the powerful Jāmbavān who once assisted the king of gods, Indra, and won many boons from him. And, you see yonder a lordly vānara whom all the other vānaras stand gazing at: he is Rambha. The gigantic form you see over there is Samnadana. That other vānara Kranthana is said to have been begotten by the god of fire. Even so is that other leader Pramāthi a vānara of incomparable might.

"The leader of yet another tribe known as Golāngulas is the mighty vānara known as Gavākṣa.

"Another tribe of vānaras inhabit the foremost among mountains; they are of different colours and of incomparable and fierce valour. All of them are assembled here.

"And, all of them are standing there filled with eagerness, in readiness to fight and destroy Laṅkā. The supreme commander Śatabalī is also seen there: desirous of victory, he worships the sun every day. All of them are utterly dedicated to the cause of Rāma to whom they are devoted. For his sake they are ready to give up their very life."

Yuddha 28–29

It was Śuka's turn and he gave a description of the other heroes in the enemy force. He said:

"Those vānaras you see over there are in truth the offspring of gods and demi-gods; they have immeasurable strength; they can even change their forms. The two commanders you see over there are known as Mainda and Dvivida; it is said that they have had a taste of the nectar of immortality. Surely, you recognise that vānara standing over there! He is the same Hanumān who burnt Laṅkā.

"You are probably aware that the two princes standing near Hanumān are Rāma and Lakṣmaṇa. The one standing next to Hanumān is Rāma who adheres to dharma and who is protected by dharma. He is a pastmaster in all branches of knowledge, and he is equipped with the supreme missile known as the Brahmā-missile. If he so desired, he could split the heavens and even split the earth, too. His anger is death; and his prowess is equal to Indra's. And, Lakṣmaṇa standing next to him is Rāma's alter ego and would not mind doing anything to secure Rāma's victory.

"No doubt you recognise that Vibhīṣaṇa is with them. I hear that Rāma has consecrated him king of Laṅkā. You see Sugrīva also there: the celestial necklace he wears, as also Tārā the wife of Vāli and the kingdom of Kiṣkindhā were all bestowed upon him by Rāma after he had killed Vāli.

"Behold, O great King, this mighty army which looks like a planet on fire; considering its strength, take such steps as would ensure your victory."

Rāvaṇa was worried. But he directed his fury at the two spies, Śuka and Sāraṇa. He said to them: "Traitors! You sing in front of me the praises of my enemies who are about to fight with me. Of what value is your scriptural learning if you do not even know how to talk to and in front of your king? I would have killed you for your misbehaviour; but I do not do so considering your past services to me. Get out of here immediately."

Rāvaṇa commanded other spies to come to him. He ordered them: "Go to Rāma's camp at once and find out without arousing anybody's suspicion, what Rāma's plans are. Watch carefully and report to me, how he sleeps, how he wakes up and what he is doing now. One who thus knows the habits and movements of the enemy easily overcomes him."

They entered Rāma's camp; but Vibhīṣaṇa detected their presence. But, merciful Rāma had them freed! At the same time, the vānaras assaulted them. Thus harassed, the spies returned to Rāvaṇa.

Yuddha 30–31

Śārdūla returned to Rāvaṇa's presence and said to him: "O King, it is not possible to spy on Rāma's army: they are very powerful and above all they are protected by Rāma. In fact, we were all apprehended immediately on entering their ranks; and we escaped with our lives only because of Rāma's mercy."

Rāvaṇa immediately summoned his counsellors for consultation. After apprising them of the latest position, he took the demon Vidyujjihvā with him and both of them went towards the Aśoka-grove. Vidyujjihvā possessed the power to materialise any object by a mere wave of his hand. Rāvaṇa said to him: "Pray, conjure up an exact duplicate of Rāma's head as well as of his weapon and missile; and give them to me."

At once the demon produced the desired articles, and received an expensive reward from Rāvaṇa. Rāvaṇa proceeded in the direction of where Sītā was seated, followed by the demon. Calmly approaching Sītā, Rāvaṇa said to her:

"O charming lady, the man for whose sake you live like this, he whom you expect to recover you from me, he who killed mighty demons like Khara, your husband Rāma has been killed by me! That is the end of your hopes, O Sītā! And the time has come for you to reconsider your position and be my wife.

"This Rāma had hoped to kill me, destroy Laṅkā and take you back. He had assembled a vast army with the help of Sugrīva; he had even had a bridge built across the ocean; and he had actually arrived at the very gates of Laṅkā. The sun had set. And, Rāma and the commanders of his army were all asleep. Some of my soldiers quietly entered the enemy's camp and killed all the commanders. While Rāma was asleep, my commander-in-chief, Prahastha severed his head with a sharp sword. Vibhīṣaṇa has been taken prisoner. Lakṣmaṇa and the army he had under his command fled. Sugrīva had his neck broken. Hanumān lies dead with his jaw broken to pieces. Jāmbavān is dead. Even so have the other heroes been disposed of without any resistance whatsoever. All the vānaras have fled for their lives; their leaders have been killed.

"I thought you would like to see your husband's head, soaked in blood and sand. Here it is."

Rāvaṇa motioned to Vidyujjihvā to place Rāma's head in front of Sītā. Rāvaṇa said: "Place the head of Rāma in front of Sītā; let her see for herself the final state of her husband!" Rāvaṇa then placed the weapon of Rāma and the missile before Sītā: "Here is the weapon used by Rāma and here is the missile. Now I am sure you will consent to be my wife."

Yuddha 32

After a moment's stunned silence, Sītā burst into tears and wailed aloud: "O Kaikeyī! Your wish has been fulfilled today. The mission that you inaugurated by disturbing the mind of king Daśaratha has come to fruition today with the death of the beloved-prince of his dynasty." Wailing thus aloud, Sītā fell down like a felled banana tree.

Sītā continued to lament: "Alas, O Rāma, you have adhered to your dharma; but I have been widowed. Widowhood is considered an undesirable tragedy in the life of a woman devoted to dharma. Oh what a tragedy! You came to save me, but gave your own life. Astrologers well versed in the study of celestial bodies and their movements had predicted that you would live long: alas, their predictions have proved false. You were ever alert and wise; and yet you have been slain in your sleep! When the time comes, even the impossible becomes possible, Time indeed is the greatest power on earth which brings everything to fruition. Moreover, you were a pastmaster in the political science as also in the use of weapons: yet, here you lie embraced by the demon of destruction. And, here lie your weapons which I used to worship every day!

"I suppose you are now happy, having rejoined your beloved father in heaven. But, why have you deserted me? Don't you remember what you said on the day of our marriage? You said then: 'We shall always practise dharma together'. Pray, take me, too, with you. It is terrible even to think of: that body which I so lovingly embraced is perhaps being ravaged by beasts! How cruel and unjust: that you who worshipped the sacred fire so regularly are denied the privilege of a proper cremation! When Lakṣmaṇa returns to Ayodhyā, alone of the party of three that left Ayodhyā, how greatly mother Kausalyā will grieve. Nay, she will give up her life, too. And, O Rāma, I am the wretched woman who has brought about all this destruction! Ah, his own wife became Rāma's death."

Turning to Rāvaṇa, Sītā said: "O Rāvaṇa, place my body over Rāma's and kill me, too. Place my head along with his, and my body with his: I shall also go along with him. Kill me. You will be rendering me the greatest service. It will be your most auspicious action, in that you bring a husband and wife together."

While she was thus wailing, a messenger urgently sought the presence of Rāvaṇa and said: "Lord, your ministers need you urgently." Rāvaṇa departed at once. When Rāvaṇa left the scene, the head and the weapons of Rāma also disappeared. Rāvaṇa conferred with his ministers and ordered general mobilisation: "Get all the demons together; but do not tell them what for," he instructed.

Yuddha 33–34

As soon as Rāvaṇa left the scene, a demoness known as Śaramā appeared on the scene. Approaching Sītā with love and affection, Śaramā said to her: "Give up your sorrow, O Sītā. Whatever Rāvaṇa said was false. Rāma's head and weapons were produced by magic. Rāma has not been killed! I am convinced that he cannot be killed. He and also his brother Lakṣmaṇa are able to defend themselves admirably. I know for certain that Rāma and the army of vānaras have crossed the ocean and arrived at the very gates of Laṅkā."

Hearing the tumultuous sound outside the grove, Śaramā continued: "O Sītā, the army of Rāvaṇa is being mobilised and troops are marching for war. The roads are blocked with the troops. They are marching to their doom, and to usher in your happiness, O Sītā. I feel convinced that soon Rāma will enter Laṅkā victoriously. Soon you will behold your beloved husband. Soon I will behold you, my very dear friend, seated on the lap of your husband. He will wipe your tears and you will be reunited. Rest assured of this, my dear Sītā. For the present, pray, adore the sun, the Lord of all beings."

This was great consolation to Sītā. Śaramā wanted to do Sītā a more concrete favour and said: "I can go where I like, unperceived by anyone, O Sītā. If you like I can go to Rāma, see him, talk to him and return to you."

Sītā said to Śaramā: "If you wish to do me a favour, O Śaramā, then please go to where Rāvaṇa is and find out what he is doing and what his plans are."

Śaramā departed at once, went to Rāvaṇa's court, and returned to the grove soon and said to Sītā: "I went to Rāvaṇa's court and heard all that took place there. Many of his ministers advised him to restore you to Rāma and make peace with him. Rāvaṇa's mother admonished him severely: 'Remember how easily Rāma disposed of thousands of demons in Janasthāna, single-handed. Remember how the heroic Hanumān performed the almost impossible task of crossing the ocean and discovering Sītā.' Even when thus advised by his ministers and his own mother, Rāvaṇa remained stubborn, not wishing to give you up. Impending death befuddles his mind. Rāma will first take his life, and then take you back, O Sītā."

At the same time, upon hearing the roaring of the vānara-forces, Rāvaṇa's army marched forward: they who had lost their lustre, and who saw no good coming out of the war, doomed by the sin of their ruler.

Yuddha 35–36

Rāvaṇa held counsel with his ministers, as his troops began to march towards the city gates. One of his counsellors who was also his maternal grandfather, spoke up:

Malayavān said: "The vital part of statesmanship is right judgement, for there are occasions when one should attack and there are others when one should make peace.

"Rāvaṇa! The Creator gave birth only to two types of sentient beings in this world, the divine and the diabolical. Dharma is the characteristic of the former and adharma that of the latter. The pendulum swings constantly between the two. In one epoch (the Satya Yuga), virtue or dharma keeps adharma under control; in another (the Kali Yuga) adharma prevails. In the present age, however, there is imbalance be-he two: and you have by your wicked actions of great de actually tilted the balance in favour of adharma. a consequence, terrible destruction awaits you and your people. You oppressed the holy sages, devoted as you were to power and pleasure. But those peaceful and holy ones carried on their religious practices: and the smoke that arises from the sacred fire worshipped by them spreads in the ten directions and brings about the destruction of the demons, O Rāvaṇa.

"You have asked for immunity only from being killed by the gods, demi-gods and demons; now you are being invaded by human beings, vānaras and other tribal people. I see terrible evil omens. Clouds rumble making terrifying sounds. Horses and elephants weep. Donkeys are born of cows, and rats of mongooses. Cats mate with leopards, pigs with dogs, and demi-gods with demons and humans. The end of the demons is near. I think Rāma is lord Viṣṇu himself, incarnate in human form. Hence make peace with him."

Rāvaṇa was furious once more. He thundered: "You do not even know what is correct and appropriate behaviour: You who belong to my court are advocating my enemy's cause! If Rāma is Viṣṇu, then I have snatched away goddess Lakṣmi herself who is in my possession now: why will I give her away? Oh, no: I may even break into two, but I shall not bow down, never! This is my native characteristic, even if it be a fault; and one's native characteristic is difficult to overcome. I assure you, I will kill Rāma in no time!" Malayavān pronounced his blessings upon Rāvaṇa and left the court.

Rāvaṇa instructed the foremost among demons to guard the three city gates, resolving to be present at the northern gate himself. Having thus assured the city's defence, hailed and adored by the ministers, Rāvaṇa dissolved the council and returned to his inner apartments.

Yuddha 37, 38, 39

Rāma and his friends had reached the outskirts of the city and were at the foot of the Suvela mountain. Vibhīṣaṇa submitted to Rāma: "O Rāma, my four counsellors have returned with the latest intelligence. They went into the palace of Rāvaṇa, effectively disguised, and have learnt that the demon has got his army ready and has also posted three mighty demons to guard the three gates of the city, while he would himself guard the fourth, the northern gate." Vibhīṣaṇa continued: "O Rāma, the forces marshalled by Rāvaṇa are of terrible strength, in fact much more than those with the help of which he invaded the stronghold of the gods and won a victory over them. I am not saying this to frighten you, hence do not be annoyed with me; I am giving you this warning so that your anger can be sufficiently aroused, for then you are invincible."

Rāma considered how his own army should be deployed and gave the following instructions: "Nīla should take the eastern gate guarded by Prahastha. Aṅgada should challenge Mahāpārśva and Mahodara at the southern gate. Hanumān should similarly attack Indrajit stationed at the western gate. I shall myself proceed towards the northern gate, along with Lakṣmaṇa, and fight with that wretched demon who is the oppressor of the world, and I shall myself kill that wicked demon. The vānara army should go, each tribe with its own distinctive appearance: by such uniform shall they be easily distinguished. They should not copy our appearance, so that Vibhīṣaṇa and his four demon-ministers, Lakṣmaṇa and I can be easily distinguished."

Followed by the vānara leaders, Rāma then climbed the Suvela mountain, and said: "We shall spend this night here. We shall from here also gain a good look at Laṅkā. Whenever I think of that evil-minded Rāvaṇa my anger is roused: he does not seem to know what dharma is, and he does not care for the code of right conduct nor for the prestige of his dynasty, and hence is devoted to base and diabolical conduct. I shall soon destroy that base and immoral demon. Alas, one person who is doomed to destruction, sins; and as a result his whole clan perishes."

When the night was past, the vānaras and Rāma looked over in the direction of Laṅkā. The vast and extensive forests around Laṅkā looked beautiful. And, the vānaras roamed that forest, raising a cloud of dust. At a distance the Trikūṭa mountain was seen; and on top of it, the golden city of Laṅkā. It was dotted with seven-storeyed mansions, palaces, fortifications and towers. Rāvaṇa's own palace had a thousand pillars and was a skyscraper. Rāma, Lakṣmaṇa and the vānara leaders surveyed that glorious city.

Yuddha 40–41

Rāma and Sugrīva, too, were surveying the glorious city of Laṅkā from atop the Suvela mountain. They saw at some distance, Rāvaṇa himself seated on the look-out on the northern gate of the city. He was attended by the royal paraphernalia—fly-whisks and a lovely white canopy. He was richly attired, ornamented and waited upon. At the very sight of Rāvaṇa, impulsively and impetuously, Sugrīva rushed towards him. Even while he was airborne, Sugrīva said to Rāvaṇa: "I am the servant and friend of Rāma, the emperor of the world, O demon! I shall seize you today, and you will not be able to escape from me." Rāvaṇa immediately gave a suitable reply; he said: "Ah, it is you Sugrīva! You were Sugrīva (one with a lovely neck) till I saw you; now you will be deprived of your neck (Hīnagrīva)."

As Sugrīva landed near Rāvaṇa, he tossed Rāvaṇa's crown down. Rāvaṇa caught hold of Sugrīva and dashed him upon the ground. Sugrīva, however, got up unhurt. There ensued a breathtaking wrestling duel.

Expert wrestlers that they were, they pinned each other to the ground. Still wrestling they fell into the wedge between two sections of the great defensive wall. Soon they regained their place on top of the wall and continued to fight each other, using the different wrestling tactics. Powerful as they both were, they did not grow fatigued. They constantly shifted their positions and the postures of their bodies. They delivered, received and dodged each other's blows. Now they pounced on each other; now they closed in on each other; and now they retreated from each other.

Rāvaṇa realised that he could not defeat Sugrīva in straight forward wrestling, and therefore he decided to use his supernatural talents. Sugrīva realised what Rāvaṇa was about to do, and he took off. While the baffled Rāvaṇa was still looking on, Sugrīva flew in the direction of the Suvela mountain. Having accomplished a difficult feat and having worn out Rāvaṇa's strength, he retired to Rāma's side.

Rāma did not appear very pleased. He said to Sugrīva: "Without duly consulting all of us, you impulsively rushed away, O Sugrīva: kings do not indulge in such rash actions You kept us all wondering. Pray, do not do like this any more: if something had happened to you, what would I do with Sītā or Bharata or the other brothers, or even with this life of mine? Surely, after killing Rāvaṇa, I would have crowned Bharata king and given up my life. Realising this, do not put your life in danger." Sugrīva replied: "Forgive me, O Rāma: but when I beheld that wicked demon who had abducted your wife, I could not restrain myself!"

Yuddha 41

Rāma said to Lakṣmaṇa: "It is time that all our troops took up their positions and remained extremely alert. It is essential that plenty of food and water should be made readily available to all and their continued supply ensured. We are on the brink of a terrible war in which I can foresee right now great destruction on both sides. Even the preparations made by both the parties are agitating the wind, and producing earth-tremors. Clouds have assumed a fearful aspect. The sun is fiercer than ever. Even the moon seems to have lost its coolness. Animals are wailing everywhere. The sky is polluted and therefore the stars are not clearly visible. It is time to invade the city."

Saying so, Rāma descended from the mountain look-out and reviewed his forces. Rāma led the siege, and he was immediately followed by the foremost among the vānara heroes, each one of them surrounded by his own division of the armed forces. Soon they reached the city of Laṅkā. The forces deployed themselves as they had been previously instructed by Rāma. Rāma and Lakṣmaṇa accompanied by their own forces stationed themselves outside the northern gate of the city which was defended by the mighty Rāvaṇa himself: the forces besieging this gate could obviously not be protected by anyone other than Rāma. Similarly other leaders took their position at the other gates, thus laying a siege to the city of Laṅkā.

The forces composed of vānaras, ṛkṣas and other tribes in their thousands and tens of thousands, organised into a hundred divisions, laid siege to the gates of Laṅkā—there were others ready to reinforce these. Rāma summoned Aṅgada and said to him: "Dear friend, please go over to Rāvaṇa and give him one final warning, the final ultimatum. Tell him: 'Surely, you are about to reap the bitter fruits of all the misdeeds you have perpetrated against the gods, sages, demi-gods and human beings. Though emaciated and weakened on account of my separation from Sītā, I shall still be able to serve you with those bitter fruits. I will rid this earth of all demons, if you do not immediately surrender yourself to me, bringing Sītā with yourself. When you and your comrades have been killed, Vibhīṣaṇa will be king of Laṅkā. If you do not accept my offer, then come prepared to die."

Aṅgada immediately sought Rāvaṇa's presence and duly delivered Rāma's message. Terribly enraged, Rāvaṇa had him captured by his soldiers. Four of them caught him. Aṅgada sprang up, along with the soldiers, dashed them on the ground, and became airborne before he could be captured again, this time breaking the dome of Rāvaṇa's palace. He returned to Rāma and reported the events.

Yuddha 42–43

The demon-leaders reported to Rāvaṇa that Rāma's vānara-army had surrounded the city and was threatening to storm the gates. Rāvaña went up the northern gate and gazed with fiery eyes at Rāma and the vānara army.

Rāma urged his army forward with great enthusiasm. As he looked at Laṅkā, his heart was afire with the thought: "Here is Sītā, undergoing untold hardships." Thus thinking of the afflicted Sītā, Rāma urged the vānaras who were themselves full of zest. The vānaras rushed forward, exclaiming: "We shall hurl thousands of rocks on Laṅkā; we shall tear the demons to pieces." Throwing trees, rocks and grass into them, the vānaras filled up the moats surrounding the city. Then they began to scale the walls of the city. Others began pounding the golden gates, shouting: "Victory to Rāma, Lakṣmaṇa and Sugrīva". Rāma and Lakṣmaṇa, supported by Vibhīṣaṇa, Gavākṣa, Dhūmra and their forces, led the attack on the northern gate.

Rāvaṇa's army was equipped with more sophisticated weapons; and even the drummers wielded golden sticks. Drums and conches sounded everywhere as the demons were urged forward to defend the city. The two armies closed in: and it looked like the legendary battle between the gods and the demons.

The demons had excellent vehicles and were clad in golden armours. The vānaras, though they did not have these, were full of personal valour and zeal. The mighty demons challenged the vānara heroes to a duel. Indrajit faced Aṅgada, Prajangha faced Sampāti, Jambumālī faced Hanumān, Śatrughna faced Vibhīṣaṇa, Tapana faced Gaja, Nikumbha faced Nīla, Praghasa challenged Sugrīva, Virūpākṣa challenged Lakṣmaṇa, and four demons, (Agniketu, Raśmiketu, Suptaghna and Yajñakopa) fought with Rāma. Even so, other demons fought with other vānara heroes. Blood from the bodies of the demons and vānaras flowed freely, with trunks and heads separately floating in it.

Jambumālī wounded Hanumān who in turn killed him. Sugrīva killed Praghasa who had taken a heavy toll of the vānaras. Lakṣmaṇa killed Virūpākṣa. Angiketu and the other three attacked Rāma who aimed four missiles at them and killed them instantly. Nikumbha injured Nīla who picked up the chariot wheel of Nikumbha himself and killed him with it.

The mighty Dvivida hit the demon Asaniprabha with a big tree and killed him. Vidyunmālī, riding a chariot, attacked Suṣena who picked up a big tree and hit the chariot with it. Then Suṣena picked up a huge rock and with that killed the demon, though the latter in the meantime delivered a powerful blow in the chest of Suṣena.

Yuddha 44–45

The battle continued during the night, too. The vānaras shouted: "Are you a demon?" and fought the demons; the demons shouted: "Are you a vānara?" and fought them. The demons who were dark could be distinguished by their shining gold armour. Yelling war-cries, all of them fought ferociously. With their missiles which were like venomous snakes, Rāma and Lakṣmaṇa killed numerous demons, whether they were visible or they were invisible. It was like the night of cosmic destruction. When six powerful demons attacked Rāma, he returned their fire, and the missiles used by Rāma illumined the night sky. They were dead. More and more demons rushed towards Rāma, and all of them were quickly destroyed.

Aṅgada continued his battle with Indrajit. Aṅdaga wounded the powerful son of Rāvaṇa, and destroyed his chariot and horses. Indrajit was tired, and hence became invisible. The gods and the sages who were witnessing this extraordinary feat, applauded Aṅgada's valour.

The infuriated Indrajit decided to use his magical powers. Still remaining invisible, he began to direct the most deadly missiles at Rāma and Lakṣmaṇa. They were poisoned missiles. They were showered in such profusion that Rāma and Lakṣmaṇa were literally covered by the wounds inflicted by them. Thus, when he was unable to stand facing them, Indrajit employed his magical powers and incapacitated Rāma and Lakṣmaṇa.

Rāma directed ten vānaras to seek the enemy. But Indrajit cleverly evaded them and directed his own powerful missiles at them, as also at Rāma and Lakṣmaṇa. The two noble princes were bleeding profusely. Still remaining invisible, Indrajit said to them: "No one on earth or in heaven can stand before me! Presently, I shall send both of you to the abode of Death!" Saying so, Indrajit directed more missiles at Rāma and Lakṣmaṇa. As each missile found its object, Indrajit roared in joy.

Very shortly, both the princes had bled so profusely that they were literally unable even to look up. Their bodies had been covered with the wounds inflicted by the dreadful poisonous missiles hurled by Indrajit. From their bodies blood flowed like water. Indrajit had used in this encounter the missiles known as nārāca (with even and circular heads), ardhanārāca (a minor type of the same weapon), bhalla (axehead), anjalika (shaped like palms held together), vatsadantas (like the teeth of a calf), simhadamṣṭra (like lion's teeth), and kṣura (like razor's edge). Struck by them, Rāma lay incapacitated; his own powerful gold-plated weapon lay by his side.

Yuddha 46, 47, 48

Rāma and Lakṣmaṇa lay on the battlefield utterly motionless. The vānaras were bewildered; they could not even see the assailant. Vibhīṣaṇa saw through the magic eye, Indrajit stationed not far off, but veiled by magic power. Still hidden from view, Indrajit proclaimed: "Struck down by my terrible and poisonous missiles, Rāma and Lakṣmaṇa lie there: no one on earth can save them. On their account, my father Rāvaṇa spent a sleepless night; he will now rejoice, now that they have been killed by me."

Sugrīva was stricken with terror, and he was shedding tears. Vibhīṣaṇa wiped his tears lovingly, and said to him: "Do not give way to grief, O King! This is a time for action: ensure that Rāma and Lakṣmaṇa are well protected during the period of their unconsciousness. They will soon be revived."

Indrajit returned to the court of Rāvaṇa, bowed to him and announced: "Rāma and Lakṣmaṇa are dead." Rāvaṇa was thrilled; and he warmly embraced his beloved and heroic son. Rāvaṇa then sent for the demonesses guarding Sītā in the Aśoka-grove and said to them: "Take Sītā in the aeroplane Puṣpaka and show her the bodies of Rāma and Lakṣmaṇa. When she sees that they are dead, she will of her own accord seek me." Sītā had already heard the news through the demonesses. Now, from the aeroplane she actually witnessed Rāma and Lakṣmaṇa lying as though lifeless on the battlefield, amidst numerous dead vānaras.

Seeing her husband and her brother-in-law lying as if dead on the battlefield, Sītā, overcome by grief, wailed aloud: "Alas, all the predictions of astrologers and other wise men concerning me have proved false. They said that I would be Rāma's queen; that we should have sons; that we should be very happy together. All the heroic endeavours of Rāma, Lakṣmaṇa and the vānaras in discovering my whereabouts, in crossing the ocean and invading Laṅkā have proved in vain. Rāma and Lakṣmaṇa both had terrible (nuclear) missiles which could bring down torrential rain, set everything ablaze, create tidal waves and flood, whip up winds to tornadoes and cyclones, and even destroy everything created: these they would not normally use, but why did not they use these when their own lives were threatened? Alas, alas, I do not grieve for any of us: but this is a terrible blow to Kausalyā!" Trijaṭā, the noble demoness who was fond of Sītā, however, said to her: "Do not give way to grief, O Sītā: Rāma is not dead. I can see this clearly from the expression on the face. Notice too that the vānaras are guarding the two princes; if they had been killed, the vānaras would flee! Grieve not, they are alive." They returned to the Aśoka-grove; and in spite of all that Trijaṭā had said, Sītā was still grief-stricken.

Yuddha 49–50

While the vānaras stood around Rāma and Lakṣmaṇa, grief-stricken, Rāma regained consciousness first on account of his mental and physical fitness and also because he was full of purity and light (because he practised sattva-yoga). But, he was greatly perturbed to see Lakṣmaṇa lying unconscious, as if dead, near him. Rāma began to lament: "Alas, what a tragedy:

It may be possible to find a wife like Sītā, but not a brother like Lakṣmaṇa. He who could single-handed kill thousands of demons has been struck down by the wicked Indrajit! Alas, I have not been able to fulfil my promise to crown Vibhīṣaṇa king of Laṅkā! O Sugrīva, return to Kiṣkindhā with all your surviving vānara leaders. All of you have done your best, but human beings cannot flout destiny. I shall give up my life now." Just then Vibhīṣaṇa was coming towards them. Mistaking him for Indrajit, the vānaras began to run.

Vibhīṣaṇa was stricken with grief at the sight of Rāma and Lakṣmaṇa; he despaired of ever gaining the throne of Laṅkā. Sugrīva consoled him and then said to Suṣena, his father-in-law: "As soon as Lakṣmaṇa regains consciousness, take both the princes back to Kiṣkindhā; I shall destroy the demons, recover Sītā and bring her to Kiṣkindhā, too." Suṣena replied: "I remember the battle which took place in days of yore between gods and demons, in which the gods had similarly been assailed by invisible demons. The sage Brihaspati administered certain remedies, accompanied by prayers, and revived the gods. Those remedies grow on the Chandra and Drona mountains in the middle of the ocean, and they are known as Sanjīvakaraṇī and Viśalya: the former brings one back to life and the latter instantly heals all wounds. Commission vānara leaders to fetch them at once."

At that moment, Garuḍa arrived there, agitating the wind. The moment he arrived, the poisons that had incapacitated Rāma and Lakṣmaṇa left them. Garuḍa passed his hands over them and felicitated them. At the touch of Garuḍa, the wounds healed, and their bodies regained their golden hue. Their radiance, virility, strength, enthusiasm, vision, intelligence as also memory, were doubled. Deeply grateful to him, Rāma asked him: "By your grace alone have we been saved. Pray, tell me who you are." Garuḍa replied: "I am your friend, your very life as it were though dwelling outside your body. I am Garuḍa. Luckily I heard of your predicament and arrived here in time: the poison with which you had been stricken could not be antidoted by anyone else. May victory attend upon you!" Garuḍa departed. The vānaras rejoiced to see Rāma and Lakṣmaṇa fully recovered.

Yuddha 51–52

Rāvaṇa heard the hilarious noise that emanated from the vānara ranks, and he asked some demons to find out the cause. Some demons leapt on the city walls and looked over the enemy army, returned to Rāvaṇa and reported: "Lo, Rāma and Lakṣmaṇa are well and the vānaras are surely celebrating their recovery from the deadly poison which Indrajit had aimed at them." When he heard this, Rāvaṇa felt terribly dejected and remarked: "If these two princes could be revived after being subjected to the deadly attack by Indrajit, I am beginning to doubt the strength of my whole army to withstand them! Our missiles which are as terrible as fire and which have taken the lives of my enemies have been proved to be useless."

Rāvaṇa then turned to the terrible demon Dhūmrākṣa and ordered him: "Proceed at once to the battlefield and destroy all the vānaras. You are indeed most powerful and capable of achieving this." Dhūmrākṣa rushed out of the palace and went towards the western gate guarded by Hanumān, after ordering the commander-in-chief to marshal all the forces in readiness.

As he flew towards the western gate, however, he was assailed by huge birds and vultures. A terrible vulture even landed on his aircraft. He saw many strange sights in the air. He saw a headless trunk flying in front of him, emitting strange sounds. The entire nature, all the elements, seemed to forebode evil.

The vānaras too were eager for a good fight. The battle that ensued between the vānaras and the demons was indeed exceedingly terrible. The demons used all their missiles against the vānaras; and the vānaras in their turn hurled trees and rocks (druma and śilā may be names of missiles, too.) All of them were roaring in fury. The vānaras crushed some demons and made others vomit blood. Some demons were torn by the teeth (danta); the bodies of others were lacerated by nails (karaja). Even so the vānaras were suffering heavy casualties at the hands of the demons. Some were mowed down by the vehicles of the demons. Others were driven out of the field by the demons. The 'twang' of weapons firing resembled the music of stringed instruments; the neighing of horses was like the music of the drum; the trumpeting of the elephants was like vocal music: the sounds of war produced a symphony.

Seeing the demons being harassed, Dhūmrākṣa advanced towards Hanumān. Seeing the vānara forces in distress, Hanumān picked up a huge rock and came towards Dhūmrākṣa. With that rock (śilā) Hanumān smashed the vehicle of Dhūmrākṣa. Hanumān assailed the demon forces, too. Dhūmrākṣa hit Hanumān with a spiked mace. Unmindful of that, Hanumān picked up a rock which looked like a mountain-peak (giri-śṛṅga) and hit the head of Dhūmrākṣa with it; Dhūmrākṣa fell.

Yuddha 53–54

Distressed to hear that Dhūmrākṣa had been slain by Hanumān, Rāvaṇa ordered another mighty demon, Vajraḍaṃṣṭra, to proceed to the front. Vajradaṃṣṭra was an adept in magic. He marched, surrounded by a colourful contingent of army commanders, and followed by a huge army. His own armoured car was thickly gold-plated and decorated with his own personal standard.

They sought to fight the vānaras outside the southern gate besieged by the forces of Aṅgada. Vajradaṃṣṭra noticed terrible evil omens: but he assumed that they forebode the death of the enemy. As this demon-army marched well set on its purpose, it shone like the clouds of the monsoon, and their gleaming weapons were like the lightning flashes that embellished such clouds.

The demons and the vānaras quickly fell upon one another and there began the most terrible battle. They fought with various weapons. They fought with their bare arms and feet. Even so, the casualties were of different categories. Some had their bodies smashed; others had their skulls smashed. When he saw that the demons were ruthlessly killing the vānaras, Aṅgada came to their rescue and killed the demons. When Vajradaṃṣṭra saw that the demons were falling in great numbers, he came to their rescue. The demons used various missiles and mystic weapons; and the vānaras pulled out trees and rolled rocks and hurled them at the demons. Both the sides lost a great number of the fighters. As their bodies lay on the battlefield some with their heads broken, some without arms, some without legs, some with their bodies smashed, the vultures and the jackals had a good time.

Aṅgada and Vajradaṃṣṭra faced each other in direct conflict. Vajradaṃṣṭra directed a thousand shots as it were at Aṅgada. With blood pouring from his whole body, Aṅgada retaliated by hurling a tree (vṛkṣam). Vajradaṃṣṭra broke that tree with a missile. Aṅgada picked up a huge rock (śailam) and threw it at Vajradaṃṣṭra's vehicle. The demon got out just in time to see the armoured car smashed to pieces. Aṅgada threw another huge rock at the head of the demon. Vomiting blood, Vajradaṃṣṭra fell down and lay on the ground hugging his mace, dazed.

The demon soon got up, dropped his mace and began to wrestle with Aṅgada. Both of them were equally powerful, of equal strength. And after a time both of them were tired. They crawled on their knees, yet they fought. At last Aṅgada drew his sword and chopped off the demon's head. With his body covered with blood, his eyes rolling, the demon fell, with his head severed from the trunk. The surviving demons fled towards Laṅkā. The vānaras rejoiced.

Yuddha 55–56

Rāvaṇa was further enraged to hear that Vajradaṃṣṭra had also been killed, and ordered the demon Akampana to be sent.

Akampana acquired that title because he could not be shaken even by the gods in war. His own car was made of solid and pure gold and was invulnerable. Though he was powerful, he was surrounded by the most powerful warriors, and though the day was bright, there was a strange depression in the air and he also experienced omens which forecast evil. As his powerful army marched towards the battlefield, the vānaras got frightened. Intense and furious activity in both the camps raised a cloud of dust in which it was difficult for the warriors even to see clearly the flags and the uniforms of the enemy they were fighting. In this confusion, vānaras killed vānaras and demons killed demons. Indiscriminate killing followed intense fury; and the battlefield was literally covered with muddied blood and dead bodies covered with dust.

Akampana ordered the driver of his armoured car: "Take me to where there is the worst fighting and where the demons are falling in great numbers." Soon Akampana was in the thick of the battle. And, that mighty warrior began ruthlessly to shoot down the vānaras.

Seeing the devastation, Hanumān came forward to challenge Akampana. This raised the morale of the vānara forces. Akampana turned the full force of his missile-power on Hanumān. Hanumān rushed forward in great fury, but he had no weapons; he therefore picked up a huge rock (śailam), whirled it around and threw it at Akampana. But Akampana broke it with his missile even while it was in the air. Hanumān was angered to see this extraordinary exploit of the demon. He uprooted a big tree known as Aśvakarna and holding it aloft he ran hither and thither in great fury. Akampana was disturbed to see Hanumān rushing towards him with the big tree held in his hand. He fired fourteen shots at the mighty vānara. But Hanumān did not even notice it! He shone like smokeless fire or like the aśoka tree in full bloom.

Reaching up to Akampana, Hanumān struck him with the tree; the demon fell down dead. The demon warriors thereupon dropped their arms and began to flee in the direction of Laṅkā. Full of panic, they stampeded out of the battlefield, crushing their own men in the confusion.

The vānaras were overjoyed. They surrounded Hanumān and roared with joy. The gods, the vānara leaders like Sugrīva, Vibhīṣaṇa and even Rāma and Lakṣmaṇa worshipped Hanumān.

Yuddha 57–58

The killing of Akampana was a terrible blow to Rāvaṇa; yet he was not overwhelmed by it. He said to the commander-in-chief Prahastha: "Many of our foremost commanders have been killed by these gigantic vānaras. I cannot think of whom to send next. The outcome of a battle is uncertain. But, then, I think sudden and unforeseen death is preferable to certain death which can be predicted. Anyhow, pray, suggest to me what should be done, whether the advice may be pleasant or unpleasant."

The brave and loyal Prahastha replied: "O King, we have indeed discussed this matter often before. And we had actually foreseen that if the wise course, which was to restore Sītā to Rāma was not adopted, war was inevitable. This has come true. I have enjoyed your affection and your favours and they have been constant; even so shall my loyalty to you be constant. Neither son, wife or wealth, nor even my life are worth preserving: behold, I shall lay down my very life for your sake."

Filled with rage and with enthusiasm, Prahastha marched to the battlefield surrounded by the picked warriors of Laṅkā. Before they departed, the brāhmaṇas performed various religious rites for their success. The demons adorned themselves not only with military hardware but with garlands duly consecrated by brāhmaṇas with the recitation of sacred texts. Prahastha mounted his armoured car which shone like the sun, which had been equipped with all sorts of weapons, which could move at great speed, and which was even provided with a bumper to avoid collision. Surrounded by several powerful generals, Prahastha marched forward, and he looked like the god of death.

Rāma ascertained from Vibhīṣaṇa the identity of this warrior and his strength. Once again, the vānaras and the demons fought a fierce battle. The commanders of the demon forces wrought havoc among the vānaras. But, soon Dvivida killed Narāntaka. Durmukha killed the demon Samunnata. Jāmbavān killed the demon Mahānāda. And the vānara Tārā killed Kumbhahanu. Enraged further by this, Prahastha fought with incredible fierceness and killed the vānaras by the thousands. The entire battlefield resembled a dreadful river of death. But the warriors fought on unmindful of the horror.

Nīla, the commander-in-chief of the vānaras, rushed towards Prahastha who showered innumerable missiles at Nīla: unable to ward them off, Nīla received them with closed eyes, calmly. They fought fiercely for a while. Prahastha used a mallet; and Nīla used rocks. While Prahastha rushed towards Nīla intent upon killing him, the latter picked up a huge rock and with it killed Prahastha. The leaderless demon-forces fled.

Yuddha 59

Rāvaṇa's fury was explosive. His grief ignited it. He said to the surviving commanders: "It is unwise to underestimate the enemy's strength. Only a warrior of no mean valour would have survived a combat with Prahastha; yet, he has been killed. I shall myself proceed to the battlefield. I shall burn up the vānara army; and I shall irrigate the earth with vānara blood." Saying so, Rāvaṇa set out for the battlefield.

Vibhīṣaṇa briefed Rāma for the new encounter saying: "Behold Rāvaṇa, who shines like the sun, wearing the crown and earrings, with a body huge and terrible looking like Vindhyā mountain, who vanquished even Indra (king of heaven) and Vaivasvata (the god of death)." Rāma looked at the enemy and could not but exclaim: "O what lustre! What radiance! It is difficult even to see him directly even as to see the sun. And, he is surrounded by dreadfully powerful demons, too. Yet, I am glad he himself comes to the battlefield today: I shall direct towards him the great anger that he has roused in me by abducting Sītā."

Before leaving the city gate, Rāvaṇa instructed the leaders of the demons: "Ensure that the gates are well guarded and that every house in the city of Laṅkā, too, is well guarded. Seeing that I myself and the foremost among our commanders have left the city, the enemy may seize it." Having said so, Rāvaṇa ploughed through the vānara army. Seeing Rāvaṇa thus devastating the vānara army, Sugrīva rushed forward. Picking up a 'mountain-top' (mahīdharā-'gram or śaila-śṛṅgam), Sugrīva hurled it at Rāvaṇa who, with his missile, broke it into pieces. Rāvaṇa then struck Sugrīva with a terrible missile, and wounded severely by it, Sugrīva fell down, writhing in agony.

Rāma grabbed his own weapon, ready to plunge into a direct confrontation with Rāvaṇa. Lakṣmaṇa intervened and said: "Let me go, Rāma: I can look after him." Consenting to this, Rāma cautioned Lakṣmaṇa: "Look for his weak-points, and remember your own weak-points and guard them, both with your weapon and your vigilance." But before he could reach Rāvaṇa, he noticed that Hanumān was engaged in a hand-to-hand combat with Rāvaṇa. Hanumān said to Rāvaṇa: "O demon, you have secured immunity only from the gods and demons; you are not immune from vānaras and humans." Rāvaṇa hit Hanumān on his chest; and Hanumān hit him back. This made Rāvaṇa reel! Rāvaṇa then said to Hanumān: "Praiseworthy is your strength and skill, O vānara!" To which Hanumān replied: "Shame on my strength, in that you still live, O demon!" Once again, Rāvaṇa clenched his fist and landed a terrible blow on Hanumān which stupified and incapacitated Hanumān for some time. In the meantime, Rāvaṇa turned to Nīla.

Yuddha 59

Rāvaṇa now directed his dreadful missiles at Nīla. Nīla jumped on to the armoured car of Rāvaṇa. Rāvaṇa warned

Nīla: "Get away before I shoot you." Shot by Rāvaṇa, Nīla fell down; but by the grace of his god-father or guardian angel, he did not die.

Abandoning him, Rāvaṇa now turned to Lakṣmaṇa who shouted at him: "Why do you waste your prowess on the vānaras; come and show me your valour!" Rāvaṇa replied in great anger: "Gladly, O Lakṣmaṇa, and I shall let you taste the fury of my fire." Lakṣmaṇa taunted Rāvaṇa: "Heroes do not brag, O King! And you who are the worst among sinners are keen only on boasting!" Rāvaṇa replied by shooting seven missiles. Lakṣmaṇa responded suitably. Whatever missile one used, the other neutralised it and replied with a more powerful missile. Rāvaṇa took an extremely deadly weapon (said to have belonged to the Creator himself) and struck Lakṣmaṇa. For a moment Lakṣmaṇa's head reeled. Regaining his consciousness, Lakṣmaṇa hit Rāvaṇa with three deadly missiles. This made Rāvaṇa swoon for a while. Recovering from the swoon, Rāvaṇa hit Lakṣmaṇa with an even more deadly weapon, a javelin of inestimable destructive power. Struck by it, Lakṣmaṇa fell down. Rāvaṇa tried to lift him presumably to carry him away: but Lakṣmaṇa's body became so heavy that Rāvaṇa could not lift it. Hanumān challenged Rāvaṇa, and hit Rāvaṇa so hard that the demon vomited blood and lost his consciousness for a while. Hanumān quickly lifted Lakṣmaṇa's body and carried it away, which became light on account of Hanumān's love for him. Lakṣmaṇa contemplated upon the truth that he was a part of the Lord himself and this healed his wounds and enabled him to regain his consciousness soon.

Rāma came forward to fight Rāvaṇa. Hanumān prayed to Rāma: "I beg of you to be seated on my shoulders and fight the demon." Rāma consented to this. He said to Rāvaṇa: "Stand, O demon: having offended me, you cannot find asylum anywhere. Remember that single-handed I killed thousands of your warriors. When he regains consciousness, Lakṣmaṇa himself will kill you and your family and followers." Infuriated by these words, Rāvaṇa hit Hanumān with several flaming missiles. Hanumān did not mind them, and his strength and enthusiasm grew. Rāma thereupon aimed a missile at Rāvaṇa. Hit by it, Rāvaṇa who could not be shaken by even Indra's thunderbolt, shook violently and dropped his weapon. With another missile Rāma knocked Rāvaṇa's diadem down. Seeing Rāvaṇa in a wretched condition, Rāma graciously said: "You have really shown great strength and skill, O Rāvaṇa; I can see you are tired and wounded; go home, rest and recuperate; when you return to the battlefield you will witness my strength and power."

Crestfallen, Rāvaṇa entered Laṅkā.

Yuddha 60

Doubt, dejection and despair overcame Rāvaṇa. He sat on his throne in his court and said: "Alas, I have been defeated by a mere mortal! I remember now Brahmā's terrible words, 'Your danger is from mortals'. King Anaraṇya of the Ikṣvāku dynasty cursed me that a descendant of his would kill me. I recall, too, the curse of Vedavatī when I violated her: surely she has taken birth as Sītā. Goddess Umā had cursed me that my death would result from a woman. These cannot but come true. Yet, guard the city gates well. Awaken Kumbhakarṇa, for he alone is capable of fighting these heroes, our enemies. He usually sleeps for nine, ten or eight months. And, he has gone to sleep only nine days ago, after our consultations. Wake him up; for only he can deal with our enemies."

The demons collected a lot of food, drink, perfumes and other articles which Kumbhakarṇa liked most. They entered the subterranean palace paved with jewels and gold, where Kumbhakarṇa slept for an unnaturally long period of time. He had a colossal form. When he exhaled, the air blew people away from him.

They blew their conches and beat their drums. They pushed his body and roared. They even struck that enormous body with clubs and maces, nay even other deadly weapons. The whole city resounded with this noise and the inhabitants and birds and beasts were frightened; Kumbhakarṇa did not wake up. Then they made a thousand elephants trample on his body; this annoyance woke him up. At once he felt the pangs of hunger. Yawning, opening his terrible mouth, he awoke. The demons directed his attention to the pile of food. When he was satisfied, they worshipped him. He asked them, why they had awakened him, and what urgent business the king had. They briefly described the war and the defeat suffered by the royal forces, and concluded: "What even the gods, and the demons could not do, that has been done by Rāma; and by him the king was spared out of compassion as it were." Springing up from his bed, Kumbhakarṇa roared: "I shall immediately proceed to the battlefield and destroy the vānara forces as also Rāma and Lakṣmaṇa, and only then shall I go to see the king. I shall please the demons by providing them with a rich repast of the meat and blood of the vānaras; and I shall myself drink the blood of Rāma and Lakṣmaṇa." The demons, however, suggested that he should first hold consultation with the king, Rāvaṇa and only then do what was appropriate.

On the instructions of Rāvaṇa, the demons politely invited Kumbhakarṇa to the king's court. After washing his face and having a drink, Kumbhakarṇa walked towards the palace. Seeing this gigantic demon striding the earth, the vānaras got the fright of their lives.

Yuddha 61–62

Rāma saw the terrible-looking Kumbhakarṇa walking the earth as if he were a cosmic person. He asked Vibhīṣaṇa: "Pray, Vibhīṣaṇa, tell who this is. Is he a demon or a goblin? I have never seen anything like this till now."

In reply, Vibhīṣaṇa told Rāma the biography of Kumbhakarṇa: "He is Kumbhakarṇa, son of the renowned sage Viśrava. He has defeated in war all the gods, demi-gods and demons. Even as a baby he devoured thousands of living beings. Indra himself defended the living beings and hit Kumbhakarṇa with a thunderbolt. He not only did not die but he pulled out the tusk of Indra's own elephant and hit Indra with it! The gods and Indra thereupon appealed to Brahmā, the creator, who was shocked by this misdeed of one of his great-grandsons. Brahmā cursed him: 'No doubt, you are born of Paulastya's son for the destruction of the world; before you can destroy the world, may you enter into perpetual sleep.' Kumbhakarṇa appealed to Rāvaṇa who pleaded with Brahmā on his behalf. He said: 'It is not right that you should thus curse your own great-grandson. Yet, your curse cannot be falsified. Pray, modify it by stipulating the period for which he would sleep at a time.' Brahmā said: 'He will sleep continuously for a period of six months, and then shall be awake for a day during which he will be ravenously hungry.' I think having been defeated by you, Rāvaṇa has awakened Kumbhakarṇa. After merely seeing him at a distance, the vānaras have fled in terror. I doubt if they would be able to face him on the battlefield. I therefore suggest a ruse: have it announced that this is just a mechanical device and is not a living being, and that should restore confidence to the vānaras."

Pleased with this account, Rāma instructed the commander-in-chief to ensure that the entire army was alert!

At the same time, Kumbhakarṇa walked into the presence of the mighty Rāvaṇa. Rāvaṇa rose from his seat and showed extraordinary love, respect and affection for his brother Kumbhakarṇa, who asked: "What can I do for you, and for what have I been awakened with such effort?" Rāvaṇa lifted him up and gave a place next to himself, and said: "O brother, you have slept for a long time. In the meantime, our enemy Rāma managed to cross the sea and has actually besieged Laṅkā. You can see for yourself that the whole of Laṅkā has been transformed into a sea of vānaras! We have tried to fight with them. But only you can deal with them. It is for this purpose that we woke you up. Our treasury is empty and our resources are at a low ebb: pray, save Laṅkā which only has children and aged ones left! I am sure you realise that I have never before asked for such a favour; pray, do this for the sake of your brother! You are our only hope; you are our last resort. No one is equal to you in strength in the whole world. If you enter the battlefield, the enemy forces will vanish like an autumnal cloud when a gale blows."

Yuddha 63–64

Kumbhakarṇa laughed aloud hearing Rāvaṇa's plea, and said: "I told you so! You indulged in an action, ignoring its obvious consequences, and without seeking our advice and help. One should certainly seek dharma, prosperity and pleasure, but each in its own time and place. Having consulted with his ministers a king who resorts to negotiation, giving presents, dissension or even a show of strength, and who seeks dharma, prosperity and pleasure with due regard to time and place, does not come to grief, O King. Yet, again, not every one can advise a king. There are unwise people who are ignorant of the scriptures, and who are really no better than beasts but who come forward to counsel a king, on account of greed or insolence. To follow their counsel would bring disaster in its train. Sometimes, the ministers might overtly or covertly enter into an alliance with an enemy and encourage the king to indulge in wrong action: the wise king should beware of them. Surely, the best thing for you to do was pointed out by me and by Vibhīṣaṇa: restore Sītā to Rāma."

Rāvaṇa was impatient with this sermon. He angrily replied: "Why do you preach as if you were my guru or father? Let us consider what should be done now; the past is past and it is no use worrying over it. Even if I have done something wrong, you can nullify the consequences by your prowess."

Kumbhakarṇa jumped up: "Fear not. Despair not. I advised you out of brotherly affection. However, you will witness my strength again today. I shall avenge the death of our heroes. I shall wipe the tears of the bereaved. Command: I shall go immediately and destroy your enemies. I can break up the earth; I can shake the firmament and create disorder in the heavens. Enjoy and be cheerful. Consider that Rāma is dead, and Sītā is yours."

The counsellor Mahodara intervened and said to Kumbhakarṇa: "You are vain and ignorant. Both the virtuous and the vicious enjoy life in this world; enjoyment of pleasure alone is worthy of pursuit. The king is right in wishing to enjoy life with Sītā. Further, I do not consider that your physical power will be of any avail before Rāma." He turned to Rāvaṇa: "You have abducted Sītā and brought her here; the important thing now is to enjoy her, to persuade her to submit to your desire. I have a nice plot. Spread word that Kumbhakarṇa along with a couple of commanders and myself have gone to fight with Rāma. If we succeed, it is all right. If we do not, we shall return to you with Rāma's missiles, clearly marked on our bodies. Spread the rumour then that we have eaten Rāma. When the rumour that we have eaten Rāma spreads, Sītā will hear it and give up her hope; at the same time, try to win her favour by secretly approaching her with presents and jewels and other temptations. Wise people in this world achieve their desired ends without even giving a battle!"

Yuddha 65–66

Kumbhakarṇa derided Mahodara for his cowardly suggestion. He said: "Cowardly ministers ruin a king's fortunes by shying away from a good fight, and by blindly assenting to all his whims."

Rāvaṇa highly applauded Kumbhakarṇa's words. Kumbhakarṇa grabbed a trident and was ready to go to war, all alone. But Rāvaṇa counselled: "Take the army with you, O hero! For the vānaras are powerful and their determination augments their power. If they find someone alone or unguarded, they might overcome him." Further to show his affection, appreciation and hope and conviction, Rāvaṇa embraced Kumbhakarṇa, placed gold necklaces studded with gems around his neck and even respectfully bowed down to him, his younger brother. Kumbhakarṇa dressed himself for the battle; he put on a pure gold armour which was unassailable. Covered with jewels on all his limbs, holding the blazing trident in his hand, Kumbhakarṇa looked verily like lord Nārāyaṇa.

Followed by mighty heroes with their armies, Kumbhakarṇa set out to go to the battlefield. He was fierce even to look at. His body was colossal; and his flaming eyes looked like the wheels of a car. He roared aloud: "I shall make a good meal of all the vānaras; I shall kill Rāma himself, who is the source of the vānaras' strength." Unmistakable evil omens appeared, but they did not deter him.

The vānaras fled in panic when they saw him. Aṅgada tried to reason with the leaders of the vānaras, and persuade them not to flee. He said: "This demon may be powerful; but he cannot face our Rāma, for no one can!" The vānaras returned. They attacked Kumbhakarṇa. But he ruthlessly crushed them. The rocks and mountain-peaks they threw at him broke on striking him! When struck by him playfully, they ran along the route by which they had entered Laṅkā. Some vānaras were drowned, others disappeared into the forests, and yet others took shelter in caves.

Aṅgada appealed to them again and again: "Why are you running, O vānaras? Even your wives will laugh at you in contempt if you run away from the battlefield. Noble vānaras though you are, you behave as if you were uncultured beings, greatly agitated by fear. If it is time for us to die, let us give up our lives here. If we win the battle, we shall enjoy on this earth; if we lose our lives, we shall reach the highest heaven! But I assure you: Kumbhakarṇa cannot escape death at Rāma's hands." But the vānaras replied: "Kumbhakarṇa has devastated our forces: this is not the time to stand up and fight, we should leave. Our lives are indeed dear to us." However, Aṅgada was able to persuade them to return to the battlefield.

Yuddha 67

Once again the vānaras attacked Kumbhakarṇa. In a very short time, eight thousand and seven hundred vānaras had fallen at his hands. Hanumān was severely wounded by Kumbhakarṇa's trident. He vomited blood and was dazed.

Nīla managed to inspire the vānaras with confidence. The vānaras, finding Kumbhakarṇa standing in front of them like a mountain, ascended that mountain, and began to bite him. Kumbhakarṇa caught hold of these vānaras and put them into his mouth, intent upon swallowing them. But, they cleverly escaped through his nostrils and his ears. However, Kumbhakarṇa continued to eat the vānaras, and kill them ruthlessly.

The vānaras appealed to Rāma for help. And, Aṅgada rushed to their relief. Aṅgada picked up a mountain-peak and threw it at Kumbhakarṇa. Enraged at this, Kumbhakarṇa hurled his trident at Aṅgada. Aṅgada dodged it, and in retaliation hit the demon on his chest. The demon fainted! On recovering, the demon clenched his fist and struck Aṅgada with all his might: Aṅgada became unconscious.

Then Kumbhakarṇa turned towards Sugrīva. Picking up a mountain-peak, Sugrīva challenged Kumbhakarṇa: "Leave the vānara warriors alone: look what I do to you now!" But that rock broke into pieces as it hit Kumbhakarṇa's chest. The demon hurled his trident at Sugrīva. But Hanumān intercepted it, caught hold of it, calmly placed it on his knee and broke it! Kumbhakarṇa was amazed, surprised and enraged at this extraordinary feat of Hanumān. He broke loose a huge rock and hit Sugrīva with it. Sugrīva became unconscious. Kumbhakarṇa walked towards where Sugrīva had fallen, picked him up, tucked him into his own armpit and walked towards Laṅkā. He knew that with Sugrīva out of the way, all the others, including Rāma and Lakṣmaṇa would surrender.

Hanumān reflected: "What shall I do now? I can assume gigantic proportions through my own supernatural powers and kill this Kumbhakarṇa and rescue Sugrīva. But, Sugrīva's reputation would thereby suffer and he may not like being rescued by me. I shall await further developments, and in the meantime restore morale to the vānara forces." Soon Sugrīva regained consciousness and realised his predicament! After careful consideration, he bit off Kumbhakarṇa's ears and nose! Surprised thus by Sugrīva, sorely afflicted with pain, Kumbhakarṇa dashed Sugrīva down. The vānara hero sprang up at once and immediately returned to where Rāma was, thus foiling the demon's plot. Dripping with blood, Kumbhakarṇa once again advanced towards the enemy.

Yuddha 67

Kumbhakarṇa took hold of a mallet and rushed into the midst of the vānara army. Lakṣmaṇa shot a number of missiles at the demon who evaded them without any difficulty. Lakṣmaṇa literally covered the demon with his missiles: but unaffected by these the demon said to Lakṣmaṇa: "I thoroughly appreciate your skill, O Lakṣmaṇa! For, no one has so far dared to oppose me: Even Indra was once routed by me. That you challenged me makes me respect you as a soldier. But I wish to kill Rāma alone: when he is dead, it will be the end!"

As Kumbhakarṇa rushed towards Rāma, the latter discharged a dreadful missile endowed with the power of Rudra, the god of destruction, and defying his powerful armour, the missile went right through to his heart. The shock was so great that his weapons fell from his hands. Yet, he ran wild, swallowing the vānaras. Kumbhakarṇa hurled another mountain-peak which looked terrible: Rāma broke that up, too, with his missiles—and its fragments fell on two hundred monkeys. Lakṣmaṇa understood the demon's nature and suggested to Rāma: "The smell of blood intoxicates the demon. And so he runs amok and kills the vānaras, though that is not his aim. Let the vānaras climb upon him and save others." The vānaras climbed upon his body. But he shook them down!

Rāma said to Kumbhakarṇa: "I am the destroyer of demons, O Kumbhakarṇa; and your death is at hand!" Kumbhakarṇa laughed aloud and replied: "I am not Virādha, Kabandha, Khara, Vāli nor Mārīca! I am Kumbhakarṇa, O Rāma! Fight with me. I shall see how powerful you are: and then I shall swallow you, too."

Rāma directed at him the same type of missiles which had instantly killed Vāli, but they had no effect on the demon. Holding his iron club aloft, Kumbhakarṇa rushed towards Rāma who discharged the 'wind' missile at the demon: It cut off the upraised arm which fell, along with the iron club, and killed a great many warriors! With his other arm, Kumbhakarṇa uprooted a big tree and rushed towards Rāma who let fly another missile which severed that arm, too. Roaring aloud, Kumbhakarṇa rushed towards Rāma. Taking up two crescent-shaped missiles, Rāma cut off both his legs. As the legs fell, the sound of their fall reverberated throughout Laṅkā. Without arms, and without legs, Kumbhakarṇa was yet able to propel himself, and came rushing towards Rāma with his mouth open. Rāma gagged him with another missile. With yet another missile, Rāma cut off his head, even as Indra had cut off the head of the demon Vṛtra in days of yore. As that huge head fell, it rolled and bulldozed a number of buildings in the neighbourhood. Thus the enemy of holy men and gods had been killed by Rāma, and they rejoiced exceedingly.

Yuddha 68–69

The demons reported to Rāvaṇa: "The mighty Kumbhakarṇa who was the terror even of the gods has been deprived of his life by Rāma's missile!" Hearing that the mighty Kumbhakarṇa had been slain on the battlefield, Rāvaṇa was consumed by grief, lost his balance and fell down. And the sons of Rāvaṇa wailed aloud. So did Rāvaṇa's other brothers. Regaining consciousness, Rāvaṇa lamented: "Alas, why have you abandoned me and gone away, my brother Kumbhakarṇa. How was it possible, I wonder, that even you could be defeated and slain in battle? What will I do even if I gain Sītā's favour now? Life is barren for me, now that you, O Kumbhakarṇa, have gone. I ridiculed Vibhīṣaṇa and lost him; and now I have lost you, too: for whom shall I live now? Ah, it is certain that my wicked action in not listening to the wise counsel of Vibhīṣaṇa has borne fruit."

While he was thus lamenting, Rāvaṇa's son Triśira tried to console the demon-king: "Undoubtedly, Kumbhakarṇa was mighty. And it is true that such a mighty warrior has been killed by this human being Rāma. But, that is surely no reason why you should lose heart! You have various weapons which the creator Brahmā himself has bestowed upon you. And, we are here, too. Stay in Laṅkā, Father; and I shall go to the battlefield and kill your enemies." This revived Rāvaṇa's hopes.

With Rāvaṇa's blessings, his four sons (Triśira, Devāntaka, Narāntaka and Atikāya) and his two brothers Mahāpārśva, and Mahodara, set out for the battlefield, taking with them their choicest weapons. Surrounded by their own armed forces, they looked formidable and invincible. They were desperate and they were determined either to win or to die on the field.

Narāntaka ploughed into the vānara-army. On the path of his advance, the vānaras fell like flies. Wielding the flaming lance, Narāntaka burnt the vānaras. The vānaras were struck with fear. They sought Sugrīva's protection. Sugrīva commissioned Aṅgada to deal with the new menace. Aṅgada challenged Narāntaka: "Leave the common vānaras alone, O demon. Here I bare my chest: try the strength of your lance on it!" Annoyed by this challenge, Narāntaka hurled the lance at Aṅgada's chest: it broke! Aṅgada struck Narāntaka's vehicle with his palm; it sank into the earth. Narāntaka brought his powerful fist to bear upon Aṅgada's skull and broke it! Unmindful of the profuse bleeding caused by this, Aṅgada hit the demon's chest with his clenched fist. His chest broken by this hit, Narāntaka fell, vomiting warm blood.

Yuddha 70

Narāntaka's brothers, Devāntaka and Triśira and Mahodara, simultaneously attacked Aṅgada. Aṅgada picked up a huge tree and hurled it at Devāntaka. But Triśira intervened and cut that tree down. In this battle, while Mahodara intercepted Aṅgada's missiles, Triśira viciously attacked Aṅgada. Though he was thus simultaneously attacked by three powerful demons, Aṅgada was not disheartened.

With a single blow, Aṅgada killed Mahodara's elephant. Pulling out its tusk, he hit Devāntaka. The demon returned the blow. At the same time Triśira also directed his missiles at Aṅgada. Finding him thus ill-matched, Hanumān and Nīla joined him. Nīla thereafter engaged Triśira.

Devāntaka fought with Hanumān. Rushing towards Devāntaka, Hanumān dealt such a deadly blow on his head that Devāntaka's skull was shattered, and he fell dead.

While Nīla was fighting with Triśira, Mahodara also began to attack the former. For a moment Nīla found himself paralysed. But regaining his strength, he hit Mahodara with a big rock. Mahodara fell. Angered by this, Triśira directed his missiles at Hanumān. Hanumān hurled a mountain-peak at Triśira but the latter broke it up into pieces. Hanumān incapacitated Triśira's horse. Triśira threw his powerful javelin at Hanumān who caught hold of it and broke it. Triśira then used his sword and severely wounded Hanumān. Hanumān slapped the demon on his chest. He fell. Hanumān wrested the sword from the demon. Triśira struck Hanumān once again. Hanumān cut off Triśira's head with his own sword.

After these, the mighty demon Mahāpārśva came forward to fight. He wielded a glittering mace which was flaming all the time. With it he had conquered many gods and demi-gods. Wielding this mace, Mahāpārśva threw the vānaras into an utter confusion. Riṣabha came forward to fight with Mahāpārśva. The demon hit Riṣabha on his chest; and the vānara's chest actually broke and blood poured from it. Regaining his strength after a little while, the vānara Riṣabha hit the demon on his chest. The demon fell down. Riṣabha pounced upon the demon and wrested the ace from his hand. Mahāpārśva got up after a few minutes and delivered a terrible blow on Riṣabha who fell down and remained unconscious for some time. Getting up later, Riṣabha struck the demon who dashed towards the vānara in an effort to retrieve the mace. However, before he could do so, Riṣabha killed Mahāpārśva with his own mace! And the demon fell down. The demon-forces began to flee.

Yuddha 71

Another son of Rāvaṇa, Atikāya, proceeded to the battlefield, in an armoured car which shone like a thousand suns. Some of the vānaras imagined that it was Kumbhakarṇa who had risen from the dead, and fled. Rāma questioned Vibhīṣaṇa: "Who is this colossal demon, O Vibhīṣaṇa? And look at his armoured car! It has gun turrets all over it, pointing in all directions. It has four drivers, twenty magazines, ten gun turrets, and it thunders like a cloud as it moves along. It is further defended by two gleaming swords. Who is this mighty demon?" Vibhīṣaṇa said: "He is Atikāya, a son of Rāvaṇa. He too is free from fear of death at the hands of gods and demons, by virtue of a boon granted by Brahmā. O Rāma, be vigilant and get rid of him soon."

Some of the vānara leaders threw rocks and trees at him; but he dealt with them all playfully. He would himself not strike anyone who was not attacking him. He went straight to Rāma and challenged him for a fight. Lakṣmaṇa responded at once. When Lakṣmaṇa readied his weapon, the terrible sound that it produced astonished and pleased Atikāya. Yet, he said to Lakṣmaṇa: "You are but a young boy, O Lakṣmaṇa! Why do you wish to provoke me to kill you?" Lakṣmaṇa retorted: "Do not boast, O demon! And, do not treat me lightly considering me to be a boy; whether I am a boy or an aged man, I am still your death."

Lakṣmaṇa aimed a powerful missile at the demon who neutralised it. In the same way, Lakṣmaṇa neutralised the demon's missiles. Next, Lakṣmaṇa aimed a flat missile and shot the demon on his forehead: it went home and severely injured the demon who said: "Ah, Lakṣmaṇa, that was excellent!" Atikāya shot Lakṣmaṇa with a terribly sharp missile which hit the latter's chest and made him bleed profusely. Recovering from it, Lakṣmaṇa let go a terrible missile dedicated to the god of fire; seeing this, Atikāya intercepted it with the missile dedicated to the sun-god. Both these missiles met in space and got burnt out completely. In the same way, one intercepted the missile that the other used. Even when Lakṣmaṇa managed to hit the demon, the missiles proved incapable of piercing his armour, studded with diamonds. Atikāya directed a missile at Lakṣmaṇa which had a zigzag course. Hit by it, Lakṣmaṇa fainted for a while. When he regained consciousness, he heard a voice say: "These conventional weapons cannot kill him, O Lakṣmaṇa: use the most powerful one, the Brahmā-missile." Thereupon, Lakṣmaṇa used the Brahmā-missile. As it was delivered from his weapon, the sun and the moon were obscured and the earth shook. Atikāya tried to intercept it. But, the Brahmā-missile severed his head.

Yuddha 72–73

Rāvaṇa's anxiety mounted to hear of Atikāya's fall. He said to his counsellors: "Many of our people whom we had regarded as invincible have been killed by Rāma and Lakṣmaṇa. When they were assailed by missiles which had the power of the creator Brahmā himself, they somehow extricated themselves from them. This indeed puzzles me. I think Rāma, by whose prowess the mighty demons have been killed, is Nārāyaṇa himself. Hence, I feel it is essential that the greatest vigilance should be exercised by all of you. Let the city be guarded with unwinking vigilance; be especially mindful of the movements of the vānaras."

Rāvaṇa's son Indrajit approached him and said: "Why do you feel depressed, O Father, while I am by your side ready to kill your enemies. Give me leave to go to the battlefield; and I promise I shall kill all of them, including Rāma and Lakṣmaṇa." Indrajit at once got ready to go to the battlefield. Indrajit performed a fire-worship, for the success of his mission. And, the god of fire himself appeared in person to receive the offerings. There were auspicious omens, too.

While Indrajit got ready the mightiest missile which had the power of the creator Brahmā, the whole world shook. He himself remained hidden, and provided cover for the demons who attacked the vānaras vigorously. The vānaras detected Indrajit's position in the sky and threw trees and rocks at him. But this only enraged him still further and made him attack the vānaras more viciously. He himself secured direct hits on the foremost among the vānara heroes: Gandhamādana, Nala, Mainda, Gaja, Jāmbavān, Nīla, and even Sugrīva, Riṣabha, Dvivida and Aṅgada had been seriously wounded by Indrajit. Remaining unseen by others, Indrajit flew over the vānara-forces, carefully avoiding his own armies, and showered bombs upon the vānaras. Indrajit released a shower of a variety of bombs—resembling pikes, swords and axes—all of them descending upon the vānaras, burning brightly and sending a shower of sparks all round, which ignited all that came into contact with them. Any vānara who dared to look up at this phenomenon had his eyes blinded or put out by the sparks and the missiles. Indrajit then turned his attention upon Rāma and Lakṣmaṇa and covered them with his fire. Rāma said to Lakṣmaṇa: "Surely, Indrajit is employing the missile dedicated to Brahmā the creator himself: its power is inviolable. Let us endure this calamity patiently for a little while. When all of us are injured, Indrajit will surely return to Laṅkā."

And so did he! When Indrajit saw that by his fire-power all the vānara leaders and even Rāma and Lakṣmaṇa had fallen upon the ground, he flew back to Laṅkā and reported to Rāvaṇa.

Yuddha 74

During that single day six million and seven hundred thousand vānaras had been slain by Indrajit, with the missile endowed with the power of nature. Vibhīṣaṇa and Hanumān went round the battlefield. They saw Jāmbavān lying wounded. Vibhīṣaṇa questioned him: "O mighty one, are you still alive, and how do you feel?" Jāmbavān replied: "I cannot see, but from your voice I believe you are Vibhīṣaṇa. Pray, tell me at once, is Hanumān still alive?" Vibhīṣaṇa was intrigued, and asked: "Why do you ask about Hanumān even before you enquire of Rāma and Lakṣmaṇa?" Jāmbavān replied: "For a very good reason, O Vibhīṣaṇa. If Hanumān is alive, then our survival is possible." Hanumān himself then spoke to Jāmbavān who was highly pleased and said: "It is time for you to show your supernormal power, O mighty hero! You can revive Rāma, Lakṣmaṇa and all the wounded vānaras: and no one else can do it. Proceed immediately to the foremost mountain covered with ice. Between the Ṛṣabha and the Kailāsa mountains you will see a blazing mountain of herbs. There you will find the four herbs, mṛtasanjīvani (which revives the dead), viśalyakaraṇi (which heals all wounds), suvarṇakaraṇi (which restores the glow of the body to its original state), and bandhani (which heals fractures of bones). Bring these with the greatest expedition."

Hanumān lost no time in leaving on this life-saving expedition. He took off with a mighty roar which struck terror in the hearts of the demons of Laṅkā. With its tail held aloft, lowering its back, pulling back its 'ears', and opening its mouth, Hanumān's aircraft blazed like fire and took to the air with a great roar. Soon, he had reached the place described by Jāmbavān. He saw the hermitages of the sages. He saw the seat of the Creator, the abode of fire, that of the god of wealth, the light of the sun, and he saw the weapon of cosmic destruction, and the very navel of the earth. He saw the Ṛṣabha and the Kailāsa mountains. He also saw between them radiant herbs. But, when he landed to collect them, he could not see them. Distressed and puzzled, Hanumān thought for a moment and came to a decision! He thought: "Since I cannot see the herbs, I shall uproot the whole hill and carry it away." And uprooting the whole hill, Hanumān was airborne again. Soon he was back in Laṅkā.

As soon as he landed on the battlefield, by merely inhaling the healing air that wafted from the hill of herbs, Rāma, Lakṣmaṇa and the millions of wounded vānaras were restored to perfect health. Alas for the demons, Rāvaṇa had decreed that the dead ones should be thrown into the ocean so that the casualties might not be known! Hanumān returned the hill to its original site.

Yuddha 75

Sugrīva said: "Now that Kumbhakarṇa is dead and even so the sons of Rāvaṇa have been killed, Laṅkā's defences have been shattered. Let us carry out an immediate incendiary attack." The vānaras broke into the city. They set fire to whatever they saw. They set fire to the gates and to the huge mansions. The jewels that adorned the gates and walls crumbled to the earth. Garments and ornaments were burnt. Fire destroyed the weapons of the warriors, and the saddles of the horses. Tens of thousands of the houses in Laṅkā were reduced to ashes, with all their secret doors, and gates and protective walls, with all their luxurious furniture. Beautiful women who were asleep in their houses were awakened by the crackling of the fire, and they ran out screaming with fear. The fire that consumed Laṅkā was reflected on the surface of the ocean and made it look as though the water had turned red.

As the incendiary bombs showered upon the city, the stables were shattered. Horses and elephants ran amok frightening one another.

Rāma and Lakṣmaṇa who had regained their health and strength, fully took up their weapons and led the invasion. The boom of their weapons struck terror into the hearts of the demons. Their missiles shattered the gates of the city. However, when the missiles of Rāma rained fire on top of the mansions of the demons of Laṅkā, they became furious. Sugrīva commanded the vānaras to enter the city, and warned: "Anyone who turns his back or slackens his effort, should be shot by others for the guilt of disobeying the king."

When Rāvaṇa saw that the vānaras and Rāma were invading the city of Laṅkā, he became furious. He commanded mighty heroes Kumbha and Nikumbha, Yūpākṣa, Śoṇitākṣa, Prajangha and Kampana, to stem the tide of the invasion. With their ornaments and their weapons gleaming in the moonlight, and radiating great splendour, these mighty heroes marched forward to meet the vānara forces. A terrible battle ensued, between the vānaras and the demons.

Aṅgada challenged Kampana. The latter hit Aṅgada with a mace. Though hurt severely, Aṅgada managed to hold himself and to pick up a mountain-peak and hurl it on Kampana. The demon was dead.

Śoṇitākṣa challenged Aṅgada, and showered a variety of missiles upon Aṅgada. The vānara hero however survived all these and attacked the demon's car. Śoṇitākṣa jumped to the ground and a hand-to-hand fight ensued in which Aṅgada dug his sword deep into the body of the demon who fell unconscious.

Yuddha 76

When Śoṇitākṣa became unconscious, Aṅgada still brandishing his sword went round looking for someone else to challenge. At the same time Prajangha and Yūpākṣa were coming towards Aṅgada. Śoṇitākṣa, too, had recovered in the meantime and he joined them. At the same time Mainda and Dvivida came to the help of Aṅgada. The three vānara heroes fighting with the three demons was a hair-raising spectacle. They fought with trees, rocks and missiles for some time. Prajangha clenched his own fist and wished to strike Aṅgada. At the same time, Śoṇitākṣa struck Aṅgada on the forehead, which made him fall down. Getting up soon, Aṅgada knocked Prajangha's head off with his fist.

Yūpākṣa picked up Prajangha's sword and began to fight. Dvivida caught hold of Yūpākṣa; Śoṇitākṣa struck Dvivida in defence of Yūpākṣa. Dvivida snatched Śoṇitākṣa's mace. Mainda came to the help of Dvivida and struck Yūpākṣa. After a fierce fight, Dvivida tore the face of Śoṇitākṣa and throwing him on the ground, crushed him. Mainda gripped Yūpākṣa in his arms and crushed him; he fell down dead.

The demons moved to where Kumbhakarṇa's son Kumbha was. Kumbha was of extraordinary strength and had supernatural powers. He surprised Dvivida by aiming a missile at him. Dvivida fell down, writhing in agony. Mainda rushed to his aid and hurled a rock at Kumbha who broke it with his missile. Hurt by Kumbha's missile, Mainda fell unconscious on the field. Similarly, Kumbha attacked Aṅgada, too, with his terrible missiles. However, Aṅgada remained unshaken. Aṅgada hurled huge rocks on Kumbha which he broke up with his missiles, and then shot Aṅgada on his eyebrows. Unmindful of the bleeding and the pain, Aṅgada continued to fight. When however Kumbha shot seven missiles simultaneously at him, Aṅgada fainted. Sugrīva himself joined the battle.

Rushing fearlessly towards Kumbha, Sugrīva wrested Kumbha's weapon from his hand and broke it. Thereupon he said to Kumbha: "Rāvaṇa's strength is the fruit of a boon he obtained from Brahmā; your father Kumbhakarṇa was strong by nature. You are equal in valour to your father, and to Rāvaṇa. Surely, you have already exhibited some of your great strength by striking the vānara heroes down. You are fatigued. Rest awhile and come back; then I shall show you my strength. I do not wish to incur ignominy by striking you when you are tired." Kumbha was enraged to hear this and attacked Sugrīva. The latter picked the demon up and threw him into the sea! Kumbha returned and landed a terrible blow on Sugrīva's chest which broke his armour and even his bones! It generated sparks of fire! Sugrīva clenched his fist and struck the demon's chest. Hit by Sugrīva, the demon fell dead; the earth shook; and the demons were filled with fear.

Yuddha 77, 78, 79

When Kumbha was killed, his brother Nikumbha rushed forward towards Sugrīva and stood gazing at him, consuming him with anger. Nikumbha had a weapon, a club (parigha). It was gold-plated and diamond-studded. When the demon wielded it, the winds that constituted the atmosphere of the earth got agitated. The club itself shone like a smokeless flame. In fact, when the club was wielded by the demon, it looked as if the whole sky with the heavenly bodies revolved around it.

But, Hanumān stepped in front of Nikumbha, bared his chest, and sought a fight. Nikumbha hit Hanumān with the club; lo and behold, the club broke into pieces. Hanumān struck the demon with his clenched fist, and this broke his armour and blood flowed from his chest. Steadying himself after this blow, the demon caught hold of Hanumān and carried him away! After a while, however, Hanumān released himself from the demon's grip, stood on the ground, struck Nikumbha down, crushed him, and sitting on his chest twisted the demon's neck. He was dead.

Rāvaṇa flew into a rage. He summoned Makarākṣa, the son of Khara, and quickly despatched him to the battlefield.

Followed by a huge army, Makarākṣa went to the battlefield. There were many evil omens; but the demon ignored them.

When the vānaras were harassed by the demons, Rāma himself came to their aid. But, Makarākṣa addressed Rāma and said: "Wait, you shall fight with me, not with these warriors. From the day I heard of your killing my father, I have been waiting for this opportunity. Fight with whatever strength you have, whatever missiles you have, or with your own arms." Rāma laughed at this boast and replied: "Victory in war is not won by vain boasting, O demon! That day the birds and the beasts of the forest had their hunger satisfied by the flesh of fourteen thousand demons and that of your father. They will have another feast today."

A terrible fight ensued. The demon's missiles were effectively intercepted by Rāma's counter-missiles. The sound that arose from the weapons filled the atmosphere, like the rumbling of clouds. Gods and the celestials witnessed this battle. Rāma and Makarākṣa hit each other with the most powerful missiles; yet, neither flagged. The fire was so intense and so constant that the ground was completely obscured. Rāma knocked down the demon's weapon. The demon jumped on the ground and brandished his flaming trident. He hurled it at Rāma who intercepted it while it was still in the air. The demon rushed towards Rāma. The latter aimed at him the missile dedicated to the god of fire. His heart pierced by it, the demon fell dead. Witnessing the death of Makarākṣa, the demons fled to Laṅkā city, afraid of the weapon of Rāma.

Yuddha 80–81

Rāvaṇa was beside himself with anger. He looked at his son Indrajit and said: "My beloved son, by your might, you have conquered even the king of heaven; is it difficult for you to kill these two humans in battle? Go and by whatever means kill them." Indrajit once again performed the religious rites connected with war, for his success in the venture. On conclusion of this religious rite, Indrajit ascended an aircarft which could go out of sight. And, he took with him the missile dedicated to the Creator. As soon as he emerged from the city, he became invisible. From high above in the sky, he directed his fire at Rāma and Lakṣmaṇa. However, though they directed their fire at the demon, remaining unseen in the sky, they could not reach him. And, the demon had effectively hidden himself behind a smoke-screen. Though he moved about constantly, he could neither be seen nor his aircraft heard. Indrajit continued to score direct hits on Rāma and Lakṣmaṇa; and once Rāma's missile scored a direct hit on Indrajit.

Seeing this, Lakṣmaṇa said to Rāma: "I shall direct the missile presided over by the Creator at this demon, Rāma; and that will be his end. I cannot see what else we can do at this juncture." Rāma, however, did not approve of this action; he said: "You cannot kill all the demons for the sake of one of them, O Lakṣmaṇa. You should not kill in battle one who does not fight, who is hidden, who comes to you with joined palms, one who seeks your asylum, one who is running away, or one who is dazed. I shall deal with him with a single powerful missile."

Indrajit returned to Laṅkā. He came back to the battlefield, but this time in an armoured car and with Sītā in it—a lifelike and exact replica of the real Sītā produced by his magic. The vānaras rushed towards him in great anger when they saw him. Hanumān saw him, too: and he saw Sītā seated in the car, a picture of grief and despair. While the vānaras were looking, Indrajit drew his sword and caught hold of the hair on Sītā's head. She wailed aloud: "O Rāma, O Rāma."

Hanumān upbraided Indrajit and admonished him: "This indeed is the worst of all sins, O demon! Though you are descended from brāhmaṇa sages, you were conceived by a demoness, and hence you exhibit this unworthy trait! The killing of a woman is universally condemned." Indrajit replied: "How true! O vānara! But, in war one can do whatever might annoy the enemy. It is for her sake that you have all invaded Laṅkā; I shall thwart your purpose by killing her." Saying so, he cut the body of Sītā into two even as the vānaras were watching. Indrajit was happy. The vānaras were grief-stricken.

Yuddha 82, 83, 84

The vānaras began to flee when they saw Indrajit: Hanumān tried to restore their morale. Under his leadership, they began to fight the demons again. He himself took a huge rock and threw it upon the vehicle of Indrajit; but the driver cleverly dodged it. The rock hit the ground and made a big hole in it. Fierce fighting ensued between the vānaras and the demons.

However, after some time, Hanumān commanded the vānara army to retreat, tearfully saying, "Sītā, for whose recovery we are fighting, is dead. We should report this to Rāma and to Sugrīva and then do as they decide." And they all did so.

At the same time, Indrajit decided that he should perform another important religious ceremony for attaining even greater power in war. He headed for a place known as Nikumbhila.

And, at the same time Rāma had despatched Jāmbavān to help Hanumān in his combat with the demons. However, Jāmbavān saw that Hanumān himself was coming to where Rāma was, with a face portraying unfathomable sorrow. Hanumān approached Rāma and said: "O Rāma, even as we were looking on and fighting, Indrajit killed the noble Sītā." Hearing this, Rāma fell down unconscious. Seeing this, Lakṣmaṇa broke down and wailed aloud: "O Rāma, if this could happen to you then surely there is no truth in the belief that happiness follows virtue. We see that the wicked Rāvaṇa prospers whereas you who have adhered to virtue all your life have experienced nothing but unhappiness! It may be said that virtue needs the protection of strength for the attainment of its own reward which is happiness; then it is weak and one should shun such weakness, and resort to might. By renouncing your right to the throne, you have renounced strength: and hence this discomfiture. In this world only a wealthy man has friends and relations; he alone is considered a man, a pundit, a hero, intelligent, blessed and virtuous. Even dharma and enjoyment are possible only to him; and all pay homage to him. Because you have renounced wealth, and because you went to the forest to honour your father's word, your wife has been abducted! . . . Ah, Rāma, get up. Why do you not know that you are the supreme being? I have been saying all this only to rouse your anger; however I shall myself presently destroy all these demons!"

Just then Vibhīṣaṇa came there. Lakṣmaṇa told him what had happened to Rāma. Vibhīṣaṇa then said to Rāma: "Rāma, I know Rāvaṇa's intentions about Sītā: he would never let her be killed. This is surely a trick by Indrajit who is an adept in magic. However, he is about to perform a great religious rite; if he concludes it he will be still more powerful. Please send Lakṣmaṇa with me, and we shall do the needful at once."

Yuddha 85–86

Still slightly dazed by the dreadful news of Sītā's end, Rāma did not clearly comprehend Vibhīṣaṇa's words, and asked him to repeat them. And, Vibhīṣaṇa did so. He added: "Indrajit is about to perform a dreadful rite at a place called Nikumbhila. If he completes this, he will obtain a terrible weapon known as Brahmaśira. And if he gets this, we are all as good as dead. I am aware of the boon he got from Brahmā the creator; it was this: 'If, before you reach Nikumbhila and before you complete the rite, someone is able to kill you, that will be your end.' Surely, therefore, now is the time, and now alone is the time to put an end to Indrajit. If he is dead, Rāvaṇa is as good as dead, too! There is no time to lose: let Lakṣmaṇa, accompanied by the army proceed immediately to Nikumbhila and he will be able to kill Indrajit."

Rāma replied: "O Lakṣmaṇa, go at once with the entire army and with all the vānara heroes. You can easily kill him in battle. And, Vibhīṣaṇa will accompany you, and he knows all the tricks of Indrajit."

Lakṣmaṇa declared: "I shall kill that terrible demon with my missiles today." Hanumān, an army of vānaras and Vibhīṣaṇa with his companions, went with him.

Vibhīṣaṇa advised the vānaras: "We have nearly reached the destination. Now, use all your strength and fight these demons with stones, rocks and trees. When you thus kill the army of Indrajit, he will himself appear before us and we can then deal with him easily." The vānaras and the demons closed in on one another and there was terrible fighting. The vānaras fought furiously and most enthusiastically. Therefore thousands and thousands of the demons fell.

Seeing the destruction of the demons by the vānaras, Indrajit was agitated and he came away from the shade of the big tree, where he was performing the religious rite and which he had not concluded. He ascended his armoured car and demanded the driver to take him to where Hanumān was, eager as he was, to kill him. The demons, too, who were with Indrajit attacked Hanumān with a variety of weapons and missiles. But Hanumān stood unaffected by them. Indrajit himself saw Hanumān standing like a mountain on the battlefield. With great anger, he shot several missiles at Hanumān: but Hanumān did not wince. He said to Indrajit: "Fight me, if you are a hero, O Indrajit! Having come near me, you will not return alive."

At the same time, Vibhīṣaṇa drew Lakṣmaṇa's attention to the demon Indrajit and said: "He wants to kill Hanumān! Before he does so, you should engage him in battle and kill him yourself."

Yuddha 87–88

Vibhīṣaṇa then guided Lakṣmaṇa to the place where Indrajit was and where he had commenced the sacred rite. Vibhīṣaṇa said to Lakṣmaṇa: "If Indrajit concludes this rite, he will become invisible and he can then destroy everyone. Kill him before that." Lakṣmaṇa went forth towards the demon and invited him to a duel. Indrajit saw Lakṣmaṇa, and also saw Vibhīṣaṇa standing near him. Addressing Vibhīṣaṇa, Indrajit said: "What a shame! You are one of us yet you are on our enemy's side. You have completely lost all sense of kinship and right judgement. Beware! He who abandons his own people and serves the enemy will, once his own people have been eliminated, be destroyed by the enemy. Disgraceful indeed is the way in which you have betrayed us."

Vibhīṣaṇa replied: "Though I was born in your race, I have never shared your nature. I am opposed to unrighteousness. One attains to happiness by abandoning the kinship of one who is unrighteous and who is bent on evil. Your father is cruel, he tormented the noble sages, and he seeks to seduce another's wife. Above all, he himself threw me out of his court and his kingdom. Well, O Indrajit, your end is near."

Indrajit then said to Lakṣmaṇa: "O Lakṣmaṇa, you will taste my power and strength today once again. Do you not remember that it was just the other day that both you and Rāma were rendered unconscious by my missiles? Today I shall complete the work." Lakṣmaṇa said: "Do not boast, O hero! But show your might in action. Remaining hidden from view, you injured us. To remain hidden and fight, is not the work of a hero but that of a thief! Here I am, standing close to you: shoot!"

Indrajit, enraged by this taunt, let loose a number of his missiles. Lakṣmaṇa was severely wounded. He returned the fire. The duel between the two heroes was hair-raising to watch, and tumultuous. After a time, Vibhīṣaṇa saw that Indrajit's face was a bit pale, and said to Lakṣmaṇa: "The demon is becoming fatigued; attack vigorously now." Lakṣmaṇa used his missiles with good effect: and Indrajit was shaken a bit. But his anger revived his strength and Indrajit shot seven missiles at Lakṣmaṇa, ten at Hanumān and a hundred missiles at Vibhīṣaṇa.

Unmindful of this devastating attack, Lakṣmaṇa aimed his missiles at Indrajit: and with them he shattered the demon's armour. Wounded and bleeding profusely, Indrajit fought on. The fight between the two mighty heroes continued unabated; and it was of unprecedented magnitude.

A considerable time went by, but the two heroes neither retreated nor did they show that they were tired.

Yuddha 89, 90, 91

Wishing to help Lakṣmaṇa and to hasten the end of Indrajit, Vibhīṣaṇa exhorted the vānaras thus; "Why are you standing and watching the duel, O vānaras? This Indrajit is the only remaining support of Rāvaṇa. His death is the death of Rāvaṇa himself. In fact, I could myself kill Indrajit: but he is my nephew, and when I approach him I feel sorry for him. All of you get together and kill his helpers so that he himself can be killed easily." Thus exhorted, the vānaras fell violently upon the demons. The demons retaliated and attacked the mighty Jāmbavān. Indrajit fought alternately with Vibhīṣaṇa and also Lakṣmaṇa. The action was so fast that no one could see them firing at one another. The sky was obscured by the fire. Later the sun set and darkness began to envelop the world.

Lakṣmaṇa shot the 'horses' (engines) of Indrajit. With another missile, he beheaded the driver of Indrajit's car. Undaunted, Indrajit drove his own vehicle, while yet fighting. The vānara heroes, however, pounced upon the vehicle and killed (silenced) the horses (engines) of Indrajit's car. The clever demon exhorted his army to keep fighting even more furiously than before and while they were doing so quietly slipped into Laṅkā to get another armoured car for himself.

Once again a fierce duel took place between Indrajit and Lakṣmaṇa. The latter knocked the former's weapon down. Lakṣmaṇa also hit Indrajit on his chest and severely wounded him. Indrajit returned the fire. Lakṣmaṇa sent a hail of missiles on all the demons and on Indrajit, too. And, once again, he killed the demon's driver. But Indrajit did not mind because the 'horses' (engines) of the new vehicle could function without a driver! All the missiles that Indrajit aimed at Lakṣmaṇa seemed to strike the latter and fall down. Indrajit assumed that Lakṣmaṇa had a shatter-proof armour on, and so hit him on the forehead. Indrajit also shot Vibhīṣaṇa at the same time. The latter, wielding his mace, killed the demon's horses (smashed the engines). Enraged at this, Indrajit hurled a javelin at Vibhīṣaṇa which Lakṣmaṇa successfully intercepted.

Both Lakṣmaṇa and Indrajit began using powerful missiles at each other. Lakṣmaṇa intercepted Indrajit's missiles in the air, neutralised them and both missiles fell on the earth. Lakṣmaṇa answered Indrajit's missile with a counter-missile: and he diverted the demon's fire-missile with his own sun-missile. Finally, taking up a missile of Indra, Lakṣmaṇa said: "If Rāma is devoted to dharma and truth, let this end Indrajit's life." That missile cut off the head of Indrajit which fell on the battlefield. The demons fled. The vānaras celebrated the event.

Yuddha 92–93

Accompanied by Vibhīṣaṇa and Hanumān and the other vānara leaders, Lakṣmaṇa approached Rāma, and Vibhīṣaṇa announced the joyous news that Lakṣmaṇa had indeed killed the mighty Indrajit. Rāma was highly delighted and extolled Lakṣmaṇa again and again: "You have done the most difficult feat!" Lakṣmaṇa was modest; out of affection for him Rāma forcibly drew him to himself, and placing him on his lap kissed his head and looked at him again and again with great pride and joy. And, again, he said to Lakṣmaṇa: "Victory is assured now that Indrajit has been killed by you in just three days. Now, Rāvaṇa himself will appear on the battlefield along with his army: and I shall easily dispose of him. With your help, O Lakṣmaṇa, I can recover Sītā and even conquer the whole world."

Rāvaṇa fainted on hearing that Indrajit had been killed. Regaining his consciousness, he lamented: "Alas, you who terrorised the gods, Indra and even the god of death, how is it that you have preceded me, instead of performing my obsequies first? But, surely, you have gone to the highest heaven to which they who lay down their lives in the cause of their master ascend. This is the path of all noble warriors. Today the gods, the ascetics and brāhmaṇas will sleep well: but today the whole world appears bleak to me."

Rāvaṇa was completely overcome by terrible anger. He thought "I still have the terrible weapon which I obtained from the creator Brahmā: with it I shall kill Rāma and Lakṣmaṇa and all their warriors." He also thought: "My beloved son Indrajit played a trick on the vānaras, and for this purpose he killed an illusory form of Sītā: I shall now turn that into a fact! I shall kill Sītā." He picked up his terrible sword and rushed to the Aśoka-grove. The demons yelling with joy followed him. His wives and also his ministers followed him apprehensively.

Seeing him approach her angrily, sword in hand, Sītā was worried and puzzled: "Is he coming to kill me? Or, has he killed Rāma and Lakṣmaṇa? What may be the cause of the shouts of joy I heard from the demons? Alas, I did a foolish thing in not accepting Hanumān's offer to take me away to Rāma." Divining Rāvaṇa's intention, his minister Supārśva admonished him: "O King, pray, do not yield to anger and commit this heinous crime. Killing a woman is entirely unworthy of your greatness. You have fulfilled all the vows of a brāhmaṇa of Vedic learning; and you are devoted to your own duties. How then do you contemplate the killing of a woman? Turn you anger on Rāma, and you will kill him without doubt; and then you can make Sītā your consort!" Rāvaṇa cooled down and accepted the minister's counsel.

Yuddha 93–94

At Rāvaṇa's request the entire army marched to the battlefield. The demons and the vānaras immediately joined in a fierce battle. The casualties were numberless on both sides. For the protection of the vānaras, Rāma himself entered the battlefield; and with his mighty weapon cut down the demons. The demons were greatly awed by the inconceivable might of Rāma. He was so swift in the discharge of the missiles that the demons could not even see where he was! They shouted: "There he is, killing the army of elephants; there he is, killing infantrymen and their horses." They even saw each other as Rāma and killed each other! Rāma used the missile which caused confusion: utterly confused by this, the demons saw thousands of Rāma all around them; and later realised that there was only one Rāma. Sometimes, they could only see Rāma's firearm and not Rāma himself. They saw Rāma's weapon flitting about like a firebrand killing the demons: they could not see Rāma. In three hours time, two hundred thousand soldiers and a great number of elephants and horses had been killed by Rāma, singlehanded, with his firearm which emitted tongues of fire. Rāma said to his companions: "Such power to use these missiles is possessed only by me and Tryambaka."

In Laṅkā, the demonesses got together in small groups and lamented: "Alas, what made that dreadful-looking, cruel and aged demoness Śūrpaṇakā cast a lustful eye on this charming prince Rāma? It was surely our doom and the doom of all the demons that prompted her to aspire for the love of Rāma. In the same way, it was surely our misfortune that tempted Virādha to have evil intentions towards Sītā. Even after that, our king Rāvaṇa had plenty of warnings: the killing by Rāma of fourteen thousand demons, of Khara and Dūṣaṇa and Triśira, Kabandha, and the killing of the mighty Vāli, the enthronement of Sugrīva— any of these should have been sufficient warning to enable Rāvaṇa to assess the might of Rāma and desist from the evil course. Rāvaṇa also had the wise advice of Vibhīṣaṇa; he could have realised the immense might of Rāma when Kumbhakarṇa was killed or at least when Atikāya was killed. Even Indrajit's fall has not made him wise! Alas we have lost all our kith and kin. Surely, Death himself has come in the form of Rāma. We have heard that in answer to the prayer of the oppressed holy men, lord Śiva granted them the boon: 'For the destruction of the demons, a woman will be born on earth.' Rāvaṇa obtained a boon-of-invincibility from Brahmā, but scornfully ignored human beings: and surely this human Rāma has come to kill him. Vibhīṣaṇa was wise: and he has in good time sought Rāma's asylum. We have no one to protect us; we have nowhere to go."

Yuddha 95–96

Rāvaṇa himself heard the piteous laments of the demonesses. He looked, with great anger, at the demon-chiefs standing around him, and ordered: "March!" All of them and their own divisions marched immediately to the battlefield. Rāvaṇa said to the demon-chiefs Mahodara, Mahāpārśva and

Virūpākṣa: "Today I shall myself kill Rāma and Lakṣmaṇa and thus avenge the killing of Khara, Kumbhakarṇa, Prahastha and Indrajit. The heads of all my enemies will roll on the ground. By their destruction I shall wipe the tears of those whose brothers and sons have been killed. Bring my armoured car. Bring my weapons. Let the army follow me to the battlefield."

There was total conscription: the demon-chiefs rounded up every able-bodied demon in Laṅkā and rushed them all to the battlefield for the final and decisive combat. Rāvaṇa got into his very special armoured car which awed even the demons. On the battlefield itself, warriors were saying to one another: "Here comes Rāvaṇa, the king of the demons, who is accompanied by his special regalia; here comes one who abducted Sītā, who is of evil conduct, and who killed the brāhmaṇas and terrorised even the gods: here he comes to fight with Rāma." Surrounded by the demon-chiefs, Rāvaṇa approached the gate where Rāma and Lakṣmaṇa were. There were many evil omens; but Rāvaṇa proceeded disregarding them.

Rāvaṇa began to attack the vānara forces who fell in huge numbers before his advance. Placing Suṣena in charge of these vānaras, Sugrīva went forward to the front ranks where the battle was. With a rain of rocks, he killed countless demons.

The demon Virūpākṣa came to their rescue, mounted on an elephant. He directed a volley of shots at Sugrīva who, undaunted by this, picked up a big tree and with it hit the elephant which retreated and trumpeted. Virūpākṣa jumped down from the elephant and rushed towards Sugrīva.

Sugrīva took a huge rock and hurled it at Virūpākṣa who, however, escaped in time, and struck Sugrīva with a sword. This made Sugrīva unconscious for a time. Recovering after a little while, Sugrīva struck the demon with his clenched fist. The demon hit Sugrīva again with his sword and broke his armour. Sugrīva actually fell down; but quickly regaining his foothold, he gave a resounding slap on the chest of the demon.

Virūpākṣa dodged that blow, but he himself hit Sugrīva with a clenched fist. Greatly enraged, Sugrīva delivered a heavy and powerful blow on the temple of Virūpākṣa: vomiting blood and with blood pouring like water from all the apertures of his body, the demon fell down dead.

Yuddha 97–98

Casualties on both sides were very heavy and the army on the battlefield was getting exceedingly thin. Rāvaṇa turned to the demon Mahodara and said: "All my hopes are now pinned on you, O Mahodara: pray, proceed to the battle."

Mahodara went to the battlefield full of zeal and enthusiasm; and he was greeted by a hail of rocks and trees hurled at him by the vānaras. While the vānaras assailed the demons, Mahodara himself began to kill numerous vānaras with his deadly missiles. Some of them fled; and others ran to Sugrīva for help. Sugrīva engaged the demon in battle. He picked up a huge rock and directed it towards Mahodara; the latter however, broke that rock to pieces with his own missile. When Sugrīva threw a huge tree at him, Mahodara tore that, too, to pieces. Sugrīva picked up a bludgeon that was lying on the battlefield and with it killed (silenced) the horses (engines) of the demon's vehicle.

Mahodara attacked Sugrīva with his mace; Sugrīva responded with his bludgeon. When Mahodara hurled his mace at him, Sugrīva intercepted it with his bludgeon. The mace fell down and the bludgeon broke. Sugrīva picked up a club from the battlefield and directed it at the demon: Mahodara responded with the mace. Both of them collided in the air and fell to the ground. The two heroes thereafter fought with their bare hands. After wrestling for awhile, Mahodara picked up a sword and fought with it. So did Sugrīva. Mahodara hit Sugrīva's armour with the sword. Undaunted by it, Sugrīva cut off the demon's head with his sword. Sugrīva was pleased; Rāvaṇa became angry; and Rāma was happy.

The demon Mahāpārśva attacked the forces of Aṅgada. Great was the destruction of the vānaras at his hands. Aṅgada was enraged and distressed. Picking up a bludgeon, he hurled it at the demon, who was temporarily rendered unconscious by the blow. Utilising this opportunity, the vānara hero Jāmbavān destroyed the demon's armoured car.

Regaining consciousness, Mahāpārśva once again attacked Aṅgada, and also the other vānara heroes, Gavakṣa and Jāmbavān. And once again Aṅgada directed his bludgeon at the demon. This knocked down the demon's weapon from his hand and tossed the helmet from his head. Aṅgada also landed a powerful blow with his hand on the demon's temple. Mahāpārśva threw a terrible looking axe at Aṅgada which, luckily, the latter dodged.

Clenching his fist firmly, Aṅgada aimed a mighty blow at the vital part of the demon. As the fist landed on his breast with the strength of a thunderbolt, his chest burst open and the demon fell dead. Seeing this, Rāvaṇa was utterly confused and enraged; and the vānaras rejoiced.

Yuddha 99, 100, 101

Rāvaṇa now said to his driver: "Drive on: I shall myself kill Rāma and Lakṣmaṇa and thus destroy root and branch this wicked army that has taken such a heavy toll of my people." Rāvaṇa took up a terrible missile which spread darkness, and killed numerous vānaras with it. Seeing this Rāma came forward to challenge Rāvaṇa. Now the demons began to fall in great numbers. Lakṣmaṇa attacked Rāvaṇa who easily neutralised all his missiles. Thereafter Rāvaṇa went over to Rāma himself and directed a hail of shots at him. But Rāma covered them all with an anti-missile known as bhalla. Rāvaṇa hit Rāma's brows with his missiles, but Rāma remained unaffected. Rāma directed the terrible missile dedicated to Rudra at Rāvaṇa who took it calmly. Rāvaṇa thereafter used diabolical missiles which seemed to have the heads of lions, tigers, vultures, jackals, serpents, donkeys, boars, dogs, cocks, alligators, etc. Rāma noticed this and used the missiles dedicated to the god of fire which had heads resembling fire, the sun, moon, comet, planets and lunar mansions. Rāma's missiles neutralised Rāvaṇa's in the air.

Rāvaṇa directed the Rudra-missile at Rāma. From this came forth diverse weapons—maces, clubs, tridents, all of adamantine strength. Rāma counteracted the effect of this missile by using the Gandharva-missile. Rāvaṇa then used the sun-god-missile. This gave rise to numerous discuses of inconceivable destructive power. Rāma dealt with them effectively with his own weapon. Lakṣmaṇa shot Rāvaṇa's flag and tore it up. He also killed Rāvaṇa's driver. He even broke the gun-turret of Rāvaṇa.

Rāvaṇa turned in all fury against Vibhīṣaṇa and hurled a terrible weapon known as śakti at him. Lakṣmaṇa intercepted it, and it fell down letting terrible sparks of fire fly from it. Enraged, Rāvaṇa now turned to Lakṣmaṇa: "Ah, since you are covering Vibhīṣaṇa, I shall take your life with this śakti." It was an extremely powerful weapon which was infallible. As it came flying towards Lakṣmaṇa, Rāma prayed! The weapon hit Lakṣmaṇa and he was made unconscious. Rāma was shocked. But he said to himself: "This is not the time for grief." And he continued to fight with great fury. But the vānaras could not extract śakti from Lakṣmaṇa's body; Rāma himself had to do it. As he was thus helping his brother, Rāvaṇa shot him several times. Angered, Rāma said to the vānaras: "Protect Lakṣmaṇa from all sides, while I turn to Rāvaṇa and rid the world of him. On account of him I have endured great sorrow; and I shall give up all that sorrow after killing this Rāvaṇa. On account of him I have had to drag numerous vānaras to the battle. Today I shall, by killing this Rāvaṇa, perform a deed which shall be remembered and recalled for all time to come throughout the world." Unable to face the terrible missiles which Rāma now used, Rāvaṇa fled.

Yuddha 102, 103, 104

When Rāvaṇa withdrew from the battlefield, Rāma returned to Lakṣmaṇa. Seeing him lying unconscious, as if dead, Rāma was stricken with despondence. He lamented: "Seeing my beloved brother, dearer to me than my own life, lying thus bathed in blood, I have no power to fight. My weapon slips from my hand; my legs have no strength to support me. There is a strong desire to give up my life. What will I gain by victory, when my brother is no more? How will I face my kinsfolk without him? He followed me to the forest; I shall follow him in death."

The vānara Suṣena tried to comfort Rāma, saying: "Lakṣmaṇa is not dead, O Rāma. Hence, give up this grief." He said to Hanumān: "Go and quickly fetch the life-saving herbs that you fetched before, growing on the Mahodaya mountain." Hanumān knew the route which had previously been pointed out to him by Jāmbavān. He went there with great expedition. He returned very soon and placing a mountain-peak before Suṣena said: "I could not see the herbs; so I have brought the peak." Suṣena discovered the herbs, crushed them and administered them to Lakṣmaṇa. Inhaling the herbs, Lakṣmaṇa regained consciousness. Rāma was happy, but he continued to be sentimental, repeating: "If you had not been revived, my victory would be useless."

Reminded of the gravity of the situation, Rāma directed his fire in the direction of Rāvaṇa's army. Soon Rāvaṇa himself appeared in his armoured car and covered Rāma with his weapon. The celestials felt that the duel was ill-matched since Rāvaṇa had an armoured vehicle (perhaps a tank) and Rāma was standing on the ground. Indra, the chief of gods, quickly despatched his own armoured car, along with his driver Mātali. This armoured car had 'green horses'. Mātali placed the car in front of Rāma and said: "Indra has sent his own car and his powerful weapons, including śakti, for your use and to enable you to gain victory."

In the fierce battle that ensued, Rāvaṇa discharged a missile that turned into venomous snakes: and Rāma neutralised them by using another missile which released eagles into the air. Greatly enraged, Rāvaṇa used even more powerful missiles and harassed Rāma, who could not even use his weapons freely. The celestials exhorted Rāma, and the demons exhorted Rāvaṇa. The latter took up a terrible weapon, a trident which was strong as adamant, fiery, with terrible spikes and which produced thunderous noise. He said: "Rāma, when I hurl this, you will be dead." As it came towards him, Rāma tried to intercept it with his missiles which were reduced to ashes by the trident. Rāma then used the śakti of Indra. Intercepted by śakti in the air, the trident was split and it fell to the ground. Rāma pursued this by attacking Rāvaṇa himself.

Yuddha 105–106

Tormented by the missiles of Rāma, the demon-chief Rāvaṇa became terribly enraged. He literally covered Rāma with his fire. However, Rāma successfully intercepted all the missiles of the demon. In that awe-inspiring battle, and in the dust and the fire raised by the battle, even Rāma and Rāvaṇa could not be seen. Laughing derisively, Rāma said to Rāvaṇa: "O Rāvaṇa, I guess that you think you are a great hero. You are not! By the very fact that you stole, without my knowledge, my wife Sītā from Janasthāna is proof that you are no hero! You laid your hands on another's wife when she was unprotected, and yet you consider yourself a hero! You will now suffer the consequences of that wicked and unchivalrous action.

Shamelessly you carried Sītā away when she was alone: if you had attempted to do so in my presence, you would have joined Khara in the other world. Luckily, you have yourself appeared before me. I shall sever your head from you body and beasts and vultures will feed on your flesh."

Rāma's anger augmented his strength and his prowess. The divine missiles, as it were, sought Rāma's presence at that time, and the joy that filled Rāma's heart at the impending and imminent destruction of Rāvaṇa enabled him to shoot the latter with great ease and speed. He also perceived good omens and was greatly encouraged by them. Rāma fought furiously; and Rāvaṇa was overwhelmed by the missiles of Rāma. Seeing the utter confusion of Rāvaṇa, his driver drove the car away from the battlefield.

When Rāvaṇa realised what the charioteer had done, he was angry. He said to his charioteer: "You have disgraced my name. You have shamed my valour. My glory has been effaced by this cowardly action of yours. When my enemy was looking on and I was eager to fight him, you drove the car away from the battlefield! If you do not take me back at once to the battlefield I shall be compelled to conclude that you have been bribed by my enemy to bring me this disrepute."

The driver explained: "Master! It is the duty of a good driver to be aware of the condition and the strength of his master, of the condition of the battlefield, the strength and the weakness of the enemy, and he should know when to attack and when to retreat. Considering all this and seeing that you were fatigued and fearing that you would be overpowered by your enemy, I acted in your own best interest. Such indeed was my duty. Now that you command me to take the car back to the battlefield, I shall certainly do so and thus fulfil my duty to my master whose favours I have not forgotten."

Yuddha 107, 108

The sage Agastya appeared on the scene of the battle along with the gods, and seeing that Rāma was fatigued by the prolonged combat with Rāvaṇa, said to him:

"O Rāma! Listen carefully to this secret. It is the heart of the sun: and its constant repetition is conducive to victory and to all auspiciousness, and to the destruction of enemies. Worship the sun, O Rāma! He is the very essence of all the gods and he alone protects all beings. He is the controller of the celestial bodies. He is the splendour of splendours. Pray to him thus:

> tejasām api tejasvī dvādaśātman namo 'stu te
> namah pūrvāya giraye paścimāyā 'draye namaḥ
> jyotirgaṇāṇāṁ pataye dinā 'dhipataye namaḥ (16)
> jayāya jayabhadrāya haryaśvāya namo namaḥ
> namo namaḥ sahasrāṁśo ādityāya namo namaḥ (17)
> nama ugrāya vīrāya śāraṅgāya namo namaḥ
> namaḥ padma prabodhāya pracaṇḍāya namo 'stu te (18)
> brahme 'śanā 'cyute 'śāya sūryāyā 'ditya varcase
> bhāsvate sarva bhakṣāya raudrāya vapuṣe namaḥ (19)
> tamo ghnāya hima ghnāya śatru ghnāyā 'mitātmane
> kṛtaghna ghnāya devāya jyotiṣāṁ pataye namaḥ (20)
> tapta cāmīkarābhāya haraye viśva karmaṇe
> namas tamo 'bhinighnāya rucaye loka sākṣiṇe (21)

"The sun, O Rāma, is the creator and the destroyer of everything. He is awake even in those who sleep. He is the lord of all actions. He who worships the sun never comes to grief and overcomes fear and calamities. You will this very moment conquer Rāvaṇa." Saying so, Agastya withdrew. Rāma sipped water, looked at the sun, recited the prayer, and advanced towards Rāvaṇa, his heart filled with delight.

At the same time, Rāvaṇa's driver also brought his car to the battlefield. Rāma said to Mātali: "Pray, be vigilant and calm. For the time has come for me to destroy this demon. Hence, it is vital that you should not be confused nor yield to anxiety, but drive the car vigilantly and swiftly. I am sure that being Indra's own driver, you need not be told all this: yet, since my whole being is concentrated on this combat, I am reminding you but not admonishing you!"

The final battle between Rāma and Rāvaṇa followed. At that time, Rāvaṇa saw many, many evil omens. And, Rāma saw many auspicious and good omens. Knowing the meaning and the significance of these omens, Rāma was happy; and this greatly augmented his strength and his valour.

Yuddha 109, 110, 111

When Rāma and Rāvaṇa began to fight, their armies stood stupefied, watching them! Rāma was determined to win;

Rāvaṇa was sure he would die: knowing this, they fought with all their might. Rāvaṇa attacked the standard on Rāma's car; and Rāma similarly shot the standard on Rāvaṇa's car. While Rāvaṇa's standard fell; Rāma's did not. Rāvaṇa next aimed at the 'horses' (engines) of Rāma's car: even though he attacked them with all his might, they remained unaffected.

Both of them discharged thousands of missiles: these illumined the skies and created a new heaven, as it were! They were accurate in their aim and their missiles unfailingly hit the target. With unflagging zeal they fought each other, without the least trace of fatigue. What one did the other did in retaliation.

Rāvaṇa shot at Mātali who remained unaffected by it. Then Rāvaṇa sent a shower of maces and mallets at Rāma. Their very sound agitated the oceans and tormented the aquatic creatures. The celestials and the holy brāhmaṇas witnessing the scene prayed: "May auspiciousness attend to all the living beings, and may the worlds endure forever. May Rāma conquer Rāvaṇa." Astounded at the way in which Rāma and Rāvaṇa fought with each other, the sages said to one another: "Sky is like sky, ocean is like ocean; the fight between Rāma and Rāvaṇa is like Rāma and Rāvaṇa—incomparable."

Taking up a powerful missile, Rāma correctly aimed at the head of Rāvaṇa; it fell. But another head appeared in its place. Every time Rāma cut off Rāvaṇa's head, another appeared! Rāma was puzzled. Mātali, Rāma's driver, said to Rāma: "Why do you fight like an ordinary warrior, O Rāma? Use the Brahmā-missile; the hour of the demon's death is at hand."

Rāma remembered the Brahmā-missile which the sage Agastya had given him. It had the power of the wind-god for its 'feathers'; the power of fire and sun at its head; the whole space was its body; and it had the weight of a mountain. It shone like the sun or the fire of nemesis. As Rāma took it in his hands, the earth shook and all living beings were terrified. Infallible in its destructive power, this ultimate weapon of destruction shattered the chest of Rāvaṇa, and entered deep into the earth.

Rāvaṇa fell dead. And the surviving demons fled, pursued by the vānaras. The vānaras shouted in great jubilation. The air resounded with the drums of the celestials. The gods praised Rāma. The earth became steady, the wind blew softly and the sun was resplendent as before. Rāma was surrounded by mighty heroes and gods who were all joyously felicitating him on the victory.

Yuddha 112, 113

Seeing Rāvaṇa lying dead on the battlefield, Vibhīṣaṇa burst into tears. Overcome by brotherly affection, he lamented thus: "Alas, what I had predicted has come true: and my advice was not relished by you, overcome as you were by lust and delusion. Now that you have departed, the glory of Laṅkā has departed. You were like a tree firmly established in heroism with asceticism for its strength, spreading out firmness in all aspects of your life: yet you have been cut down. You were like an elephant with splendour, noble ancestry, indignation, and pleasant nature for parts: yet you have been killed. You, who were like blazing fire have been extinguished by Rāma."

Rāma approached the grief-stricken Vibhīṣaṇa and gently and lovingly said to him: "It is not right that you should thus grieve, O Vibhīṣaṇa, for a mighty warrior fallen on the battlefield. Victory is the monopoly of none: a hero is either slain in battle or he kills his opponent. Hence our ancients decreed that the warrior who is killed in combat should not be mourned. Get up and consider what should be done next."

Vibhīṣaṇa regained his composure and said to Rāma: "This Rāvaṇa used to give a lot in charity to ascetics; he enjoyed life; he maintained his servants well; he shared his wealth with his friends, and he destroyed his enemies. He was regular in his religious observances; learned he was in the scriptures. By your grace, O Rāma, I wish to perform his funeral in accordance with the scriptures, for his welfare in the other world." Rāma was delighted and said to Vibhīṣaṇa: "Hostility ends at death. Take steps for the due performance of the funeral rites. He is your brother as he is mine, too."

The womenfolk of Rāvaṇa's court, and his wives, hearing of his end, rushed out of the palace, and, arriving at the battlefield, rolled on the ground in sheer anguish. Overcome by grief they gave vent to their feelings in diverse heart-rending ways. They wailed: "Alas, he who could not be killed by the gods and demons, has been killed in battle by a man standing on earth. Our beloved lord! Surely when you abducted Sītā and brought her to Laṅkā, you invited your own death! Surely it was because death was close at hand that you did not listen to the wise counsel of your own brother Vibhīṣaṇa, and you ill-treated him and exiled him. Even later if you had restored Sītā to Rāma, this evil fate would not have overtaken you. However, it is surely not because you did what you liked, because you were driven by lust, that you lie dead now: God's will makes people do diverse deeds. He who is killed by the divine will dies. No one can flout the divine will, and no one can buy the divine will nor bribe it."

Yuddha 114

Inconsolable in grief, Maṇḍodarī, Rāvaṇa's wife lamented: "O Lord, no one in the three worlds could conquer you. Even the gods and their chief, Indra, could not face you: how is it that a mere mortal has killed you? Surely, this Rāma is none other than the supreme being, without beginning, middle or end, greater than the greatest, eternal and unshakable: he alone has assumed this appearance of a human being for the welfare of all beings. He, surrounded by the gods in the disguise of the vānaras, and, having previously conquered the senses, has now slain you. It was evident even when Khara was killed by him, and when Hanumān devastated Laṅkā by the grace of Rāma. Alas, it was because you were doomed that you sought to seduce Sītā. You were not immediately burnt on that occasion, because the god of fire was afraid of you. But the fruits of one's deeds cannot be cheated: Vibhīṣaṇa who took refuge in Rāma, enjoys good fortune and you who sinned against him are dead. It was unnecessary for you to have sought Sītā: she is by no means my equal in beauty, ancestry or culture. But you sought your death by seeking her. Alas, how happily we roamed together on mountains: now your beautiful form has been shattered by Rāma's missiles. It is difficult to believe that you who were a terror to the gods, demons, sages, ascetics, and who were an adept in magic, could reach this end. Alas, you have departed carrying your own karma with you: but we live forlorn. My heart is obviously hard: how is it that I live when you are dead? Widowed, see how all of us have rushed out of the inner apartments without our veils: why is it that you are not angry at this? I have heard it said that the tears of a faithful wife are never shed in vain. I can see now that the tears that Sītā shed have brought about your end. The curses of all the good ladies whom you molested have borne this bitter fruit." While she was lamenting thus, the other women tried to console her with the words: "Pray, do not give way to grief. Do you not know that the fortunes of kings are fleeting?"

Rāma urged Vibhīṣaṇa to carry on with the funeral rites. Vibhīṣaṇa felt: "Rāvaṇa was vicious and if I honour him by performing his funeral rites, people will hold me in contempt, too." Rāma, however, repeated his arguments: "Hostility ends with death. He is your brother and he is mine, too. Let the funeral rites proceed."

The brāhmaṇas who knew the scriptural injunctions prepared the funeral pyre in strict accordance with Vedic ordinanace. Towards the conclusion of the ritual, Vibhīṣaṇa set alight the funeral pyre.

All of them returned to the city. When the womenfolk had re-entered the inner apartments of the palace, Vibhīṣaṇa stood near Rāma humbly gazing at him. Rāma had laid down his weapon and the missiles once and for all and was once more gentle and sweet.

Yuddha 115, 116

Rāma returned to the camp where the vānara troops had been stationed. He turned to Lakṣmaṇa and said: "O Lakṣmaṇa, install Vibhīṣaṇa on the throne of Laṅkā and consecrate him as the king of Laṅkā. He has rendered invaluable service to me and I wish to behold him on the throne of Laṅkā at once."

Without the least loss of time, Lakṣmaṇa made the necessary preparations and with the waters of the ocean consecrated Vibhīṣaṇa as king of Laṅkā, in strict accordance with scriptural ordinance. Rāma, Lakṣmaṇa and the others were delighted. The demon-leaders brought their tributes and offered them to Vibhīṣaṇa who in turn placed them all at Rāma's feet.

Rāma said to Hanumān: "Please go, with the permission of king Vibhīṣaṇa, to Sītā and inform her of the death of Rāvaṇa and the welfare of both myself and Lakṣmaṇa." Immediately Hanumān left for the Aśoka-grove. The grief-stricken Sītā was happy to behold him. With joined palms Hanumān submitted Rāma's message and added: "Rāma desires me to inform you that you can shed fear, for you are in your own home as it were, now that Vibhīṣaṇa is king of Laṅkā." Sītā was speechless for a moment and then said: "I am delighted by the message you have brought, O Hanumān: and I am rendered speechless by it. I only regret that I have nothing now with which to reward you; nor is any gift equal in value to the most joyous tidings you have brought me." Hanumān submitted: "O lady, the very words you have uttered are more precious than all the jewels of the world! I consider myself supremely blessed to have witnessed Rāma's victory and Rāvaṇa's destruction." Sītā was even more delighted: she said, "Only you can utter such sweet words, O Hanumān, endowed as you are with manifold excellences. Truly you are an abode of virtues."

Hanumān said: "Pray, give me leave to kill all these demonesses who have been tormenting you so long." Sītā replied: "Nay, Hanumān, they are not responsible for their actions, for they were but obeying their master's commands. And, surely, it was my own evil destiny that made me suffer at their hands. Hence, I forgive them. A noble man does not recognise the harm done to him by others: and he never retaliates, for he is the embodiment of goodness. One should be compassionate towards all, the good and the wicked, nay even towards those who are fit to be killed: who is free from sin?" Hanumān was thrilled to hear these words of Sītā, and said: "Indeed you are the noble consort of Rāma and his peer in virtue and nobility. Pray, give me a message to take back to Rāma." Sītā replied: "Please tell him that I am eager to behold his face." Assuring Sītā that she would see Rāma that very day, Hanumān returned to Rāma.

Yuddha 117, 118, 119

Hanumān conveyed Sītā's message to Rāma who turned to king Vibhīṣaṇa and said: "Please bring Sītā to me soon, after she has had a bath and has adorned herself." Immediately Vibhīṣaṇa went to Sītā and compelled her to proceed seated in a palanquin, to where Rāma was. Vānaras and demons had gathered around her, eager to look at Sītā. And Vibhīṣaṇa, in accordance with the tradition, wished to ensure that Sītā was not seen by these and rebuked them to go away. Restraining him, Rāma said: "Why do you rebuke them, O Vibhīṣaṇa? Neither houses nor clothes nor walls constitute a veil for a woman; her character alone is her veil. Let her descend from the palanquin and walk up to me." So she did.

Rāma said sternly: "My purpose has been accomplished, O Sītā. My prowess has been witnessed by all. I have fulfilled my pledge. Rāvaṇa's wickedness has been punished. The extraordinary feat performed by Hanumān in crossing the ocean and burning Laṅkā has borne fruit. Vibhīṣaṇa's devotion has been rewarded." Rāma's heart was in a state of conflict, afraid as he was of public ridicule. Hence, he continued: "I wish to let you know that all this was done not for your sake, but for the sake of preserving my honour. Your conduct is open to suspicion, hence even your sight is displeasing to me. Your body was touched by Rāvaṇa: how then can I, claiming to belong to a noble family, accept you? Hence I permit you to go where you like and live with whom you like—either Lakṣmaṇa, Bharata, Śatrughna, Sugrīva or even Vibhīṣaṇa. It is difficult for me to believe that Rāvaṇa, who was so fond of you, would have been able to keep away from you for such a long time."

Sītā was shocked. Rāma's words wounded her heart. Tears streamed down her face. Wiping them, she replied: "O Rāma, you are speaking to me in the language of a common and vulgar man speaking to a common woman. That which was under my control, my heart, has always been yours; how could I prevent my body from being touched when I was helpless and under another person's control? Ah, if only you had conveyed your suspicion through Hanumān when he came to meet me, I would have killed myself then and saved you all this trouble and the risk involved in the war." Turning to Lakṣmaṇa, she said: "Kindle the fire, O Lakṣmaṇa: that is the only remedy. I shall not live to endure this false calumny." Lakṣmaṇa looked at Rāma and with his approval kindled the fire. Sītā prayed: "Even as my heart is ever devoted to Rāma, may the fire protect me. If I have been faithful to Rāma in thought, word or deed, may the fire protect me. The sun, the moon, the wind, earth and others are witness to my purity; may the fire protect me." Then she entered into the fire, even as an oblation poured into the fire would. Gods and sages witnessed this. The women who saw this screamed.

Yuddha 120, 121

Rāma was moved to tears by the heart-rending cries of all those women who witnessed the self-immolation of Sītā. At the same time, all the gods, including the trinity—the Creator, the Preserver, and the Redeemer (or Transformer)—arrived upon the scene in their personal forms. Saluting Rāma, they said: "You are the foremost among the gods, and yet you treat Sītā as if you were a common human being!"

Rāma replied to these divinities: "I consider myself a human being, Rāma the son of Daśaratha. Who I am, and whence I am, may you tell me!"

Brahmā the creator said: "You are verily lord Nārāyaṇa. You are the imperishable cosmic being. You are the truth. You are eternal. You are the supreme dharma of the worlds. You are the father even of the chief of the gods, Indra. You are the sole refuge of perfected beings and holy men. You are the Om, and you are the spirit of sacrifice. You are that cosmic being with infinite heads, hands and eyes. You are the support of the whole universe. The whole universe is your body. Sītā is Lakṣmi and you are lord Viṣṇu, who is of a dark hue, and who is the creator of all beings. For the sake of the destruction of Rāvaṇa you entered into a human body. This mission of ours has been fully accomplished by you. Blessed it is to be in your presence; blessed it is to sing your glories; they are truly blessed who are devoted to you, for their life will-be attended with success."

As soon as Brahmā finished saying this, the god of fire emerged from the fire in his personal form, holding up Sītā in his hands. Sītā shone in all her radiance. The god of fire who is the witness of everything that takes place in the world, said to Rāma: "Here is your Sītā, Rāma. I find no fault in her. She has not erred in thought, word or deed. Even during the long period of her detention in the abode of Rāvaṇa, she did not even think of him, as her heart was set on you. Accept her: and I command you not to treat her harshly."

Rāma was highly pleased at this turn of events. He said: "Indeed, I was fully aware of Sītā's purity. Even the mighty and wicked Rāvaṇa could not lay his hands upon her with evil intention. Yet, this baptism by fire was necessary, to avoid public calumny and ridicule, for though she was pure, she lived in Laṅkā for a long time. I knew, too, that Sītā would never be unfaithful to me: for we are non-different from each other even as the sun and its rays are. It is therefore impossible for me to renounce her."

After saying so, Rāma was joyously reunited with Sītā.

Yuddha 122, 123

Lord Śiva then said to Rāma: "You have fulfilled a most difficult task. Now behold your father, the illustrious king Daśaratha who appears in the firmament to bless you and to greet you."

Rāma along with Lakṣmaṇa saw that great monarch, their father clad in a raiment of purity and shining by his own lustre. Still seated in his celestial vehicle, Daśaratha lifted up Rāma and placing him on his lap, warmly embraced him and said: "Neither heaven nor even the homage of the gods is as pleasing to me as to behold you, Rāma. I am delighted to see that you have successfully completed the period of your exile and that you have destroyed all your enemies. Even now the cruel words of Kaikeyī haunt my heart; but seeing you and embracing you, I am rid of that sorrow, O Rāma. You have redeemed my word and thus I have been saved by you. It is only now that I recognise you to be the supreme person incarnated as a human being in this world in order to kill Rāvaṇa."

Rāma said: "You remember that you said to Kaikeyī, 'I renounce you and your son'? Pray, take back that curse and may it not afflict Kaikeyī and Bharata." Daśaratha agreed to it and then said to Lakṣmaṇa: "I am pleased with you, my son, and you have earned great merit by the faithful service you have rendered to Rāma."

Lastly, king Daśaratha said to Sītā: "My dear daughter, do not take to heart the fire ordeal that Rāma forced you to undergo: it was necessary to reveal to the world your absolute purity. By your conduct you have exalted yourself above all women." Having thus spoken to them, Daśaratha ascended to heaven.

Before taking leave of Rāma, Indra prayed: "Our visit to you should not be fruitless, O Rāma. Command me, what may I do for you?" Rāma replied: "If you are really pleased with me, then I pray that all those vānaras who laid down their lives for my sake may come back to life. I wish to see them hale and hearty as before. I also wish to see the whole world fruitful and prosperous." Indra replied: "This indeed is an extremely difficult task. Yet, I do not go back on my word, hence I grant it. All the vānaras will come back to life and be restored to their original form, with all their wounds healed. Even as you had asked, the world will be fruitful and prosperous."

Instantly, all the vānaras arose from the dead and bowed to Rāma. The others who witnessed this marvelled and the gods beheld Rāma who had all his wishes fulfilled. The gods returned to their abodes.

Yuddha 124, 125

Vibhīṣaṇa approached Rāma and said: "Pray, O Rāma, a bath is ready for you as also raiments and ornaments for you to wear." Rāma, however, replied: "What shall I do with bath, raiments and ornaments, O Vibhīṣaṇa, without first seeing the noble Bharata? Can you find a way by which we can return to Ayodhyā with expedition?"

Vibhīṣaṇa replied: "Surely, there is, O Rāma. I shall see that you return to Ayodhyā within the course of a single day. I have the celestial aircraft called Puṣpaka which my brother Rāvaṇa had wrested from the possession of Kubera, the lord of wealth. It is with me, but for your sake. It looks like a cloud and is capable of flying like a cloud in the sky; and with it you can easily reach Ayodhyā without any anxiety."

Vibhīṣaṇa had the aircraft Puṣpaka brought at once. It was like a big mansion. It shone like the sun. It was made entirely of gold and diamonds. Even Rāma was wonderstruck to see it. Rāma then said to Vibhīṣaṇa: "All these vānaras and others have helped you in the accomplishment of your great mission. It is, therefore, proper that you should honour them and reward them suitably with wealth, jewels, etc."

Vibhīṣaṇa complied with Rāma's command. After witnessing this, Rāma got ready to leave for Ayodhyā. He was about to board the aircraft. He said to the assembled vānara leaders: "You have regarded me as your friend, and you have all rendered me a very great service. Now you may return to your own abodes. O Sugrīva, you too, may now return to Kiṣkindhā accompanied by your troops. O Vibhīṣaṇa, pray consolidate this kingdom of Laṅkā which is now yours. And I shall with your leave return to Ayodhyā."

On behalf of the vānara leaders and the principal demons, Vibhīṣaṇa submitted to Rāma: "Rāma, we, too, wish to accompany you to Ayodhyā. We are eager to witness your coronation. We wish to pay our homage in person to mother Kausalyā, too. Grant us this prayer." Rāma was happy to hear this and replied: "Surely, what you have said augments my joy and intensifies my delight. Certainly, if I return to Ayodhyā surrounded by all of you my friends, we shall be enhancing the joy and the happiness of Bharata and the other kinsmen there."

Delighted to have Rāma's permission, the vānara leaders and Sugrīva, and also Vibhīṣaṇa and his ministers, boarded that excellent aircraft Puṣpaka.

Yuddha 126, 127

With Rāma's permission the aircraft Puṣpaka took off giving off a mighty roaring sound. As the aircraft flew over the city of Laṅkā, over the battlefield and so on, Rāma pointed out to Sītā and said: "Behold this Laṅkā built on top of the mount Trikūṭa, O Sītā!" He continued to show her all the important landmarks. They were flying over Kiṣkindhā territory, and Sītā said to Rāma: "I would like to return to Ayodhyā in the company of the wives of Sugrīva and the other vānara leaders, O Lord."

Rāma ordered the aircraft to land and then said to Sugrīva: "Let the wives of the vānara chiefs come on board as soon as possible, so that they may also accompany us to Ayodhyā." Sugrīva announced the delightful command to the womenfolk of Kiṣkindhā: "We shall all witness the triumphant re-entry of Rāma into Ayodhyā." Immediately they came on board, the aircraft took off again.

Once again, Rāma showed Sītā the various places connected with his wandering. The Ṛṣyamūka hill, the Pampā lake, the site of Śabari's hermitage, Janasthāna from where Sītā was abducted, and also the spot where Jaṭāyu fell. He also showed Sītā where their own hermitage was. Later he showed her the river Godāvarī, the hermitage of Agastya, the hermitages of Śarabhaṅga and Sutīkṣṇa and that of the sage Atri, the Citrakooṭa where Bharata met him, the hermitage of Bharadvāja, the river Gaṅgā and the abode of Guha, and finally pointing out Ayodhyā, he said: "Yonder is Ayodhyā, O Sītā, pray, bow down to Ayodhyā, now that you have safely returned."

But even before he reached Ayodhyā, Rāma landed once again near the hermitage of the sage Bharadvāja and bowed down to him and enquired of Bharata and other members of the family in Ayodhyā. Bharadvāja said: "Bharata, clad in ascetic robes, is eagerly awaiting your return, with your own sandals placed on the throne. All are well in Ayodhyā." He also revealed that he knew all that had happened between his previous meeting with Rāma and now. "I was unhappy to see you proceeding to the forest then; I am delighted to see you return to the kingdom now," he said, and added: "Choose a boon, Rāma, and I shall grant it." Rāma asked: "May all the trees on our route from here yield fruits, even if this is not their season. And, may there be plenty of honey en route." The sage said: "May it be so". Lo and behold, immediately all the trees in the neighbourhood were laden with fruits and honey. The vānaras enjoyed to their hearts' content. At the command of the sage, Rāma spent a day at the hermitage.

Yuddha 128, 129

Though Rāma gladly agreed to spend a day in the hermitage of the sage Bharadvāja, he was greatly concerned about Bharata and contemplated seriously what he should do. Calling Hanumān to himself, he said to Hanumān: "Pray, O Hanumān, proceed to Śṛṅgaverapura at once; and you will meet Guha there. He is a great friend of mine; he is as good as my own self. He will also tell you the route to Ayodhyā. Proceed to Ayodhyā and meet Bharata and tell him all that happened to me between his meeting with me fourteen years ago and now. Please also inform him that I shall be coming to Ayodhyā tomorrow, along with Sugrīva and also Vibhīṣaṇa. Please note very carefully how he feels on hearing all this. Watch every gesture and every expression on his face, whether he is pleased or displeased at the news. It is very difficult for one who has enjoyed the powers of rulership not to be influenced by a desire to keep them. If you feel that Bharata wishes to continue to rule as king, then I shall be delighted to let him rule the whole world."

With the blessings of Rāma, Hanumān immediately proceeded to Śṛṅgaverapura. He saw Guha and introduced himself to Guha, and then he conveyed to him the joyous news of Rāma's return.

Hanumān flew onwards again and reached the little village known as Nandigrāma not far from the city of Ayodhyā, and there he saw the noble Bharata, the very picture of grief and sorrow, living as an ascetic, clad in ascetic garments and living an extremely ascetic life. Approaching Bharata with joined palms Hanumān said to Bharata, who was well versed in dharma, who appeared to be Dharma itself embodied: "The blessed Rāma is well and enquires after your welfare. You will soon behold him here." Bharata fainted with joy. On regaining consciousness, he shed tears of joy and said to Hanumān: "You may be a god or a man, but surely out of great compassion to me, you have come here." He also offered to Hanumān thousands of cows and other objects as his joyous gift.

Bharata enquired: "Pray, tell me everything. How did Rāma acquire the friendship of the vānaras and what happened then?" In response to that enquiry, Hanumān told Bharata the entire story of Rāma in brief. Hanumān concluded: "At the request of the sage Bharadvāja, Rāma decided to spend a day at the sage's hermitage and hence sent me to convey the glad tidings to you. Tomorrow during the auspicious hour known as Puṣyayoga, you will behold Rāma who has already reached the banks of the holy Gaṅgā and who is living at the hermitage of sage Bharadvāja."

Hearing this, Bharata was exceedingly happy.

Yuddha 130

Bharata immediately made the reception arrangements. He instructed Satrughna: "Let prayers be offered to the gods in all temples and houses of worship with fragrant flowers and musical instruments."

Satrughna immediately gave orders that the roads along which the royal procession would wend its way to the palace should be levelled and sprinkled with water, and kept clear by hundreds of policemen cordoning them. Soon all the ministers, and thousands of elephants and men on horse-back and in cars went out to greet Rāma. The royal reception party, seated in palanquins, was led by the queen-mother Kausalyā herself; Kaikeyī and the other members of the royal household followed—and all of them reached Nandigrāma.

From there Bharata headed the procession with the sandals of Rāma placed on his head, with the white royal umbrella and the other regalia. Bharata was the very picture of an ascetic though he radiated the joy that filled his heart at the very thought of Rāma's return to the kingdom.

Bharata anxiously looked around but saw no signs of Rāma's return! But, Hanumān reassured him: "Listen, O Bharata, you can see the cloud of dust raised by the vānaras rushing towards Ayodhyā. You can now hear the roar of the Puṣpaka aircraft."

"Rāma has come!"—these words were uttered by thousands of people at the same time. Even before the Puṣpaka landed, Bharata humbly saluted Rāma who was standing on the front side of the aircraft. The puṣpaka landed. As Bharata approached it, Rāma lifted him up and placed him on his lap. Bharata bowed down to Rāma and also to Sītā and greeted Lakṣmaṇa. And he embraced Sugrīva, Jāmbavān, Aṅgada, Vibhīṣaṇa and others. He said to Sugrīva: "We are four brothers, and with you we are five. Good deeds promote friendship, and evil is a sign of enmity."

Rāma bowed to his mother who had become emaciated through sorrow, and brought great joy to her heart. Then he also bowed to Sumitrā and Kaikeyī. All the people thereupon said to Rāma: "Welcome, welcome back, O Lord."

Bharata placed the sandals in front of Rāma, and said: "Rāma here is your kingdom which I held in trust for you during your absence. I consider myself supremely blessed in being able to behold your return to Ayodhyā. By your grace, the treasury has been enriched tenfold by me, as also the storehouses and the strength of the nation." Rāma felt delighted. When the entire party had disembarked, he instructed that the Puṣpaka aircraft be returned to its original owner, Kubera.

Yuddha 131

The coronation proceedings were immediately initiated by Bharata. Skilled barbers removed the matted locks of Rāma. He had a ceremonial bath and he was dressed in magnificent robes and royal jewels. Kausalyā herself helped the vānara ladies to dress themselves in royal robes; all the queens dressed

Sītā appropriately for the occasion. The royal chariot was brought; duly ascending it, Rāma, Lakṣmaṇa and Sītā, went in a procession to Ayodhyā, Bharata himself driving the chariot. When he had reached the court, Rāma gave his ministers and counsellors a brief account of the events during his exile, particularly the alliance with the vānara chief Sugrīva, and the exploits of Hanumān. He also informed them of his alliance with Vibhīṣaṇa.

At Bharata's request, Sugrīva despatched the best of the vānaras to fetch water from the four oceans, and all the sacred rivers of the world. The aged sage Vasiṣṭha thereupon commenced the ceremony in connection with the coronation of Rāma. Rāma and Sītā were seated on a seat made entirely of precious stones. The foremost among the sages thereupon consecrated Rāma with the appropriate Vedic chants. First the brāhmaṇas, then the virgins, then the ministers and warriors, and later the businessmen poured the holy waters on Rāma. After that the sage Vasiṣṭha placed Rāma on the throne made of gold and studded with precious stones, and placed on his head the dazzling crown which had been made by Brahmā the creator himself. The gods and others paid their homage to Rāma by bestowing gifts upon him. Rāma also gave away rich presents to the brāhmaṇas and others, including the vānara chiefs like Sugrīva. Rāma then gave to Sītā a necklace of pearls and said: "You may give it to whom you like, Sītā." And, immediately Sītā bestowed that gift upon Hanumān.

After witnessing the coronation of Rāma, the vānaras returned to Kiṣkindhā. So did Vibhīṣaṇa return to Laṅkā. Rāma looked fondly at Lakṣmaṇa and expressed the wish that he should reign as the prince regent. Lakṣmaṇa did not reply: he did not want it. Rāma appointed Bharata as prince regent. Rāma thereafter ruled the earth for a very long time.

During the period of Rāma's reign, there was no poverty, no crime, no fear, and no unrighteousness in the kingdom. All the people constantly spoke of Rāma; the whole world had been transformed into Rāma. Everyone was devoted to dharma. And Rāma was highly devoted to dharma, too. He ruled for eleven thousand years.

Yuddha 131

Rāma's rule of the kingdom was characterised by the effortless and spontaneous prevalence of dharma. People were free from fear of any sort. There were no widows in the land: people were not molested by beasts and snakes, nor did they suffer from diseases. There was no theft, no robbery nor any violence. Young people did not die making older people perform funeral services for them. Everyone was happy and everyone was devoted to dharma; beholding Rāma alone, no one harmed another. People lived long and had many children. They were healthy and they were free from sorrow. Everywhere people were speaking all the time about Rāma; the entire world appeared to be the form of Rāma. The trees were endowed with undying roots, and they were in fruition all the time and they flowered throughout the year. Rain fell whenever it was needed. There was a pleasant breeze always. The brāhmaṇas (priests), the warriors, the farmers and businessmen, as also the members of the servant class, were entirely free from greed, and were joyously devoted to their own dharma and functions in society. There was no falsehood in the life of the people who were all righteous. People were endowed with all auspicious characteristics and all of them had dharma as their guiding light. Thus did Rāma rule the world for eleven thousand years, surrounded by his brothers.

This holy epic Rāmāyaṇa composed by the sage Vālmīki, promotes dharma, fame, long life and in the case of a king, victory. He who listens to it always is freed from all sins. He who desires sons gets them, and he who desires wealth becomes wealthy, by listening to the story of the coronation of Rāma. The king conquers the whole world, after overcoming his enemies. Women who listen to this story will be blessed with children like Rāma and his brothers. And they, too, will be blessed with long life, after listening to the Rāmāyaṇa. He who listens to or reads this Rāmāyaṇa propitiates Rāma by this; Rāma is pleased with him; and he indeed is the eternal lord Viṣṇu.

LAVA AND KUŚA said: Such is the glorious epic, Rāmāyaṇa. May all recite it and thus augment the glory of dharma, of lord Viṣṇu. Righteous men should regularly listen to this story of Rāma, which increases health, long-life, love, wisdom and vitality.

Uttara Kāṇḍa
Period after Coronation

While Rāma was ruling his kingdom, one day a deputation of several great sages waited upon him, with the sage Agastya at their head. Agastya said to the palace guard: "Pray, tell Rāma that we the Ṛṣis are eager to see him." At the request of Rāma, the Ṛṣis were immediately conducted to his presence.

The king received the sages with due honour. After they had been seated in the royal court, they said to Rāma: "O Rāma, we are well and happy. We consider ourselves fortunate that we see you well and happy. Fortunately, Rāvaṇa, the enemy of the world, has been slain by you. It is no wonder, O Rāma, that you killed Rāvaṇa; when you take up arms you are capable of conquering the three worlds. We are particularly happy that you despatched the son of Rāvaṇa. When we heard of the death of Indrajit who was invincible by all other beings in the universe, we rejoiced and we offer our special felicitations to you. That indeed was the most praiseworthy achievement. By this you have freed us all from great fear." Rāma asked them: "Pray, O sages, tell me why you consider that victory over Indrajit as even more praiseworthy than victory over Rāvaṇa? How did he become so powerful?"

The sages replied: "Before we narrate the story of Indrajit, we shall have to narrate the story of Rāvaṇa. Hear, O Rāma. In the Kṛta age, there was a brāhmin-sage known as Pulastya; he was the son of God and was the peer of Brahmā, the creator. He practised intense austerities in the hermitage of Tṛṇavindu. In those days, the daughters of holy men and demi-gods used to sport in the vicinity of the hermitage. This disturbed Pulastya's austerities. He pronounced a curse: 'Whoever will come near me will become pregnant.' Whoever knew of this curse avoided going near him. But the daughter of the royal sage Tṛṇavindu did not know of this curse. One day she went in search of her friends. Pulastya was engaged in the recitation of the Vedas. The girl sat down near him to hear this. Soon, she noticed a change coming over her. Frightened, she ran to her father and in answer to his question told him what had happened. Tṛṇavindu thereupon took her to Pulastya and offered her in marriage to Pulastya: 'Holy one, when you are fatigued on account of austerities, she will comfort you.'

"Pulastya accepted her. She served him with great love and devotion. Pleased with this, the sage said to her: 'I am delighted with your devoted service. I therefore bless you with this boon: you will give birth to a son who is equal to me in all respects, and will be known as Paulastya, and also Viśravā since you conceived while listening to my recitation of the Vedas.' "

Uttara 3–4

"Pulastya's wife soon gave birth to a son and he was duly christened Viśravā. The sage Bharadvāja heard of the noble virtues of Viśravā and offered the hand of his daughter in marriage to the ascetic.

"Of them was born a radiant son. The grandfather Pulastya was highly delighted by the birth of this son whom he christened Vaiśravaṇa.

"Vaiśravaṇa resolved to tread the path of virtue even while he was a mere boy. For, he thought: 'Dharma is indeed the noble path, hence I shall pursue dharma.' He engaged himself in intense austerities for a period of a thousand years. Brahmā, the creator, and all the gods appeared before him and asked him to choose a boon. Vaiśravaṇa said: 'Lord, I wish to be a protector of the world and the guardian of the wealth of the world.' Pleased with this, Brahmā replied: 'In fact, I myself had intended to appoint four protectors of the world, of whom three have already been chosen by me—and they are Yama, Indra, and Varuna. You will indeed be the fourth protector of the world, and you will be the guardian of wealth. You will be equal to the gods in heaven.' Brahmā also bestowed upon him the gift of an aerial vehicle, the Puṣpaka.

"Vaiśravaṇa returned home, sought his father's presence and requested him to indicate where he should dwell. Viśravā replied: 'There is a mountain named Trikūṭa on the shores of the Southern Sea. On top of this mountain the divine architect Viśvakarma has built a city called Laṅkā which is equal to the capital of heaven in splendour, for the dwelling of the demons. However, since the demons have fled that city for fear of lord Viṣṇu, it remains uninhabited. I think you should make that your abode.' He obeyed."

In response to Rāma's question concerning the origin of demons the sage Agastya said:

In the beginning Brahmā created water, and then other beings. The latter, oppressed by hunger and thirst, prayed: "Pray, tell us what to do?" Brahmā said to them: "Protect by all means." Some of them responded: "We shall protect"; others said: "We shall worship." "They who said: 'rakṣāma (protect) will be demons," said Brahmā, "And they who said 'yakṣāma' (worship) will be demi-gods."

Among Rākṣasas arose two brothers Heti and Praheti. Heti's daughter-in-law was expecting a son; she prematurely induced the delivery, and discarding the baby on a hill, went away with her husband to enjoy herself. That baby began to cry. Rudra and Pārvatī happened to pass nearby and blessed that baby to reach instant adulthood. Pārvatī decreed: "Henceforth, demonesses will give birth the very moment after conception to babies who will become instant adults."

Uttara 5–6

This boy was Sukeśa who grew up to be a noble young man by the grace of the boon he had obtained from Rudra. In due time a Gandharva named Grāmaṇi gave him his daughter Devavati in marriage. She gave birth to three sons—Mālyavān, Sumāli and Māli. These three demons immediately went to the forest and practised the most intense austerities, having come to know of the boons conferred upon their father by the Lord.

Pleased with their devotion and austerity, Brahmā the creator granted them the boon they asked for—which was "We should be invincible, long-lived, and united." The moment they realised the full significance of the boon they had thus obtained, they became fearless and began to oppress both the gods and the demons.

A celestial named Narmadā had three daughters whom she gave in marriage to the three demons, and they gave birth to more demons.

The gods and the sages who were oppressed by these demons resorted to lord Rudra for protection. Rudra, however, said: "I cannot kill them, but I shall give you my counsel. Approach lord Viṣṇu abandoning all other activities; and take refuge in him. He will surely destroy all these demons." So they did. They narrated to him the atrocities of the demons. Lord Viṣṇu consoled them and, after granting the boon of fearlessness, said: "I know already that Sukeśa is proud of having obtained a boon from Rudra. I also know the wrong-doing of his three sons. But, be free from anxiety; I shall surely destroy them all." The gods returned to their abode.

Mālyavān had come to know of this and he informed his brothers of the plot of the gods. The other two brothers, however, were undaunted by these stories. They were confident that no power in the universe could defeat them. Moreover, they said: "We have given no cause for the displeasure of lord Viṣṇu; surely, he has lost his head on account of the mischief of the gods." Hence, they sought to fight the gods.

Thousands upon thousands of the demons gathered in Laṅkā to wage a war against the gods. Ascending their own aircrafts, armed to the teeth with deadly weapons, protected by armours, these terrible looking demons all of whom were extremely powerful, flew towards heaven (the world of the gods.) Placing the three brothers at their head, and roaring with uncontrolled anger, they entered the abode of the gods.

Lord Viṣṇu came to know of this invasion and soon he himself appeared on the battlefield, holding his divine weapons and riding his divine vehicle the Garuḍa who was as big as a mountain. The gods and the sages sang his glories. The demons surrounded him. He began to assail them with his divine weapons.

Uttara 7–8

The demons rushed towards the holy hill known as Nārāyaṇa Giri and closed in on lord Nārāyaṇa or Viṣṇu even as insects rush towards a flame. The Lord routed them by a shower of missiles and blew his powerful conch. This sound stupefied the demons; they could not stand and they were thoroughly confused. Lord Viṣṇu destroyed the demons by their thousands.

Sumālī came to the rescue of the harassed demons and shielded them from the might of the Lord. Lord Viṣṇu fought back the demon and cut off his ear-rings and also his horses. The horses got out of the demon's control and ran in several directions, even like the senses of an uncontrolled man.

Mālī rushed to his brother's aid. A fierce battle ensued between him and lord Viṣṇu. The Lord's missile struck the demon and drank his blood as it were. Mālī hit the Lord's vehicle Garuḍa and forced Garuḍa to turn away from the battlefield, to the supreme delight of the demons. Unmindful of the discomfiture, lord Viṣṇu hurled his discus which had the brilliance of the sun itself upon the demon Mālī who fell dead instantly.

When Mālī fell dead, Sumālī and also Mālyavān retired from the field and headed towards Laṅkā. Garuḍa in the meantime regained his vitality and drove to despair the demons by the force of the wind which emanated from his wings.

When lord Viṣṇu pursued the fleeing army of the demons, Mālyavān said to him: "Nārāyaṇa! Do you not know the code of a warrior's conduct? Contrary to that code, why do you wish to kill those who have retired from the battle and who are therefore non-combatants?" The Lord replied: "You are cruel, and the gods are living in fear of you. Their protection is dearer to me than my own life. Hence I shall destroy you wherever you are."

These words roused the anger of Mālyavān who immediately attacked the Lord with his powerful weapons. The Lord received those missiles and hurled them back at the demon himself: gravely hurt by them, Mālyavān was stunned for some time, though he soon regained his strength. He roared mightily and hit both Viṣṇu and Garuḍa. In great fury, Garuḍa turned the full blast of wind against Mālyavān who fled to Laṅkā. Seeing him retire to Laṅkā, Sumālī also went away to Laṅkā. Unable to stand the supreme might of lord Viṣṇu, the demons with Mālyavān and Sumālī at their head, went away to the netherworld, leaving Laṅkā in charge of the lord of wealth.

Whenever there is loss of dharma on earth, the Lord incarnates himself in order to destroy the demons and to restore dharma.

Uttara 9–10

Sumālī reflected long and deeply over his position. He looked at his beautiful daughter who had attained marriageable age. He wondered whom she would obtain as her husband. A girl fills the families of her father, her mother and her husband with anxiety: the reputation of these families depended upon her right conduct. He therefore said to her: "Pray, seek the presence of Viśravā, the son of sage Pulastya, and you yourself persuade him to be your husband."

Kaikasī immediately sought the presence of the sage Viśravā who was then engaged in a great Vedic ritual. Upon conclusion of the rite, the sage asked her: "Who are you and why are you here?" Kaikasī replied: "I am Kaikasī, daughter of Sumālī; why I am here, I am sure you will know by your own intuition." The sage contemplated for a while and divined the reason why she was there. He said to her: "Since you sought my presence at an inauspicious time when I was engaged in a fearsome rite, you will give birth to terrible sons of great cruelty, yet your last child will be noble and righteous, after me."

In due time, Kaikasī gave birth to a ten-headed child or a monster; the sage christened him Daśagrīva. Then was born Kumbhakarṇa. After him the girl Śūrpaṇakhā. Lastly was born the pious Vibhīṣaṇa. They grew up rapidly.

One day, Vaiśravaṇa (also known as Kubera) came to visit his father Viśravā, and Kaikasī introduced Daśagrīva to him. The young boy became jealous of Kubera and resolved to excel him in every way. Thereupon all the three boys took to austerities.

Kumbhakarṇa did the Pañcāgni tapas in summer and stood in freezing water in winter. Vibhīṣaṇa stood upon one leg for five thousand years. Daśagrīva fasted for a thousand years after which he offered in sacrifice one of his heads; thus he had sacrificed nine heads. As he was about to offer the tenth, Brahmā appeared before him and offered all of them a boon. "Ask for a boon," he said: "for your efforts should not go in vain." Daśagrīva said: "Lord, all beings in this world are afraid of nothing but death; there is no enemy like death; hence I ask for immortality." When Brahmā said that it was impossible for created beings not to die, he modified his prayer by asking that he should not be killed by gods, demi-gods, demons, etc., and contemptuously left out man. Vibhīṣaṇa prayed: "May my mind not swerve from dharma even in the face of the worst danger." Before offering a boon to Kumbhakarṇa Brahmā asked the goddess of speech to ensure that he would not ask for a boon which might result in universal destruction. She entered into him and clouded his mind. He asked: "May I sleep many, many years." And Brahmā granted them the boons of their choice.

Uttara 11–12

Sumālī approached Daśagrīva and said: "Luckily, young man, has the covetable boon been obtained by you, by which you will surely be the lord of the three worlds, We had to flee Laṅkā on account of lord Viṣṇu; and that fear has now left us. Laṅkā belongs to the demons; it is our territory. When we left, you brother Kubera occupied it. It is proper therefore that you should reclaim it from him, by negotiation, by persuasion or if necessary by violence."

Daśagrīva's first reaction was negative; he said: "Kubera is my brother; how can I fight with him?" But Sumālī's minister Prahasta replied: "There is no brotherly affection among heroes. In days of yore there were two sisters Diti and Aditi whose sons were demons and gods respectively. These brothers fought among themselves, and with the help of Viṣṇu, the gods won and became lords of the worlds."

Daśagrīva was convinced. He sent Prahasta himself as his emissary to claim Laṅkā from Kubera. Without hesitation Kubera said: "Indeed, Laṅkā was given to me as my abode by my father. But, pray, go to Daśagrīva and tell him that from this moment Laṅkā is his." Daśagrīva thus got Laṅkā without a fight.

Kubera went to his father Viśravā and informed him of all this. The sage said to Kubera: "In fact, Daśagrīva has mentioned this to me, and I scolded him for it. Since however you have left Laṅkā, please go to Kailāsa which upholds the earth, and live there along with your people."

Daśagrīva was crowned king of Laṅkā. Soon after that, he gave his sister Śūrpaṇakhā in marriage to the demon Vidyutjihvā. After this, one day he went to the forest for hunting. There he met Maya, one of the sons of Diti, and enquired why he was thus roaming the forest. Maya replied: "Once upon a time, the gods gave me the nymph Hemā with whom I enjoyed life for a long time. She left me about fourteen years ago, on the mission of the gods. Pining for her I am roaming this forest, along with this my daughter. I also have two sons by her, Māyāvi and Dundubhi." Daśagrīva revealed his identity. Maya offered him the hand of his daughter, Maṇḍodarī, in marriage and Daśagrīva gladly accepted the offer.

Maṇḍodarī gave birth to a son who cried so loudly at birth that even Laṅkā shook: hence Daśagrīva name him Meghanāda.

For Vibhīṣaṇa, Daśagrīva obtained the daughter of the demi-god Sailūṣa, named Śaramā. This girl was born on the banks of the Mānasa lake. Her mother commanded the lake: "Saro mā vardhata" (Lake, do not swell); hence, the girl was named Śaramā.

All of them lived in Laṅkā, enjoying their life.

Uttara 13

At Kumbhakarṇa's request Daśagrīva had a palace built. Delighted, Kumbhakarṇa entered this palace and entered into a deep sleep for a very long period of time.

In the meantime, mighty Daśagrīva commenced his campaign of destruction. He ravaged the gardens and playgrounds of the demi-gods. He uprooted their trees and polluted their rivers.

The chief of the demi-gods, Kubera, came to know of his brother's misdeeds, and full of familial concern, and wishing to dissuade him from further sinful pursuit, Kubera sent an envoy to the court of Daśagrīva with a message. The envoy was lovingly and honourably received by the noble Vibhīṣaṇa and presented to Daśagrīva, the king.

The envoy said: "O King, I have a message for you from your brother Kubera. Lend ear to it as I read it out to you: 'I think it is good that you should stop your destructive activities—you have done enough in this direction. I also think that you should tread the path of dharma, if you can do so. I have seen the destruction of the celestial gardens which has been brought about by you; and I have also heard that you have killed many sages, and that you have been harassing the gods.

'You have spurned me on many occasions; yet, one does not disown a member of one's own family, even if he is guilty of an offence. I have retired to the Himālaya. There I performed intense austerities. Lord Śiva was highly pleased with my austerities and appeared before me; and he said: "O Lord of wealth, I am highly pleased with your austerities and your devotion. As the fruit of your austerities I have come to regard you as a very dear friend; you have won this friendship by your devotion. Be my friend from now." When I returned to my abode after having thus been blessed by lord Śiva, I heard of your destructive pursuits. Hence, I beseech you to abandon this course of conduct.'

Hearing the words of the envoy, Daśagrīva grew terribly angry. He clenched his fist and gnashed his teeth and shouted: "Neither you nor he is my well-wisher. Only a fool will boast of his friendship with lord Śiva. Till now, O envoy, I felt that I should not harm my own brother. Having heard your words and his message, I feel I should abandon that resolve: I am ready to conquer the three worlds and despatch to the abode of Death all the lords of creation!" Saying so, Daśagrīva cut off the head of the envoy and delivered the body to the demons to eat.

Uttara 14–15

Daśagrīva immediately gathered his ministers around him—Mahodara, Prahasta, Mārīca, Śuka, Sāraṇa, and Dhūmrākṣa. Surrounded by his demoniacal forces, he proceeded towards the abode of Kubera, as if he were ready to burn down the entire world. In a few hours he reached the abode known as Kailāsa.

The sentries posted at the borders quickly informed Kubera that his own brother Daśagrīva had invaded Kailāsa. Kubera ordered the defence of Kailāsa. There ensued a fierce battle between the demons and the demi-gods.

When Daśagrīva forced entry into the palace, the guards stopped him and hit him with all their might; but the boon that he had obtained from the Creator made him immune to all these. When Daśagrīva returned the blows, the demi-gods collapsed.

Seeing this, Kubera despatched the demi-god Manibhadra to defend Kailāsa. In the meantime, Daśagrīva's lieutenants had felled thousands upon thousands of demi-gods: where is the righteous warfare of the demi-gods and where is the deceit and strength of the demons—and what comparison is there between the two? Manibhadra was defeated.

Kubera stepped up and spoke to Daśagrīva who, deluded by the boon of invincibility he had obtained from the Creator, was perpetrating the most sinful deeds: "O sinful one! You do not heed my wise counsel; but in course of time you will realise the evil consequences of your wicked actions. He who insults his mother, father, the holy ones, and the teachers gets the fruits of such actions when he enters the abode of Death. With the help of this impermanent body, if one does not practise austerities (tapas) here, later that fool is burnt (tapyate) after leaving this world. However, this is certain: everyone inevitably gets the fruit of his actions here."

Hearing these words, the lieutenants of Daśagrīva turned away from battle. But, Daśagrīva himself came forward to fight with Kubera. During that spectacular battle, when Kubera hurled the fire missile, Daśagrīva neutralised it with the water missile; Daśagrīva assumed various forms and fought and defeated Kubera. When Kubera fell down, defeated, Daśagrīva got hold of Kubera's vehicle the Puṣpaka (a spacecraft which could fly at the speed of thought, as it were, and which was built of precious jewels and metals and which was proof against heat and cold) and considering himself the conqueror of the three worlds, turned to go to his abode.

Uttara 16

While Daśagrīva was returning to Laṅkā in the Puṣpaka suddenly, the spacecraft stalled. Daśagrīva was bewildered. There appeared near the spacecraft a strange-looking being. It was dwarfish, bald, short-armed, but powerful. It was Nandi, the divine vehicle of lord Śiva.

Nandi said to Daśagrīva: "Turn back, O Daśagrīva. On yonder mountain, lord Śiva is sporting. No one is allowed to go beyond this point." Hearing these words and looking at the appearance of the strange creature, Daśagrīva laughed derisively.

The angry Nandi cursed Daśagrīva in the following words: "Because I have the face of a vānara, you have behaved thus with contempt towards me. Hence, in order to kill you, vānaras will be born, endowed with my strength and vitality, and with my form and equal to me in might. I could myself have killed you this very moment; but I do not do so, for you have destroyed yourself by your own evil actions." While Nandi was uttering these words, the gods and the sages sang the glories of the Lord and released a shower of flowers.

Daśagrīva was terribly annoyed, and he proceeded to uproot the mountain itself, for it had stood as an obstacle to the smooth flight of his spacecraft. The mountain shook; all the beings that dwelt on the mountain shook; even Pārvatī, the consort of lord Śiva, was afraid. Seeing this, lord Śiva playfully pressed the mountain down with his toes.

The mountain was stabilised. The pressure of lord Śiva's toes was so great that Daśagrīva's arms were caught underneath! Daśagrīva yelled in pain. The gods, demi-gods, demons and sages were frightened to hear this thunderous sound. They came to Daśagrīva and advised him to propitiate lord Śiva and assured him, "The Lord is an ocean of mercy and he will surely bless you."

Daśagrīva thereupon sang the glories of the Lord. Pleased with this, lord Śiva appeared before him; released from the pressure of the mountain, Daśagrīva rescued his arms. Lord Śiva said to him: "I am pleased with your devotion. Since you cried aloud and your cry made all beings run in several directions, you will henceforth be called Rāvaṇa (ravaḥ-noise)."Daśagrīva prayed to lord Śiva for other boons: "Pray, grant me the boon that I would not be killed by anyone except a human being: I am not afraid of a human being. Also, please bestow upon me a divine weapon which I may use in war." The Lord conferred these boons upon Rāvaṇa and gave him a divine sword known as Candrahāsam. Rāvaṇa returned to his abode.

Uttara 17–18

While roaming the forest, one day, Rāvaṇa saw a beautiful young woman in the garb of an ascetic. He was filled with passion for her. He approached her and asked: "Who are you,

O beautiful woman? You are young and you have the appearance of an ascetic: these two are contradictory!"

The girl replied: "I am the daughter of the royal sage Kuśadhvaja who was the son of Bṛhaspati. My father instructed me in the recitation of the Vedas; and I was known as Vedavatī. Many gods and demi-gods sought my hand. But my father desired to have lord Viṣṇu as his son-in-law and no one else. Hearing this, a demon named Śambhu killed my father, and my mother, too, ascended the funeral pyre after her husband. Since then I am engaged in intense austerities in order to fulfil my father's desire and attain lord Viṣṇu as my husband."

Rāvaṇa introduced himself and boasted: "What is this Viṣṇu before me? Come, become my wife and enjoy life." Rāvaṇa grabbed her by her hair. Greatly enraged at this behaviour, Vedavatī cursed Rāvaṇa in the following words: "I do not wish to preserve this body which has been touched by you; I shall therefore enter into the sacred fire. O sinful one, since you touched me, and thus caused my death, I shall be reborn for your destruction. If there is any merit left in me, I shall be reborn without being conceived by a woman." Saying so, she entered into the sacred fire. That Vedavatī is Sītā, your wife, O Lord, and you are lord Viṣṇu himself.

Later, Rāvaṇa came to a place where a king Marutta was performing a sacred rite assisted by the sage Samvartta, the son of Bṛhaspati. When they saw him, all the gods disguised themselves: Indra became a peacock, Yama became a crow, Kubera became a lizard, and Varuṇa became a swan.

Rāvaṇa challenged Marutta who was about to fight; but the preceptor reminded Marutta: "If you leave the rite incomplete then your family will perish; moreover, since you have undertaken this sacred rite, you shall not engage in fighting." He kept quiet. The demons declared Rāvaṇa victorious. Rāvaṇa ate up all the sages in the place and went away. The gods, pleased at having so cleverly escaped the wrath of Rāvaṇa, conferred boons on the animals whose forms they had assumed: thenceforth the peacock had eyes on its feathers, the crow was granted freedom from the pangs of death, the lizard got golden hue, and the swan its pure white colour.

Uttara 19–20

After the victory in the rite of the king Marutta, Rāvaṇa continued to roam the world, eager to defeat all the kings of the world. Most of them yielded to his claim without as much as a challenge.

In course of time, Rāvaṇa reached Ayodhyā, and there he challenged the king Anaraṇya who however accepted the challenge and fought with Rāvaṇa. There ensued fierce fighting between the two. Rāvaṇa destroyed the best part of Anaraṇya's forces; while the latter routed Rāvaṇa's lieutenants. In fierce rage, Rāvaṇa delivered a mighty blow on Anaraṇya's head, and the latter fell from his vehicle. As if smiling, Rāvaṇa said: "What have you done, O King? In all the three worlds there is no one who is my equal in a hand to hand fight." Anaraṇya replied: "What can I do, O demon: for Time is indeed supreme, and I have to bow to the inevitable. I have not been defeated by you, but by Time alone have I been defeated, and you have merely served as an excuse. But, I tell you this: in my own dynasty will arise a prince, Rāma son of Daśaratha, who will avenge my death and will bring about your destruction." Saying this, Anaraṇya ascended to heaven, and Rāvaṇa continued his exploits.

Seeing the wanton destruction of human beings by Rāvaṇa, the sage Nārada approached him, and said to him: "O king of demons, you have earned the extremely rare boon of invincibility by gods, demi-gods and demons. Listen, I would like to offer a piece of advice to you. The world of human beings is subject to death; why then do you indulge in killing these human beings? Is it not waste of time killing these foolish human beings who are already subject to old age, disease and death? Surely, all these beings have to enter the abode of Yama, the lord of death. Therefore, challenge Yama himself. If you conquer Yama, all other beings are automatically conquered."

Nārada's reasoning appealed to Rāvaṇa and he immediately set out to go to the abode of Yama. He said to Nārada: "Indeed, I shall be able to destroy even the Lords of creation." After he had left, the sage was intrigued: all beings are afraid of death and no one can conquer death; what could Rāvaṇa do to Yama? He, too, proceeded immediately to the abode of Yama.

Uttara 21–22

Nārada said to Yama: "The demon named Daśagrīva is coming to defeat you who are extremely difficult to overcome.

Hence I have come here, too." Even while he was saying this, the sound of Rāvaṇa's spacecraft descending nearby was heard.

In the light shed by the spacecraft, Rāvaṇa himself beheld with his own eyes the fate of the evil-doers, sinners as also the pious people's fate. He saw how the sinners were tortured in hell. He also saw how the pious people rejoiced in heavenly abodes.

Forcibly, he had the sinners released from the grip of the servants of Yama; and they rejoiced exceedingly. But the servants of Yama were annoyed and they fought with Rāvaṇa. And, Rāvaṇa discharged a volley of the most powerful missiles; standing on bare ground, he used the most powerful missile known as Pāśupata which came as a blazing fire surrounded by smoke. The servants of Yama were falling in great numbers.

Yama heard the pitiable cries of his own servants, and he surmised that they were suffering defeat at the hands of Rāvaṇa. He emerged from his court, preceded by Death in its own form, and armed with various infallible missiles. Seeing Yama emerge in great anger, all beings in the whole universe trembled in great fear.

Rāvaṇa was the only one who was unafraid. Approaching Yama, Rāvaṇa hit him with various weapons; and Yama in his turn assailed Rāvaṇa with various weapons. Thus they fought for seven days and nights. Rāvaṇa hurled several powerful missiles at Yama. Seeing this, Death spoke to Yama: "Pray, give me leave to destroy this wicked demon. No one who comes within my sight ever survives even for an hour."

Yama replied: "Stay, now see my prowess." Saying so, Yama lifted up the most powerful weapon known as kāla-daṇḍa, the very sight of which kills all beings. Just at that moment Brahmā the creator appeared on the scene and pacified Yama with the following words: "Yama, you should not kill Rāvaṇa who is protected by my boon. Put the kāla-daṇḍa away. It is infallible. If you use it against Rāvaṇa, after that, whether he survives the blow or dies of it, my word would have been proved false." In obedience to Brahmā's advice, Yama put the kāla-daṇḍa away. Yama could not be defeated either. So, he merely vanished from the spot. Considering himself the victor, Rāvaṇa ascended the Puṣpaka and went his way.

Uttara 23–24

Next, Rāvaṇa conquered the Nāgas. He then went to where the Nīvātakavacas dwelt. They, too, had a boon from Brahmā the creator and so had been specially favoured by him. Rāvaṇa went to them and invited them for a fight. The two forces were engaged in a battle for over a year, but neither could win.

Brahmā the creator appeared on the scene and said to the Nīvātakavacas: "You cannot conquer this Rāvaṇa in battle. I think it is a good idea for you to be united in mutual friendship. It is only through friendship that people can attain prosperity." Thereupon, Rāvaṇa concluded friendship with the Nīvātakavacas, with the sacred fire as the witness.

Emerging from there, Rāvaṇa encountered the beings known as Kālakeyas. In a fight with them, Rāvaṇa lost his brother-in-law Vidyutjihvā (husband of Śūrpaṇakhā) and also very many of his soldiers. But Rāvaṇa exterminated the Kālakeyas.

From there he went to the abode of Varuṇa. Though he was met there by the sons of Varuṇa who gave him a good fight, they said to him that Varuṇa himself had gone away to the court of Brahmā the creator to listen to a music concert. However, since he had defeated the sons of Varuṇa, Rāvaṇa considered himself the world-conqueror and returned to Laṇkā.

Wherever he went, whenever he saw a beautiful girl, Rāvaṇa abducted her and carried her away. Thus very many girls had been forcibly carried away by him. Nāgas, celestial musicians, daughters of sages, demonesses and goddesses—the Puṣpaka had carried all of them, and had been flooded by their tears. All of them wailed: "This indeed is incomparable sin—the violation of the wives of others and Rāvaṇa revels in it. Therefore, he will die on account of a woman."

When he re-entered Laṅkā, he found that his sister Śūrpaṇakhā was inconsolable with grief. On enquiry, she said: "O King, you are the cause of my widowhood; you are responsible for the death of my husband. You are supposed to protect me; but in fact you have ruined my life." Rāvaṇa calmly replied to her: "Your husband was killed in battle, and I did not intend that he should die. Anyhow, all that is past. I shall do everything to please you now. Go and live with our brother Khara and all the fourteen thousand soldiers of his army will be like brothers to you. You will be like their mother."

Uttara 25

A little later, Rāvaṇa entered one of the pleasure-gardens of Laṅkā, named Nikumbhila. There he saw his own son Meghanāda engaged in an elaborate religious rite. He also saw that Meghanāda was clad in deer-skin and bore the appearance of one engaged in an orthodox religious rite. He fondly embraced his son and then asked him: "What is this that you are doing, my son?"

The officiating priest Uśanā replied: "Sir, your son has successfully completed these seven sacred rites—agniṣṭoma, aśvaṁedha, bahusuvarṇakaḥ, rājasūya, gomedha, vaiṣṇava and māheśvara. And he has earned the blessings of the lord Śiva himself, by which he will be able to move about at will, fly in the air, and also perform many magical tricks."

Rāvaṇa expressed a slight displeasure thus: "All this is unworthy of you, my son; you have been offering sacrifice to our enemies, the gods. However, whatever you have done is well-done. Let us go home."

On reaching his palace, Rāvaṇa brought down from the Puṣpaka the numerous women whom he had abducted. Seeing them, Vibhīṣaṇa was sore distressed and gently admonished his elder brother: "Surely, it is sinful to thus abduct others' wives. We shall have to pay dearly for this sin. And it is already evident! Brother, our cousin sister Kumbhinasī has been abducted by the demon Madhu. Surely, this is directly connected with the sin of your abducting these good women. Meghanāda was engaged in the sacred rite; I was engaged in meditation, and Kumbhakarṇa was in deep sleep. Madhu took Kumbhinasī away. When I heard, I thought that perhaps they were a good match for each other."

But, Rāvaṇa reacted differently. He ordered the army to get ready to invade the territory of Madhu. He even had Kumbhakarṇa awakened. With all of them—except Vibhīṣaṇa who looked after Laṅkā in the absence of the other brothers—he invaded Madhupura.

Rāvaṇa could not see Madhu. However, Kumbhinasī rushed towards Rāvaṇa and fell at his feet and cried. She pleaded with him: "Pray, grant me this boon—that you will not make me a widow. To a good women there is no greater misfortune than widowhood; it is the greatest cause for fear and sorrow." Rāvaṇa agreed to spare Madhu's life. Whereupon Kumbhinasī went inside and awakened her sleeping husband.

She introduced Rāvaṇa to Madhu: "Here is my brother, Rāvaṇa, who needs your help in his fight with the gods." Madhu received Rāvaṇa with great affection and hospitality.

Uttara 26

On a full moon night Rāvaṇa was resting on mount Kailāsa. The armed forces were asleep. The full moon and the cool breeze, the fragrance of the wild flowers and the music of the love-intoxicated celestials roused his own passion.

At the same time, there appeared on the scene a celestial nymph named Rambhā. She was seductively dressed; her looks and her gait were such as to rouse the onlooker's passion. Rāvaṇa approached her and questioned: "Where are you going, O beautiful woman? Who is that most fortunate person who is going to enjoy sensual pleasure with you today? Nay, do not go away leaving me here. Come, let us enjoy ourselves. Who is equal to me in the three worlds?"

Thus accosted by Rāvaṇa, Rambhā began to tremble in fear. She said: "Be gracious to me, O Lord! You are the protector of all; will you not protect your own daughter-in-law? I am going to meet your own brother's son Nalakūbara, and therefore I am your daughter-in-law. Pray, let me go."

But, Rāvaṇa was in no mood to listen to this sermon. Overcome by lust, he grabbed Rambhā and violated her. After this violation, when he released her, Rambhā was like a soiled garland or muddied water.

Still shaking with fear and shame, she approached Nalakūbara and narrated to him all that had happened to her on the way. She fell at his feet, weeping. She craved his pardon.

Nalakūbara went into deep meditation for a while, when he heard that Rāvaṇa had dared to violate Rambhā. He 'saw' all that had happened to Rambhā. Overcome with great anger, he took water in his hands and pronounced the following terrible curse: "Since he violated you, O Rambhā, who did not desire him, he will not be able to enjoy any woman who does not desire him. If he should ever try to violate a woman who does not desire him, his head will break into seven pieces."

As Nalakūbara pronounced this terrible curse, the gods right from Brahmā the creator were delighted and they rained a shower of flowers.

When Rāvaṇa came to know of this unfailing curse, he began to refrain from molesting any woman who did not desire him.

Uttara 27–28

Rāvaṇa turned his eyes upon heaven and decided to conquer the heaven, too. He entered the realm of the gods with his mighty army. The heavens shook, and bewildered Indra shook on his throne. He ordered all the gods to get ready to fight Rāvaṇa.

Indra, the god of heaven, then approached lord Viṣṇu trembling with fear. Humbly he submitted to lord Viṣṇu as follows: "Pray, O Lord, tell us what we should do. Rāvaṇa, who considers himself invincible on account of the boons he has gained, has come here to give us battle. You are our only refuge, our only strength and support. You are the supreme Lord, and in you are the worlds established. In you the universe has its origin and to you it returns. Pray, tell me what you would like us to do with this Rāvaṇa."

Lord Viṣṇu replied: "Rāvaṇa's misdeeds are already known to me. But I shall not now engage Rāvaṇa in battle. I, Viṣṇu, can never return from the battlefield without killing the enemy; but this is impossible now since Rāvaṇa is protected by the boon he has gained from Brahmā. However, I promise that soon I shall destroy him for the redemption of the gods. Hence, you yourself give him battle, along with the gods for the present."

All the gods marched out to the battlefield with Indra at their head; and at the same time the demons with Rāvaṇa at their head marched into heaven.

In the meantime, the mighty demon Sumālī also entered the battlefield. He wrought great destruction among the forces of the gods. The eight Vasu known as Savitra, destroyed the vehicle of Sumālī. Wielding an extremely powerful missile known as gada, the Vasu hit Sumālī with it. The fire that the missile emitted entirely consumed the demon. The demons fled in all directions, seeing that Sumālī their leader had been killed.

Meghanāda now took the field. Indra consoled the gods by saying: "Fear not: there you see my son Jayanta proceeding to the field, to face Meghanāda." The battle between Meghanāda and Jayanta was exceedingly fierce. When Meghanāda used his magic power, there was utter confusion, and the gods even killed other gods!

Indra himself entered the battlefield in his celestial spacecraft. The battle rose to a new peak with Kumbhakarṇa and other demon-warriors fighting to their very best. There was great destruction on both sides.

Uttara 29–30

During that fearsome battle, once Indra surrounded Rāvaṇa with the divine forces. Hearing of this, Meghanāda rushed to the scene. He used his magic powers. No one could see Meghanāda. He bound Indra by his deluding power and took him prisoner. He turned to his father, Rāvaṇa, and said: "Come, let us go home: I have captured Indra himself."

The gods, with Brahmā the creator himself at their head, went to Laṅkā. Brahmā pleaded with Rāvaṇa: "Highly praiseworthy is your son's valour. Since by him Indra himself was conquered, he will henceforth be known as Indrajit. Let Indra be freed so that he can continue his function in heaven. Let Indrajit choose any boon in return."

Highly pleased with this, Indrajit asked for the boon of immortality. Brahmā pointed out: "Immortality is impossible in this mortal world, either for birds, beasts or other beings. Hence, please modify your request." Indrajit responded: "I shall regularly perform the sacred rites before undertaking an important task. If I complete them in time, I should be invincible; if I do not I should be vulnerable. And as long as I am seated in my vehicle, I should also be invulnerable." Brahmā granted him the boon. Indrajit said: "People seek to become immortal through austerities and by propitiating the gods; but I shall become immortal by self-effort and vigilance."

Indra was freed from captivity. Brahmā said to him: "I shall narrate to you the reason why you were thus taken captive. In the beginning, I created all beings, and I created them all equal, of the same colour and of the same form. I then contemplated my own creation and I desired to create a special being. I wished to ensure that this special being would be absolutely flawless (a: without, halya: flaw). This was a woman, and she was Ahalyā. She became the wife of Gautama, the sage. Once, overcome by passion for her, you seduced her in the absence of her husband Gautama. The sage surprised both of you; and, when he discovered the mischief you were up to, he cursed you: "Because my wife was thus seduced fearlessly by you, you will be taken captive by your enemy." He also cursed his own wife: "Because your were proud of your beauty and did this, you will not be the only beautiful woman in the world and thus lose your uniqueness." Hence, remember your own misdeed, O Indra; by your own misdeed you were defeated, not by anyone else. Immediately adore the Lord through the sacred Vaiṣṇava rite, and by that will you be purified of all sin." Indra followed Brahmā's advice.

Uttara 31, 32, 33

Once, Rāvaṇa went to the city named Mahiṣmatī the capital of the Haihaya kingdom whose ruler was Kartavīrya Arjuna. He shouted: "Who is that Arjuna who rules this city?" He was told that Arjuna was sporting in the river Narmadā.

Immediately Rāvaṇa proceeded to the river Narmadā. After his bath, Rāvaṇa adored the Lord through the Liṅga which he placed on the sands.

Rāvaṇa then noticed an inexplicable phenomenon: the flow of the river had suddenly been arrested. Through his spies, he learnt that Kartavīrya Arjuna, who was sporting with women in the stream, had dammed the river with his own bare hands and created an artificial lake for his pleasure. Hearing this, Rāvaṇa wished to challenge Kartavīrya Arjuna for a fight. The latter's ministers, however, prayed that Rāvaṇa should accept their hospitality, spend the night there and challenge the king the next morning. They argued: "It is not heroic to challenge a warrior who is frolicking with women!"

Rāvaṇa was inclined to agree. However, at the same time, his forces had already begun to fight with the forces of Kartavīrya Arjuna, and they raised a great hue and cry. Rāvaṇa's foremost lieutenants joined the fight. Kartavīrya Arjuna's ministers informed him of the battle. And he too rushed to the battle.

A fierce fighting ensued. Kartavīrya Arjuna delivered a powerful blow with his gada and rendered Prahasta senseless.

All the other demons and Rāvaṇa too rushed to help Prahasta. Kartavīrya Arjuna then directed his attention to Rāvaṇa. With great ease, he caught hold of Rāvaṇa. And he bound Rāvaṇa, even as Nārāyaṇa bound the demon king Bali. At that time, the gods and the demi-gods released a shower of flowers saying: "Well done." The demons vainly shouted: "Release him, release him."

The sage Pulastya heard of Rāvaṇa's capture through the gods, and he came in person to intercede with Kartavīrya Arjuna. The latter received the sage with due honour and reverence, and after prayerfully offering his hospitality asked the sage: "What can I do for you, O holy one?" The sage praised Kartavīrya Arjuna's prowess and prayed that his son Rāvaṇa might be released from captivity. Kartavīrya Arjuna did so immediately.

Uttara 34

Undaunted by the ignominy sustained at the hands of Kartavīrya Arjuna, Rāvaṇa continued to roam the world in search of fresh fight and fresh conquest.

Once he reached the kingdom of Kiṣkindhā, ruled over by the vānara Vāli of great prowess. He loudly hurled a challenge at Vāli to come forward and fight with him. Vāli's minister, however, informed Rāvaṇa that Vāli had gone out of his capital city in order to perform the daily evening worship. "If you care to wait for a little while, you can see him, surely," he said. "But I might just as well forewarn you! Do you see that mountain of bones: they belonged to other heroes who similarly challenged Vāli. Even if you have drunk the nectar of immortality, its effect lasts only till you confront Vāli. If you are in a hurry to die, then go to the Southern Ocean where you will behold Vāli."

Rāvaṇa was not impressed by this threat. He ascended the Puṣpaka and headed southwards. He saw Vāli there engaged in offering his evening prayers. He approached Vāli without making the least sound. Accidentally, Vāli saw him, too. Without much ado, Vāli engulfed Rāvaṇa in his armpit and leapt in the air. The other demons wailed aloud and pursued Vāli, in vain.

After going to the oceans in the four directions and offering his prayers at each of those oceans, with Rāvaṇa still held in his armpit, Vāli returned to Kiṣkindhā. There, in the garden, Vāli dropped Rāvaṇa. Then he asked Rāvaṇa: "From where did you come?"

Rāvaṇa then said to Vāli: "What strength; what prowess; and what majesty! Amazing that someone could hold me in his grip like a small animal and carry me to the four oceans in the four quarters. You are indeed a supreme hero. Having thus witnessed your extraordinary might, I wish to conclude a treaty of friendship with you. Henceforth, we shall enjoy undivided between ourselves, i.e. in common, wives, sons, cities, kingdom, pleasures, shelter and food."

Then they raised the sacred fire and in front of it held each other's hands and concluded a treaty of friendship. Rāvaṇa dwelt in the abode of Vāli for a month, enjoying his hospitality and then returned to his own abode.

Such was the prowess of Vāli, O Rāma, whom you killed very easily. Thus concluded the sage Agastya.

Uttara 35–36

Rāma said to Agastya: "Wonderful is your description of the strength of Vāli and Rāvaṇa. But surely Hanumān was more powerful than all these heroes. I have attained Laṅkā, Sītā, victory, friendship and also the kingdom, all on account of the strength of Hanumān; but for him we might not even have known the whereabouts of Sītā. Yet, how was it that he could not kill Vāli or Rāvaṇa or the others?"

Agastya replied: If it is your will I shall narrate the story of Hanuman in detail. On the hill known as Sumeru there was a king known as Kesari whose wife was Añjanā. Of her Hanumān was born as the son of the wind-god. While she had gone away to bring fruits for his food, the baby mistook the sun for a fruit, and sprang up in the sky to pick it. Though the baby was close to the sun, the latter did not wish to burn the innocent baby. At Rāhu's complaint, Indra intervened and struck the baby who fell down on the earth: as he fell, his chin was broken and hence he came to be known as Hanumān.

Seeing this, the wind-god grew angry and withdrew himself from the world. No one could breathe. All beings thereupon sang the praises of the wind-god and sought to propitiate him. All of them, with Brahmā himself, waited upon him. Vāyu the wind-god emerged from the cave with the unconscious baby.

At the touch of the Creator the baby was revived. The wind-god once again began to move amongst beings, as their life.

All the gods then glorified Hanumān and gave him all kinds of boons: health, freedom from illness, a very long life, invincibility when assailed by the thunderbolt and such other weapons, the gift of a powerful gada, the ability to change his form and roam where he like, etc.

Blessed with these boons, Hanumān had lost his head, and began to ravage the forests, hermitages of the sages and even the sages themselves. The sages knew that he was invincible and that he enjoyed the divine protection of the boons that the gods had bestowed upon him. Hence, they pronounced a curse: "You harass us, depending upon your great strength; you will not be aware of your strength for a long time from now." And, realising the great role he had to play in your service, they modified the curse thus: "When you are reminded of your strength, however, you will regain it."

Hence, though he was on the side of Sugrīva in his fight with Vāli, he did not remember his strength. It is only for your sake that Hanumān was born in this world, and the gods created him.

After narrating all these stories, Agastya and the sages took leave of Rāma.

Uttara 37–40

The day after Rāma's coronation, the bards of the court sweetly sang his glories in order to rouse him from sleep: "Lord, if you sleep the whole world will sleep, too. Hence, wake up." Rāma woke up and after performing his ablutions worshipped the holy ones and God.

The kings and other honoured guests who had come to witness the coronation left Ayodhyā one by one, after being duly honoured by Rāma. Rāma said to them: "The wicked Rāvaṇa was killed in truth by dharma, truth and righteousness, and the spiritual glory of which you are embodiments: I was a mere instrument, an excuse." They in their turn praised him and considered themselves fortunate and blessed indeed.

Rāma bestowed gifts of precious jewels upon the vānara chiefs who had helped him in the great battle with Rāvaṇa and who had come to Ayodhyā to witness the coronation. They enjoyed their stay in Ayodhyā; a month passed by as if it were but an hour. Rāma was happy in their company, too.

Rāma then gave leave to Sugrīva and the other vānara leaders to depart and return to their own realm. He gave leave to Vibhīṣaṇa to return to Laṅkā, and "rule Laṅkā in accordance with the code of dharma." He emphasised: "May your mind never seek unrighteous behaviour, O King of Laṅkā; wise men adhere to the path of dharma and thus enjoy the rulership of the kingdom for a long time."

Hanumān then bowed to Rāma and offered the following prayer: "Lord, may there be in me supreme devotion to you; may my heart never waver in its devotion. And, may I live just so long as your story and your glory are sung in this world."

Rāma said: "Even so be it, O Hanumān. My stories shall be narrated in this world so long as the world lasts; and your glory will endure so long as my stories are narrated in this world. For just one of the great services you have rendered to me, I am bound to give you my very life; for the numerous others I shall ever remain indebted to you. One who has received help reciprocates in times of the other's difficulties: but I wish that you may never stand in need of my help, and that you may never find yourself in difficulty." Saying so, Rāma embraced Hanumān and bestowed upon him the precious gift of a necklace he himself had worn around his neck.

All the vānara and other chiefs then tearfully took leave of Rāma.

Uttara 41–42

One day, while Rāma was sitting with his brothers, he heard an ethereal voice. It said: "Rāma, I am the spacecraft Puṣpaka. At your command, I went to the abode of Kubera. But he has returned me to you, since you conquered Laṅkā and destroyed the wicked Rāvaṇa. Kubera is highly pleased to hear of your victory and he prays that you should use this Puṣpaka spacecraft to move about in this world. Hence I have come back to you. Pray, accept my services."

Rāma worshipped the spacecraft and then commanded it thus: "Very well, go where you like now, and return to me when I shall think of you."

Bharata marvelled at the supernormal powers of Rāma, and said to him: "Brother, even inanimate things become sentient beings in your presence. People in your kingdom are free from illness; life-span is prolonged. Infant mortality is unknown. Everyone enjoys good health. And even the rain and the wind favour you. People are saying among themselves: "May we have such a ruler for all time to come." Rāma was pleased to hear this.

Later in the day, Rāma entered the Aśoka-grove along with Sītā. This lovely garden was full of fragrant flowers and lovely green lawns, and in it also dwelt beautiful birds whose songs delighted the listeners.

Rāma and Sītā seated themselves in that garden. With the greatest of love and affection. Rāma himself handed to Sītā the sweet drink known as maireyakam. Soon, the servants brought there well cooked meat and various other delicacies. The royal attendants entertained Rāma and Sītā with music and dance.

Thus, Rāma spent the forenoon in the affairs of the royal court; and the evenings he spent in the company of his wife. Sītā, too, spent the forenoon in the service of her mothers-in-law and the afternoons with her beloved husband.

One day, Rāma said to Sītā: "I see that you are expecting a baby, my dear: tell me, what can I do for you to make you happy during this auspicious period." Sītā replied: "Lord, my only desire is to revisit the forests and the sacred hermitages of the holy ones on the banks of the holy river Gaṅgā." Rāma immediately replied: "Certainly and we shall go tomorrow itself."

Uttara 43–45

In Rāma's court, the clowns were entertaining Rāma and the other princes and dignitaries with humorous stories. Later, Rāma asked the spies and secret agents: "Tell me, what do people say about me, about Sītā, about my brothers? Tell me everything without any reservation."

After much hesitation Bhadra conveyed to the king what some citizens were saying: "Rāma has done what no one else has done: he built a bridge over the ocean, went over to Laṅkā with the vānara forces and others, killed Rāvaṇa and regained Sītā. I do not know how he still loves Sītā so much, after her abduction by Rāvaṇa who placed her on his lap and kept her in the Aśoka forest for such a long time. Well, well, I suppose that hereafter we cannot object to such conduct on the part of our wives, too."

Rāma's face showed deep concern and anxiety. He dismissed the court, and asked his messengers to request his brothers to come to his presence at once. Thus urgently summoned, the three brothers rushed to the court and were bewildered to see Rāma's anxious face. They bowed to him and stood respectfully at a distance.

Rāma gravely turned towards them and said as follows: "Pray, listen to what I have just heard. Public scandal is eating my heart. For I belong to the great Ikṣvāku dynasty. Sītā, too, belongs to a respectable family. You know how she was abducted by Rāvaṇa from the Daṇḍaka forest and how I eventually regained her. In order to convince me of her purity, Sītā even entered the fire; Lakṣmaṇa, you were witness to the declaration by the fire-god himself that Sītā is pure. In my own innermost being I know she is pure. Hence I brought her back to Ayodhyā with me.

"Yet, there is public scandal concerning her. He who is thus subjected to public scandal in this world goes down to the lower worlds so long as the scandal lasts. Infamy is ridiculed by the gods, and fame is adored in this world. Indeed it is for the sake of fame that people undertake various activities. For fear of scandal I can even give up my life and all of you, my dear brothers; what to speak of Sītā? Hence, do as I tell you and do not even counsel me against it. Take Sītā immediately and leave her in a far-off place: take her to the hermitage of the sage Vālmīki and leave her there. In fact, she herself wanted to go to visit those hermitages.

"I swear by my own feet, I will not change my mind, and please do not even try to make me change my mind."

Uttara 46–47

When that night was past and the next day dawned, Lakṣmaṇa asked Sumantra to get ready the royal chariot. When the chariot was ready, Lakṣmaṇa said to Sītā: "You had requested the king Rāma to let you visit the hermitages of the sages on the banks of the river Gaṅgā. The king has been graciously pleased to accede to that request and has commanded me to take you thither. Hence, O Sītā, ascend this chariot."

With a joyous heart, Sītā ran into her apartments, gathered clothes and jewels and other presents which she wished to give the sages and their consorts, and returned to where the chariot stood ready. The chariot sped forward.

However, Sītā noticed ill omens and was anxious on account of her husband and her mothers-in-law: she offered a prayer for their safety.

They spent the first night on the bank of the river Gautami in an Aśrama. The next morning they continued the journey. When they neared the river Gaṅgā, Lakṣmaṇa looking at the river wailed aloud, to the surprise of Sītā. She asked him: "Why do you cry thus, O Lakṣmaṇa? Surely, because you miss your brother Rāma so much. So do I. We shall visit the hermitages and spend tonight there and return to Ayodhyā as soon as possible."

Sītā and Lakṣmaṇa got into the ferry to cross the river Gaṅgā. Lakṣmaṇa began to weep and wail once again. He said to Sītā: "My heart is heavy, O Sītā. I know that the world will blame me for this. In fact, I would have preferred death at this very moment. Be gracious, for it is not my fault." Saying so, he fell at the feet of Sītā, weeping bitterly.

Sītā grew anxious and was greatly worried. She requested Lakṣmaṇa to tell her everything without reserve. Lakṣmaṇa got up and continued to address Sītā: "In the presence of the members of his assembly, Rāma heard a terrible public scandal. It is something which the citizens of Ayodhyā and the country are saying. Rāma was greatly upset and he told me something and retired to his apartment. I cannot repeat those words to you. It is on account of that scandal that the king has decided to abandon you. Pray, bear in mind that he does not accuse you, but he is afraid of public scandal. This is the command of the king: I should take you to the hermitage of the sage Vālmīki and leave you there. The sage is a great friend of our father and he will surely look after you very well."

Uttara 48–49

When Sītā heard Lakṣmaṇa's terrible words, she fainted, overwhelmed by grief. After a considerable time, she regained consciousness and in a sorrowful tone spoke to Lakṣmaṇa thus:

"My body has surely been created for suffering; and I am an embodiment of endless suffering. What great sin should I have committed in a previous birth, and whom did I deprive of his spouse, that I should be subjected to this fate though I am pure and innocent? Earlier in life I lived in the forest, but then I had my lord Rāma with me. Now deprived of him how shall I live in this forest?

"When I enter the hermitages of these sages, what shall I tell them; for what reason have I been banished by Rāma? It would have been better for me to drown myself in the Gaṅgā; but my lord would accuse me of having destroyed his dynasty, for I am with his child.

"O Lakṣmaṇa, do as you have been commanded by the Lord to do. When you return to Ayodhyā convey my prostrations to lord Rāma and also to my mothers-in-law, and assure him of my eternal devotion to him, of my purity. I am quite sure that I have been thus banished only on account of public scandal and not because my lord suspects my chastity. Indeed, the husband is the god, relative and guru for a chaste woman; he is dearer to her than even her life; hence his mission is all-important to her. It is in this spirit that I give you leave: you may now go." When he went out of sight, Sītā burst into tears, sitting on the bank of the Gaṅgā.

Vālmīki came to the bank of the Gaṅgā and greeted Sītā with due respect and honour. He said: "I know that you are Sītā, the daughter of king Janaka and the daughter-in-law of Daśaratha; you are the beloved queen of Rāma. I knew that you would be coming; and I also know the reason why you are here. By the eye of intuition gained by the practice of intense austerities I know that you are utterly chaste. I know all that happens in the three worlds. Come: at a little distance from here you will see a convent of female ascetics who will look after you from now on. Grieve not. Treat this as your own home."

Vālmīki led Sītā to the hermitage of the female ascetics and introduced her to them and entrusted her care to them.

Uttara 50–51

When Lakṣmaṇa saw that Sītā had duly entered the hermitage of the sage Vālmīki, he was afflicted by grief and said to the driver of the chariot, Sumantra: "Behold, O Sumantra, he who conquered the gods, demi-gods and the demons, himself suffers such misfortune. Previously, he was banished from his kingdom. And now he is separated from his beloved wife on account of public scandal. This action appears to me to be improper."

Hearing all this, Sumantra replied: "O Lakṣmaṇa, all this was known to the holy ones long ago. And one day the sage Durvāsa told all this to your father king Daśaratha—that Rāma would undergo a lot of suffering, that he would banish Sītā, and later you, too. The king warned me not to reveal this secret to anyone. Anyhow, I have told you."

Lakṣmaṇa was eager to hear the whole truth, and Sumantra continued: "At that time the sage Durvāsa was living in the hermitage of sage Vasiṣṭha. King Daśaratha went there to see him and to ask him about his and his children's life.

"At that time, the sage Durvāsa said to your father: 'I shall narate to you something which took place long ago. A war took place between the gods and the demons; the gods sought the protection of the sage Bhṛgu, but Bhṛgu's wife granted asylum to the demons. Viṣṇu became very angry and in a fit of anger cut off the lady's head with his revolver. This greatly annoyed the sage Bhṛgu who cursed lord Viṣṇu himself: "Since you killed my wife, you will be born as a human being and there you will be separated from your wife!" Instantly the sage regained his composure and felt very sorry that he had cursed the lord Viṣṇu himself. However, lord Viṣṇu assured him that he would make the best use of that curse for the benefit of the gods and the worlds.' As a result of that curse, Viṣṇu was born as Rāma and had to banish his wife Sītā. Durvāsa also predicted that Rāma would rule the world for a very long period, and give birth to two sons."

Lakṣmaṇa felt consoled by the words of Sumantra. The sun set; and they decided to spend the night on the bank of the river Kosi.

Uttara 52–53

The next morning Lakṣmaṇa and Sumantra set out to go to Ayodhyā which they reached about midday. There Lakṣmaṇa saw Rāma who was the very picture of grief. Catching hold of Rāma's feet, Lakṣmaṇa offered the following advice:

"O Rāma, in accordance with your command I have taken Sītā and left her on the other side of the river Gaṅgā in the care of female ascetics. Pray, O Rāma, do not grieve over this incident; for wise men like you do not grieve. All objects in this world must perish, all things that go up must fall, all meeting must end in parting and life must end in death. Hence one should not be too greatly attached to one's wife, sons, friends and wealth, for one is certain to part from them. Give up this grief: for if you grieve, there may be more public scandal, the very thing you wish to avoid."

Rāma felt uplifted. His grief had gone. He thanked and praised Lakṣmaṇa for his timely advice.

Rāma continued: "For the past four days, on account of this grief, I have neglected my royal duties. Pray, summon the ministers and other members of the royal court. For it is unwise to leave the royal duties unattended to. The king who does not attend to them every day falls into a fearful hell.

"In this connection I have heard the following story: Once upon a time there was a king named Nṛga. After a sacred rite, he gave away thousands of cows in charity to the priests. A cow that belonged to a brāhmaṇa somehow got mixed up in this charity and had been given away to a brāhmaṇa in Kankhal. The brāhmaṇa whose cow it was somehow found this out. He claimed it, and the other rightly asserted that it was a royal gift. Both of them went to the court of the king to have the dispute settled. But the king was absent; and the dispute could not be heard. The brāhmaṇas waited for a few days and when even then the king did not appear, they cursed that he would be born as a lizard and would lie unseen in a hole (even as he had remained unseen during those few days), and that when lord Viṣṇu incarnated as Vāsudeva, he would be liberated from that curse. Such is the fate of the kings who neglect their duties.

Uttara 54–55

Rāma continued: "Nṛga summoned his ministers and said to them: 'Pray, install my son Vasu on the throne immediately and let him be king. Also, order our royal architects to build for me a hole in which I can live in relative comfort during the whole period of my accursed life as a lizard. There I shall spend my days till I am freed from the lizard body by the grace of the lord Vāsudeva.'

"Nṛga also said to his son, the king: 'Pray, my beloved son, adhere to the code of dharma strictly. Do not swerve from the path of righteousness. Let my own fate be a warning unto you: see what even a minor transgression has brought about in my case! But, do not grieve on my account. It is as it should be; every action is followed by its appropriate reaction. One gets what one should get, one goes where one should go, and one obtains here (both pleasure and pain) that which he should so obtain. All this is in strict accordance with divine justice, for one's own good.' Having thus counselled his son, Nṛga went away to his hole."

Rāma continued to tell Lakṣmaṇa similar stories to illustrate the way in which even sages cursed others and how such curses proved to be a blessing in disguise to all concerned. The next was the story of king Nimi.

Rāma continued: "Nimi was the twelfth son of the great king Ikṣvāku. Once he entered his capital city known as Vaijayantī along with the sage Gautama and others. As he entered the city, he resolved to perform a sacred rite. He invited his father Ikṣvāku and requested the sage Vasiṣṭha to officiate at the rite. The sage said: 'I have a previous engagement to conduct Indra's sacred rite; I shall come to you as soon as I conclude that one.'

"However, Nimi carried on with his sacred rite for a full five thousand years. When Vasiṣṭha returned to that place after the conclusion of Indra's ritual, he discovered that his (Vasiṣṭha's) place at Nimi's rite had been taken by the sage Gautama. At this Vasiṣṭha was greatly angered. Moreover, he saw that Nimi was fast asleep during the day-time. This further angered him. In uncontrolled rage, he cursed Nimi: 'You have insulted me by first inviting me and then ignoring me; may your body become insentient.' Nimi felt that it was unjust on the part of the sage to curse him and pronounced a counter-curse: 'May you also be deprived of sentience.'

"Both of them were immediately disembodied."

Uttara 56–57

At the request of Lakṣmaṇa, Rāma continued: "The radiant sage Vasiṣṭha went to the abode of his father, Brahmā the creator and there submitted to Brahmā as follows: 'Lord, great unhappiness is the lot of those who have been deprived of their body, and without the body, no action can be performed. Hence, please indicate how I can get another body.'

"Brahmā replied: 'Obtain a body from the combined energies of Mitra and Varuṇa, and you will also be embodied without being conceived by a woman. With that body, you will perform great righteous deeds and return to me.'

"At that time, Mitra and Varuṇa were living together, duly worshipped by all the gods. And, at that time, one day the celestial nymph Ūrvaśī happened to come there. Varuṇa saw her and promptly fell in love with her and asked her to stay with him. However, she said that she had already been sought for a wife by Mitra: 'I love you with my heart,' she said to Varuṇa, 'but my body belongs to Mitra.'

"Unable to control himself, Varuṇa let fall his energy in her presence into a pot (which already contained the energy of Mitra).

"Mitra was annoyed with Ūrvaśī even for this much transgression and cursed that she would be born as a human being on earth, and marry Purūrava (the son of Budha) and live on earth for some time. She fell from heaven to earth.

"From the pot there emerged a radiant sage, the sage Agastya, who said to Mitra: 'I am not your son!' and went away. After some time, however, from that pot there arose the sage Vasiṣṭha.

"Elsewhere, the sages who saw that Nimi had become lifeless, preserved the body embalmed, and continued their rite. Upon conclusion of the rite, the sage Bhṛgu said: 'I shall bring Nimi back to life.' At this miracle, even the gods were delighted and asked Nimi: 'Where would you like to abide?' Nimi replied: 'I shall dwell in the eyes of all beings.' The gods granted that boon and decreed: 'On account of you all the beings will blink, open and shut their eyes, in order that the eyes may enjoy some rest in between.'

"They still had Nimi's body to deal with. The gods 'churned' that body and a being arose from it. Because he was born (janana) of the churning (mathana) and from the bodiless (videha) Nimi—he who was thus born has come to be known as Janaka Vaideha of Mithilā."

Uttara 58–59

Lakṣmaṇa asked Rāma: "Even though he was engaged in a religious rite, how was it that Nimi could not restrain his anger and refrain from pronouncing his counter-curse?"

Rāma replied: "Forbearance is not common to all, O Lakṣmaṇa; anger is hard to restrain for most people. To illustrate this, I shall tell you the story of king Yayāti, please listen.

"In the days of yore there was a king named Yayāti who was the son of Nahuṣa. Yayāti had two wives—the first one was called Śarmiṣṭā, the daughter of Vṛṣaparvā, and the other one was Devayāni the daughter of Uśanā. He had a son by each of these two wives: Śarmiṣṭā gave birth to Puru, and Devayāni gave birth to Yadu.

"The king Yayāti was more fond of Śarmiṣṭā than he was of Devayāni. One day Yadu said to his mother Davayāni: 'You are born of noble sages and you are noble, too. How is it that you endure all this insult from the king without a word of protest or displeasure? I think that both of us should enter the fire, and burn ourselves to death; let the king enjoy life with Śarmiṣṭā, without the least hindrance. Well, if you wish you may endure all this insult and ill-treatment; I cannot—and hence I shall take leave of you.'

"Hearing the words of her son, she sought the help of her father—the sage Bhārgava, or Uśanā. When he heard the story, he was very angry and cursed: 'May Yayāti who, in the enjoyment of the pleasures with Śarmiṣṭā thus neglects your welfare, be overcome by old age immediately.'

"On account of the sage's curse, Yayāti reached old age at once. However, to put off the evil day, he approached his young sons to take over the curse for some time, while he continued to enjoy the pleasures of life. He approached Yadu: but Yadu would not even listen. He then approached the other son Puru: and Puru readily agreed and considered himself blessed.

"Yayāti became young again, while Puru bore his old age. After enjoying himself for a long long time, Yayāti returned the youth to Puru and took back his old age. In return for this favour, Yayāti crowned Puru king in his stead. But, as for Yadu, Yayāti cursed him: 'You had no respect for me, your own father: you will therefore by the father of very many demons.'

"After some time, Yayāti ascended to heaven; and Yadu gave birth to very many demons."

Uttara 60–61

One day, while Rāma was seated in his court, the palace guard announced to him: "Many sages have arrived at the gate, O King, to meet you." At Rāma's earnest request, the sages entered the court.

Rāma addressed them, after duly honouring them: "Holy ones! What can I do for you? May I know the purpose of your visit? Pray, command me and all that you desire of me I shall do with the greatest delight. This kingdom, my life and everything I maintain only for the service of the holy ones. This I say in truth."

After such an assurance, the sages said to Rāma: "In a bygone age there was a great demon known as Madhu, son of Lola. He was, however, a very righteous person. Hence he was beloved of the gods and the sages. Highly pleased with him, lord Śiva presented him with a trident which had the powers of the trident of lord Śiva himself.

"The Lord said to Madhu: 'Highly pleased with you, I am presenting you with this trident. As long as it is not used against the holy ones and the gods, so long will it be yours; otherwise it will disappear.'

"Madhu was highly pleased and he prayed for another boon: 'Lord, may this trident by the property of all my descendants.'

"The Lord, however, granted a slightly modified boon: 'Your prayer should not go unheeded. Hence, you will beget a son to whom you will present this trident. So long as he holds the trident in his hand, he will remain invincible.'

"Pleased with this boon obtained from lord Śiva, Madhu returned home. His wife Kumbhinasī soon gave birth to a vicious son named Lavaṇa. Right from his childhood Lavaṇa indulged in terribly wicked deeds. Seeing this, his father Madhu became very annoyed and displeased; yet, he could not do anything. Therefore, he left the house and went away. Before he did so, however, he gave the young man lord Śiva's trident and also conveyed the gist of the boon.

"With the help of that trident, Lavaṇa began to ravage the three worlds.

"All the kings of the world and the holy ones are terribly afraid of Lavaṇa. O Rāma, you are our only refuge. We have truthfully told you of the demon and of the weapon which he wields. We were happy to hear that you killed the wicked Rāvaṇa. We therefore consider that you alone can save us."

Uttara 62–63

Rāma enquired: "Where does this demon Lavaṇa live? What does he eat? What does he do?"

The sages replied: "The demon, O Lord, lives in Madhuvana. He eats everything, and he is particularly fond of eating ascetics. His doings are cruelty!"

Rāma reassured the sages: "Go in peace, O holy ones; the demon is surely killed already; there is no doubt about this." Then turning to his brothers, Rāma asked: "Who is willing to undertake this?"

Bharata volunteered. Śatrughna however intervened and said: "My beloved elder brother Bharata has had more than his share of unhappiness in life. Let this task be allotted to me."

Rāma agreed and replied: "Well said, Śatrughna. I shall send you to fight Lavaṇa. Nay, I shall immediately have you crowned king of Madhuvana. Kill Lavaṇa and install yourself on the throne of Madhuvana and rule that kingdom righteously."

This sudden turn of events upset Śatrughna who replied: "Alas, what have I done! This seems to be unrighteous to me that while the elder brother lives the younger is crowned. On the other hand, your command should not be disobeyed. You yourself have often taught me the holy scriptures dealing with human conduct, and I know that it is improper for a youngster to argue with an elder. I know that to argue with what an elder has said, even if it appears to be unrighteous, is improper. Hence, O Rāma, I shall not argue with you, but I shall do exactly as you command me to do, and destroy any unrighteousness that may be found in me."

Rāma performed Śatrughna's coronation as the king of Madhuvana immediately, even before sending him to fight the demon. The sages and other holy men proclaimed the demon dead, even at the moment of Śatrughna's coronation! Rāma took Śatrughna on his lap and handed him a weapon of incomparable might: "This, my dear brother, was created from the great ocean by Brahmā the creator himself; but it has remained hidden from view so long. The Lord used it against the first demons, Madhu and Kaiṭabha; and after their destruction he used it to create the world. Though I knew it, I did not use it against Rāvaṇa as that would have caused untold destruction . . . You know that Lavaṇa keeps the trident of Śiva in his home and worships it daily. Later he roams about for his food. If you challenge him before he re-enters his home and before he lays his hand again on the trident, you will easily overcome him."

Uttara 64–65

Rāma continued: "Take a big army to support you in this venture, O Śatrughna. Take enough money and foodstuff and distribute them to the armed forces to keep them happy with their morale high. Station the army at a distance from the city and go alone into Madhuvana, so that the demon does not suspect your intention. That is the only way in which you can kill him. Now is the best time to go: for it is summer when the Gaṅgā is easier to cross."

With the blessing of the queens and of Rāma, Śatrughna left. After spending two nights en route, Śatrughna reached the hermitage of the sage Vālmīki. He bowed down to the sage and submitted: "O holy one, permit me to stay here for one night. Tomorrow, I shall leave on my mission." The sage heartily welcomed Śatrughna and said to him: "This indeed is your own hermitage, O Śatrughna; it belongs to Rāma and his family."

After thus offering the hospitality of the hermitage, the sage Vālmīki narrated to Śatrughna the following story concerning a neighbouring hermitage:

"Once upon a time there lived a king named Saudāśa whose son was Vīryasahā. While hunting one day, Saudāśa saw two demons in the forest, enjoying their meal. In great anger, he killed one of them. The other demon cursed Saudāśa in the following words: 'You have killed my friend who did not give you any offence; hence I shall take revenge upon you in due time.'

"Some time later, Saudāśa performed the horse-rite. At its conclusion, the demon disguised himself as sage Vasiṣṭha and asked for meat to eat. The king asked for the meat to be prepared. The demon himself, this time in the disguise of a cook, prepared a dish of human flesh.

"The king then entertained sage Vasiṣṭha with that food. The sage angrily cursed the king: 'Since you have served human flesh for me to eat, such shall be your own food.' (i.e. you will become a cannibal). The king was about to counter-curse the sage, but the queen restrained him. His anger flowed from him and bathed his feet which grew dark. Hence he was called Kalmaṣapāda. Vasiṣṭha thereupon modified his curse and said: 'It would be effective only for twelve years.' After living as a cannibal for twelve years, the king once again regained his former state and his former kingdom. That famous sacred rite was performed in that yonder hermitage, O Śatrughna."

Uttara 66–67

That night when Śatrughna was in Vālmīki's hermitage, Rāma's sons were born to Sītā.

In the middle of the night some people from the convent of the female ascetics where Sītā resided, came to the sage Vālmīki and announced: "Holy sir, Rāma's wife has given birth to two sons; pray, come and bless them and protect them from evil spirits."

The sage Vālmīki immediately went over to where Sītā was, along with several elderly sages. He took a bunch of kuśa-grass, consecrated them with mantras for the protection of the boys from evil spirits and had them touched with those blades of grass. The elder boy was touched with the kuśa-grass and hence Vālmīki christened him Kuśa. The younger boy was touched with the lower end (lava) of the grass and hence he came to be known as Lava. All the people in the hermitage then sang the glories of Rāma and Sītā.

The next morning, Śatrughna approached the sage Chyavana and wanted to know from him the strength and the weakness of Lavaṇa and the famous trident that he had in his possession.

To bring home to Śatrughna the terrible power of the trident, the sage narrated the story of Śatrughna's own ancestor, Māndhātā—which was as follows.

"Once upon a time, your own ancestor Māndhātā went to heaven with the intention of conquering it. Indra humbly said to him: 'O King, why do you not conquer the whole of the earth before attempting to invade heaven like this?' Māndhātā angrily questioned: 'The earth has been conquered; who is there on earth who does not recognise my sovereignty?' Indra quietly replied: 'Lavaṇa'.

"Māndhātā at once returned to the earth and sent an emissary to Lavaṇa to ascertain if indeed he did not recognise Māndhātā's sovereignty. Lavaṇa's response was quick and summary: he made a meal of the messenger. Greatly angered by this affront to his prowess, Māndhātā himself went forward to fight with Lavaṇa. Undaunted by this challenge, Lavaṇa took his trident and hurled it at Māndhātā: the infallible weapon took the great king's life, and returned to the demon."

"However," said the sage Chyavana, "tomorrow you will kill the demon Lavaṇa, when you challenge him before he has time to take hold of the trident."

Uttara 68–69

Early the next morning, Śatrughna set out to go alone to the city known as Madhuvana. Having reached the city, he stood blocking the entrance to Lavaṇa's abode.

Lavaṇa who had gone out to gather food returned before long with a huge load of carcasses of various animals. Seeing Śatrughna standing at the entrance to his palace, blocking it, he shouted: "Who are you, O fool? What do you want to do here? Thousands of people like you have been killed and eaten by me, even though they were fully armed and were heroic in battle. Surely, the meat that I have brought with me is incomplete, and you have come to complete it for me: I shall presently kill you and make a meal of you, too."

Śatrughna thereupon revealed his identity: as the brother of Rāma who had killed the mighty Rāvaṇa. The demon replied: "Ah, that is marvellous. Rāvaṇa is a close relative of mine, and how very lucky I am that I can thus easily avenge his death!"

Śatrughna challenged the demon for a hand-to-hand fight, since the demon was unarmed. Lavaṇa accepted it, and picked up a few huge trees and began to hit Śatrughna with them. Undaunted, Śatrughna fought. By hitting him with a huge tree, Lavaṇa rendered Śatrughna unconscious. Seeing Śatrughna fallen, Lavaṇa thought he was dead and hence without even bothering to take up his trident, sat down to eat his meal.

In the meantime, however, Śatrughna had regained his consciousness; and, without wasting any more time, fixed the deadliest missile that Rāma had given him, ready to fire, at the same time blocking the entrance to the palace so that Lavaṇa could not get hold of his invincible trident. The force of the missile was such that it frightened even the gods who waited upon the Lord in a deputation. The Lord assured them: "This great energy which has frightened you all is none other than the missile that Śatrughna is about to use in his fight with Lavaṇa. It was first fashioned by the Creator of the universe to destroy Madhu and Kaiṭabha. Go quickly and witness this dreadful battle." And the gods came to the earth to witness the great fight.

Śatrughna directed the divine missile at Lavaṇa who instantly fell down dead.

And, the trident returned that very moment to lord Śiva.

Uttara 70–71

When Lavaṇa had been killed, the gods congratulated Śatrughna on his superhuman feat. "This demon had mercilessly oppressed many gods and demons," they said, "and fortunately you have killed him."

Śatrughna prayed that the gods might enter the city of Madhupuri; and the gods consented to do so and blessed that the city would flourish thenceforward. From that very day prosperity and peace returned to the city; everyone was healthy, happy and peaceful. With Śatrughna as king, righteousness prevailed and roads and gardens were laid everywhere.

Thus had twelve years rolled by when Śatrughna felt eager to see the divine feet of Rāma.

On the way to Ayodhyā, he again spent a day at the hermitage of the sage Vālmīki. The sage had, in the meantime, composed the famous epic known as Rāma Carita (the History of Rāma). And, he recited it for Śatrughna to hear.

The epic was perfect in every respect. Its words were truthful and the narration was truthful. Hearing it, Śatrughna shed tears of love, and sighing again and again he lost consciousness for some time.

The soldiers also heard the moving story and were entranced by it. They then questioned Śatrughna: "Whose story is this? On what is this poem based? Is it real or are we dreaming? Kindly ask the sage concerning this."

But Śatrughna, however, declined to do so. He replied: "Warriors! It is not proper for us thus to question the sage. Surely there are numerous wonders in this hermitage of the sage Vālmīki." Saying so, he retired to his own camp.

Uttara 72–73

Soon Śatrughna was at the abode of Rāma, and to his great delight beheld Rāma surrounded by his ministers. He bowed to Rāma and submitted as follows: "Rāma, I have duly carried out your commands. Lavaṇa has been slain and I have also ruled over Madhuvana for a very long period of twelve years. The administration has been very well established there. Bless me, Lord, for without you I am like a calf without the cow; allow me to stay here at your feet."

Rāma fondly embraced Śatrughna and replied: "Even so are you very dear to me, O Śatrughna. But men of the warrior clan do not feel sorry to be separated from their kith and kin; for to them the protection of the people is of the utmost concern. Hence, stay with me here for seven days and then return to your kingdom."

Śatrughna spent seven blissful days with Rāma and his other brothers; and on the eighth day he left for Madhupuri along with Bharata.

One day, while Rāma was holding court in Ayodhyā, an aged man appeared at the gate, carrying the dead body of his little son. The aged brāhmaṇa was wailing aloud:

"Alas, what have I done to deserve this? I have never uttered falsehood; I have never harmed any living being. I do not remember having done any sinful action towards any being. Yet, on account of what sin has this my little son died before performing the funeral of his parents?

"Ah, my son, you have departed after a very short span of life here, leaving myself and your mother sunk in sorrow. We shall soon follow you, too.

"Such a calamity is unheard of and I have not seen another instance like this. There must surely be a reason for it. And surely it is due to the unrighteousness of the king that a thing like this happens. There is no doubt that king Rāma is responsible for this untimely death of a boy.

"Let the king bring this boy back to life or I shall give up my life at this gate. Let the king along with his brothers enjoy life after having been responsible for the death of a brāhmaṇa.

"Calamities befall the nation unrighteously ruled by a king of defective or immoral conduct; it is only in such a state that people experience untimely death."

Uttara 74–75

Greatly distressed to hear the brāhmaṇa's words, Rāma immediately summoned the wise sages of his court. After receiving them with great reverence and honour, Rāma conveyed to them all that had happened.

The sage Nārada, noticing the great distress which afflicted Rāma, said to him as follows:

"Rāma, I shall tell you the real reason for this untimely death of this boy.

"In the epoch known as Kṛta Yuga or Satya Yuga only brāhmaṇas or wise and learned men who were self-controlled and righteous undertook austerities. Time rolled on and during the age known as Tretā Yuga even they who were not so wise and learned, so righteous and self-controlled—even they who were warrior-like and martial-spirited—began to practise austerities. Surely during this period, unrighteousness had begun to invade the earth. With the onset of the third age known as Dvāpara the unrighteousness of the previous age had become doubled as it were. And even they who were given to trade, commerce, industry and agriculture and who were therefore farther removed from the course of righteous conduct began to indulge in austerities, surely for unedifying reasons. Now, already one who is none of these, who on the other hand was born in the servant-class is engaged in austerities: surely he does not possess any of the qualifications necessary for it. In this age, the śūdra (servant-class) is characterised by unrighteousness; and such a one taking to austerities is the cause of the death of this boy. If you are able to remedy this state of affairs then this boy will regain his life."

Rāma's spirit was revived on hearing this. He ordered that the boy's body be embalmed, and the old man consoled. Immediately he thought of the spacecraft Puṣpaka which instantly arrived upon the scene. Ascending this spacecraft, Rāma scoured the east, the north, and the west but found no unrighteous action which could have caused the great calamity. Then he turned southwards. There near a great mountain he saw a large lake. Standing in that lake, someone was practising intense austerities. Looking at him, Rāma asked: "Who are you, O ascetic? In what community were you born—I wish to know out of curiosity. Why are you practising these austerities—for the attainment of heaven or some other motive; for getting a boon are you practising austerities which are difficult for others? Tell me truly, are you a brāhmaṇa, or a warrior, a trader or a servant?"

Uttara 76–77

The ascetic replied to Rāma: "I shall not utter falsehood, O Rāma: I tell you the truth. For, I wish to attain divinity through this penance. I am a śūdra. My name is Śambuka."

As soon as Śambuka said this, Rāma unsheathed his radiant sword and cut off his head. The gods were delighted and offered boons to Rāma. Rāma chose a boon: "O gods, if you are pleased with me, may the brāhmaṇa's son live: this is the only boon I ask for."

The gods replied: This has already been accomplished. For the moment you cut off the head of Śambuka, the brāhmaṇa's son rose to life. Good, let us now proceed to the hermitage of sage Agastya. He has been lying on water for the past twelve years and he has just now concluded his penance. Let us go visit him."

When the gods entered his hermitage, Agastya received them with worshipful devotion. Later, they left. Rāma descended from the spacecraft Puṣpaka and bowed to the sage. The sage welcomed him heartily and said: "The gods told me that you have killed the śūdra-ascetic and revived the brāhmaṇa's son. You are indeed lord Nārāyaṇa, and in you all things abide; you are the lord of all gods and you are the eternal puruṣa, person. Pray, spend the night here and you may depart tomorrow. Also, accept this ornament which is radiant and which you alone deserve. It is said that one who gives away what has been given to him obtains a rich reward of merit."

Rāma asked: "How did you happen to get this ornament in the first place? Pray tell me that for I am curious to know."

Agastya continued: "Long, long ago, I was living in a forest. One day I entered deep into the forest. There I saw a beautiful hermitage. I spent one night there. The next morning I saw a dead body near that hermitage. As I was wondering whose body it could have been, I saw another marvellous sight. A spacecraft descended upon that spot. In it was a radiant celestial surrounded by nymphs, singing and dancing. Even as I was looking, he descended from the spacecraft and sat down to eat that corpse. After finishing the meal, he went to the lake to wash himself. Then he was about to board the spacecraft; and I asked him: 'Who are you; you look like a god. But you are eating a corpse. Why is it so? Kindly enlighten me.' "

Uttara 78–79

When I enquired thus, the celestial told me his story which is as follows: "When I lived on this earth I was the son of the king of Vidharbha known as Sudeva. He had two wives and through them two sons. I was known as Śveta and my brother was Suratha. On the death of our father, the citizens crowned me king. I ruled the kingdom justly for some time. Later, I went to the forest and practised intense austerities. However, on leaving this world, when I went to the highest celestial realm, Brahmaloka, I discovered that I was still subject to hunger and thirst. When I enquired of the reason, Brahmā the creator said to me: 'You did penance only with your body; hence you will satisfy your hunger by eating human flesh. Since you did not give anything to anyone—neither food nor drink—you are still subject to hunger and thirst even in heaven. However, you will be freed from this state when you are blessed with the sight of the sage Agastya.' "

That celestial was delighted to see me, for that very moment he was freed from his wretched condition. As a token of gratitude, he pressed upon me to accept this celestial ornament.

Rāma then enquired of the sage Agastya: "Why is it that the forest known as Daṇḍaka is devoid of beasts and birds? Pray, enlighten me on this, too, O sage."

The sage Agastya continued:

In days of yore, Manu gave birth to a son known as Ikṣvāku. Manu installed him on the earth as its sole emperor. Manu also instructed Ikṣvāku on the art of righteous administration. He said: "Here is the rod of punishment, my son. With this protect the people. The king who uses this rod to punish the criminals goes to heaven. Therefore, use the rod judiciously. Righteousness is supreme in this world." Manu then returned to his abode.

A hundred sons were born of Ikṣvāku. The last of them was a fool who grew up to be an illiterate person. His name was Daṇḍa, for the father thought: surely his body will receive the rod (daṇḍa). Ikṣvāku entrusted to him the land between Vindhya and the Śaivala hills. Daṇḍa built his capital city and named it Madhumantam and appointed Uśanā as his personal priest.

Uttara 80–81

While Daṇḍa was thus ruling his kingdom, one day he happened to meet Araja, the daughter of Uśanā (sage Śukra). She was exceedingly beautiful. When Daṇḍa saw her, immediately he was overcome by lust. Approaching her, he asked: "Who are you, O beautiful girl? At your very sight, I am filled with desire for you."

Araja, however, was terribly frightened and she replied meekly: "O King, pray, do not touch me or seek me by force. For, a virgin is in the custody of her father. My father, Śukra, is my elder and guru, and you are his disciple, too. If he is angered, you will come to great grief. Hence, it is proper that you should ask him for my hand; otherwise, great will be your misfortune. When angered, my father can burn the three worlds. On the other hand, if you ask him he will give me to you in marriage."

Daṇḍa, however, was unmoved by all this. He held his hands over his head, in a gesture of salutation and submission and repeated his plea for immediate satisfaction of his lust. "I want you," he said, "and even if it costs me my life; if it means a great sin on my part. I love you intensely. Come to me, O timid girl!" Then, he took her by force. Afterwards, he returned to his palace; and Araja returned to the hermitage, weeping.

When the sage Śukra came to know of Daṇḍa's deed, he was beside himself in uncontrollable anger. He turned to his disciples and roared: "Look at this terrible misdeed of the fool Daṇḍa. Surely he has reached the end of his own life that he thus dares to play with fire that I am. Since he has dared to commit such a heinous crime, surely he should reap the fruits of his action. In seven days, the king with his kith and kin will meet his death. And for seven days it shall rain incessantly devastating his kingdom."

And so it happened. The sage's own disciples quit their hermitage and went away to a neighbouring forest. Śukra, however, commanded his daughter Araja to stay put in the hermitage, assuring her of his protection; even the plants and trees that were near her were protected by the sage's blessings.

Thus was Daṇḍa's kingdom, the Daṇḍakāraṇya, rendered uninhabited. Later on, however, sages began to live in it and practise austerities.

Uttara 82–83

The next day, Rāma got up early in the morning and said his morning prayers. Then he approached the sage Agastya, bowed down to him, and asked for his permission to return to his palace. "I consider myself truly blessed by your sight, O sage!"

The sage Agastya replied: "I am amazed at your words, O Rāma; for, in truth, you are the supreme purifier and redeemer of the whole world and all beings in it. He who beholds you even for an hour is purified completely, and comes to be worshipped even by the gods. On the other hand, he who looks upon you with evil eyes, he is subjected to the punishment of Yama, the god of death. Go back to your kingdom and protect the subjects in strict accordance with dharma. For you are indeed the goal of all beings on earth."

Rāma ascended the spacecraft Puṣpaka and soon returned to his palace. He entered the palace and dismissed the spacecraft.

Soon after this, Rāma summoned his brothers to his presence and said to them:

"I have fulfilled my duty towards the old brāhmaṇa who has got back his son. I wish to pursue the path of dharma and do something more to earn religious merit. I have in mind the Rājasuya rite, along with all of you who are my own self externalised. We have heard that Mitra performed that sacred rite, and also Soma performed the rite and obtained eternal fame."

Hearing this, Bharata submitted to Rāma with great love and devotion:

"Rāma, all the kings of the world look upon you as the lord of the universe. They regard you as their father. You are the sole refuge of all beings on this earth, O Rāma. But the Rājasuya rite is fraught with conflict with kings, subduing them, and such acts of violence. When you know that all of them are in your virtual control, there is no need even to challenge them. Hence, pray, give up the idea of performing the Rājasuya rite."

Rāma was pleased with this and said:

"I am delighted with your brave words of wisdom, O Bharata. I have given up the idea of performing the Rājasuya rite which does involve one in some violence. Surely, good men should not engage themselves in actions which involve harm or suffering to living beings."

Uttara 84–85

Lakṣmaṇa then said to Rāma:

Instead of the Rājasuya, O Rāma, I think we should perform an Aśvamedha rite. Aśvamedha is a great rite and purifies one of all sins; hence please consider it.

I have heard it said that in days of yore Indra himself performed that sacred rite in order to earn the merit to destroy his enemy, the demon Vṛtra. This demon Vṛtra was indeed a good and noble king of the whole world; and he ruled the world righteously and justly. There was peace, plenty and prosperity in the world.

Entrusting the kingdom to his son, Vṛtra once decided upon practising austerities. Even as he commenced his austerities, Indra approached the lord Viṣṇu and submitted: "Lord, Vṛtra is about to commence austerities. If he succeeds in it he will become supremely powerful and no one will be able to subdue him for as long as the world lasts. Your grace is his only strength, O Lord; and I pray to you, think of some way to get rid of him."

The Lord, however, replied: "I have been the friend of Vṛtra so long, hence I shall not be able to kill him. But I shall do what you pray for. I shall divide myself into three parts. One will enter Indra, the other will enter his weapon, the thunderbolt, and the third will enter the earth. With the help of these, you will be able to destroy Vṛtra."

As the gods were thus standing bewildered, Indra caught hold of his thunderbolt and hurled it at the demon Vṛtra, and the demon's head instantly rolled on the ground. Surely this was the divine energy of lord Viṣṇu himself which enabled this to be achieved.

Vṛtra was a brāhmaṇa by birth. And the dreadful sin of having killed a brāhmaṇa pursued Indra and haunted him. Once again, the gods went to lord Viṣṇu and prayed to him repeatedly; "O Lord, by your grace, the mighty demon Vṛtra has been killed; but the terrible sin of having killed a brāhmaṇa haunts Indra. Kindly liberate Indra from this sin."

Lord Viṣṇu replied: "Worship me through the sacred Aśvamedha rite, O gods, and I shall free Indra from the fear born of the killing of a brāhmaṇa."

Uttara 86, 87, 88

When Indra was thus afflicted by the sin of the killing of a brāhmaṇa, great calamities overtook the earth. Lakes dried up, and rivers were dry; there was no rain and drought prevailed. At that time, the gods remembered the words of lord Viṣṇu.

Soon the gods got together to celebrate the great Aśvamedha rite. At the conclusion of this rite, the great sin of the killing of a brāhmaṇa appeared before them, having left Indra. This 'sin' split itself into four parts: one part lives in the waters of rivers during the four months of the rainy season, one part lives in barren lands, one part lives in young women during their monthly period, and the fourth part lives in those who scandalise or kill a brāhmaṇa.

Thus had Indra been purified and redeemed from the sin of having killed a brāhmaṇa, by the power of the great Aśvamedha rite.

Rāma was delighted to hear this narrative, and said to Lakṣmaṇa:

"O Lakṣmaṇa, the story you have narrated is indeed wonderful to hear. Even so, I have heard another story which brings out the glory of the Aśvamedha rite. I shall relate that story to you."

In day of yore, the sage Kardama had a son known as Ila. He had conquered the whole world and he ruled the earth justly and wisely, treating all beings as his own children.

One day he set out to go to the forest for hunting. In the course of that expedition, he went to where lord Skanda was born. In that region, lord Śiva was sporting with devi Pārvatī, having ordained that all beings in that area should turn into females.

When king Ila entered that area, he found that he had mysteriously lost his manhood and had been turned into a woman. He discovered that it was the doing of lord Śiva. Distressed by this, he sang the glories of lord Śiva who, pleased with him, said: "Ask for any boon other than the return of your manhood." But Ila had no other desire!

Seeing his pitiable plight, devi Pārvatī said: "I am the other half of lord Śiva, and in exercise of that privilege I give you manhood. You will therefore be a man for a month and a woman for another, alternatively. You will forget your manhood while you are a woman, and vice versa."

Uttara 89

Rāma continued the story of Ila.

During the first month, Ila, the beautiful woman roamed about with 'his' retinue who had all been transformed into women. One day, Ila saw there the beautiful son of the moon-god (Soma) named Budha. She fell in love with Budha, at first sight.

Budha also saw Ila and fell in love with her. He said to himself: "I have never seen such a beautiful woman in the whole world; not among the goddesses, not among mortal women." He went to the hermitage where Ila and the retinue dwelt. He questioned them about Ila, but they replied: "She is our leader, she is not married, and she lives in this hermitage with us all."

Through his own intuitive wisdom, Budha, however, came to know the whole story. He understood that they were all male (puruṣa) and had been transformed into females. Hence, he called them Kimpuruṣa-women, and said to them that they would obtain Kimpuruṣa-men (a sort of celestials) for their consorts.

Then Budha approached Ila and revealed his identity and sought her hand. Ila, too, readily consented to be his wife. Together they enjoyed life for a whole month.

One day, after the conclusion of the first month, Ila woke up as a man. Anticipating this, Budha had commenced to practise an intense austerity. Ila said to Budha: "I came to this forest along with a retinue; and I fell asleep. I do not see my retinue. My friend, do you know what happened to them?" Budha, realising that Ila had forgotten the happenings of the previous month, said: "There was a terrible storm which killed all of them; and you, too, took shelter here from the storm. Never mind: you can continue to stay here, eating the fruits, roots, etc."

Ila believed it and said: "Well, I would not like to go back to my palace without my retinue. My son Śaśabindu is there, and he will surely rule the kingdom in my stead."

Once again, after a month, Ila became a woman. Thus time rolled by. In nine months' time, Ila and Budha had a son, known as Purūrava.

Uttara 90–91

One day, after the birth of Purūrava, Budha asked the wise sages: "Pray, O sages, listen to me. This Ila was a great and noble king. And you know how he was transformed into a female. Please consider some way by which his manhood could be restored."

The sage Kardama (father of Ila) said: "I can see no remedy except the adoration of lord Śiva; and there is no greater rite than the Aśvamedha rite which can earn his blessing."

Soon all of them organised the Aśvamedha rite for the propitiation of lord Śiva. Highly pleased with the performance of the Aśvamedha rite, lord Śiva manifested himself in their midst and asked them: "I am highly pleased with your devotion, O holy ones; ask for a boon." They prayed: "Pray, O Lord, grant manhood to Ila." Highly pleased, lord Śiva bestowed manhood on Ila once again.

The holy ones returned to their abodes and king Ila, too, returned to his palace.

Such is the glory of the Aśvamedha rite—concluded Rāma.

Then Rāma said: "In the presence of holy sages like Vasiṣṭha, Vāmadeva, Jābāli and Kaśyapa, and the holy brāhmaṇas, and with their advice and blessings I shall release a well-adorned sacred horse, in preparation for the sacred rite."

Lakṣmaṇa, on hearing these words of Rāma, had the sages and the brāhmaṇas assembled immediately in the palace. Rāma also sent for Śatrughna, Vibhīṣaṇa, all the neighbouring kings, and the holy ones from everywhere.

As these guests began to arrive, Rāma gathered mountains of foodstuff for the service of these guests. Bharata and Śatrughna received the guests and gave them costly presents. Vibhīṣaṇa and others worshipped the holy ones and served them. The vānaras served all the guests and ensured that nothing was neglected.

The Aśvamedha rite commenced with indescribable grandeur.

Uttara 92–93

When all the arrangements had been completed, Rāma let go a beautiful horse which was in the charge of Lakṣmaṇa. Then he entered the place in Naimiṣaṁ where the sacred rite was to be held, along with his retinue.

The sacred rite commenced and lasted a whole year. Food, drinks, clothes, gold and ornaments flowed ceaselessly in that place. Bharata and Śatrughna were in charge of these and they ensured that no one who expressed the least inclination was denied anything. The vānaras spared themselves no pain in the service of all the guests. And, the noble Vibhīṣaṇa served the holy sages zealously.

No one was weak, dirty, or in want. No need remained unfulfilled. Before the need was expressed it was supplied. They who wanted gold, got gold; they who wanted clothes, got clothes. Sweets and other delicacies were always available to all.

All the guests said to one another: "We have not seen the like of this, neither Indra, nor Soma, nor Varuṇa, no one else has performed a rite like this."

Elsewhere, escorted by Lakṣmaṇa, the horse continued to roam the earth.

To this great sacred rite came the sage Viśvāmitra along with his disciples. Among the latter were the two boys Kuśa and Lava. The sage had told them: "Joyously sing the great epic poem Rāmāyaṇam which I have taught you. Sing it in the presence of sages or brāhmaṇas, in the palaces of princes and along the main roads. Sing it at the gates of Rāma's palace, and in front of the priests officiating at the sacred rite. Here, take these fruits: these will prevent fatigue and keep your voices from getting tired.

"Should Rāma call upon you to sing the poem, please do so without hesitation. Do not even expect a reward; for of what use is gold or wealth. Should Rāma ask you whose sons you are, merely reply: 'We are the disciples of Vālmīki.' Take this musical instrument and sing the poem to its accompaniment."

Thus instructed by the sage, the young sons of Sītā eagerly awaited the opportunity to sing the Rāmāyaṇam.

Uttara 94–95

The two boys got up early the next morning and offered their morning prayers. Just as the sage had instructed them, they began to sing; and Rāma made them sing the poem. The king assembled all the holy men, kings, heroes, pandits, storytellers, grammarians and all other brāhmaṇas who were interested in hearing the great poem, and requested the two boys to sing the poem in their presence. All the members of this august assembly drank the nectarine poem with their ears, and the beautiful personality of the two young boys with their eyes. They said to one another: "These two boys are very much like Rāma, like the very image of Rāma. Had they not been clad in ascetic garments, with matted locks and so on, we would have concluded that they were in fact Rāma's sons."

When they had completed the twenty chapters according to the instruction of sage Vālmīki, they paused; and the king asked his brother to give them a bag of gold—which they politely declined to accept, saying: "We are forest-dwellers, and gold is useless to us."

Rāma asked them who the author of the poem was and whether it was authentic; and they devoutly replied that it was the composition of sage Vālmīki and it was entirely truthful.

At the end of the day, Rāma gave them leave to return to the sage's camp. The next day again he had them recite the poem. Thus very many days passed. Rāma made them recite the poem in the presence of the sages and kings. And from the way in which it was recited, he concluded that they were the children of Sītā.

Rāma then sent messengers to the sage Vālmīki with the message: "If Sītā is free from unchaste conduct, then let her come here, escorted by the sage Vālmīki and prove her purity. Let her therefore present herself tomorrow morning here in this august assembly."

This message was duly conveyed to the sage Vālmīki who replied to the messengers: "Surely, Sītā would agree to do as instructed by Rāma; for she regards her husband as God himself."

When this was conveyed to Rāma, he addressed the sages and kings, and said: "You will witness tomorrow the purity of Sītā." And they, in their turn, applauded his decision: "This is entirely in accordance with your glorious and pure nature, O Rāma."

Uttara 96–97

When the night was past, and the day dawned, Rāma assembled all the sages and the holy men like Vasiṣṭha, Vāmadeva, Jābāli, Kaśyapa, Viśvāmitra, Dhīrghatamā and Durvāsa, and others. All of them were eagerly awaiting the developments, and looked forward to witness the noble Sītā prove her chastity.

Sage Vālmīki entered the assembly followed by Sītā. There was instant restlessness in the assembly, as everyone noticed the picture of sorrow and grief that Sītā was.

Vālmīki spoke: "Here, O Rāma, is Sītā who is devoted to her marital vows and whose conduct is perfectly righteous. Abandoned on account of public scandal she has been living near my hermitage. These two sons of Sītā are your sons, O Rāma: I speak the truth. I do not remember having uttered falsehood in my life. I have practised austerities for a very long time: I swear by them that Sītā is pure."

Rāma said: "I am also convinced of Sītā's purity, O sage. However, mighty is public scandal on account of which I had to abandon Sītā, even though I myself knew that she was pure. I know, too, that these two boys are my sons."

In the meantime, even the gods entered the assembly.

Sītā then said: "If I never even mentally thought of another, other than Rāma, then O Earth, receive me. If in thought, word and deed I have always worshipped Rāma, then O Earth, receive me."

When Sītā said these words, a celestial throne arose from the earth. In it was mother Earth; she received Sītā in her arms, and embracing her with great love, re-entered the earth.

All beings—the gods, the sages, the brāhmaṇas, the priests who had assembled to conduct the Aśvamedha rite, the birds, the beasts, and even the trees and insentient beings—all of them expressed their admiration, their devotion and their wonder in their own way. They were all wonderstruck, stunned, by the miraculous way in which Sītā disappeared into the earth.

Some praised and glorified Rāma; some praised and glorified Sītā. Everyone was filled with awe and wonder.

Uttara 98–99

When Rāma saw the descent of Sītā into the earth, he was completely overwhelmed with grief. He wept aloud. He cried: "Alas, even as I was looking, Sītā has been taken away. I rescued her from Laṅkā years ago; why should I not bring her back from the bowels of the earth? O Earth! Return Sītā to me immediately; or I will let you taste my anger. Wherever Sītā may be now, bring her back to me at once; if you do not, I shall destroy you along with the hills and forests, and the whole earth will be covered with water."

Seeing Rāma's anger, Brahmā the creator said: "O Rāma, do not lose your temper. The chaste and devoted Sītā has naturally gone ahead of you to the other world; and you will soon be reunited with her. Hear, again, O Rāma: your story till this period has been beautifully narrated in the great poem by the sage Vālmīki. There is some more left which concerns what is to come. Listen to that section, too." After saying so, Brahmā departed for his abode.

Rāma requested Vālmīki to recite the story of coming events. This was later recited by Kuśa and Lava.

Not seeing Sītā, Rāma regarded the world as empty, and overwhelmed by sorrow, he did not enjoy peace of mind. He did not consider looking upon another as wife, and for the performance of religious rites, he therefore used a golden image of Sītā.

Rāma ruled the earth for a very long time. During this entire period, all beings enjoyed health and long life. There was justice and righteousness everywhere. The earth was prosperous. There was adequate and timely rain. No one suffered any kind of misfortune.

After enjoying her life with Rāma, his children and his grandchildren, Rāma's mother Kausalyā ascended to heaven. After leading a righteous life, Sumitrā and Kaikeyī also went to heaven. All of them were reunited in heaven with the king Daśaratha. And, Rāma propitiated them all by the due and regular performance of the anniversary ceremonies performed for the welfare of the departed ancestors.

Uttara 100–101

After the lapse of several years, Rāma's uncle Yudhājit sent his own guru to Rāma with a message and a huge load of woollen blankets, precious stones, dresses, and also horses as his present to Rāma.

The holy messenger was received by Rāma with the greatest of respect, reverence and love. After this, Rāma bade him sit on a seat appropriate to a distinguished visitor and enquired after the welfare of his uncle. Then, Rāma asked the brāhmaṇa: "What was my uncle's message to me?"

The holy messenger said to Rāma: "On the banks of the river Sindhu a Gandharva known as Śailūṣa lives with thirty million soldiers of extraordinary strength. Pray, conquer them with your own might and enter that city of the Gandharvas. We have no other person to achieve this task."

Rāma immediately consented and sent for Bharata along with his two sons Takṣa and Puṣkala. Pointing to them, Rāma said to the brāhmaṇa: "These two boys, along with their father Bharata, will soon conquer the Gandharva hordes." Having said so, Rāma had the two boys crowned kings of the Gandharva territory, in anticipation of their victory.

The holy mnessenger thereupon returned to the Kekaya kingdom (of Yudhājit) and Bharata with his two sons set out on his expedition. In a fortnight's time, Bharata reached the Kekaya kingdom and linked up his armies with those of Yudhājit.

The combined armies then attacked the Gandharvas. The fierce battle that ensued lasted seven days. Wishing to terminate the fight, Bharata used a deadly missile known as Samvarta; and in the twinkling of an eye the thirty million Gandharvas were destroyed.

Bharata then entered the Gandharva territory along with his two sons. He established his son Takṣa as the king of Takṣaśila, and his son Puṣkala as the king of Puṣkalavata. The two cities greatly prospered under their sovereignty.

Bharata spent five years with his sons in their new territories, and after stabilising their administration, returned to Ayodhyā. He bowed down to Rāma and informed him of all that had happened. Rāma was highly pleased.

Uttara 102–103

Then Rāma desired to establish the two sons of Lakṣmaṇa (Angada and Candraketu) as the rulers of two suitable principalities. Rāma said to Lakṣmaṇa: "These two sons of yours, O Lakṣmaṇa, are strong and valiant and are fit to be rulers of their own principalities. I shall anoint them kings; think of a suitable territory for each of them. It should be such that the rulers are free from trouble, and the hermitages are free from molestation.

As soon as such territories were found Rāma himself anointed the two boys kings: the territory ruled by Angada was known as Angada; and Candraketu was installed on the throne of Candrakānti. Lakṣmaṇa stayed for some time with them, and when the administration was functioning smoothly, he returned to Ayodhyā and to Rāma.

As Rāma was thus administering his empire, Time (or Death) appeared at the gate of Rāma's palace in the guise of an ascetic. The ascetic said to Lakṣmaṇa: "Pray, inform Rāma that a messenger from one who is supremely powerful has arrived and that I would like to speak to Rāma."

Lakṣmaṇa informed Rāma of the arrival of the ascetic. Upon Rāma's instructions Lakṣmaṇa led the ascetic to Rāma's presence. Rāma received the ascetic with great reverence and made him sit on a golden seat. Then, Rāma requested the ascetic to convey the message he had.

But the ascetic replied: "I can only reveal the message in private, O Rāma. And, whoever hears it or observes the two of us talking should be immediately put to death."

Rāma consented to this condition. He installed Lakṣmaṇa outside the chamber with the strict instruction: "Do not let anyone come in and interrupt this important conversation; anyone who enters the chamber will suffer death." He then turned to the ascetic: "Pray, convey the important message that you have for me."

Uttara 104–105

When they were alone, the ascetic revealed his true identity as Time (or Death) and submitted to Rāma: "O Lord, the creator Brahmā sent me to you with this message: Once upon a time, you had withdrawn the universe into yourself and were resting on the great ocean. By your own Māyā you then created the two powerful beings, Madhu and Kaiṭabha. Upon their destruction, this earth was fashioned from their own flesh. You yourself entrusted the work of protecting this world, to me who was born of the lotus that had sprung from your navel. And I have endeavoured to do my duty, placing the burden upon your shoulders. In course of time, for the destruction of the demons like Rāvaṇa, you incarnated on the earth, along with other divine beings. All that has been accomplished and the time for your return is at hand. If, however, you wish to continue to live on the earth, of course you can. If you wish to return to heaven so that heaven could have you as its sovereign, may it be so."

When Rāma heard this, he replied: "My manifestation is for the protection of the three worlds, not only of this earth; hence I shall soon depart from this earth. I shall do exactly as the creator, Brahmā, says."

As they were thus engaged in the conversation, there appeared at the entrance to the chamber Durvāsa, the great sage of terrible anger. He demanded of Lakṣmaṇa: "Take me to Rāma at once." When Lakṣmaṇa humbly questioned: "May I take a message to Rāma, for he is engaged in an important meeting? Or, would you care to wait for a few minutes?" the sage grew terribly angry and said: "Tell Rāma this moment that I am here. If you do not, I will curse him, you, your brothers and the whole royal family. I cannot contain my anger."

Hearing these terrible words, Lakṣmaṇa reflected for a moment: "It is better that I die rather than that this sage should curse the entire royal family." Having thus made up his mind, Lakṣmaṇa entered the chamber where Rāma and the ascetic were engaged in their conversation, and informed Rāma of Durvāsa's visit.

Rāma dismissed the ascetic and came out, bowed to the sage who said to him: "I have fasted for a thousand years; I wish to break the fast just now. Give me food." Rāma worshipfully served him with food. He ate and went away.

Thinking of his own terrible promise to the ascetic (that anyone interrupting the conversation would die), Rāma became moody.

Uttara 106–107

Lakṣmaṇa understood Rāma's predicament and approached him reverently and said: "Do not be worried on my account; all this is predestined to happen. Throw me out, O Rāma, and honour your promise; for when people dishonour their promise they go to hell."

Rāma summoned the ministers and the sages in council and informed them of all that had happened. The sage Vasiṣṭha then said: "O Rāma, I see that the end is coming: and now even Lakṣmaṇa has to be banished. It has to be done, for the sake of dharma. If dharma is abandoned, there will be universal destruction."

Rāma then said to Lakṣmaṇa: "Banishment is equal to execution, O Lakṣmaṇa. I banish you from the kingdom." Without even entering his house, Lakṣmaṇa went away. He reached the bank of the river Sarayū, ready to give up his life, sighing again and again. All the gods appeared in the heaven. Unseen by any human being, Indra took Lakṣmaṇa bodily to heaven. The gods were delighted that Lakṣmaṇa, who was inseparable from Rāma, had returned to heaven, thus indicating that Rāma would soon be with them.

Rāma was inconsolable with grief and he said: "I wish to abdicate the throne and retire to the forest; I wish to follow Lakṣmaṇa." He asked Bharata to ascend the throne.

But the noble Bharata replied: Oh, no, Rāma, I have no desire for the kingdom without you. Install your sons Kuśa and Lava on the throne. Let Śatrughna also be informed of our decision."

Vasiṣṭha said to Rāma again: "Rāma, look at these citizens who are all grief-stricken." Rāma was overcome by sorrow and sighed: "Ah, what shall I do?" All of them with one voice said to Rāma: "With our wives and children, we shall all go where Rāma goes; we shall follow him."

Reflecting over the devotion of the citizens and also the imminent end of his career on earth, Rāma that very day installed Kuśa and Lava on the throne, apportioning to them suitable territory. He also sent fast messengers to inform Śatrughna of his decision.

Uttara 108–109

The messengers conveyed to Śatrughna all the news of the events in Ayodhyā: "Rāma has abdicated his throne, having installed Kuśa and Lava on the throne; Kuśa rules from his capital Kuśavati, and Lava from his capital Śṛavasti. All the citizens of Ayodhyā have decided to follow Rāma: the capital is therefore totally deserted. Rāma asked us to convey all this to you."

Hearing of the destruction of the family, Śatrughna instantly installed his sons on the throne and, alone on his vehicle, drove in great haste to meet Rāma. Upon reaching Rāma's presence, Śatrughna said: "I have enthroned my two sons on the throne, O Rāma, and I have decided to follow you." Rāma saw the firmness of his determination and acquiesced.

Coming to know of Rāma's abdication and of his imminent ascension to heaven, all the vānaras came, led by Sugrīva, and even so the gods and the sages rushed to where Rāma was. Sugrīva had installed Aṅgada on the throne and decided to follow Rāma.

When Vibhīṣaṇa arrived, Rāma quickly said to him: "O Vibhīṣaṇa, rule the kingdom of Laṅkā so long as the people wish you to do so, so long as the sun and the moon shine, and so long as my story is narrated in this world. Pray, do not argue." Vibhīṣaṇa consented.

Rāma blessed Hanumān: "Live and rejoice in this world as long as my story is narrated, and adhere to my instructions, O Hanumān." Hanumān bowed his acceptance.

All of them, thereupon, began to move out of Ayodhyā. All the weapons, the sages, the brāhmaṇas, the goddess of wealth, the holy scriptures, the holy mantras—all these followed Rāma. Bharata and Śatrughna went. All the ministers and the civil servants went. And all the citizens went, too. Not even the smallest creature stayed behind in Ayodhyā: all of them followed Rāma.

Uttara 110–111

Rāma approached the river Sarayū and touched its waters with his feet. To witness this most glorious and auspicious ascension of Rāma, all the gods had come in their space vehicles, and the creator Brahmā himself came in person in his own celestial vehicle.

Then, the Creator said to Rāma: "Come, O Viṣṇu, enter your own divine bodies along with your brothers. Whatever be the form which you wish to assume, that you may assume. Freed from the Māyā with which you had covered yourself, you are once again beyond the reach of mind and speech. Pray, ascend to your own abode."

Rāma then entered into the spirit of lord Viṣṇu, along with his brothers. Hence, the gods and the sages worship Rāma as lord Viṣṇu himself.

Rāma said to Brahmā the creator: "Assign a celestial region for these, my devotees and followers, O Brahmā." Accordingly, Brahmā ordained a celestial region known as Śantanaka (or Śaantanaka), and decreed: "Even subhuman creatures that leave their physical body thinking of you, O Lord, will reach this celestial region."

Sugrīva entered the orb of the sun. And the other vānaras who were born of the various divinities re-entered their source. All the citizens and devotees of Rāma entered the river Sarayū and were instantly transported to heaven.

Brahmā the creator and all the gods in heaven were delighted at the return of Rāma and all the divine beings.

This is the Rāmāyana; the main parts of it were composed by the sage Vālmīki and approved by Brahmā the creator. It is extremely auspicious, and it destroys the sins of one who is able to read even a small part of it. In fact, this Rāmāyana is recited and listened to even in heaven. One who reads this daily obtains whatever he desires.

Printed in the United States
40611LVS00003B/55

9 780887 068638